Shakespeare Refashioned
Elizabethan Plays on Edwardian Stages

Theater and Dramatic Studies, No. 5

Bernard Beckerman, Series Editor
Brander Matthews Professor of Dramatic Literature
Columbia University in the City of New York

Other Titles in This Series

No. 1	*The Original Casting of Molière's Plays*	Roger W. Herzel
No. 2	*Richard Foreman and the Ontological-Hysteric Theatre*	Kate Davy
No. 3	*The History and Theory of Environmental Scenography*	Arnold Aronson
No. 4	*The Meininger Theater: 1776–1926*	Steven DeHart
No. 6	*The Public and Performance: Essays in the History of the French and German Theater, 1871–1900*	Michael Hays
No. 7	*The Theatre Theory and Practice of Richard Boleslavsky*	J.W. Roberts
No. 8	*The Teatro Olimpico: An Analysis of Design Sources*	J. Thomas Oosting
No. 9	*Georges Feydeau and the Aesthetics of Farce*	Stuart E. Baker
No. 10	*The Theatre Director Otto Brahm*	Horst Claus

Shakespeare Refashioned
Elizabethan Plays on Edwardian Stages

by
Cary M. Mazer

UMI RESEARCH PRESS
Ann Arbor, Michigan

The author would like to thank the Society of Authors for permission, on behalf of the Bernard Shaw Estate, to quote from the works of Shaw, and for permission, as the literary representative of the Estate of Harley Granville-Barker, to quote from the published and unpublished works of Granville-Barker. The extracts from previously unpublished Barker letters on pp. 129, 130, 146, and 148 are © 1981, The Estate of Harley Granville-Barker.

Copyright © 1981, 1980
Cary M. Mazer
All rights reserved

Produced and distributed by
UMI Research Press
an imprint of
University Microfilms International
Ann Arbor, Michigan 48106

Library of Congress Cataloging in Publication Data

Mazer, Cary M.
  Shakespeare refashioned: Elizabethan plays on Edwardian stages.

  (Theater and dramatic studies ; no. 5)
  Revision of thesis (Ph.D.)–Columbia University, 1980.
  Bibliography: p.
  Includes index.
  1. Shakespeare, William, 1564-1616–Stage history–1800-1950. 2. Theaters–Stage-setting and scenery–History. 3. Theater–England–History–20th century.
I. Title. II. Series.
PR3099.M3 1981   792'.0941   81-13048
ISBN 0-8357-1236-2   AACR2

To Deborah Rohr

Frontispiece. Garden Scene of Tree's *Twelfth Night* (1901).

Contents

List of Illustrations   *ix*

Acknowledgments   *xiii*

Introduction   *1*

1 Shakespeare and the Traditional Stagecraft   *7*

    Traditionalist Aesthetics
      The Illusion of Reality
      Unity
      Narrative Interpolations
      Character and Environment
    The Special Demands of Shakespeare's Plays
      Continuity
      Organizational Determinants
      Localization
      The Alternation System
      Time
    Convention

2 Shakespeare and the Elizabethan Revival   *49*

    Theory
      Elizabethanism and History
      Elizabethanism and Traditionalism: Reality, Unity and
        Dramatic Form
      Elizabethanist Scholarship
      Perception
    Practice
    Limitations and Contradictions

3 Shakespeare and the New Stagecraft   85

    Theory
        The Special Demands of Shakespeare's Plays
        Traditionalism and Convention
        Fantasy and Reality
    Practice
        Pictorial Experiments: Craig and Ricketts
        Spatial Experiments: Modified Elizabethanism
        Picture and Space: Harvey's *Hamlet*

4 Shakespeare and Granville Barker   *123*

    Theory
        Convention
        Space
        Decor
    Practice

5 Epilogue: Shakespeare and the Director   *151*

Illustrations   *161*

Appendix: Shakespeare Productions in Greater London and Stratford, 1890–1916   *195*

Notes   *213*

Bibliography   *239*

Index   *255*

List of Illustrations

Frontispiece. Garden Scene of Tree's *Twelfth Night* (1901). Photographed during a performance on tour in Germany in 1908 (*The Stage Door Year Book*, 1911)

Following Page 159:

1. A front scene from Tree's *Antony and Cleopatra* (1906): the exterior of the monument. (*Play Pictorial*, 1906, Free Library of Philadelphia)

2. A full scene from Tree's *Antony and Cleopatra:* the interior of the monument. (*Play Pictorial*, 1906, Free Library of Philadelphia)

3. Alma Tadema's designs for Irving's *Coriolanus* (1901): the proscenium arch (*Architectural Review*, 1901)

4. The single set for Tree's production of Phillips' *Herod* (1900): solidity and realism impossible in productions of Shakespeare (*Architectural Review*, 1900)

5. Design by Alma Tadema for Irving's *Coriolanus* (1901): a street (*Architectural Review*, 1901)

6. Design by Alma Tadema for Irving's *Coriolanus* (1901): the Forum of Antium (*Architectural Review*, 1901)

7. Design by Alma Tadema for Irving's *Coriolanus* (1901): the exterior of Aufidius's house (*Architectural Review*, 1901)

8. Garden Scene of Tree's *Twelfth Night* (1901). Photographed during a performance on tour in Germany in 1908 (*The Stage Door Year Book*, 1911)

x   List of Illustrations

9. A rendering of the Garden Scene

10. The Grand Tableau from Act I of Waller's *Henry V* (1901). (*Sketch,* 9 January 1901. Library of Congress)

11. Current events illustrated: the relief of Ladysmith (*Illustrated London News,* 21 April 1900)

12. The Battle of Angiers: a tableau from Tree's *King John* (1899). (Courtesy of the Beerbohm Tree Collection, University of Bristol Theatre Collection)

13. Poel's use of curtains: a scene from *Hamlet* (1900)

14. Localization and Edwardian Elizabethanism: a cartoonist's view of Tree rehearsing *Hamlet* (*Tatler,* 29 December 1906, by courtesy of the Beerbohm Tree Collection, University of Bristol Theatre Collection)

15. Brodmeier's plan for the Elizabethan stage

16. The stage used by Granville Barker for *Iphigenia in Taurus* (1912) at the Greek Theatre, Bradfield (*Bristol Times,* 10 June 1912, Harvard Theatre Collection)

17. Plan of the stage, derived from the photograph

18. Reconstruction by Walter H. Godfrey and William Archer of the Fortune Theatre (*Quarterly Review,* 1908)

19. Conjectural plan for Poel's *Measure for Measure* (1893), based on Arthur J. Harris' analysis of photographs

20. Poel's *Twelfth Night* (1897): the traverse curtains used for a "front" scene (British Museum)

21. Darrell Figgis's plan for an Elizabethan stage

22. George Pierce Baker's Elizabethan Stage at Harvard (Harvard Theatre Collection)

23. Byam Shaw's drawing of the Dance from Craig's *Much Ado About Nothing* (1903), from the *Souvenir Programme given by the*

Theatrical and Musical Professions as a Tribute to Miss Ellen Terry on the Occasion of her Jubilee Tuesday Afternoon June 12th 1906; (Billy Rose Theatre Collection, The New York Public Library at Lincoln Center; Astor, Lenox and Tilden Foundations)

24. Designs for II.iii of Craig's *Much Ado About Nothing* (1903) (The Theatre Museum)

25. Design by Charles Ricketts for *King Lear* (1909) (The Theatre Museum)

26. The playing area for Max Reinhardt's *Oedipus* (1912) at Covent Garden (Harvard Theatre Collection)

27. Plan of the playing area, derived from the photograph

28. Photograph of the apron stage, under construction, for Poel's *Two Gentlemen of Verona* (1910), His Majesty's Theatre. (Courtesy of the Beerbohm Tree Collection, University of Bristol Theatre Collection)

29. Photographs of the Palace for *The Winter's Tale* and the Garden for *Twelfth Night* (1912) (*Country Life,* 10 May 1913, Harvard Theatre Collection)

30. A drawing of the Garden set, *Twelfth Night* (1912) (*Everyman,* 29 November 1912, Harvard Theatre Collection)

31. II.iii of Barker's *Twelfth Night* (1912) (*Play Pictorial,* 1913, Free Library of Philadelphia)

32. Two forest scenes from Barker's *A Midsummer Night's Dream* (1914) (*Illustrated London News,* 28 February 1914)

33. Albert Rutherston's costume design for Leontes in Barker's *The Winter's Tale* (1912) (Harvard Theatre Collection)

Acknowledgments

My research has been assisted by numerous curators and librarians at theatre collections in England and the United States. These include Ann Brooke Barnett and Christopher Robinson of the University of Bristol Theatre Collection, Martha Mahard of the Harvard Theatre Collection, Miss Tracy and Miss Langstrith of the British Drama League, Louis Rackow of the Player's Club; the librarians of the Shakespeare Centre Library, The London Museum, the British Film Institute, the Folger Library and the British Library Department of Manuscripts; and George Nash, who guided me through the temporarily inaccessible reaches of his former domain, the Theatre Museum. I would also like to thank my many correspondents for their information, guidance and advice. These include J. C. Trewin, Martin Holmes, Cathleen Nesbitt, Eric Jones-Evans, Edward Craig, Laurence Irving and Marvin Rosenberg. My special thanks to Jennifer Aylmer, who encouraged me to interview her father, Sir Felix Aylmer, and Miss Betty Andraea, who showered me with hospitality and with memories of her father, Otho Stuart Andraea, whose unpublished autobiography she allowed me to read.

I would like to thank the Society of Authors for permission to quote from the works of Bernard Shaw and Granville Barker, Mrs. D. W. Linley for permission to quote from the published and unpublished writings of William Archer, and the Beerbohm Tree Collection, University of Bristol Theatre Collection, for permission to draw from their inexhaustible files of production documents. The sources for the photographic illustrations are acknowledged in the List of Illustrations. The diagrams were executed by Kitty Anderson and Gerald K.B. Esyaman, Jr.

I would particularly like to thank Professors Bernard Beckerman and Martin Meisel for their support, encouragement and criticism, and Professors Daniel Dodson, Carl Woodring and Michael Hays, who made several useful suggestions in response to an earlier version of the text. I am most grateful to Dr. Beckerman for his continued interest in this book, which he read in manuscript in virtually every version. And I extend my deep personal thanks to Deborah Rohr, to whom this work is dedicated.

Introduction

The Edwardian period was a cultural and theatrical watershed between the values of high Victorianism which preceded it and those of the postwar years which followed it. Samuel Hynes likens the period to the English Channel, "a place made turbulent by the thrust and tumble of two opposing tides."[1] During the Edwardian period the old and the new coexisted, engaged in perpetual conflict, but sharing many common assumptions and underlying principles. Literary and theatrical historians tend to see the Edwardian period either as a coda of the Victorian period or as the prelude to postwar Modernity; however it was neither the one nor the other; the Edwardian period was both Victorian and Modern at the same time. And, as Hynes has shown, the Edwardians themselves were acutely aware of the attitudes and conditions that defined their own age, sensing the end of one era and the beginning of another.[2]

Yet theatre historians, and Shakespeare Production Historians in particular, have undervalued many of the crosscurrents of the Edwardian period, and so have failed to appreciate many of the period's ambivalent and contradictory tendencies, viewing the period instead as a steady progression from the old-fashioned to the truly modern. This is partly due to the fact that historians tend to read history backwards, projecting onto the past the values which the historian holds dear in his own day and age. The decades subsequent to the Edwardian period have been dominated by the Director's Theatre, a system of artistic organization which had its roots in the Edwardian period, when the stage director emerged as a discrete functionary within the theatre company and was able to articulate his role as the controlling artistic force in the production process. Consequently, theatre scholars living in the age of the Director have tended to seek out only those aspects of the Edwardian period which confirm the aesthetics and prejudices of the Director's Theatre. Having concentrated our historical studies of the period on those theatre practitioners who functioned as directorial innovators, we have, in effect, fallen prey to the system of critical values invented by the directors of the period. Today we commonly view the Edwardian period through the filter of the values and prejudices of an artistic system which grew out of the period. Clearly a new, more comprehensive, synthetic approach is necessary.

According to the standard view of the changes in the staging of Shakespeare during the Edwardian period, the actor-manager system, which so dominated the theatre industry in the last quarter of the nineteenth century, fell into a state of decadence during the Edwardian period and then virtually disappeared after the first World War. Edwardian actor-managers created extravagantly spectacular productions of Shakespeare, which employed elaborate scenery in the current style of pictorial realism and featured heavily cut and rearranged texts. The stage director, who emerged during this period, ushered in an age of nonrepresentational scenic decor, continuous action, and virtually uncut texts. The decline of the actor-manager and the rise of the director, who would ultimately replace him, has been described as a revolution.[3]

We tacitly reinforce this standard picture every time we choose to concentrate our studies on the insights and contributions of individual theatrical innovators. Actor-managers, such as Henry Irving and Herbert Beerbohm Tree, are considered old-fashioned vestiges of an earlier age, while directors, such as William Poel, Edward Gordon Craig and Harley Granville Barker, are portrayed as creative and innovative harbingers of the future. This focus on the individual theatrical innovator is a product, in part, of common methods of theatre scholarship. One of the more prevalent formats for theatre history, on which the more comprehensive studies are based, is the critical biography; in this form, the scholar emphasizes the importance of the individual contributions of his subject and draws lines of influence to contemporaries and successors. Biographical studies of Poel, Craig and Barker have successfully presented such a picture.[4] Even the older, more "old-fashioned" generation of theatre artists has been examined afresh in several mid-twentieth-century biographies, designed to prove that their subjects were either titans of a golden age, or else unrecognized pioneers of the new order.[5] The biographical format of many doctoral dissertations in theatre history has contributed to this tendency. The concentration on the contributions of the period's individual theatre artists has helped to confirm the values of the Director's Theatre.

Although the age of the Director's Theatre is not yet over, we are now increasingly aware of the fact that the Director's Theatre is neither the ultimate nor necessarily the best system of theatrical rehearsal and performance. John Russell Brown has argued in *Free Shakespeare* that the Director's Theatre is merely one system of many, the product of a particular set of organizational and historical conditions.[6] Brown has further shown that the present system is in many ways antithetical to the essential nature of the

Shakespearean text and the system of performance for which it was designed.

Our new perspective on the historical nature of the Director's Theatre enables us to view many of the developments of the Edwardian period in a new light. As Brown has demonstrated, the very notion of "production" as a finished product, the translation of a living text into an encapsuled statement of a single conception or interpretation, belongs exclusively to the age of the Director's Theatre. It is, therefore, misleading to trace the development of theatre art through the sequential contributions of individual productions and directors.

This book is based on the assumption that variations in modes of performance are more significant than any single production, and that the organizational system under which the performance is created is more significant than the contribution of the director who creates it. It is more important to examine how a whole generation of theatre artists understood Shakespeare than to praise any one director's superior insights. Individual directors or individual productions cannot be studied out of context; they must be seen as only single parts of a broad spectrum of theatrical activity.

Such an approach is, in fact, true to the spirit of the Edwardian period. The struggles between conservative and innovative practitioners during the period were subsumed within a broader, and more significant, set of changes in theatre aesthetics. And these changes in aesthetics were in turn part of a larger trend in the structure of the theatre industry. The period saw several fundamental changes in the financial organization of the industry, changes which directly or indirectly affected the theatre both in the front of house and backstage. Edwardians were aware of these organizational changes, and consequently became increasingly interested in the effect of organizational structures on theatre art. Theatrical practitioners, conservatives and reformers alike, either developed new reasons for the retention of existing organizational structures or proposed new structures to take their places. We will see that this organizational self-awareness informed their understanding of theatre aesthetics in several crucial ways.

The Shakespeare productions of the Edwardian period provide a particularly rich body of documents through which one can trace the fundamental changes that took place in theatre art and organization. One reason for this is the fact that the role of Shakespeare in the context of theatrical activity at large was changing. One elaborate and established system of organizing the theatre industry was slowly evolving into a new and modified system, and the role of the Shakespearean repertoire was changing along with it.

In the 1870s and 1880s, an aesthetic system for the production of Shakespeare's plays was fully articulated by Henry Irving at the Lyceum Theatre. Irving specialized in the romantic costume repertoire, and left the modern-dress drawing-room repertoire to the Bancrofts, John Hare and the Kendals, who developed the production aesthetic for those plays to an equally high level of perfection. Irving produced relatively few Shakespeare plays in his final years.[7] His increasing dependence on the non-Shakespearean productions in his repertoire is characteristic of a decline in the number of full-scale London productions of Shakespeare during the final decade of the nineteenth century. While some allowance must be made for the long run system, which often limited the actor-manager to a single major production a year, it is clear that the theatregoer of the 1890s was able to see only a limited number of productions of a limited number of plays. On seeing an amateur production of *All's Well that Ends Well* in 1895, William Archer complained of the lack of any opportunity in his theatre-going lifetime to see such plays as *The Tempest, Coriolanus, Timon of Athens, Richard II, Henry IV part two*, all of *Henry VI, The Comedy of Errors,* and *Two Gentlemen of Verona;* and the next year he cited as works of Shakespeare "seldom or never produced" *Richard II, Coriolanus, Antony and Cleopatra* and *The Tempest*[8]

The first decade of the new century saw a substantial increase in both the number of Shakespeare productions and the breadth of the canon produced. While 29 full professional London productions of 18 plays were produced between 1890 and 1899, between 1900 and 1909 there were 53 productions of 25 plays, and numerous experimental amateur and professional matinees (raising the number of plays from the canon to 27.)[9] From 1905 to 1909, the annual Shakespeare Festival at His Majesty's Theatre produced 27 revivals of 10 different plays, with two more plays produced by guest companies.[10] While Archer had only to wait one year to see *Two Gentlemen,* by 1910 he could have seen *The Tempest, Coriolanus, Timon of Athens, Richard II, Henry IV part two, The Comedy of Errors, Love's Labour's Lost* and *Troilus and Cressida* in London and all three parts of *Henry VI* in Stratford.[11] New audiences were being generated for Shakespeare's plays, and nationwide play-reading organizations, such as the British Empire Shakespeare Society (B.E.S.S.) boasted chapters in every major community.

Furthermore, Shakespeare ceased to be the exclusive domain of actors or producers specializing in the costume repertoire, and many managements, including Tree's, moved freely between Shakespeare and modern-dress plays. New organizational formats, such as repertory and the annual Festivals, featured Shakespeare's plays prominently in their prospectuses. The most ambitious, though least successful, organizational reform movement, the Shakespeare Memorial National Theatre (S.M.N.T.) Committee, officially linked Shakespeare's plays with the ideals of the endowed theatre. The connection of Shakespeare with these organizational experiments indicates that Edwardians still considered Shakespeare a valued prize, a symbol of managerial status. So long as Shakespeare was not the exclusive property of any single actor-manager or particular school of production, each production of his plays was an assertion of the validity of a particular aesthetic school or system of theatrical organization, and a conscious attempt to define what the theatre should be.

The most important reason that Edwardian Shakespeare productions deserve historical analysis is related to the nature of the texts themselves in performance. The plays have been produced during virtually every period of English theatre history since Shakespeare's own day, and the abundance of data from many periods enables the historian to make fruitful comparisons of theatre practice and attitudes from one period to another. Furthermore, Shakespeare's texts, written according to Elizabethan dramatic and theatrical conventions, are fundamentally incompatible with the conventions and conditions of later periods; the scripts must be "translated," adapted or willfully transformed in order to be presented on these later stages for later audiences. Consequently, the degree and nature of the translation of a play in production in a later period reveals the fundamental nature of the theatrical experience of that later period; a period writes its own theatre history through its productions of Shakespeare.

Of all of the aspects of Shakespearean staging, this book concentrates on issues of stagecraft and scenic design. These were by no means the only areas of change during the Edwardian period, when entire systems of theatre management, acting and dramaturgy were modified and revised. But the theory and practice of scenography deserves particular attention because it has experienced the greatest degree of historical misinterpretation. Scenic decisions are always immediately perceptible by audiences, and the smallest change in method consequently receives disproportionate attention in journalistic reviews and eye-witness accounts. These records, along with production designs and photographs, constitute a wealth of documents relating to scenery which have made Edwardian scenography a frequent focus of attention and consequently a frequent victim of inherited misconceptions, received opinions, and half-truths.

The accepted historical account of the changes in scenic art during the Edwardian period is that pictorially representational scenery was challenged, and ultimately replaced, by non-illusionary, nonrepresentational decor. But if we examine the scenography of the period in detail more closely, particularly as it was applied to the special problems posed by Shakespeare's texts, a different picture emerges. The rival "schools" of scenic art, though competitors, contributed equally to the diversity of the period. The schools shared several assumptions regarding the definitions of theatrical space, the stage event, and the fictive reality of the world presented on the stage. These assumptions, as they functioned within the more traditional schools, actually encouraged and welcomed the diversity of approaches offered by the other schools. Conversely, the more advanced schools were limited in many ways by the realistic premises which they inherited from more traditional scenic modes. No single scenic movement succeeded in supplanting the others during the period; they all coexisted, and together forged a language of production which later generations would inherit.

Our goal, then, is to examine the full range and variety of scenic activity in the production of Shakespeare during the Edwardian period. By examining the work of minor and anonymous figures as well as major contributors, of conservatives as well as innovators, we should be able to free our understanding of the period from the prejudices of the Director's Theatre to which it gave rise.

1

Shakespeare and the Traditional Stagecraft

The first step toward an understanding of the scenography of the Edwardian period is to examine in detail the values and methods of staging elaborated during the late Victorian period, and in particular the scenographic vocabulary and aesthetic assumptions which provided a referential frame for the number of experimental departures made by other Edwardian schools of stagecraft and design.[1]

I use the term "traditional" to describe the mode of scenic presentation that dominated the work of the accepted theatrical practitioners of the period, the scenic mode that was supplanted by supposedly more advanced, sophisticated and aesthetically valid systems of scenic display which developed later in the period. Certainly many of the techniques of tradititional staging were supplanted by newer ones, and the traditional mode of production did not outlive the period. But there was nothing particularly outmoded or untenable about the system as it was practiced in its heyday. The accepted critical notion that the work of Irving represents the pinnacle of the form and the work of Tree its decadence does justice to neither artist nor to their contemporaries. There were excesses, illogicalities and absurdities in the later works of the tradition. As a system of staging, however, it was internally consistent with its own goals and aesthetics; and while the understanding of Shakespeare and his plays on which it was based is not the same as our own, it is nonetheless coherent and, according to its own terms, valid. Nor was the traditional stagecraft necessarily considered to be outmoded or old fashioned among its supporters during the Edwardian period. Indeed, the practitioners of the traditional stagecraft often referred to it as the "modern" style of scenic presentation, priding themselves both on the superiority of the methods of the nineteenth century to those of Shakespeare's day, and on the improvements within the traditional stagecraft introduced at the end of the nineteenth century and the beginning of twentieth.

Our goal, then, is to look beyond the absurdities of the system, and, indeed, to look beyond those superficial features of the stagecraft, such as pictorial representationalism, which were rejected by Edwardian reformers.

Beneath the surface features of the stagecraft was a set of assumptions about life, theatre and dramatic literature which provided the cornerstone of all Edwardian scenographic thinking; we shall see that a great number of the root assumptions of the traditional stagecraft were retained in several of the ostensibly more radical Edwardian schools of design.

The underlying assumptions of the traditional stagecraft can be divided into three general categories. The first involves the nature of the theatrical event itself, and the corollary issues of the definition of the stage reality created behind the proscenium arch and the demands for a "unity" of effect in the creation of that separate world. The second category involves the assumptions of the Edwardian traditional stage practitioners regarding the dramatic material in hand, i.e., the special demands of the Shakespearean text and the extent to which the texts can be adapted and modified in production in order to fulfill what were felt to be the more important structural and aesthetic features of the plays in performance. The third set of assumptions concerns the nature of theatrical communication and the problems of internal consistency within the system of theatrical conventions generated to create the stage event. Many of the absurdities of the traditional stagecraft were a direct result of contradictions among these three categories. It will be seen, however, that the practitioners of the traditional stagecraft were always aware of the conventional nature of their art, and that the exploitation of the paradoxes built into the stagecraft paved the way for the formal experimentation of the Edwardian scenic reformers.

Traditionalist Aesthetics

The Illusion of Reality

The underlying premise of the traditionalist Edwardian definition of the nature of the theatre event was twofold. First, it was assumed that the world depicted on the stage was something crucially separate and apart from the world of the spectators in the auditorium of the theatre; secondly, the separate world thus created on the stage was a complete, internally consistent and conventionally "real" space, obeying historical, environmental, behavioral and dramatic laws bound together according to the principles of "unity." These two aspects are interrelated, for the sense of separation between spectacle and spectator is necessary for the establishment of the reality and the unity of the stage world.

The development of realism and naturalism in both modern and romantic drama corresponded to the increasing definition of the proscenium frame and the gradual elimination of the vestigial stage apron. The concept of the fourth wall in naturalist drama is equivalent to the "mystic gulf" in

Wagner's romantic theatre: both assure the complete visual and spatial separation of the stage environment from the world of the audience. The audience was cast in the role of passive spectators, viewing other worlds from a distance; and the stage event itself became either a vehicle for escapist presentation of distant localities, or else an educational device, a means of showing distant worlds and past ages. In England, the separation of stage and auditorium was structurally built into the playhouses; several theatres, most notably the Haymarket (after the Bancrofts' renovation of it in 1880), Wyndham's (1899) and the Aldwych (1905) featured proscenium arches which continued the decorative motif of the frame along the stage floor, masking the footlights and deliberately suggesting a four-sided picture frame. The world of the play was viewed much as an easel painting would be viewed: as a glimpse into a separate world, which defined its own reality in terms of period, locale and environment.

Edwardian reformers were quick to see the connection between the physical separation of the proscenium theatre and the premise of the fictive reality of the stage event; and in order to modify, if not to completely reject that premise, they called for the alteration or abolition of the proscenium. It is little wonder that Edwardian traditionalists recognized the threat to the sanctity of stage reality posed by such suggestions. William Telbin, the veteran scene-painter, responding negatively to Hubert Herkomer's suggestion that the footlights be abolished, recalled an experiment undertaken by D'Oyly Carte years before at the English Opera House in which the footlights were replaced by side lighting: Telbin complained that "the auditorium seemed only to end where the scenery blocked the way, and the singers appeared to form part of the audience."[2] And J. H. Barnes, who acted for both the old schools and the new, similarly complained about Max Reinhardt's *Oedipus* (1912), which broke through the proscenium and placed much of the action in the area usually occupied by stalls: "I very gravely doubt if any production *in the body of a theatre* can give more unalloyed pleasure than what can be (and has been) done behind the proscenium arch."[3] For both Telbin and Barnes, the validity of the stage event depended upon the complete separation of the dramatic universe from the real world of the audience and the auditorium.

The physical separation of the stage from the auditorium allowed the theatre artist to create, and to manipulate, the reality of the time, place and event taking place upon the stage: he could create a complete illusory world with the premise of real events taking place, involving ostensibly real characters in a real imaginative environmental context. Historical "archaeological" details, popularized in the 1850s through the pedantry of Charles Kean, were the means of creating a "real" environment and of assuring the veracity of the stage event. Certainly by the late Victorian period, it became increasingly clear that archaeology *per se* was not an end in itself but a means of creating and supporting an illusion of reality. The philosophy behind the archaelogical side of the traditional stagecraft was best expressed by E. W. Godwin, the architect and occasional scene and costume designer, who maintained

> that we do not go to the theatre simply to hear passionate recitations and funny speeches, but to witness such a performance as will place us as nearly as possible as spectators of the original scene or of the thing represented, and so gain information of man, manners, customs, costumes and countries—and this result is only obtainable where accuracy in every particular is secured.[4]

If effect, Godwin wished to create in performance "the illusion of the first time" that the historical event took place, a concept which, as a philosophy of acting, also dates from this period.[5] Godwin's educational tone is evidence of the Victorian obsession with pictorial information, but it also demonstrates that the educational function of stage archaeologism was directly related to the Victorian belief in creating a fictive reality of the stage event. It is important to note that the principles of archaeology were applied to nonhistorical plays. When Beerbohm Tree produced *The Winter's Tale* in 1906, he did not need to follow Charles Kean's 1856 emendation of Bohemia to Bithynia: folkloric Bohemia, though historically discontinuous with Classical Sicily, was historical enough so long as it held the stage in the fourth act of Shakespeare's play. Like the Greeks, who considered myth a synonym for history, the Edwardian traditionalists historicized their theatrical fantasies, investing them with the fictive reality of their separate stage world. Archaeology became a means of creating this reality, not an end. Writing about Godwin, Oscar Wilde subordinated the independent importance of archaeology to its role in the creation of an artistic product: "to attack [archaeology] for any reason is foolish . . . one might just as well speak disrespectfully of the equator. . . . We look to the archaeologist for the materials, to the artist for the method."[6]

The Edwardian traditionalists believed that the fictive reality on the stage was an intrinsic feature of their dramatic text. If Shakespeare was not able to create such a verisimilar world on the stage, this was, according to the traditionalist, the fault of his theatre, not of his dramatic vision. Henry Irving believed that the aim of modern production must be "to realise the *locale* of the action."[7] This Victorian belief in specific localization of scene was projected onto Shakespeare's intentions; Alfred Darbyshire, an apologist and explicator of Victorian scenic conventions, recorded Irving's compliment to Robert Courtneidge on his Manchester *As You Like It* (1902): "Well, my boy, I have seen exactly what Shakespeare saw as he wrote the immortal comedy."[8] Darbyshire added his own assertion that Shakespeare's "great mind dwelt on actual scenes, whether historic or ideal," when he wrote his plays.[9] The premise in both these statements is that Shakespeare's inspiration preceded his consideration of theatrical realization, that he first envisioned a specific locale for his action and then turned to the theatre to recreate it as best it could. A supporter of this belief was William Archer, the theatre critic and supporter of the new drama, who averred "that scenery should as nearly as possible express to the eye the locality which was present to the author's imagination."[10]

A large repertoire of theatrical techniques was available to the traditionalist for the verification of the reality of the stage world. One means was the creation of the illusion of the 360 degree reality of the stage space, the suggestion that the proscenium arch offers only one view of a room or vista. The box-sets of modern realistic comedy contained a built-in verification of three-dimensional reality: the three walls of the room imply the existence of the fourth wall. But traditional romantic scenery needed to create the illusion of three-dimensional reality through other means. One common device was to take a view of a realistic space and, in the next scene, to revolve it 180 degrees, thereby verifying the 360 degree reality of the locale. The tomb scene in Irving's *Romeo and Juliet* (1882) provides the best early example of the technique: Romeo slays Paris in a front scene and drags his body upstage through the gate of the tomb. The scene changes, and Romeo is seen dragging Paris toward the front of the stage down a steep flight of steps into the tomb, the floor of which is now at stage level.[11]

Tree similarly shifted the dramatic locale in the middle of the church scene in his production of *Much Ado About Nothing* (1905): the ceremony took place in the cathedral, while the Beatrice/Benedick duologue took place in the adjoining cloisters, suggesting a three-dimensional plan to the cathedral precincts. Tree's most striking use of this technique was for the difficult stage direction in *Antony and Cleopatra* (1906), in which Antony's body is borne upwards into Cleopatra's monument. Tree employed a front scene for the exterior of the monument, with a window cut into it; the lights faded as Antony was being lifted upwards toward the window. The next scene was the interior of the monument, with the window upstage, and when the lights went up, the audience saw Antony being brought foward into the room through the window.[12] (See illustrations 1 and 2.)

The implication of 360 degree reality was created through different means in Irving's *Coriolanus* (1901). Alma Tadema employed a false proscenium which, painted *trompe l'oeil*, implied that the audience was sitting within an architectural unit out of which it could watch the events of the play (see illustration 3). The intention of this design is clearly to make the audience believe that they are within a Roman room, under the lintels and barrel vault of the portico, looking out onto Rome, Antium and Corioli. Not only does this design imply a 360 degree reality of the stage world, but it specifically defines the spatial locality of the audience and their relationship, as spectators of an historical event, toward the stage action.

A second means of creating the illusion of the reality of the stage space is the suggestion of offstage space in which persons or activities crucial to the onstage action are taking place, a technique which Shakespeare himself exploited to great effect in the second scene of *Julius Caesar*. As early as 1884 Wilson Barrett introduced the offstage sounds of the court's carousing during Hamlet's first soliloquy; Hamlet looked offstage in their direction throughout the speech, and a burst of offstage laughter inspired his line, "that it should come to this."[13] The comedy of the letter scene in Tree's *Twelfth Night* (1901) depended upon the constant suspicion on Malvolio's part that he was indeed being overheard.[14] And a remarkable effect was created in two of the scenes in Tree's *Macbeth* (1911). The act I, scene 7 dialogue between Macbeth and Lady Macbeth was performed with the repeated punctuation of Duncan and the court at dinner directly offstage, as implied by the Folio dumbshow stage direction which precedes the scene. If the audience failed to notice the effect of Duncan's offstage presence on Macbeth's scheming, Tree made it clear by bringing on Duncan and his nobles at the end of the scene to give a blessing to his hosts and their house. And, in the scene after the murder, Tree and Violet Vanbrugh spoke entirely in whispers, constantly aware of the offstage presence of the sleeping court.[15] Bridges-Adams describes at great length a similar device of H. B. Irving in a crime play called *Markheim* which he adapted from Stevenson: the murder took place in a shuttered antique shop in complete silence, while the murderer was constantly aware of the least noise he made, and froze in his tracks as each passerby casually, but audibly, walked by.[16]

These theatrical devices, then, were employed in the creation of an illusion of the isolated, fictive reality of the stage world. The traditionalists did not disguise the fact that this scenic world was illusory; the reality created on the stage was a shared premise of theatre artist and audience, based on a repertoire of scenic conventions. The only mandate of the theatre artist, according to the traditionalist vocabulary, was the internal consistency of the component elements of the stage environment. The credo of scenographic traditionalism was most clearly expressed by Beerbohm Tree. For Tree, the prime function of the theatre was to create a world of illusion; illusion is "the very alpha and omega of dramatic art."[17] "It may be broadly laid down that whatever tends to quicken the imagination of the audience—in fact, to create illusion—is justifiable on the stage. Whatever detracts from the appreciation of the author's work and disturbs the illusion is to be deprecated—is, in fact, bad art."[18] For Tree, painted representational decor was the only scenic mode which did not disturb artistic illusion. He acknowledged that there may have been a time when painted scenery did distract the attention of the audience from the total illusion but "now appropriate illustration is the normal condition of the theatre."[19] Note Tree's equation of two words with similar linguistic roots: illusion and illustration. His half-brother, Max Beerbohm, agreed that illusion is the prime goal of dramatic art, and uses the verb "to illude" to describe the process.[20] The belief in illusion was not confined to the traditionalists. It is interesting to note that Shaw's original advocacy of Poel's experiments was not on the grounds of Elizabethanism but on the basis of the need to create a theatrical illusion: "I do not, like the Elizabethan Stage Society, affirm it as a principle that Shakespeare's plays should be accorded the build of stage for which he designed them. I simply affirm it as a fact, personally observed by myself, that the modern pictorial stage is not so favorable to Shakespearean acting and stage illusion as the platform stage.[21] Though Shaw's definition of dramatic "illusion" is undoubtedly more complex than Tree's, it is clear that Shaw, too, was placing the concept of illusion at the center of the theatrical event.

Unity

Dramatic and theatrical unity was an important means of establishing and maintaining the stage illusion: each element contributed to the total illusion of stage reality, and the illusion of reality in turn reinvested each artistic and dramatic element with a reality of its own. There were several means by which the physical environment of the stage could be unified with the dramatic event: these included unifying the scenic environment with the nature of the dramatic activity, the dramatic mood, the physical presence of the actor, the dramatic integrity of the character, and the symbolic content of the drama.

The first type of unity involved the relation of the scenic environment to the dramatic activity taking place within the scene. There is evidence that traditionalist practitioners scoured the text for some minor contextual indication of how the scene should be set, or else found excuses in the text to justify scenic choices actually made for other reasons. One example of this was Irving's decision to set the Osric scene in his 1878 *Hamlet* out of doors, ostensibly to justify Hamlet's gentlemanly suggestion to the fop that he put on his hat.[22] Dramatic activities of more central importance were used to determine the character of the dramatic environment. One example is the so-called church scene in *Much Ado About Nothing,* often used as an excuse for scenic display or as a travelogue of Messina. Percy Fitzgerald, author of several books on the theatre of his day, complained that the church in question need not be a specific church, since Shakespeare merely demanded "a place where people come to—a church, a chapel, a hall in a palace—anywhere. The point for him was a marriage that was interrupted."[23] Notwithstanding Fitzgerald's complaints, it was precisely the visual relationship between the scenic environment and the dramatic activity in this scene which drew the attention of A. B. Walkley, who, in his critique of Irving's 1891 production of the play, noted that the characters "are so much alive that they go a-courting at the very foot of the high altar . . . amid organ-peals and frankincense."[24] Surely this contrast between action and locale can be used to great effect, but it was precisely because of this disunity that Tree decided on a scenic change (already noted above) between the two parts of the scene; as he explains in his program note:

> . . . a love scene occurs between Beatrice and Benedick, a scene which in the minds of many strikes a somewhat jarring note, taking place as it does in the precincts of the Cathedral, and I have, therefore, transferred the love scene to the cloisters adjoining. Not only do I think that these scenes gain dramatically by the change, but I believe it was so intended by Shakespeare. There are no instructions in the Folio as to where the scenes take place and, therefore, the license I have taken may be held justifiable.[25]

In such instances, archaeological specificity and gratuitous pictorial beauty take second place to dramatic concerns. An example from the end of the period in question reveals how archaeological issues could be rejected altogether without breaking from the illusory values of the traditional stagecraft; in defense of his production of *The Merchant of Venice* (1915), Matheson Lang explained his unconventional decision of not setting the trial scene in a replica of the Doge's council chamber in Venice:

> By laying the trial in an imaginary Court, the producer is not tied to a definite reproduction of a well-known historic room, but can get what effect he thinks best for the play. So in a play where rich, bright colour and gorgeous sunlit views of beautiful Venice set off the lighter scenes, the more fitting setting for the grim drama of the trial scene is the lofty dark hall, with its great pillars stretching to an invisible ceiling, its massive arches and great coloured windows, through which struggle dim, mysterious lights.[26]

Lang clearly preferred visual dramatic contrast to historical or geographical accuracy.

Traditionalists were aware of their ability to manipulate the nature of the dramatic event through their control over the scenic context of the action. Scenes could be shifted from private to public environments by the mere introduction of gawking extras, as the Benson 1914 *Richard III* film indicates: the wooing of Lady Anne is played before the entire populace of London; conversely, the scene in which Richard consents to be King is played in a small private interior. In Asche's *Antony and Cleopatra* (Australia), Antony's confessional speech (act 3, sc. 11) is spoken before his entire army, and in the Asche/Stuart *Measure for Measure* (1906), the final scene is set in the private council chambers rather than before the gates of the city.

The principle of stage unity further enabled the theatre artist to use the scenic environment as an extension or reflection of the tone of the dramatic event. The preparation copy for Tree's *Hamlet* in the Folger Library reveals how the producer's mind, even at this early date (1892), was already controlling his stage environment in this way. For the battlement scene (act 1, sc. 4), Tree marginally suggested to himself "snow"; Horatio's speech to Hamlet, "What if it tempt you toward the flood, my lord, / Or to the dreadful summit of the cliff / That beetles o'er his base into the sea..." (act 1, sc. 4, lines 69-71) inspired Tree with his picture of act 1, scene 5, as he marginally noted, "realise this"; in the margin of that scene, he queried, "?the sea beyond"; and, at the end of act 5, scene 1, he suggested a scenic transformation matching the state of Hamlet's mind: "the sun rises—the northern light—like blood." In the play scene, Tree considered the idea of having the scene gradually darken from a gathering thunderstorm outside, first noticeable when Lucianus has entered to poison the Player King; this motivates Claudius's call for lights, and it is explicable according to naturalistic meteorology, but it also reflects the sinister tone of the moment, Claudius's impending explosion, and the excitement of Hamlet's confirmation of the Ghost's information. Throughout his career Tree introduced locales, or details within them, to illustrate the state of the characters or the nature of the action taking place within the scene. As Richard II is being led to the tower, a drunken man in the stocks visually reflects the fallen state of the King. To emphasize their kinship, Tree further introduced a piece of illustrative business, as recorded in the promptbook: "When they are off Richard turns & notices man in the stocks, who is holding out his hand (begging). Richard looks to see if he has anything to give, finds that he has nothing, shakes hands with the man in the stocks who then points to the sun. King looks up at it, then bows taking hat off. Then exit laughingly." Tree unconventionally set the opening scenes of *Much Ado About Nothing* (1905) in military battlements, in order to "convey the impression of a warlike atmosphere in contrast to the piping time of peace in which the love plot is woven" in later scenes.

Other traditional producers of the period introduced pantomine characters and pieces of local color illustrative of dramatic tone, mood, or situation. An old blind man playing a doleful tune on a shepherd's pipe is introduced into the scene of "The Street before the Prison" in the Asche/Stuart *Measure for Measure* (1906), reflecting the doleful state of the characters being brought there as prisoners.[27] Arthur Bourchier's *Merchant of Venice* (1905), the first managerial venture into Shakespeare by an actor-manager who was most experienced as a producer of modern light comedy, featured several such insertions. One critic complained that the business "appears to be derived rather from Mr. William Gillette than from Shakespeare."[28] Bourchier boasted of the details in his opening pantomime:

> In the scene described in the original as a Public Place, I have sought to profit by the opportunity afforded for offering an animated picture of the busy life of Venice. Here the

spectator is shown the loading of a ship, the gondoliers and fishermen plying their trades, fruitsellers actively engaged in theirs, and a group of Jews bargaining amongst themselves to the unconcealed scorn of Christians of all grades.[29]

Bourchier's textual citation is, of course, not Shakespeare's but his later editors', and the producer's concern for local detail sounds as archeology-minded as the Bancrofts' production of the same play in 1876. But Bourchier's collaborator, his Oxford colleague Alan Mackinnon, explained the dramatic effect thus obtained:

> The opening scene we placed in a balcony overlooking a lagoon. The intention was to suggest the heat and brilliance of an Italian sun without, viewed from the shade within. The voice of a singing girl from the water at the rise of the curtain was meant to emphasize the effect of the former in contrast with the shadow on the mind of Antonio, the premonition of impending trouble expressed in the opening lines of the play.[30]

The goal of the scenography of this production, then, was not archaeological accuracy *per se* but an evocation of a dramatic tone which the producers thought relevant to the dramatic action.

One can often turn to the most forward looking Edwardians for the clearest statement of traditional principles. And so, the most interesting exposition of the traditional principle of the dramatic value of the pictorial environment can be found in the opinions of Bernard Shaw. Though Shaw supported Poel and the Elizabethanists, he strongly believed in the importance of a scenic environment which could create the illusion of reality appropriate to dramatic action, character and situation. After advising Ellen Terry about the playing of Imogen in *Cymbeline,* Shaw found his carefully planned dramatic effects ruined by an incompatible scenic background. He wrote to her in protest:

> The scene of the waking up should be in moonlight: a full bank holiday sunlight is too prosaic to make Imogen's dreamy condition & the uncanny effect of the mysterious body covering with flowers credible. . . . I am furious at myself for having omitted to urge upon you the importance of the scenic setting—I ought to have known that without a vigorous protest you would be put off with something between Bellinzona & Tintern, and two nice young men out of a studio, instead of a land of lions, murderers and hobgoblins, with dreadful lonely distances and threatening darkness. Why should you ask for a drop of pity on a nice pretty warm comfortable reassuring lovely day in the country, with "tea for tourists" obviously around the corner? Great Lord, if I were a scene-painter I'd have painted such an endless valley of desolation for you that at your appearance in its awful solitude, lost and encompassed by terrors, everybody would have caught their breath with a sob before you opened your mouth.[31]

Shaw's *Saturday Review* article made these sentiments common knowledge, expressed in similar terms.[32] In like manner, Shaw boasted to Terry of having advised Forbes Robertson on his *Hamlet* (1897), claiming that were he the designer, he would "make short work of that everlasting 'room in a castle.' You should have the most beautiful old English garden to go mad in, with the flowers to pick fresh from the bushes and a trout stream of the streamiest and rippliest to drown yourself in."[33] Shaw urged Robertson to restore the Poland scene for the pictorial effect of "the ghostly twilight march" of Fortinbras's army, and he boasted that he could create a picture of "Hamlet in his travelling furs, on a heath like a polar desert, and Fortinbras and his men 'going to their graves like beds'—as shall never be forgotten."[34] (Robertson adopted Shaw's suggestion for Ophelia's mad scenes, and restored Fortinbras's entrance at the end of the play, but decided not to restore the fourth act soliloquy or Shaw's accompanying picture.) Shaw's review of the production reveals that he believed that the smallest detail was crucial in creating the atmosphere of the dramatic moment: he complained of the hollow wooden sound of the floor in the ghost scene, set unconventionally on a beach, suggesting as a corrective "a sea-weedy looking cloth on it, with a handful of shrimps and a pennorth of silver sand."[35]

The technical complexity of traditionalist "built-up" scenes has often been blamed for the textual rearrangement in traditional productions, wherein scenes taking place in a given locality are placed together and played sequentially. In fact, these rearrangements, while dictated by technical demands, were often justified in terms of the tonal and environmental unity of the traditionalist aesthetic. The act divisions of Tree's production of *The Winter's Tale* (1906) did not call for any major rearrangement of scene order, and yet created environments appropriate to the dramatic flavor of each of the play's major sections. Each act had a single national locale (Sicilia, Bohemia, Sicilia); each locale could be both archaeologically accurate and dramatically unified, with little risk of undermining the credibility of either through the unlikely juxtaposition of anachronistic periods and places.

Two seasons later, Tree radically altered the scenic sequence of a Shakespeare play in order to achieve much the same effect. In *The Merchant of Venice* (1908) he arranged his text so that the sequence of scenes taking place in the Jewish Ghetto, representing Jessica's elopement and Shylock's reaction to it, were run together into one scenic unit. This allowed him to make his single set more elaborate for this act; but it also enabled him to have greater control over the environmental details which affect the characters. Tree wrote in his program notes:

> In the present arrangement of the play, I have placed the second act entirely in the Ghetto, in order to bring the story of Shylock into greater cohesion. This, I believe, has not been done before. It enables us to see much of the life of the Jews and the customs and manners of the day. For many of the details of this scene I am indebted to the courteous assistance of high Jewish authorities.

While Jewish sacred music was played during Shylock's scene with Tubal in Bourchier's production, Tree introduced the Kol Nidrei as an entr'acte and as a periodic sound wafting from the synagogue at the corner of the set. The language of Tree's description of the Ghetto scene smacks of archaeological reverence, and certainly he carried this far in his promotional notices, one of which boasts that "the pains which have been taken to secure actuality are indicated by the fact that each member of the various groups which compose the picture is a veritable Hebrew."[36] But Tree's concern was characteristically more than archaeology. The life of the Ghetto which Tree pantomimically inserted succeeded in underscoring what he decided were fundamental issues of the play: race hatred and the vengeance it inspires. When the Jews leave the synagogue, a fight breaks out between them and rowdy Christians which, after momentarily subsiding with the ringing of the curfew bell and the entrance of a nightwatchman (*vide Die Meistersinger*), becomes a full-fledged pogrom, during which the dummy likeness of an old Jew is thrown over a footbridge into the canal. Just as Tree's Malvolio was supported by four mimic servants in identical dress, Tree's Shylock was shadowed and supported by the sinister monkey-like Tubal; and in the "Hath not a Jew eyes" speech, he was supported by a full chorus of his "veritable Hebrews" who echo his call for "revenge" with a vociferous "Ay, Revenge!!"

Another important aspect of traditionalist stage unity was the integration of the actor into the stage picture. This had been important ever since the emergence of the romantic stage aesthetic in the late eighteenth and early nineteenth centuries.[37] As the pictorial theatre of the late nineteenth century was equally or significantly more an actor's theatre, so the integration of the actor and the character into the fictive reality of the stage environment drew upon another system of scenic unities.

One of the means by which the actor is set into the contextual frame of the picture is through costume. Costume was a major concern of the theatrical archaeologists, and Godwin's principal written contribution to contemporary staging was a long series of articles on historical costumes for Shakespeare's plays. Ellen Terry, echoing Wilde in stating that "Archaeology is not a pedantic method, but a method of artistic illusion," defined costume as "a means of displaying character without description, and of producing dramatic situations and dramatic effects."[38] The goal of the actor was to convey an illusion of the reality of the dramatic situation within the pictorial stage environment. Costume mediates between the internal reality of the actor and the unity of the total theatrical effect; as Henry Irving put it, "when you are getting into the skin of the character you must not neglect the wardrobe."[39] The interrelation of the actor and the physical environment via costume was summarized by Sarah Bernhardt in a conversation with Tree during the run of the latter's *Henry VIII* (1910):

> A theatre is a place where art seeks to present to the mind a real and living drama, something that once took place, something that was once as actual as our life to-day, a thing that happened. To do this three things are necessary—the genius of the actor, the genius of the painter, the genius of the costumier. The illusion is not complete without the truth of the impersonation, the truth of the place, the truth of the dress. The whole thing must be there. I could not play L'Aiglon in a dressing gown; you could not play Wolsey in a frock-coat; Monsieur Bourchier, in spite of his beard, would be absurd as Henri Huit in a silk hat![40]

Note how Bernhardt makes the "truth" of the dress a prerequisite of the total theatrical illusion, which is in turn designed to create the illusion of "something that once took place."

As costume allowed the actor to be unified with the stage spectacle, the choice of costume was governed by the same rules of unity as those of the stage set. Certain actors who undertook the design of their own costumes emphasized the relationship between the dramatic activity and tone of their role and the particulars of costuming. Forbes Robertson designed his own costume for Buckingham in Irving's *Henry VIII* (1892). And Ellen Terry drastically altered the costumes designed for her for Tree's *Winter's Tale* (1906), substituting for an amethyst colored dress one of white tableau-net in order to convey Hermione's "physical weakness" and "stainless purity" in the trial scene; and for Tree's *Merry Wives of Windsor* (1902), she substituted a red and yellow dress for one of black panne velvet, since "farcical comedy would be impossible in such a dress."[41]

The actor was further integrated into the historical picture through carefully controlled details of behavior and comportment. Here again, archaeology was not used as an end in itself, but as a means of achieving the illusion of a unified, historical event. And so Alma Tadema, who designed for Irving, Tree and Benson, also advised them on manners, carriage and deportment: for Tree's *Julius Caesar* (1898), he taught the cast the wrist-grip of the Roman handshake, and opened his house to Tree on weekends so that the actor could wear his toga in daily life.[42]

But perhaps the most important way in which the actor was united with the fictive world of the stage was through strictly pictorial, compositional values. It is here that the scene-painter's theatre and the actor's theatre merge. The actor-manager, meticulously controlling the stage picture as he was regulating his own performance, created an artistic totality by maintaining a careful balance between the physical, histrionic presence of the actor and the total pictorial values of the stage environment. Henry Irving in one generation of the traditional stagecraft and Beerbohm Tree in the next created this balance in different ways, leading many to associate Irving with the height of a scenographic style and Tree with its decadence. But the two solutions worked equally well in maintaining the pictorial and environmental integrity of the stage environment, and, as complementary principles of staging, show us the gamut of the scenic language of the traditional stagecraft.

Irving, the most magnetic actor of his generation, integrated the actor into the scenic environment by compositionally subordinating the intensity of the picture to the visual prominence of the actor. In doing so, Irving was able to place the character amidst his scenic milieu without sacrificing the human value of the drama or the histronic values of the performance. Martin Harvey, a lifelong admirer of Irving's scenic style, contrasted Irving's technique with that of productions which were excessively archaeological:

> This "archaeological method" of production . . . has a serious drawback—a play itself is sometimes buried beneath a mountain of antiquarian detail. This was never the case with the Irving productions, for he was a master of "tone" (painters will know what I mean), and though he would spend months of research over correct historical detail, he could, with his feeling for "tone," reduce all this detail to a mere background—a subtle gift denied to those who followed or imitated his method, including myself.[43]

Irving's compositional skills included the subordination of detail to a central focal point in the composition. Tom Heslewood recalls that Irving would take scene drawings from his designers and smudge out the edges with his wet thumb, complaining of "no mystery, no dark corners."[44] Each composition had its focal point on the principal actor, usually Irving himself, which Laurence Irving calls the "nub" of the composition.[45]

Irving's effects depended upon the magnetic reality of the star actor as seen against a darker, less defined, scenic background. These effects were aided by the creative use of stage lighting. "The history of the Lyceum Theatre during Henry Irving's management" wrote Irving's business manager and biographer Bram Stoker, "is the history of modern stage lighting."[46] The truth of Stoker's assertion has less to do with technical innovation than with the use to which these innovations were put. Among the innovations were the division of the footlights into individually operable sections, so that the focal segment of the stage composition could be highlighted. Irving and Forbes Robertson both stayed with gas lighting longer than their contemporaries, partly for the air of mystery which resulted from the waves of heat it produced, but more for its limited range, which forced the producer to light individual pieces of scenery separately, and so obliged him to control the visual intensity of each section separately. The result, in the case of Irving, was gloomy scenes and an emphasis on the actor standing before them.[47] Harvey achieved an effect similar to Irving's when a production of *Richard III* in a traditional mode was revived with tour-worn scenery: "I bade my lieutenants 'keep the lights off the scenery and concentrate it on the centre of the stage' and left them to it, with my blessing. To our amused amazement, the staging called forth a chorus of wonder at its beauty."[48] Harvey credited the success of the shoddy decor to "the imagination of an audience," but it demonstrates instead the degree to which the actor needed to be differentiated from the visual pictorial space.

Irving's visual differentiation between actor and scenic environment was adopted by many traditionalists and members of the avant-garde alike in the succeeding generation. Forbes Robertson believed that "the scenery . . . should always remain a background only, taking its place in subordination and proper proportion to the actor."[49] Charles Ricketts, a Royal Academician and scenic reformer, called for a greater spatial separation between the actor and scenery: "I am convinced that, if scenery is to be retained, and I for one hope that it will, in duty to the actors and the designer of the setting, a greater space should be allowed, and the scenery should begin where it usually has to end, namely, twenty or twenty-five feet away from the proscenium. I might add that this is the rule, not the exception, abroad."[50] And W. Bridges-Adams, an admirer of Irving's lighting techniques, rejected the front-of-house lighting of the reformist school, and retained traditional footlights in his Stratford productions in the 1920s so as to separate the scenic space from the acting space: "the golden rule . . . is to keep all projected and focussed light on the actors and off the set; this brings the actors into relief and pushes the set back."[51] This was best achieved, claimed Bridges-Adams, through the use of perch limes, a key device of the traditional stagecraft, which "put[s] an edge on the actors without hitting the scenery."[52]

While each of these practitioners adopted Irving's technical practice of heightening the visual intensity of the actor in the overall scenic composition, it is important to remember that Irving's techniques were not designed to separate the actor from the scenery, but rather to integrate the living actor into the pictorial environment, an environment created by painted decor lit by gaslight.

Beerbohm Tree integrated the actor into the scenic environment through slightly different means. Histrionically unable to assume the focal point of his compositions, Tree created elaborately detailed worlds, illuminated by electricity, in which his characters took a dominant part. While Irving integrated himself into the stage environment through skillful composition and histrionic magnetism, Tree integrated himself into the stage environment by embellishing his performance with a myriad of naturalistic details of both character and environment. This was not a negation of Irving's scenic philosophy; Tree was merely modifying an existing language of scenography and consequently exploring that language's limits. Alfred Darbyshire, a defender of Irving's generation and its scenography, asked: "what is the proper method of stage representation? Before such a question can be answered it is necessary to arrive at a conclusion as to what is comprehended in the term *histrionic art?* Is it the art of *acting* only, or does it include the complete art of stage representation?"[53] Darbyshire suggested that the total theatrical picture is an extension of the actor's art. The traditional stagecraft of both Irving and Tree unified the artistic effect by integrating the actor's art with the art of the scene-painter, enabling them to create together the illusion of a separate world behind the proscenium arch.

Narrative Interpolations

Just as the goal of the traditional stagecraft was the verification of the fictive reality of the stage world through pictorial means, the goal of the traditionalist actor and director was the verification of this same reality by means of realistic, illustrative histrionic business. Moreover, since Darbyshire and others considered acting to be only part of the complete art of stage representation, non-textual narrative interpolations—pantomime sequences, transformation scenes, pageants and tableaux—should be considered to have been as much a part of scenic art as they were the products of the histrionic and directorial arts. Such interpolations were not aberrations from traditional scenography; they were a crucial part of the scenic vocabulary. Like technical devices used to establish the 360 degree reality of the stage world, narrative interpolations verified the fictive reality of the stage world. The traditionalist use of tableaux, in the sense of frozen stage pictures appended to the end of a scene or act, will be discussed in a separate context. But it is important to examine the use of tableaux, in the more general sense of interpolated pantomime moments, not frozen in motion, but filled with narrative business. Such moments were used to embellish the narrative line of the drama in such a way as to verify the fictive reality of the stage space and to unify the artistic elements into a scenic whole.

The validity of the tableau was debated by many Edwardians. Darbyshire defended the use of tableaux in productions of Shakespeare: "They give point and accentuate the value of the poet's meaning, and are perfectly legitimate, so long as they are done in silence and no words are introduced beyond what the author has set down for utterance."[54] Darbyshire further claimed that "when a realistic scene or episode will assist in the accentuation of the author's idea, it is not only admissable but desirable."[55] William Archer felt that tableau scene endings were inevitable in the drama, and presupposed some historical validity for them in the Elizabethan drama, on the grounds that "it is inconceivable that a playwright should never have discovered the convenience of the tableau ending to an act or scene—the ending which leaves a group of characters on the stage and simply draws the curtain on them."[56] Tableau business, as defended by Darbyshire and Archer, represents an assertion that the world of the stage has significance beyond the words and rarefied situations of the dramatic text. Since the world of the play is conventionally "real," the personages and events of that world need not be confined to the narrow view of that world presented by the playwright. Characters can behave and incidents can take place independently of the specific dictates of the playwright's text, provided that they confirm or extend the reality created jointly by the playwright and the designers and directors. Archer believed that when the audience's perception of an historical event exceeded the treatment given by the playwright, then an interpolated tableau came under the category of an "obligatory scene":

> Where legend (historic or otherwise) associates a particular character with a particular scene that is by any means presentable on the stage, that scene becomes obligatory in a drama of which he is the leading figure. The fact that Shakespeare could write a play about King John, and say nothing about Runymede and Magna Charta, shows that that incident in constitutional history had not yet passed into popular legend. When Sir Herbert Tree revived the play, he repaired the poet's omission by means of an inserted tableau.[57]

Archer, then, appears to sanction Tree's interpolation on the grounds that the validity of the characters and the historical events in the play, as measured against the historical preconceptions of the audience, would be thereby strengthened.

The use of tableau strongly affected the audience's perception of the fictional world of the play, and its relation to the fictive time of performance. One example of a tableau sequence, written into an ambitious Edwardian verse play, helps to illustrate a special form and function of the tableau. Stephen Phillips's *Herod* was his second play, and while his first, *Paolo and Francesca,* was written along more strictly Shakespearean lines, *Herod* was tailor-made for Beerbohm Tree and Her Majesty's Theatre, and so embodied many of the dramatic values of the theatre and its manager. In the final act, Herod has gone mad from grief over the murder of Mariamne. At the fall of the curtain, he has become virtually catatonic before her corpse which, like Lear, he refuses to acknowledge as dead. The curtain falls with Herod transfixed. A few moments later it rises, revealing Herod, with eyes still fixed, unmoved; but the sun has set beyond the pillars of his place and the stars are shining. The curtain falls, and rises a few moments later to reveal Herod again frozen in position, with the first light of dawn illuminating the sky. By implication, should the curtain rise again, the stage would continue to show Herod, forever transfixed. The curtain tableau implies that the life of the play continues behind the curtain without the audience's participation or perception.

The implications of this device, when applied to Shakespeare, as it was so consistently during the Victorian and Edwardian periods, are profound. To some extent it parallels the novelistic treatment of Shakespeare's characters in the criticism of A.C. Bradley, wherein the characters are assumed to have a life before and between the scenes presented in the play; what Cowden Clarke's *The Girlhood of Shakespeare's Heroines* implies as to a character's life before the play begins, the curtain tableau implies as to his life, and the persistent existence of his world, after the performance ends. A famous tableau sequence in Tree's *Tempest* (1904) illustrates this implication, as is described in the "souvenir" promptbook: Prospero has spoken his epilogue (not that of the text, but his speech from act 4, scene 1 transplanted), and the Italians have exited and boarded their ships:

> Caliban creeps from his cave, and watches the departing ship bearing away the freight of humanity which for a brief spell has gladdened and saddened his island home, and taught him to "seek for grace." For the last time Ariel appears, singing the song of the bee.... The voice of the sprite rises higher and higher until it is merged into the note of the lark—Ariel is now as free as a bird. Caliban listens for the last time to the sweet air, then turns sadly in the direction of the departing ship. The play is ended. As the curtain rises again, the ship is seen on the horizon, Caliban stretching out his arms towards it in mute despair. The night falls, and Caliban is left on the lonely rock. He is a King once more.

The curtain falls again, and when it rises, the scene and the pose are retained, but the ship is no longer in sight. As in the *Herod* sequence, the lives of the characters continue; the implication is even more stongly stated here: "the play is ended" before the characters achieve their final state of being; the theatre event continues after the end of the play in order to show this to us.

Such uses of the tableau or interpolated pantomime were not confined to the ends of plays, though they were often placed at the end of scenes. This was not merely a means of provoking applause. Rather, it was a means of increasing the illusion of the reality of the stage events. This could be accomplished through several different types of interpolated pantomimes and tableaux. One type verifies the reality of the stage world by showing us that the world continues after the characters have left the scene or the action of the scene has ended. The best example of this type of scenic interpolation is the elaborate pantomime at the end of the kitchen scene in Tree's *Twelfth Night* (1901), described at length by Max Beerbohm:

> As the two topers reel off to bed, the uncanny dawn peers at them through the windows. The Clown wanders on, humming a snatch of the tune he has sung to them. He looks at the empty bowl of sack and the overturned tankards, smiles, shrugs his shoulders, yawns, lies down before the embers of the fire, goes to sleep. Down the stairs, warily, with a night-cap on his head and a sword in his hand, comes Malvolio, awakened and fearful of danger. He peers around, lunging with his sword at the harmless furniture. One thinks of Don Quixiote and "the notable adventure of the wine-skins." Satisfied, he retraces his footsteps up the staircase. A cock crows, and, as the curtain falls, one is aware of a whole slumbering household, and of the mystery of an actual dawn.[58]

This interpolation carried with it the implication that the life of the great household, in which the play is set, goes on around the clock.

Another standard type of narrative interpolation extends the action of the scene, exploring its repercussions and implying possible consequences.

Characters that have died are buried or cremated, bodies are borne aloft (as in the final moments of *Hamlet*, though this implied action was usually cut in traditionalist productions of the play), and newly crowned monarchs are raised onto the shoulders of their followers.[59] Narrative interpolations were also used to prepare the way for action which followed, either by creating a sense of foreboding or by showing characters already engaged in preparing for succeeding scenes.[60]

By leaving characters onstage after the scene has ended or by bringing them back onstage, the traditionalist director could comment upon the action of the scene by showing how the character reacts to the preceding events, how he was emotionally involved in the action, or how he secretly feels about what has just transpired.[61] One common motif involved one character mourning over the death of another.[62] Perhaps the most elaborate example of this type of pantomime was a sequence in Matheson Lang's *Romeo and Juliet* (1908), in which the bridesmaids, bedecked for Juliet's wedding to Paris, enter to find her apparently dead. Max Beerbohm described the moment, laughingly underscored Darbyshire's rule that interpolations are legitimate so long as no words other than the playwright's are introduced: the leader of the bridesmaids "says nothing—because, I suppose, the managers of the Lyceum, Messrs Smith and Carpenter, have not been able to agree as to just what Shakespeare would have made her say—but it is evident that she thinks the worst. 'O Juliet, Juliet, Juliet, thou are dead' is the language of her eyes."[63]

Pictorial and narrative interpolations could be used to bring out the symbolic values of the drama as well, and Tree was once again a prime practitioner. Previously, Irving introduced a skeletal, drooping "fate tree" into virtually every one of his productions. Tree's *Antony and Cleopatra* (1906) opened and closed with a gauze effect of the Sphinx appearing and disappearing. Tree described the effect to the press:

> The major part of the drama is laid in Egypt, that wonderful civilization which has been for some centuries buried beneath the sands of time. There remains through the centuries the calm figure of the Sphinx, still gazing across the desert of to-day, as it did in the days of Egyptian greatness; so I propose at the rise of the curtain that this Symbol shall be the opening note of the play. At the close of our falling night we see looming once more through the darkness the clam, indifferent figure of the Sphinx in the desert. The play ends, as it begins, with this symbol of eternity.[64]

The preparation copy for *The Merchant of Venice* (1908) in the Folger demonstrates how Tree could use illustrative business in a symbolic manner: in the Ghetto scene, as Shylock comes on stage, "he kicks Launcelot who is asleep outside. When Shylock is gone Launcelot kicks a little Jew boy who is asleep." Tree appends to this description the following note: "Jew kicks Christian—Christian kicks Jew—this is the story of the play." Tree's *King*

John (1899) ended with a spectacular dawn effect, meant to symbolize the hope associated with the new reign.[65] And the division of stage space could also be used symbolically; Tree described in an interview one such device in *Henry VIII:*

> In the scene at the end of [Wolsey's] career as statesman, which puzzled me greatly for a long time, for I could not understand how Shakespeare imagined it, I have overcome the difficulties which I found by dividing the stage in two. I hope to have symbolised the tragic episode of his farewell and his entry into monastic life by my treatment. You will see Wolsey quietly disappear from the world, knocking at the door of heaven, as it were.[66]

The stage was divided into an antechamber and an adjoining chapel; the latter remained in darkness until Wolsey's exit from one room to the other.[67] Note also Tree's belief that Shakespeare must have had some localized physicalization of the scene in mind when composing his drama.

Narrative interpolations, then, could be used by the traditionalist theatre practitioner to extend the reality of the stage world and to augment the dramatic and symbolic values of the drama. This is not to say that Edwardian traditionalists were not guilty of using pictorial elaborations and irrelevant interpolations irresponsibly.[68] Indeed, pageantry was often made an end in itself, justified by Shakespeare's supposed interest in pure pageantry and the supposed conventions of the Elizabethan playhouse.[69] But the pictorial elaborations of the late Victorian and Edwardian stages were, in their purest forms, instruments of illusion designed to verify the independent reality of the stage world and to work in conjunction with other artistic elements on the stage toward the creation of a unified artistic effect.

Character and Environment

As we have seen, Victorian and Edwardian stage realism often attempted to integrate the character into the stage environment. But the stage picture was often employed to demonstrate the degree to which a character was alienated from his environment. The internal reality of the stage environment could be used to heighten the plight of the central character; or, through the use of several common traditionalist techniques, the stage picture could be made to represent the world as perceived by the alienated character. Many traditionalist Edwardian Shakespeare productions used either or both of these techniques.

Several of Tree's dramatic impersonations depended upon the juxtaposition of the character with a hostile or uncontrollable environment. This in part informed the diablerie of his many Jewish chacters (Macari, Svengali, Fagin and Shylock). But it also accounted for his interpretation of several

Shakespearean roles, in particular Hamlet and Richard II. Tree's program note to *Richard II* compared the situation of the two characters:

> It may well be imagined that the tragic figure of Richard served the poet as a model for the development of the character of Hamlet, with whom the ill-fated king has many points of resemblance. In both instances we have the spectacle of a young prince thrown into surroundings of barbarism and corruption, both incapable of grappling with the stern facts of life.

Tree then noted temperamental and poetical similarities between the two.[70] Behind this comparison was the notion that the character was fundamentally incompatible with the forces of his environment. Tree's teutonic Hamlet, usually compared with Werther, here had more kinship with the romantic idea of Hamlet defined in *Wilhelm Meister*. In his *Richard II* (1903) Tree used decor and illustrative business to illustrate the character's separation from the personal and political forces at work around him. The first scene of the play was enlarged by an extended pantomime involving the King and his favorites at croquet. The King did not heed any of the angry pantomime messages whispered to him until John of Gaunt took the matter into his own hand. The scenic environment thus created was one of political unrest surrounding the enclosed garden retreat into which the King had walled himself.

In these cases, the stage scene represented an immutable environment which directly affected the character's own nature. But the traditional stagecraft further allowed the scene to reflect the character's psychological state through its mutability, its capacity to be visually transformed according to a character's changing perceptions. The mutability of the stage environment was borrowed, in several instances, from the contemporary Christmas pantomime, which invariably included a major "transformation scene." Several Shakespeare productions borrowed directly from the Christmas pantomimes. In Tree's 1900 *Midsummer Night's Dream,* the final scene in the Palace of Theseus was transformed for the entrance of the fairies; this change was described in the publicity material: "the picture will be suddenly flooded with light, massive pillars becoming translucent, and the stage full of dancers."[71] Tree also staged *The Tempest* (1904) during Christmas season, and amateur critic Richard Dickins noted the use of a pantomime device on the first entrance of Caliban: "A very tall fairy entered, and the scene changed, disclosing a cardboard rock, a portion of which slid aside in true pantomime fashion, discovering Mr. Tree as a sort of Demon King."[72] But Tree introduced a far more elaborate transformation scene into the production when Caliban and his confederates are pursued by the hounds of Prospero's conjuring; the souvenir promptbook describes the scene:

> Prospero's magic wand is once more at work. To Caliban, Stephano and Trinculo is now revealed a monstrous cave. At first there is an uncanny silence. The three are paralyzed with

fear. They attempt to creep off, but are met at every turn by strange shapes which, appearing from behind the rocks, bow to the drunkards with a mocking and haunting politeness. The three men rush up the steps, but are again met by divers spirits with terrible and unearthly shapes. They are hunted about and tortured as Shakespeare directs. Once more they seek to rush from their tormentors, but the air itself is now inhabited by the denizens of the nightmares which affect conscience-stricken men. The shapes laugh a hollow laugh. The punishment of the drunkard is now complete—the comic inferno dissolves and we are once more in Prospero's cave.

The transformations, and in particular the final vision of the nightmarish images, were achieved through the traditional use of gauzes. The implication of the sequence is that Prospero has conjured with his magic only those creatures of fantasy which are already present in the recesses of the conspirators' imaginations.

The use of gauzes for subjective visions dates back to well before the middle of the century; early examples within Edwardian memory include the visions of the Dei Franchis in *The Corsican Brothers,* and Matthias's vision of his murder of the Polish Jew, and his later fantasy trial and hypnotism in *The Bells.* Both of the pieces remained in the active repertoire of Irving, and of his sons and imitators, well into the Edwardian period. And the device reappeared in newer romantic plays: *Nelson's Enchantress* (1897) ended with Mrs. Hamilton's vision of Nelson's death onboard the Victory.[73] And when H. B. Irving produced *For the Soul of the King* in 1910, Max Beerbohm complained that the device was inexcusably old fashioned:

> reality ... [when] we saw a "transparency" meant to represent the execution of King Louis, utterly collapsed. Yes, actually, in a would-be realistic play produced in 1910, a transparency! ... It is lamentable that so gifted an actor as Mr. Irving should submit to this ludicrous device. His father submitted to it in *The Bells.* That was a great pity. But in the 'seventies a dramatic absurdity did not seem so absurd as it does now. I refuse to believe that any stage-manager with a method formed since the 'seventies would solemnly go out of his way to introduce a "transparency." Mr. Irving's stage-manager must, accordingly, be well-stricken in years.[74]

In fact, Irving had retained in his company the services of many theatre artists who had worked for his father for decades. By maintaining the scenic traditions of the romantic drama performed by his father, H. B. Irving was taking advantage of devices well within the scenic repertoire of the romantic drama, inclusive of Shakespeare, in the Edwardian period.

Tree's most effective use of the subjective vision transparency was at the end of *Richard II* (1903): the final scene was cut, but Bolingbroke's coronation was seen in pantomime through a transparency in the wall of Richard's prison; the promptbook describes the sequence:

> ... the KING falls mortally wounded just in the ray of light in front of the column.— EXTON & ATTENDANT slink off up steps. The KING continues dialogue "Exton, thy

fierce hand," etc., struggling up until he rests at the base of the column in a sitting position, and speaks remaining lines of the play. At the words "sink downward here to die" he drops dying—The death bell of the Castle now peals out in unison with plaintive music from the Orchestra; and the Choir are ready set behind back of the Dungeon in the Coronation set, and take it up in song.—Every light fades out except one faint pencil light on the KING's face from the O. P. perch, and the gauze and back cloth are taken up. Then the limes and electrics grow, disclosing the congregation gathered in the Abbey for the Coronation. The ceremonial of the crown being placed on BOLINGBROKE's head then takes place—He rises, turns, bows to the people R. and L., and at the end of the first part of the Te Deum the lights and all fade again to blackness, leaving the KING just sinking in his last death agony, and the Curtain falls on the end of the strain of music from the Orchestra.

By implication, the visual reality of the stage event is a projection of the perception of the focal, pin-spotted character. Here stage reality transcends mere environment and becomes a reflection of psychological stage. Tree used this same device again, by implication at least, when he arranged the text of *Henry VIII:* the play ended with the coronation of Anne Bullen, and all the rest of the play was cut, with the exception of Katherine's death scene, which was transposed to a point directly before the coronation. The coronation became, in effect, Katherine's second death vision; and as the observations of the two gentlemen are cut, the juxtaposition of her fall and Anne's rise is as direct as Richard's death and Bolingbroke's rise in the earlier production. In Tree's *Macbeth* (1911), the physical environment was similarly transformed at key moments to represent, through the techniques of traditional pictorialism, a phantasmagorical projection of Macbeth's tortured psyche.[75] The production was originally to have been designed by Gordon Craig. Given Tree's penchant for using the stage world as a subjective vision of the character's mind, it is not surprising that he was an admirer of Craig's Moscow *Hamlet,* which he saw on 22 February 1913.[76] Viola Tree recalls that her father "described this as a wonder of gold kings and courtiers from which background the tiny black figure of Hamlet detached itself."[77]

Tree's admiration of at least one aspect of Craig's work is indicative of the aesthetic and conceptual similarities between the traditional stagecraft and the New Stagecraft. These similarities will be examined in detail in Chapter 3. Taken by itself, however, the traditional stagecraft certainly had great integrity of purpose. It was an elaborate system devised for the creation of the illusion of a complete, separate historical world, in which lifelike events occurred. The quality and nature of the environment was directly supported by the dramatic activity, the mood of the drama, the psychology of the actor and the symbolic content of the drama. And the stage event was unified either by means of visual composition or through the elaboration of visual narrative material, which also served to verify the fictive reality of the stage world.

The Special Demands of Shakespeare's Plays

The traditional stagecraft was not static and unchanging during the Edwardian period. As the demands for scenic realism became greater, the traditional conventional means of creating the illusion of realism became less effective. This was particularly true for Shakespeare, for the plays demanded a scenic treatment which made them technically unsuitable to strictly realistic treatment. To produce Shakespeare in a manner in keeping with the contemporary demands of scenic realism, Edwardian traditionalists had either to alter the texts and stagecraft of the plays, or to modify the principles of their own stagecraft. The resulting theatrical products were often paradoxical compromises of Edwardian scenic principles. Traditional productions of Shakespeare, therefore, were at the center of the Edwardian conflict between dramatic ends and theatrical means. It is useful to define what the Edwardians regarded to be the special demands of Shakespeare's texts, and to examine the ways in which the practitioners of the traditional stagecraft dealt with them.

The scenic reforms of the late nineteenth century involved the perfection of the means used to create an illusion of stage realism. Such reforms included an increasing use of three-dimensional built-up scenes in place of painted wings and flats, box sets with working fixtures, and sophisticated stage lighting. These innovations were most suitable to the growing naturalist repertoire of plays, which often involved interior localities and a single scene per act. The romantic repertoire carried with it a very different set of scenic demands. Though most of the Edwardian adherents of the traditional stagecraft did not fully understand the rhythmic nature of the structure of Shakespeare's plays, they did realize that the rapid changes of scene (necessitated by the specifically designated scene locales of the eighteenth-century editors) made the solid one-act/one-set realism of most modern stagecraft impossible for Shakespeare. If the naturalist reforms of the elite modern drama were to be applied to Shakespeare, it was necessary either to change the rhythmic patterns of Shakespeare's texts or to make compromises in the consistency of the naturalistic three-dimensionality of the stage.

Continuity

The most conservative Edwardian traditionalists were aware of the special demands of Shakespeare's plays. And while the advocates of Elizabethanism and New Stagecraft claimed that the traditional stagecraft was fundamentally ill-equipped to deal with these demands, the traditionalists nevertheless made their own handling of these problems part of their publicity. According to the Edwardians, Shakespeare's plays demanded flexibility of scenery and continuity of action. Matheson Lang, the young star of the Smith-Carpenter management of the Lyceum, described his acting version of *Romeo and Juliet* (1908) as having been "arranged for speed and continuity of action."[78] Even Beerbohm Tree claimed that he was meeting the special demands of the plays. In using a three-act division for *Julius Caesar* (1898), Tree claimed, "a nearer approach is thus made to the Shakespearean ideal than could be given by presenting the play with long waits, nowadays inseparable from a five-act tragedy."[79] Tree certainly did not fully understand the type of continuity which Shakespeare, according to Edwardian scholarly notions, required. He justified his cuts in *Antony and Cleopatra* (1906) on the grounds that "the loose construction of Act III., involving as it does the necessity of no fewer than eleven changes of scene, could hardly have fulfilled the ideal dramatic requirements even of those days."[80] It was beyond Tree's comprehension that such an act on the Elizabethan stage would not have required any physical change of scene at all. And while Tree's use of a three-act division of Shakespeare's plays was based on other issues, including the imposition of Aristotelian form, it did not necessarily alter the rhythmic structure of the plays in performance, as the scene waits within each act removed any advantages which may have accrued to one or two fewer act intervals. Richard Dickins noted that "the divisions at His Majesty's are of little or no consequence, as the curtains fall and there is an interval after every scene, so that the arrangement of the plays would be better and more correctly described as being, not in acts, but in so many scenes."[81] The productions in the traditional style by many of Tree's contemporaries had a similar structure. The programs for Harvey's *Hamlet* (1906), Bourchier's *Macbeth* (1906) and Asche's *Julius Caesar* (Australian tour), for example, reveal that designated intervals were frequent but short—often only five or six minutes—so that the divisions between the scenes and between the four or five acts resembled each other in length and rhythmic effect upon the structure of the plays. The typical Edwardian traditional production of Shakespeare progressed evenly but in fits and starts, with an irregular but consistent continuity. This continuity was certainly un-Shakespearean, but the traditionalist producer's claims for "Shakespeare's intentions" have some validity nonetheless.

Organizational Determinants

The technical and conventional systems employed by scenic traditionalists were to a great extent dictated by organizational determinants, the conditions of finance, repertoire and touring facing any artist-manager. These organizational determinants invariably affected the specific proposals which were designed to solve the problem of integrating Shakespeare's stagecraft and the contemporary scenic vocabulary.

Although the romantic drama aspired to long runs, the repertoire as a whole was dependent upon its stars, and stars could best attract, both in London and the provinces, by displaying their versatility in a repertory of new and old roles. So, while Irving performed a single play in a given Lyceum season, during the final month a repertory of works was taken out on tour of the number one provincial towns or to America. Similarly, companies relying predominantly on provincial touring which carried a "classical" repertoire of Shakespeare or Old Comedy needed several plays to fill their weekly bill, in contrast to other companies which travelled with one piece, usually the latest London comedy or musical. The so-called "repertoire" companies resembled, in many ways, the old stock companies in terms of their scenic demands: scenery needed to be reusable in a variety of productions, and so a specific design for each piece was not as important as versatility and relative simplicity. In the 1880s, the Compton Comedy Company, playing the seconds and the smalls, could still travel without most of the scenery they required, relying on the stock pieces in local theatres left over from the stock company and circuit days.[82] The major London classical companies travelled heavy, even with a medium to large size repertoire; for example, Tree carried 418 pieces of scenery on his 1895 American tour (which included *Hamlet* and *The Merry Wives of Windsor*).[83] By contrast, in 1906, Benson's number one company (of three on the road in England and one in the West Indies) travelled with only four backdrops, eighteen pieces (wings, cut cloths, doorways, all presumably two dimensional), six ground rows, one set tree, and four raking platforms.[84] Benson had purchased the physical effects of Forbes Robertson's *Macbeth* (1898), and though he was using pieces and rostra from it throughout the Edwardian period, the pieces were distributed among every company and rarely used as a scenic unit. Oscar Asche's Australian and South African tours were relatively heavy, and yet many scenic details reappear in each production: the ground-plans in his prompt-books reveal that a pair of tiger skins were used, not only for the Cyprus interiors in *Othello* and Alexandria in *Antony and Cleopatra*, but for the Antony/Octavius/Lepidus scene in *Julius Caesar* and the Belmont scenes of *The Merchant of Venice*. The stock pieces left over from Matheson Lang's companies served the Old Vic for both its Shakespeare and its opera productions through the 1920s.[85]

Theatre theorists and practitioners were aware of the financial and practical demands of touring, or of maintaining a repertory of plays in one theatre. In 1912 William Poel could suggest that, because labor, cartage and railway rates were increasing, a replica of an Elizabethan stage might well be attractive to the touring manager.[86] And Archer and Barker incorporated a scheme for a reusable stock of conventionalized scenery into their prospectus for a National Theatre.[87] A frequent managerial practice for producers of the costume and Romantic repertoire was to recycle, in whole or in part, scene units from one production to another. Benson toured for many years with the unit set from his undergraduate production of the *Agamemnon* at Oxford, using it for the palace of Theseus in *A Midsummer Night's Dream*.[88] A pencilled note in the promptbook for Tree's production of the same play (1900) states that the male costumes were "used & altered & cut up" for his production of Nero (1906), and "cut up again & altered" for *The Winter's Tale* (1906). The scene vamp for Tree's 1908 Festival revival of *Hamlet*, a year when he did not resort to his Elizabethanist tapestried version, reveals the degree to which Tree recycled his scenery. Act 1, scene 1 featured the backcloth and balustrade from the last act of *Much Ado;* the Palace set (used repeatedly throughout the play) used flats from the church scene of *Much Ado*, a stage cloth from the crypt scene of *Edwin Drood*, a rostrum and steps from the Ghetto scene of *The Merchant of Venice* and draperies from the other *Hamlet* production; Act 1, scene 3 added *Winter's Tale* wood borders to *Much Ado* castle wings, balustrades and backcloths; the horizon backcloth in the second battlement scene was from *Much Ado*, and had already been used in *Twelfth Night;* Act 3 featured Windsor Castle flats and backings for one scene and Ely House flats and backings for another; and the graveyard scene featured a backdrop and church wings from *King John*, with wings and borders from *The Winter's Tale* and a flight of stairs from *Antony and Cleopatra*.

Localization

It should be noted that these organizational considerations did not deter the traditionalist from using localized scenes created through techniques of pictorial realism. The notion of a verisimilar and consistent world created on the stage was, as we have seen, an unshaken assumption of the traditional stagecraft. The organizational difficulties of repertory, touring and finances were, along with the rhythmic demands of flexibilty and continuity, simply another factor which prevented Edwardian traditionalists from fully applying the stagecraft of the modern realistic drama to the romantic and Shakespearean repertoire. Traditionalists clung to their assumption that Shakespeare must be treated with concrete and specific locations and environments. And it was in this insistence upon concrete localization that many of the absurdities of the traditional stagecraft appeared, as the result of a direct clash between traditionalist scenic notions and the demands of Shakespeare's dramaturgy.

The precise localization of scenes often created problems of logic undreamt of by Shakespeare. Shaw's criticisms of Augustin Daly's Shakespeare productions are often cited: Proteus leaves his father and makes a sea voyage only to arrive in the place he has just left, and Malvolio catches up with

Viola to give her the ring in precisely the place he began.[89] Dickins criticized Tree's placement of the shipwreck of Viola and Sebastian in the Garden of Olivia, Waller's placement of Bianca's meeting with Cassio in Othello's living room (1906), and Benson's placement of the Battle of St. Alban's in *Henry VI Part Two* (1899 and 1906) in a street in London.[90] The promptbook for the Asche/Stuart *Taming of the Shrew* (1904) reveals that Tranio intercepted the Pedant of Mantua in the middle of Baptista's garden. Often extreme localization, devised for the purpose of evocative effect, led to unexpected inconsistencies: Asche's *Merry Wives of Windsor* (1911), given in a snowy setting, prompted the *Era* to wonder whether the characters posing as fairies before Herne's Oak wore warm underclothing.[91] While Shakespeare rarely worried about the time necessary for certain events to take place within a flexible or multiple time scheme, the Edwardians often created more inconsistencies which, within their verisimilar time scheme, challenged probability; for example, the excision of act 4, scene 2 in Benson's *As You Like It* and the conflation of the first and third scenes in the act posed the question of when Orlando had had the time to be wounded by the lioness.

The Alternation System

The adherence of the traditional stagecraft to strictly localized scenes, and the demands for an elaborate and unified stage picture of the locality, created the biggest dilemma in resolving Shakespeare's dramaturgy within the traditional conventions of staging: how does one obtain some continuity of action of the stage, in keeping with the constant change of scene in Shakespeare's texts, while harnessing all of the theatre's technical means toward the creation of a convincing illusion of scenic reality? The resolution of this dilemma generated a modified system of scene change, caused the retention of several superseded conventions of scene painting and construction, and inspired an awareness of the conventionality of the theatrical spectacle which helped to spawn the reformist schools of decor that ultimately replaced the traditional stagecraft.

The late Victorian stage inherited from earlier nineteenth-century stages a perfectly feasible way of assuring the continuity in a production without sacrificing the illusion of solid reality. The solution was found in the "alternation" system. This system allowed for every other scene to be scenically solid, covering the full stage and employing three-dimensional set pieces. The intervening scenes were played downstage against a painted drop, which would mask the activities of the stage carpenters upstage and would allow sufficient time for them to change the set. The principles of alternation are best and most simply described by William Archer:

> Playgoers whose memory carries them back twenty years or so can recall a general practice, in plays requiring frequent changes of scene, of alternating what were called "front" or

"carpenter" scenes with full "sets." Thus, in "Othello," the curtain would rise on a moderately deep scene representing the exterior of Brabantio's house. Then a painted "cloth" would be let down in front of this (or two "flats" would be shoved on), representing a street in Venice; and on the shallow space between this "cloth" and the footlights the first encounter between Othello and Brabantio would take place. This over, the "cloth" would be raised, or the "flats" withdrawn, and it would be found that Brabantio's house had been cleared away, and the whole depth of the stage called into requisition for a "set" representing the Venetian Senate chamber.[92]

To a great extent this practice of alternation was in use in the late Victorian period for Shakespeare productions. Ellen Terry remarks upon Irving's persistent alternation of full and front scenes, and Odell further notes Mary Anderson's use of the device.[93] Alternation worked effectively only if an act required a single built-up scene, or if the two or more built-up scenes required for the act could be set and struck simply and efficiently during an intervening front scene. In 1896, Benson's policy, according to W. J. Lawrence, was that "no play should be elaborately mounted when a change of scene takes place in the middle of an act."[94] When Benson did need to alternate full and front scenes within a given act, the full scenes would be relatively simple, consisting of one-surface painting with a minimum of ground-rows, raking pieces and heavy properties.[95] Benson's scenery lists in 1906 reveal that he did use more scenery than Lawrence accounted for, but the promptbooks from the period reveal a thorough use of alternation. The alternation of front and full scenes enabled Benson to maintain some momentum in the battle sequences of the tragedies and histories, as, for example, with the approaching armies in *Macbeth* and *Richard III;* the latter alternation sequence is documented in the 1914 silent film. The relative simplicity of Benson's sets can in part be ascribed to the demands of provincial touring with a large Shakespearean repertoire; but the alternation which this scenic simplicity facilitated certainly contributed to the rhythmic continuity of Benson's production.

Even the more elaborate and complex productions of London producers continued to employ alternation. Irving's *Coriolanus* (1901), a production reputed for its extensive use of *trompe l'oeil* two-dimensional painted scenery, employed the alternation system extensively. In the case of one scene in that production (act 3, sc. 2), the interior set for Coriolanus's house was probably deeper and more permanent than Irving had anticipated; Irving simply divided the first section of act 3, scene 3 into a separate scene and had Alma Tadema, the scene designer, prepare a shallow scene representing a street to cover the scene change to the Forum. This change was probably made late in the production process, as the extra scene was pencilled into the promptcopy, while other scenes are printed in the acting text prepared by Irving years before the production went into rehearsal. Irving had already interpolated just such a front scene, constructed from the observational dialogue between Sicinius and Brutus at the end of act 2 scene 1 to cover the change from the

Forum, the locale of act 2, scene 1 to the Capitol, the full scene for act 2, scene 2.

As I have shown, the increasing use of realistic built-up three dimensional sets was the result of the developments made in the popular drawing-room repertoire of plays. These plays were usually constructed so as to require only one scene per act. The romantic repertoire, calling for several changes of locality per act, was ill-suited to this type of scenic treatment. In the quest for greater stage realism, many sets became so solid or technically complex that they could not be struck while another scene was in progress. In such cases, the scenic scheme of the act had to be designed around the single set: either the text would have to be altered, so that only a single set and, therefore, a single scenic locale need be employed, as in the cases of Tree's *Winter's Tale* (1906) and *The Merchant of Venice* (1908) noted above; or else the built-up scenes in the production would be limited to a single set, with all other scenes played as front scenes alternated with it, as was the case in Tree's *Twelfth Night* (1901), in which the set for Olivia's Garden dominated the production and was used for virtually every event taking place in Olivia's household.

Useful as it was, however, the entire practice of alternation gradually fell into disuse. In 1897 Archer had already complained that "the simple devices known as a 'cloth' and a 'carpenter-scene' appear to have slipped not only out of use but out of recollection," and he criticized a production which tried to impose "the one-act-one-scene system" into plays which were not constructed for the purpose.[96] And B. Iden Payne recalls that by 1909, his use of alternation in his Manchester Rep production of *Much Ado About Nothing* was viewed as something unconventional: "simple and obvious as this may seem nowadays, at that time it appeared to our company as a daring and doubtful innovation."[97]

The reason for the "seeming disuse" of the alternation system was that, according to Archer, the system had been replaced by another, one more suitable to the Edwardian preference for built-up, heavy scenes: "managers generally drop a curtain, or plunge the stage in darkness, while the scene is being changed."[98] The alternation system obliged the producer to present every other scene as "light" front scenes, employing two-dimensional drops and shallow depth. However convincing the verisimilar effect of the built-up full scenes, the overall effect of the production would be lessened by the relatively unsophisticated scenic technique of the front scenes. Producers who wished to present two "heavy" scenes in a row had either to drop the tableau curtains for a scene wait, or else to devise some other technique for changing the full set quickly and efficiently. Such a technique was devised by Henry Irving. According to Bram Stoker, Irving was the first to make scene change on a darkened stage without lowering the curtain:

> It used to be necessary, when one "full" scene followed another [i.e., when alternation was impossible], to drop a curtain temporarily so that the stage could be lit sufficiently for the

workmen to see what they were doing. But later on, when the workmen had been trained to do the work as Irving required it to be done, darkness itself became the curtain. The workmen were provided with silent shoes and dark clothing, all of which were kept in the house and put on before each performance. Then, in obedience to preconcerted signals, they carried out in the dark the prearranged and rehearsed work without the audience being able to distinguish what was going on. Later on, when electric power came to be harnessed for stage purposes, this, with different coloured lights, was used with excellent effect.[99]

The practice of making changes in darkness seems to have been fairly widespread among Shakespeareans. Lawrence noted of Benson in 1896:

> Hence, finding it absolutely necessary, in accordance with his principles, frequently to exhibit a couple of set scenes in the same act without making use of an intercalary front scene, Mr. Benson had little or no compunction in pressing into service a certain grateful mechanical device hitherto the sole prerogative of melodrama. This ingenious revolving system of scene-shifting permits of one heavy set being transferred bodily in place of another, the whole creating little disturbance when performed on a darkened stage.[100]

While Benson was using a wagon stage to simplify the changes, he did not attempt to conceal them by any means other than darkness. Other producers began to use darkness to cover scene changes. A review of Forbes Robertson's *Macbeth* (1898) reveals that, not only were the scene changes made in darkness, but they were executed without the traditional accompaniment of musical interludes.[101] For scene changes in *A Midsummer Night's Dream* (1900), Tree made the effect of darkness more complete by turning off the music-stand lights in the pit, obliging Raymond Rôze to conduct the players from memory with a lighted baton.[102]

In many ways, this practice was far from satisfactory. William Archer remarked that "the fashion of changing the scene on a pitch-dark stage, without dropping the curtain, is much to be deprecated."[103] Perhaps his reaction was based on his need to retain the illusion of reality of the stage event, an illusion undoubtedly shattered by the transformation of the stage world without its being conventionally hidden from the audience for an interval by the fall of the curtain. It is difficult to imagine what the effect of a scene change would be like in full or near darkness, let alone under colored light; the picture truly falls outside traditional notions of late-Victorian staging. Fortunately Percy Fitzgerald has left a description of the effect:

> How barbarous and pristine are the invariable methods of changing scenes! A shrill whistle is heard; then follow a clatter and flappings, as of a ship in a storm; great screens are seen tottering and twisting; the hands, arms, often figures, of men doing this thing sometimes visible; other screens are brought forward, and the thing is complete. This is rude to a degree, and destroys all sense of illusion. Sir Henry Irving, I believe, was the first to introduce the practice of suddenly and completely darkening the stage, though the noise and flappings still continued.[104]

An entire scenic system, devised to create an illusion of reality in a stage world which presumably represented a real space with real events occurring on it, was being undercut by an accepted technical system which exposed, or at least barely concealed, the mechanism of that illusion's creation. This paradox, as we shall see, was characteristic of several features of Edwardian manifestations of the traditional stagecraft.

Another shortcoming of this new method of scene change was that, although it was designed to facilitate rapid scene changes without using the alternation system, it encouraged a less continuous rhythm of scene change. Traditionalist producers seem to have gotten out of the habit of conceiving their productions according to the alternation system; there are several instances in Edwardian productions when the simple alternation of front and full scenes could have easily facilitated scene changes and eliminated substantial waits. The program for Waller's *Henry V* (1900) notes that "the Tableau Curtain will be dropped for 2 minutes" between act 3, scene 3 (the English lesson scene) and act 3, scene 5 ("In Picardy—the English line"), and the Asche/Stuart *Taming of the Shrew* (1904) promptbook indicates a ten-minute break between the first and second scene on the Induction; in both cases, the waits could have been eliminated by making the earlier scenes front scenes and the later full scenes. The preparation copy for Tree's *Henry VIII* (1910) reveals that he had considered a front scene as a scenic anticipation of the Coronation procession (act 4, sc. 1). The text itself provides the opportunity, as it begins with the dialogue of the two gentlemen, who then provide a running commentary on the various participants. Tree wrote in the margin of his preparation text: "Part of this scene might be played as a front scene, a street or a parapet from which the actors are looking down to a lower level through wh[ich] the procession is passing:—the change c[ould] be instantaneous & the scene w[oul]d prepare the audience for the coronation & w[oul]d fill up the inevitable two minutes wait." It is characteristic of the period that Tree chose to cut the gentlemen's dialogue completely and to dovetail the Coronation with the transposed scene of Queen Katherine's death, undoubtedly interrupted by the two-minute wait he had hoped to avoid.

Time

The scenic and rhythmic continuity of Shakespeare's plays were further interrupted in Edwardian stagings due to modifications in the theatrical means of presenting changes in time. As the extreme localization of the scenic environment created extraneous problems of logic in stagings of Shakespeare, so too the traditionalist premises of the reality of the stage world were incompatible with Shakespeare's fast and loose treatment of the passage of time. The nineteenth-century romantic stage, with its relatively swift alternation of front and full scenes, could handle the often rapid passage of time from one scene to the next in Shakespeare. The episodes in the sequential course of events which the earlier traditional stage chose not to present for scenic or histrionic reasons were not missed by contemporary audiences, thanks to the convention of serial discontinuity. According to this convention, the stage need only show significant moments in the narrative line; between the scenes depicted, any amount of time can be assumed to have passed, and sequentially important events can be assumed to have occurred, though unseen by the audience. Such a convention allowed for the excision of scenes in Shakespeare which were believed to contribute only to the progression of the plot, and not to spectacular, poetic or dramatic purposes. For example, Hamlet's banishment, his confrontation with Claudius after the closet scene, and the circumstances of his return to Denmark, were omitted in performance. Similarly, Bottom's reunion with his comrades and the final preparations for the mechanicals' performance in the final scene were cut, leaving the action of the scene implicit in the fact of the later performance. Another common cut was act 5, sc. 2 of *The Winter's Tale,* in which the reunion between Perdita and Leontes, so narrowly avoided in the previous scene, is described rather than depicted, so as not to detract from the more theatrically stunning reunion between Leontes and Hermione which follows. With the intervening scene removed, the audience must assume that the Perdita/Leontes reunion has taken place, though little reference is later made to it.

In direct contrast to this practice, the Edwardian traditionalists, with their obsession with narrative embellishment, tended to flesh out the scenes or sequences traditionally omitted earlier in the century. Irving showed Shylock returning from dinner after Jessica's elopement; Tree felt obliged to show Shylock entering the house and discovering her absence. With an acute sense of real time, missing events in a causal chain could no longer be conveniently omitted. For example, Tree rehearsed the above mentioned scene for his 1906 production of *The Winter's Tale,* and only cut it shortly before the first performance. To communicate the impending reunion between Leontes and Perdita, however, he introduced a pantomime at the end of the previous scene (act 5, sc. 1): "Leo. move to go to R. He is looking at Perd., who takes a step forward to follow him . . . Leo. stands for a moment undecided, then goes slowly up to Perdita, looks steadily at her face, then with both hands strokes her hair. Leo. slowly backs towards R exit. . . ." Picture replaces narrative, and while the traditionally excised textual passage is not restored, the serial discontinuity of the sequence is avoided.

This concern for narrative accuracy and the reality of the supposed time scheme made certain features of the older conventions of the traditional stagecraft unworkable. One limitation of painted decor is that, when a scene reappears, the temporal details, painted onto the canvas, cannot change with the implied passage of time; Irving made Alma Tadema paint out a fish hanging from a shop in his front scene of a street in Rome in *Coriolanus,* on the grounds that the fish would have spoiled between the time of the scene's first appearance, when the soldiers go off to Corioli, and time of the scene's reappearance, after their return.[105]

With built-up scenes, the possibilities of temporal transformation within the course of each scene were far greater through the use of sophisticated lighting effects. The full scenes in *Coriolanus,* though mostly consisting of painted wings and flats, nevertheless were designed to accommodate changes in atmosphere and time of day: the backcloth, traditionally consisting of both the sky and the landscape, here was divided into a cutout of the distant buildings and a neutral skycloth which could be illuminated separately. Tree employed a single built-up set for Stephen Phillip's *Herod* (1900), and with lighting changed the time of day throughout the play and in the sequence of tableaux with which the play ended (see illustration 4). During the scene in the English camp before Agincourt in Waller's *Henry V* (1900), "the dawn breaks slowly, revealing the landscapes in the cold grey light of early morning."[106]

Scenic transitions from one time of day to another helped to denote the passage of time when no change of scene occurred. In Irving's *Coriolanus,* act 5, scene 2 (in which Menenius fails to dissuade Coriolanus) and act 5, scene 3 (in which Volumnia succeeds) were set in the same locale; to denote the passage of time, the scene slowly changes, after a pause, from night to morning, and the sentinels in Coriolanus's camp are changed. The most striking, and superflous, time transformation sequence in Edwardian Shakespeare productions was in Tree's *Much Ado About Nothing* (1905). Many critics locate the famous dawn transformation at the end of tomb scene, based on Shaw's ironical note that Don Pedro's speech at the end of that scene was cut as superfluous.[107] But the sequence actually took place at the end of the masked ball in the first act. Tree describes the effect in his program note:

> The lanterns are extinguished, the silent night is only broken by the high notes of the lovesick tenor subsiding in the distance. The clock strikes one, and in the appropriate darkness which now enshrouds the scene, the plot of Don John and Borachio is hatched. Here I have introduced an Intermezzo which illustrates the passing of a summer's night and in which the sounds of nature are blended with those of the orchestra. At first the hoot of the night owl is heard, then the song of the nightingale. The clock strikes two and three and as the music progresses we see the first faint dawn, and with it nature begins to awaken; chanticleer is heard and the hoarse croak of the raven. The clock strikes four, the sun has risen and the birds twitter a thousand welcomes to the coming day; the cowbells tinkle and the dogs bark, all nature is astir, it is full morning; the sound of the hunter's horn tells us that man is once more bent on killing; Benedick enters fresh from hawking and in turn becomes himself the sport of love.

The irrelevance of this sequence need hardly be mentioned, and yet it is clear that Tree's extravagance was a direct product of his setting of certain scenes within a definite time scheme: the party in the evening, the plot at night, and the love-sport in the morning. Given this scheme, and the employment of a single set, his interpolative inspiration was inevitable. A similar transition is worked into two scenes in Asche's *Antony and Cleopatra*. The third act of the production ends with a spectacular bacchanalian revel after the second day of the battle. The next act begins with the identical scene the morning after, with the entire court and company of extras asleep about the stage. A herald enters to rouse them for battle, and it takes three trumpet blasts before Antony and the court begin to stir and scatter. This pantomime replaces act 4, scene 3, in which the soldiers notice the departure of the spirit of Hercules, a scene not surprisingly beyond Asche's theatrical understanding; yet Asche was able to preserve the dramatic effect of this scene in the way the court responded to the implied passage of time between the two scenes.

In each of these cases, the traditionalist producer has gone to great length to demonstrate the coherence of time on stage. This obsession with the verisimilitude of stage time is analogous to the traditionalist obsession with the illusion of physical reality in the stage environment. Both concerns are revealing, for they indicate the Edwardian belief that time and place, as well as character and events, are rational, ordered, and causally linked. By illustrating the passage of time, the traditionalist was demonstrating that time can both establish reality and dramatically transform it.

Another way of demonstrating the passage of time was to drop the tableau curtains, thereby momentarily cutting off the audience from the world of the stage. When Tree conflated all the Ghetto scenes in *The Merchant of Venice*, he was obliged to note in the program that "the curtain will descend momentarily to make a lapse of time." Similarly, Irving dropped the curtain in *Coriolanus* between act 2, scene 2 and act 3, scene 1, set in the same streetscene, to denote the passage of time, with the result that, given the localization of the scene, the citizens encountered Coriolanus in precisely the place they had just left. The use of the curtain to denote the passage of time became a common device of the traditional staging, and was even reintroduced into the structure of modern realistic plays. Though Pinero uses his traditional one-act/one-scene system in *Iris* (1901), the events of the third act are sequentially separated by the use of what A. B. Walkley labelled the "episodic curtain."[108] Clearly this increasing use of the tableau curtains, like the increasing use of scene waits which accompanied departures from the alternation system, accentuated the incompatibilities of Shakespeare's dramaturgy with the newer manifestations of the traditional stagecraft.

Convention

With the increasing number of inconsistencies within the language system of the traditional stagecraft resulting from technical and scenic developments, and the increasing incompatibility of Shakespeare with the conventions of the stagecraft, it became clear to a great number of Edwardian traditionalists that their method of staging was in fact one of several possible conventional systems, a semiotic code whereby a collection of scenic devices could be made to stand for a depiction of the natural world. The nature of theatrical artifice began to interest many Edwardians, traditionalists and innovators alike. Traditionalists used this sense of artifice to defend the theatrical potential of their idiom: while pictorial representationalism might not be the only means of presenting a scene, it is still the best means. Scenic innovators welcomed this recognition of the artifice of theatrical language so as to justify their choices of other scenic idioms which they felt were more appropriate for the staging of Shakespeare.

Traditionalist attitudes toward the artifice of the theatre took two complementary forms. On one hand was the belief that the theatrical means of creating the illusion of a real world should not be evident in the final illusion as perceived by the audience. As the *Era* commented in 1900, "In mounting Shakespeare our scenery cannot be too beautiful, our appliances for creating illusion too elaborate. But art must conceal art. The machinery should never be seen at work."[109] On the other hand is Ellen Terry's unveiled recognition of the artifice of the stage:

> "What is really natural should not, in nine cases out of ten, be done on the stage." Think of the scorn attached to the word "theatrical," and the honour of the word "natural," in stage affairs! To a certain extent we of the theatre are responsible; our lifeless actors and producers are to blame—those whose works are of artificiality instead of works of art. The word "theatrical," if the air of the theatre were rightly understood, ought to have an honourable sense. It is through theatrical means, not natural means, paradoxical as it may sound, that a play is made to hold the mirror up to nature.[110]

It is small wonder that Terry, steeped in aestheticism in her private life, should have been sympathetic to the innovations of her son, Edward Gordon Craig. And it is precisely Terry's type of recognition that opened the door for other scenic schools. On the one hand, it is only a small step beyond this recognition to the threshold of Elizabethanism. For Shaw, the artificiality of the stage could only be transcended by abandoning any attempts to conceal it; he praised Poel's experiments because "we are less conscious of the artificiality of the stage when a few well-understood conventions, adroitly handled, are substituted for attempts at an impossible scenic verisimilitude."[111] Take away the pretence of reality and the artificiality of the stage does not intrude into the dramatic illusion; Shaw praised William Morris, who proved, in his amateur theatricals, "that no more was necessary for stage illusion than some distinct conventional symbol, such as a halo for a saint, a crook for a bishop, or, if you liked, a cloak and dagger for the villain, and a red wig for the comedian."[112] And from this set of assumptions it was not far to some forms of the New Stagecraft, as represented by the assumptions of Albert Rutherston, one of Granville Barker's designers at the Savoy: "The whole art and charm of the Theatre is its artificiality, which should stimulate the decorator in making the most flighty, fantastic, dramatic, or tragic use of his imagination by presenting that which is frankly artificial, and all the more beautiful for that reason."[113] Clearly the traditionalist recognition of theatrical artifice and their acknowledgment of the conventionality of their aesthetic system opened the door to the rival Edwardian schools which coexisted with it.

The artifice of theatrical convention was all the more apparent to Edwardians due to the problems of integrating the living actor into his relatively artificial scenic environment. One point on which there seems to have been some agreement was the belief that the true theatrical illusion was vested in the actor. Martin Harvey, who practiced both traditional techniques and new techniques inspired by Max Reinhardt and William Poel, summarized this belief:

> There has been a great clamour lately against what is known as the "picture stage," where the action progresses behind a frame when a curtain is raised. This, it is argued, takes from the vivid reality of the play. Does it? And, if it does, why should it not? What we see on a stage, whether there is a frame and a curtain or not, is not real and we know it is not. It is creating the *semblance* of reality which is the aim of our art and this is within the scope of the actor to achieve according to his power of self-identification with his part.[114]

The problem, then, was to provide a scenic environment for the actor which did not detract from the actor's ability to convey an illusion of reality. And here again the newly acknowledged conventionality of the traditional stagecraft led to fundamental inconsistencies. Joseph Harker, spokesman for the last generation of Edwardian scene painters, claiming that the "background should be forgotten the moment the play begins," called for "real people with a background of real scenery; not muddled symbolism."[115] Of course, by "real" scenery Harker means wood and canvas painted to resemble three-dimensional reality. But clearly this type of analysis contains within it its opposite, for the definition of reality on the stage depends upon the language and vocabulary of technical means used to create this reality. An opposite view to Harker's was held by Albert Rutherston, who felt that "it is wrong that the actor, alive, moving, and speaking, should have as his (or her) background a thing which, though lifeless, pretends to live."[116] William Poel rejected scenery, not on the grounds of Elizabethan accuracy, but because of its relation to the real presence of the actor, noting that "the inappropriateness of scenery for Shakespeare lies, mainly, in its unreality."[117] And Shaw sarcastically remarks that Harker's traditional pictorialism could not be improved upon if the actor could only be ignored: "if Mr. Harker could do as he pleased with the stage and the lights without the least regard to the actors, ... and raise the curtain on his painted picture for its own sake solely, there would be nothing for any school to advance on."[118]

Thus far we have seen how Edwardian traditionalists used their awareness of theatrical conventions to define and justify the illusion of reality which they hoped to realize in their productions. This same awareness of theatrical conventions, however, allowed the traditionalists to use the artifice of their theatrical language in several ways which went blatantly in opposition to their usual demands for the illusion of stage reality. Side-by-side in the same production could be examples of extreme realism and frank conventionality; in fact, the conventionality would often be used in transparently theatrical ways to achieve traditionally realistic effects. Such instances point to the paradoxes inherent in Edwardian traditional scenic practice.

One such technical paradox in Edwardian staging involves the relative merits of two- and three-dimensional scenery in creating the requisite illusion of stage reality. As we have seen, traditionalist Shakespeare productions during the Edwardian period employed a greater number of built-up scenes, and relied less and less on the alternation system, which demanded a large number of scenes whose effects are created almost exclusively through frontcloths painted in *trompe l'oeil*. But even built-up scenes employed two-dimensional surface painting to create the illusion of three-dimensional forms. This is particularly true of exterior scenes. For interiors, so often the scene for modern drawing-room comedy, the illusion of three-dimensionality could be created simply and effectively. But exterior scenes, with the recession of detail into the deep background, and with trees and geological features to depict, required a more elaborate combination of technical effects to create a scenic illusion of three-dimensionality.

The result of these difficulties was that many Edwardian traditionalists, working within the romantic repertoire, continued to endorse the use of two-dimensional effects in their productions. Ellen Terry joined Forbes Robertson, among others, "in favor of everything possible being painted," preferring built-up effects only for certain interior scenes, where "it is better to have your details real."[119] The demands of touring with a repertoire of plays kept two-dimensional decor popular among touring managers. In 1896, Lawrence observed that "the provinces are now alone in upholding the great traditions of one-surface painting ... indeed, the growing demand for built-up work indicates that with us this elemental principle will soon be a lost art."[120] Certain productions in London continued to rely heavily upon painted decor.

In 1901, *The Architectural Review* praised Alma Tadema's designs for Irving's *Coriolanus* (commissioned 20 years before) for achieving with painted scenery what Tree achieved with his single built palace set for Stephen Phillips's *Herod* the same year:

> We are inclined to press his claim to be a great designer of scenes in that he has been able, with the ephemeral materials of canvas and strips of wood, to produce the illusion of solid architectural forms. . . . he was able to convey to the spectator that appearance of solidity which from every point in the house suggests a truthful representation of the built-up scenes which of late have been employed on the modern stage.[121]

And Arthur Bourchier credited the scenic success of Irving's productions, Tree's *Henry VIII* (1910), and Asche's *Kismet* (1911) and *Chu Chin Chow* (1914) to their employment of "the art of the scene-painter, not that of the stage carpenter."[122]

Joseph Harker was a vehement spokesman for painted, rather than built, effects, and he collected many statements from his contemporaries in support of his views in his book, *Studio and Stage*. Harker countered Shaw's statement that scenery was inappropriate to Shakespeare by claiming that he could "see no reason why Shakespeare should not be staged in its entirety, that is to say, adequately mounted in every way, with all the scenery I contend is asked for by Shakespeare, providing that the necessary changes are carried out simply, as I maintain they can be with the aid of mainly well-painted backgrounds."[123] He further claimed that built-up scenery was usually indicative of inadequacy on the part of the play:

> A scene-painter is always suspicious when a manager or producer concentrates his energies on built-up scenic effects. It suggests that he does not think much of the picture he proposes to frame; that he seeks to distract attention from the shortcomings of the play by mounting it so extravagantly that the defects will be overshadowed.[124]

A similar claim was made by opponents of representational scenery of any form, painted or built.

Front scenes relied almost exclusively upon two dimensions for their effects. Odell claimed, with regard to the use of front scenes by Henry Irving and Mary Anderson, that he "never received from them much sense of illusion, especially if the subject be a landscape."[125] But Ellen Terry assures us that the illusion of front scenes was often, for Edwardian audiences, virtually complete; two of Irving's front scenes, the Apothecary scene in *Romeo and Juliet* (1882) and the exterior of Aufidius's house in *Coriolanus* (1901), were singled out by her for their "remarkable beauty."[126] Certainly many front scenes created little illusion; floors and streets merged awkwardly with the stage floor, and distant views hovered over actors standing only a few feet in front of them. But Alma Tadema's designs for several scenes in *Coriolanus* demonstrate various ways in which the front scene could be employed without destroying the illusion of reality. In all three cases, Tadema chose to create a visual separation between the acting space (i.e., the stage floor in front of the cloth) and the scenic space (i.e., the painted cloth). In the street scene (illustration 5), the street leading us into the depths is angled sharply upwards and separated from the stage floor by a row of stones. In the Forum of Antium (illustration 6), the foreground consists of a painted flight of steps up to a broad plaza, with the actual floor of the plaza hidden by the steep angle of the view. And in the exterior of Aufidius's house (illustration 7), so admired by Ellen Terry, the rear illumination of the objects in the foreground and the network of branches of the "fate"-tree visually prevent the viewer from entering into the plane of the painting.

The contention between advocates of painted scenery and those of built-up scenery only proves that the Edwardian traditionalists themselves were torn between the flexibility of their pictures and the demand for greater verisimilitude. The premises of pictorial accuracy and scenic localization were not questioned. A large number of successful Shakespearean scenes were composed of a combination of two- and three-dimensional elements: Tadema's forum scene for Tree's *Julius Caesar,* for example, was both architectural and, in its wings, middle-distance buildings, and vistas, painted; and his senate scene in Irving's *Coriolanus,* with its semicircular tiers of seats, was architectural in a production consisting almost exclusively of painted scenes. Even single scenic features of a set could be composed of both built and painted effects. Irving's tomb scene in *Romeo and Juliet* showed a practical flight of steps behind which was the eerily lit painted flight of stairs down which Romeo had presumably just descended. The boldest example of this device was Hawes Craven's scene for Olivia's Garden in Tree's *Twelfth Night* (1901), which featured a long tiered flight of terraced grass steps receding into the distance. The construction of this scene is described in the *Era:*

> It is an example of how much effect may be obtained with very little actual modelling. Almost the only parts of the set which are real and solid are the holly hedges at the right entrance, the seat at the left, and two "rakes" of grass-covered steps. Beyond this the garden walk stretches up and away, seemingly for nearly half a mile. The effect is achieved by pure scene-painting.[127]

An unusual photograph of the scene, taken from a side angle rather than from the front, reveals precisely how unsatisfactory this effect could be (see illustration 8). It is remarkable that only Gordon Craig appears to have been bothered by the contrasting effects of real and feigned three-dimensionality (see below, p. 94). This testifies to the mutual agreement between the designer and the audience during the period to accept a pictorial imitation of reality according to whatever devices were employed to create it. The extent to which the designers were confident of the audience's acceptance of the contrivances is illustrated by a picture of the set in the souvenir program: Malvolio is seen in the middle-distance, on the fourth tier of steps, a position which the audience could quickly see was physically impossible on the painted cloth of the set. (See illustration 9.)

This hybrid use of both two-dimensional and three-dimensional scenery was yet another way that the demands of Shakespeare's texts (the need for nearly continuous action, the number of different localities, and the prevalence of exterior scenes) compelled the Edwardian traditionalist producer of Shakespeare to compromise the premises of stage reality and to accept frankly the conventional nature of his scenic language. The theatrical result is a seeming contradiction between new techniques, and an oblique confession of the nonrealistic basis for the supposed reality of the stage event. Another such contradiction appears in the continued use, during the Edwardian period, of the curtain tableau in its purest Victorian sense: a static picture which freezes the action on the stage into an ordered and memorable composition. Such a device seems to contradict the intent of Edwardian narrative interpolations, which were designed to increase the illusion of stage reality. Ironically, the frozen tableau was usually employed for interpolated moments which would, naturalistically, call for the most action, e.g., battles. George Colman introduced a static tableau of Agincourt into his Manchester *Henry V* in the the 1860s, which later toured the world for years with George Rignold; and Tree copied this device with a motionless tableau of Shrewsbury in *Henry IV part one* (1896). Each group martial scene in Waller's *Henry V* (1900) ended with a static "grand tableau"; and the occasional nature of this production, which was produced at the outbreak of the Boer War, reveals an interesting feature of the Edwardian tableau. While early- and mid-Victorian tableaux duplicated in style or content popular Academy paintings, engravings or chromolithographs, the later manifestations of the device imitated journalistic photography and illustration: illustrated weeklies would often contain renderings of key battles in the same issue as photographs of tableaux from the latest Shakespearean revivals. (See illustrations 10 and 11.)

We have seen how Tree, in *Herod* and *The Tempest*, employed a repeated static image to represent the persistence of a physical state over time. Conversely, he could transform a fleeting, active moment into a sequence of static pictures. The Battle of Angiers was one of two tableau sequences introduced into *King John* (1899) (the other was the irrelevant picture of the signing of the Magna Carta). The battle tableaux were described by Mario Borsa:

> In *King John*, Tree causes the curtain to be raised between two scenes, displaying for a few minutes a battlefield with its combatants, both horse and foot, and its dead and wounded.

> None of the characters either speak or move. . . . The curtain rises once more; those who figured a moment ago as wounded are now dead. Those who were fighting on foot have fallen, and the public testifies its satisfaction by thunders of applause.[128]

A photograph of the tableau (illustration 12) reveals an interesting function of Edwardian traditional stagecraft: beyond the tangle of principals and supers in the foreground rises, in the middle ground, a two-dimensional painted hillock covered with a tangle of painted soldiers and horses receding into the distance. Here, the palpable presence of the actor, robbed of some of his reality by being deprived of motion, is united with a two-dimensional, painted artistic illusion of humanity. While interpolated pantomime extended the reality of the character and situation beyond and between the moments presented in the play, the static tableau reduces the action and reality of the drama to a timeless, self-contained, composed and internally meaningful picture.

The central paradox of traditional romantic staging, then, is the pretence of verisimilitude concurrent with an acute awareness of and enjoyment of the artistic means by which the illusion of reality is created. This paradox permeates every aspect of the stagecraft: the rhythmic flow of the play is continuous though episodic; the curtain preserves the illusion of the changing scenery, though changes in darkness or under colored lights convey the excitement and the trickery of the technical scene-change; built-up scenes are alternated and juxtaposed with two-dimensional *trompe l'oeil* front scenes; and pictorial interpolations both extend the reality of the drama and reduce it to complete pictorial artifice.

The traditional stagecraft of the nineteenth century reached a crucial point in its history during the Edwardian period. The realistic premises of the stagecraft remained true to the last, and directly influenced the rival scenic schools which were assertively non-realistic. Still, the traditional stagecraft suffered a crisis from within, from its inability to find the theatrical means to achieve its realistic dramatic ends. This inability generated contradictory and ambivalent attitudes toward the flexibility of theatrical convention, attitudes which in turn generated a theatrical self-awareness that distinguishes Edwardian traditionalists from their Victorian predecessors.

This self-awareness stimulated the experimentation of the other Edwardian scenic schools, the attempts to redefine the scenographic language which ultimately led to the decline of traditionalist methods after the first world war. These rival schools shared many of the dramatic premises of the traditional stagecraft, as will be illustrated in the following chapters. It was the freedom of theatricality, however, newly rediscovered by Edwardian traditionalists, that enabled the rival schools to exist, and gave them the freedom to offer other solutions to the challenges posed by Shakespeare's plays.

2
Shakespeare and the Elizabethan Revival

The traditionalist mode of production was, by definition, a practice which developed slowly and organically and adjusted itself to changing attitudes and practices. The other Edwardian scenic movements were, by contrast, deliberate, dogmatic and doctrinaire, arising not from evolutionary trends but by willful assertion. They were designed to meet the demands of particular dramatic material, or to redefine the aesthetics of the stage experience. Nevertheless, a great many of the assumptions of these schools were adopted unquestioningly from traditional contemporary attitudes. While emphasizing different features of the dramatic event and experimenting with new conventions of staging, these radical movements often reasserted and reaffirmed received ideas about theatre space, the reality of the dramatic event, and the relation of dramatic text to theatrical presentation.

Of all the reform movements in Edwardian scenography, the Elizabethan Revival was most strongly linked to social, philosophical and scholarly issues. The movement actively encouraged the activities and findings of Shakespearean scholars who, as J. L. Styan has pointed out, were beginning to examine the details of Shakespeare's stage and to appreciate the theatrical dimension of Shakespeare's playtexts.[1] But the relationship between the scholarly and practical sides of the Elizabethan Revival movement was not accidental: the desire to return Shakespeare's plays to Shakespeare's own stage, both in the theatre and in the scholar's study, was in fact a manifestation of broader Edwardian attitudes toward history and the effect of ongoing historical forces on the present. In order to understand the incidental details of Edwardian Elizabethanism, it is first necessary to examine the interrelationship of the theoretical and scholarly attitudes of the movement, and to trace the similarities between the aesthetic assumptions of the movement and contemporary modes of Shakespearean staging. It will then be clear how Elizabethanism was able to contribute to the evolution of a new aesthetic of staging beyond the confines of the movement proper.

Theory

Elizabethanism and History

We have seen that the increasing incompatibility of Shakespeare's dramaturgy with Edwardian traditional stagecraft gave rise to a deepening awareness of theatrical conventions. The Edwardians were further aware of the interrelation of theatrical art and theatrical organization. It is not surprising that Edwardian reformers who called for new systems of organization, such as subsidized theatres and the repertory system, were at the forefront of artistic reform in dramaturgy and scenography.

The Elizabethan Revival movement, calling for a return to the stagecraft of Shakespeare for the staging of his plays, was a product of this same Edwardian self-awareness. As modern thinkers noted the correlation between the special conditions of the time and the resulting theatrical product, the Elizabethanists noted a correlation between Shakespeare's art and the special conditions of Shakespeare's day. The self-awareness of the Edwardians corresponded to the new "historical sense" cultivated by the Elizabethanists with regard to the theatre of the past. As Captain Shotover says in Shaw's *Heartbreak House,* "A man's interest in the world is only the overflow of his interest in himself." Similarly, the interest of the Edwardians in the dynamics of the Elizabethan stage was an overflow from their interest in the theatre of their own time. The Edwardians hoped, in understanding the way in which the Elizabethan drama was affected by the conditions of the Elizabethan theatre, to achieve a greater understanding of the ways in which their own drama and theatre were related and could be reconceived and reshaped. History was a mirror in which the Edwardians looked to see an image of themselves. But as with all mirrors, the Edwardians saw only what they wished to see. Their image of the past was, in many ways, constructed from reflected fragments of the present. By defining their relationship with the theatre of the past, the Edwardians asserted their attitudes toward the theatre of the present.

Both Elizabethanists and traditionalists defended their scenic approach to Shakespeare by attempting to define the relation between the dramatic art of the past and the scenic resources of the present day. They did so by citing what they thought was Shakespeare's own attitude toward the theatrical conditions of his day as expressed in the chorus of *Henry V,* perhaps the most quoted passage in a period obsessed with the issue of theatrical realization. On the one hand, the Chorus speech could be interpreted as Shakespeare's elaborate apology for the failure of his theatre to realize the illusion of reality that he dramatically desired, and it was so interpreted by Edwardians sympathetic to the aesthetics of the traditional stagecraft. Tree saw the speech as proof that "Shakespeare . . . not only foresaw, but desired, the system of production that is now most in public favour," i.e., verisimilar scenic embellishment.² "Shakespeare," according to Tree, "not only counted upon the potentialities of his own theatre to give point and life to his text, but . . . he also, with the prophetic eye of his genius, foresaw the time when a later stage would achieve for him, in the way of scenery, costumes, and effects, what the playhouse of his own day was powerless to accomplish."³ In other words, Shakespeare, had he lived in 1900, would have been an aide-de-camp of Tree at Her Majesty's Theatre. Arthur Bourchier, citing the same authority, averred that Shakespeare "wrote his plays in the hope that some day they would be acted and staged better than they could be acted and staged in his own time."⁴ This view found a surprising number of supporters in the Edwardian period. William Archer, no friend to Poel or the Elizabethan Stage Society, firmly believed that the modern theatre could accomplish the scenic intentions of Shakespeare which his own stage, regrettably, could not: "the great majority of the pictures he suggests are such as, with our modern resources, we can easily realize. That the public should take a vivid interest and delight in such realizations, even if a little too ostentatious, is neither to be wondered at nor to be deplored."⁵ E. K. Chambers, while encouraging the study of Shakespeare's stage, by no means advocated its use in modern productions: "It is difficult, in view of Shakespeare's apologies in the choruses to *Henry V.* . . . to feel that he would not have gladly welcomed more spacious and decorative opportunities."⁶ Henry Arthur Jones found in the chorus "a safe guide to his desires and aspirations in the matter of mounting a play," suggesting that "Shakespeare would be very tolerant" of making changes in his plays' structure in order that his plays can receive "superior" scenic mounting; for example, thirteen scenes in Act 4 of *Antony and Cleopatra* could hardly be presented without curtailment or rearrangement. But, to Jones, "it is impossible to suppose Shakespeare is raising objections in the shades if he knows what is being done to and for his plays on the London stage to-day."⁷

Naturally the speech from *Henry V* was taken by other Edwardians as justifying the opposite view: that Shakespeare, though frustrated with the scenic limitations of the theatre, relied instead on the powers of imagination. Sidney Lee believed that Shakespeare "is reminding his hearers that, though scenery can do much to aid the illusion which is essential to the success of representations of life in the theatre, it cannot do all."⁸ Lee continued elsewhere to assert that Shakespeare is rejecting any attempt at scenic illusion:

> Those who read into these words any regret on Shakespeare's part that his plays were in his own day inadequately upholstered in the theatre, or would have us believe that modern upholstery and spectacular machinery do them the justice that was denied to them in his lifetime, assume the hopeless position of affirming that the theatre has now conquered all ordinary conditions of time and space, that a modern playhouse can actually hold the

"vasty fields of France," and that within its walls "two mighty monarchies" can, if the manager so will it, actually be confined. We know this to be impossible.[9]

Granville Barker concurred, seeing in the speech a "formal confession,... as if Shakespeare had distressfully realised that he had asked his theatre—mistakenly; because it must be mistakenly—for what it could not accomplish."[10] While Tree, Bourchier and the rest read into the speech Shakespeare's prophetic approval of the Edwardian theatre, Lee and Barker read into it a condemnation of theatrical illusionism, prophetically applicable to any theatre including, perhaps especially, the Edwardian.

The Edwardians turned not only to Shakespeare's opinions, as expressed through the Chorus, but to the historical changes in the theatre of Shakespeare's day as a mirror of their perceptions about their own theatre. Barker cited the advent of the Masque, with its machinery and painted scenery, as the precipitating agent of the decadence of the drama. "Man and machine," Barker wrote, "are false allies in the theatre, secretly at odds; and when man gets the worst of it, drama is impoverished; and the struggle, we may add, is perennial."[11] By contrast, Gordon Craig, enamored of the Italian renaissance, found in the same historical transition a different message for his contemporaries: "I don't care a rap what Shakespeare liked, but I may tell you that I have seen evidence in Italy during the last seven years that the fifteenth and sixteenth centuries didn't like their boards bare." The introduction of masque decor in England was, to Craig, the fulfillment of the artistic yearnings of Shakespeare and his contemporaries, not the negation of them. Appropriately, William Poel, founder of the Elizabethan Stage Society (E.S.S.), criticized Craig's decor by quoting Ben Jonson's "Expostulation with Inigo Jones."[12]

The Edwardian appreciation of the interrelationship of art and history led the Elizabethan Revivalists to the conclusion that the art and craft of a dramatist belongs to the particulars of the theatre for which his plays are written. "Our newly cultivated historic sense," as Barker called it, enables us to see that the virtues of the theatre "are the virtues of its time."[13]

> The surprising discovery had been made that the varieties of stagecraft and stage were not historical accidents but artistic obligations, that Greek drama belonged in a Greek theatre, that Elizabethan plays, therefore, would, presumably do best upon an Elizabethan stage, that there was nothing sacrosanct about scenery, footlights, drop-curtain or any of their belongings.[14]

In his contribution to Joseph Harker's symposium on scenery, Shaw stated axiomatically that "every play should be performed as its author intended it to be performed," qualifying the statement only by allowing advancements in technology to supplement the mechanics of staging, provided that the fundamental relationship of actor to audience is conserved.[15] Martin Harvey could similarly assert (when the occasion suited him) that Shakespeare should be staged according to the method of Shakespeare's day.[16] And this view was the cornerstone of Poel's artistic creed: "there is no excuse for changing the environment for which the plays were written;" for Poel this imperative is all the stronger because "the author is not now with us to himself reconstruct his works to suit a different stage."[17] Nothing short of complete dramatic reconstruction would be necessary, Poel felt, for Shakespeare to fit the picture-frame stage.

The desire to find a stage historically suited to the plays of Shakespeare led many supporters of William Poel to hold a symposium on the subject of "the best method of presenting Shakespeare's plays" at Guildhall in 1905. The proceedings of this symposium reveal the complexity and confusion of Edwardian historical thinking. W. S. Gilbert, for example, having no fondness for "modern," i.e., traditionalist, productions of Shakespeare, suggested that Elizabethan reconstructions could only be effective if carried to the extreme of assigning female roles to boy actors.[18] And Arthur Bourchier, normally unsympathetic to Poel and his disciples, suggested a return to the simplicity of the Greek stage for the staging of Shakespeare.[19] Bourchier's suggestion does not make logical or theatrical sense, but it does allude to yet another theatrical revival movement of the Edwardian period: the attempt to find a stage for the Greek drama. The particulars of the movement, headed by Gilbert Murray and Granville Barker, lie, for the most part, outside the scope of this study. Nevertheless, the inconsistencies in contemporary attitudes toward the Greek revival and the Elizabethan revival reveal the extent of the ambivalence of Edwardians toward the issue of classic plays and their stages. The exemplary spokesman for this ambivalence is Max Beerbohm.

Beerbohm was no friend of the E.S.S., which he described, in an extended metaphor in his review of their 1903 *Twelfth Night,* as an "owlish" bunch of pedants, blinking, twittering and hooting in the dark, advocating the methods of the dark ages for the pleasure they afford rather than for their instructional utility.[20] But elsewhere Beerbohm was able to recognize the differences in the aesthetic and cultural assumptions of the period of a play's composition and those of the period of its contemporary revival. He responded negatively to John Hare's revival of Robertson's *School* set in modern dress, and positively to one of *Ours* set in the costume of the 1860s, because of the need to place the values and manners of the plays in their proper historical context.[21] And he was whole-heartedly in favor of the Greek revival, critical only when the plays were not staged outdoors, or when the weather was not sufficiently Attic when they were. Beerbohm tried to explain away the inconsistency of his attitudes towards the Greeks and the Elizabethans: Shakespeare is spiritually close to the present, in the spirit of "romantic realism;" Aeschylus and the Greeks are not, as they are "classic idealists." As a Romantic realist,

> Shakespeare may be—ought to be, I think—elaborately mounted; for he wrote with romantic realism for a stage which was already struggling (even without his guidance) towards elaboration of scenic effect. The romantic realism of his method could not, in his day, find its full expression on the stage. We, after the lapse of three centuries, are finding its full expression.[22]

Shakespeare, then, was at the beginning of a theatrical tradition which could only find its fullest realization in the present. The ideas of the present day are thus embryonically present in Shakespeare's transcendent art, as they are not in the very different art of the Greeks; and so Shakespeare belongs more to the present than to his own benighted age. Once set upon the modern course by Shakespeare and his similarly enlightened contemporaries, the theatre has progressed steadily and advantageously to the present day.

The idea of the arts progressing to the present is found more dramatically in the opinions of William Archer, whose attitude toward the Elizabethan reconstructionists is otherwise inexplicable. Though Archer acknowledged the educational value of experiments in Elizabethanism, he rejected it as a viable modern solution:

> If a piece of music was composed for the harpsichord, we are interested in hearing it played on the harpsichord, because we thereby fully realise the composer's intentions—not because we consider the harpsichord inherently superior to the grand piano. In the case of the Elizabethan theatre, indeed, the argument for superiority is not only irrelevant, it is self-contradictory.[23]

It is difficult to discern the true causes for Archer's chronic impatience with the E.S.S., as he was an avid, and often enlightened, scholar on the subject of the Elizabethan stage, and had asserted, on the discovery of the De Witt Swan drawing in 1888, that "our efforts to force" the works of the Elizabethans "into a frame and treat them pictorially, inevitable though it be, necessarily warps them from their original intent."[24] The key lies in Archer's imperative to the Shakespearean producer that he have "regard to the altered conditions of the theatre both before and behind the curtain,"[25] i.e., not only stage mechanics, but the society of the day and the relation of the theatre to it. Archer was concerned with the forward progress of the theatre as a cultural institution; and in his belief that culture and society can and must progress inexorably forward, he felt that the theatre has no choice but to follow suit, or, if possible, to lead. Archer contemptuously summarized the goal of the E.S.S.: "Because scenery is stupidly overdone, because archaeology in costumes, arms, etc. is apt to run to pedantry and ostentation, we are forcibly to put the clock back, and, instead of refining a living art, make hopeless efforts to revive a dead one!"[26] Such a rejection of the principle of progress was abhorrent to Archer.

Archer's objections to Poel, and Shaw and Barker's support of him, boil down to the classic struggle in Edwardian England between the traditions of enlightened Victorian liberalism and the new radicalism. On the one hand was the Roebuck Ramsden belief that society is identical to its institutions, and that while those institutions may be bettered, their very existence in their present form is proof of the evolutionary process toward better things which has carried us to the present day. The view of the new Edwardian radicalism held that man is as much shaped by his institutions as he shapes them, and that these institutions are therefore neither sacrosanct nor permanent, but valuable only to the extent that they are utile. Each new set of conditions, each new understanding of human personal and economic need, must be met by corresponding new institutional structures, just as each type of drama needs its appropriate stage; and these institutions can and should be changed through deliberate, controlled means. The Elizabethan revival, then, was a revival only in that it returned to the techniques of a past age; but it was also anti-progressive, and as such it was as radical as the political movements that were based on a new definition of institutions and the relation of society to them. Revivalism and radicalism are not unrelated; William Morris, the pre-Raphaelite and "revivalist" of medieval arts and crafts, was a major figure in British socialism. Similarly, the Elizabethan revival was an Edwardian statement about the present and future as well as about the past.

Elizabethanism and Traditionalism: Reality, Unity and Dramatic Form

To the doctrinaire Elizabethanist, then, the fact that Shakespeare's plays were best suited to Shakespeare's own theatre took greater dogmatic precedence than any single dissatisfaction with specific features of the contemporary theatre. Elizabethanists did complain about the picture-frame stage, the tableau scene endings and the pictorial representationalism of the traditionalist stage; but their biggest complaint was that the traditionalist stage was not Shakespeare's stage. This partly explains the lack of theatrical sophistication among many members of the Elizabethan revival movement. It also explains why the few genuine differences between Elizabethanist and traditionalist methods of staging, e.g., attitudes toward pictorial representationalism, should be accompanied by significant similarities in underlying assumptions about the dramatic event. It is important to note how Elizabethanist conceptions of the stage were derivative of contemporary traditional attitudes, and how these attitudes affected Elizabethan scholarship and revivalist stage practice.

As we have seen, the proscenium picture-frame stage of the traditional stagecraft was used to convey an illusion of the fictive reality of the stage event. Though Elizabethanists rejected the proscenium stage in favor of the open platform stage, it is crucially important to note that they did so, not to reject the notion of the reality of the stage event, but to redefine and strengthen it. The concept of stage reality was raised during a meeting of the Royal Society of Arts in 1915 at which Poel was presenting a paper with Sir Squire Bancroft in the chair. Shaw opened the discussion with an elaborate joint compliment to Bancroft and Poel. Bancroft, according to Shaw, had taken the existing stage of his day to the farthest point of perfection, and Poel had taken it beyond it; Bancroft had affirmed the reality of character within the world behind the proscenium, and Poel had established a new reality of character on the platform stage.[27] Shaw's somewhat baroque analogy can be partially dismissed for its complimentary purpose, but it does reveal a truth about the Edwardian view of the stage: the Elizabethanists believed, not in the greater theatricality of the platform stage, but in its greater reality. To Shaw, the Elizabethan stage had a greater "sense of reality" than the proscenium stage.[28]

Poel's belief in the reality of the platform stage is summarized in his description of the Elizabethan stage event: "This was the realism of an actual event, at which the audience assisted, not the realism of a scene, to which the audience is transported by the painter's skill, and in which the actor plays a somewhat subordinate part."[29] The source of this statement, first cited by Poel in an 1893 lecture (reprinted in *Shakespeare in the Theatre*), was John Addington Symonds; but so well did it represent Poel's views that he appropriated it as his own, without quotation marks or citation, in a 1916 pamphlet.[30] Styan is troubled by the statement, seeing in it a contradiction of the concept of non-illusionism.[31] But non-illusionism was Poel's goal only insofar as the illusion of the picture frame created a world of "make-believe" distinct from the "actual event" of the Elizabethan stage. In fact, Poel claimed that his advocacy of the Elizabethan stage stemmed, not from any desire for historical authenticity, but from the desire to stage Shakespeare as "naturally and appealingly . . . as in a modern drama," for which he found the platform stage indispensable.[32] The few genuine experiences with open stages which theatregoers were to have during the Edwardian period confirmed this belief in the increased sense of reality of the stage event: Max Reinhardt's 1912 *Oedipus* at Covent Garden showed Edwardians "the action of everyday life passing beside you and about you."[33] The Elizabethanist concept of reality was, then, a modification of traditionalist concepts. The traditional pictorial stage recreated the context of the historical event, allowing the spectators to pretend that they were present when the event was occurring for the first time. The Elizabethanist stage took the event out of its historical context and enacted it on the open platform in the midst of the spectators, creating instead the illusion that the "first time" of the event was in fact the moment of its theatrical presentation.

As the traditionalist concept of stage reality called for a particular type of stage unity, the "realism of the actual event" of the Elizabethanists called for its own type of unity. One means of creating a unified effect was costume, and as the dramatic event was removed from the pictorial context of the picture-frame stage, the Elizabethanists had to depend far more on the delineating and elaborating effects of dress. Shaw remarked that William Poel's greatest contribution to contemporary production was his increased sensitivity to costume, as the actor had to create his effect without the pictorial context "and go through his part with no greater advantage in the way of illusion than a quadrille party at a fancy ball enjoys."[34] Poel's conception of reality was based on the congruence of character, costume, situation and incidental details. Poel found an inconsistency in the logic of a single costume in a 1919 *Romeo and Juliet* sufficient for the play to "lose all reality."[35] Poel rejected togas for the Roman plays, and criticized the relatively abstract costumes of Charles Ricketts's *King Lear* (1909), not on the grounds of period accuracy or Elizabethanism, but because these costumes failed to delineate and verify the character within the context of the dramatic situation and the stage environment:

> Costume is an essential adjunct in drama, as an indication of character. We know at a glance a man's rank, his wealth, and taste, by aid of his clothes, provided always that we are familiar with the period in which the apparel was worn. But put the man into bath-sheets or into night-shirts, and we cannot tell the master from the servant.[36]

According to one of his actresses, Poel selected the costumes for his productions "with the sole idea of expressing the character of the part," and showed the costumes to the actors early in rehearsal so that they could properly conceive their roles.[37]

So high were Poel's expectations of unity on the stage that he absolved Shakespeare of inconsistencies in narrative logic, blaming these on the inability of modern producers to discern the logic found deep within the text; narrative consistency became, for Poel, a crucial factor in creating a unified stage event. For example, Poel here attempts to explain Valentine's pardoning of Proteus in the final scene of *Two Gentlemen of Verona:*

> In the reconciliation scene between Valentine and Proteus, it should be remembered that Valentine has become King of the Outlaws and has, as his prisoners, the Duke of Milan and his daughter, and all the courtiers. As these prisoners are disarmed and perfectly helpless it is easy for Valentine to secure Sylvia as his prize and to forgive Proteus, already defeated.[38]

Poel added that it was the first responsibility of the stagemanager "to make this situation intelligible to the audience."[39] Similarly, the producer of *Henry V* had to show, if nothing else, the numerical superiority of the French army to the English before Agincourt if the story was to retain any reality for the audience.[40] The internal reality of the Elizabethan play rested, for Poel, not only in narrative details of the story, but in the manner in which the story was told on the stage. The traditional stagecraft's emphasis on "stage-picture" at the expense of Shakespeare's "word-pictures" "takes the reality out of the drama" because the interpolated pictures "mutilate the 'fable' " of the play, i.e., the internal logic of the narrative as it unfolds according to Shakespeare's stagecraft.[41]

As the traditional stagecraft called for unity between the scenic environment and the nature of the dramatic event, the Elizabethanists, despite their non-illusionistic approach to the stage environment, nonetheless retained the belief both in the appropriateness of the stage environment to the dramatic action and in the specificity of the locality of the stage action. Although the dramatic locale would not be pictorially presented, they reasoned, it should nevertheless be specifically identified in the mind of the producer, and should be conveyed indirectly through the selective use of furniture and props. Rarely were localities left neutral on the Elizabethan revivalist stage. Furthermore, there was a vague belief in the importance of defining the scale and ambience of the stage space in relation to the dramatic action: indoor and outdoor locales, public and private activities, had to be delineated in the size and shape of the stage space. It will be seen how such attitudes led to the creation of a zone theory, which crucially affected the shape and use of stage reconstructions.

We have already seen that Edwardian traditionalists recognized the need for continuity of action in the presentation of Shakespeare, a demand which they were not fully equipped to meet. The Elizabethanists adopted this belief as well, recognizing that the contemporary inability of the traditionalist stage to provide sufficient continuity for Shakespeare was the result of fundamental differences in the understanding of dramatic form. In traditional productions of the Edwardian period, Shakespeare's texts were edited in such a way as to make them conform to contemporary notions of dramatic form, to make up for their "ill-made" features. The Edwardian version of the well-made play was as strongly based upon the one-act-one-scene principle and the tableau scene-ending of the modern stage as the Elizabethan play was based upon the physical dynamics of the Elizabethan stage. Elizabethanists, reacting to the distortions of the modern theatre, sought to establish a model of the Elizabethan stage which most strongly removed Shakespeare from the formal strictures of the well-made play. W. J. Lawrence asserted that the entire notion of "well-made" construction could only be invented once the theatre had moved from the platform into the picture-frame; the major difference, as Lawrence perceived it, was that the picture stage allowed for the tableau scene ending, from which evolved the sequence of climaxes behind the structure of the well-made play.[42]

Poel adopted the notion that a modern stage for Shakespeare must reflect the dramaturgical structure which was influenced by Shakespeare's theatre.

So different were the Elizabethan and the Edwardian stages, and the stagecraft that went along with them, that it was impossible to criticize Shakespeare's plays according to the rules of "construction" followed so meticulously by Edwardian dramatists:

> Pinero would no more know how to set about writing a play for the Elizabethan stage, in which the characters appear in the course of the story in twenty-six different localities during twenty-six years, than Shakespeare would know how to make twenty-six persons live their lives through a whole play in one room or on one day.[43]

Poel called upon his contemporaries to admire the Elizabethan peculiarities of Shakespeare's dramatic construction as they already admired his poetry and characters, and called for the publication of the texts of the plays which did not, like the ones currently available, alter the very construction of the plays by the addition of locality and act divisions.[44]

Poel's rejection of pictorial and narrative interpolation was accompanied by a firm belief in the continuity of action on the Elizabethan stage. The "unity of fable" which he considered of paramount importance could only be preserved through "continuity of action" and "variety of movement."[45] Noting the absence of scene headings in the Quartos, Poel deduced an uninterrupted flow of action; "Shakespeare," he wrote, "abhorred the vacuum of an empty stage."[46] A stage for Shakespeare had to allow for the type of continuity that Poel perceived in the early printed texts.

One final aspect of the Elizabethan revival movement was the singularly conservative attitude of Elizabethanists toward the liberating power of theatrical conventionality. Though they recognized the nonrepresentationalism of the Elizabethan stage, the Elizabethanists, obsessed with questions of stage reality, either failed to recognize the freedom of flexible conventions, or else actively tried to deny it. While traditionalists were beginning to recognize the arbitrary conventionality of representational scenery and were increasingly prepared to display the artifice of their theatrical devices, the Elizabethanists were establishing a model of Elizabethan stage convention which deliberately concealed the theatrical means of creating dramatic effects.

Elizabethanist Scholarship

The Edwardian conceptions of the Elizabethan stage (the reality of the stage event, the unity of the stage event, localization, continuity, and an ambivalence toward convention), all of them derivative of traditionalist attitudes, directly affected contemporary scholarly research into the Elizabethan stage and stage practice. Although J. L. Styan notes a new relationship between stage practice and theatre scholarship during the Edwardian period, and cites Poel and his colleagues as examples, he neglects to consider that such a relationship may have been crippling, that theatrical preconceptions may in fact have fueled a half century worth of scholarly misconceptions about the Elizabethan stage.[47]

The Elizabethanists clearly projected Edwardian notions of stagecraft and stage space onto their understanding of the Elizabethan stage. The De Witt Swan drawing was discovered in 1888, and the quantity and quality of the resulting scholarship added fresh impetus to the Elizabethan revival movement, as demonstrated at length by Styan. But the scholarship itself was affected by the prejudices and shortsightedness of the scholars whose understanding of the theatre was, to a great extent, limited to the nineteenth-century stage. The Swan drawing was a Rorschach, into which Victorian scholars projected their own theatrical needs and impressions. As the Elizabethan stage revival was so closely tied to advances in scholarship, it is necessary to examine the limitations of this scholarship, with particular attention to those features of the reconstructed stages which are Victorian in conception: localization of scene, the use of curtains, pictorial representationalism, and the alternation system.[48]

The incorporation of features of the traditional Victorian stage into the model of the Elizabethan stage was not purely coincidental; scholars often looked to the contemporary theatre for evidence of Elizabethan stage practice, on the assumption that theatrical tradition is continuous, and that change only takes place due to the gradual acceptance of minor innovations. W. J. Lawrence frankly pleaded for the validity of *a posteriori* argumentation in theatrical scholarship; and Victor Albright, who went so far as to call the tiring house doors proscenium doors, similarly argued for continuity in theatrical tradition in support of his *a posteriori* scholarship; he prefaced his discussion of the uses of the Elizabethan stage by an examination, not only of Restoration stage practice, but of the scenic alternation used in a melodrama entitled *The Outlaw's Christmas* which he saw at the American Theatre in New York in 1907.[49]

This faulty scholarly methodology was augmented by a few initial misguided assumptions. The first, and most influential, of these assumptions was the placement of a traverse curtain between the two stage pillars halfway down the platform stage. This was first proposed by Karl Theodor Gaedertz, in the essay which introduced the Swan drawing to the world. It is an excellent example of the scholar supplementing inconclusive data with his own preconceptions. Noting the absence of any curtain in the Swan drawing, and citing the recurrence of Elizabethan stage directions which refer to curtains, Gaedertz conjectured that the curtains of the Swan existed, contrary to the evidence of the drawing; they were merely out of sight, bunched behind the two pillars from which, he presumed, they were suspended. Traverses at the stage pillars became a standard feature of the theatre models of Cecil Brodmeier, Sidney Lee, and George Pierce Baker, and can be found in the reconstructed stages of

Baker, and, most significantly, William Poel. With curtains at the traverses, before the "inner stage," and on the "above," Poel's stage was a mass of imitation tapestry (see illustration 13).

Gaedertz's conjecture received wide acceptance during the Edwardian period because it satisfied a number of specific theatrical assumptions of the day. The traverse curtains allowed for the differentiation of public and private space, as the square footage of the stage space and the ambience of the scenic picture were different when the curtains were closed and when they were open; in other words, it reinforced the belief that the scenic environment could be modified to reflect visually the tenor of the dramatic action. This traditionalist concept was only one step away from a belief in pictorial representationalism, and it is not surprising that many Edwardian reconstructions of the Elizabethan stage featured devices for primitive pictorialism, used in tandem with either the front traverse curtain or the conjectural curtains before the "inner stage" and the "above." Baker used painted drops on the above for his 1904 *Hamlet* with Forbes Robertson at Harvard, and from his success with the technique conjectured that the hut above the shadow was used as a fly space for the backcloths. Albright's model featured a painted cloth on the inner stage.

The Edwardians' retention of contemporary concepts of localization can be seen in their scholarly ambivalence toward the Elizabethan use of placards to indicate locales, which was derived principally from Sidney's reference in his *Apology for Poetry*. Archer and others attempted to argue from the dramatic texts against any consistent use of them. William Poel rejected them outright, but from a characteristically faulty premise: if the placards, as Sidney suggested, had been placed on a door, they would have been hidden from the audience for most of the action, as the tiring house doors were masked by the traverse curtains between the pillars during outer scenes.[50] Shaw, for one, believed in the Elizabethan use of placards, mentioning "A street in Mantua" as a typical example in 1895, and used this example again in an article published in 1950, the year of his death.[51] Scene placards were a crucial stumbling block of the Edwardians; the placards represented their ultimate inability to part with their notions of specific locale. Their adherence to this belief led them to the untenable position of most Elizabethan revivalists that the Elizabethan audience actively conjured pictures of the scene in their imaginations as the locale was poetically described to them, that painted cloths were regularly used behind curtains, and that each location needed to be announced in writing. This last position was carried to the point of absurdity by a cartoonist commenting on Tree's forthcoming *Hamlet* (1905) without scenery (see illustration 14). Tree himself had already parodied the convention of placards and the implicit spurious convention of localization, in the Pyramus and Thisbe sequence in *A Midsummer Night's Dream* (1900), during which Quince entered with a sign stating "This is a wood."[52] Few Edwardians could fully accept Reynold's analogy of scenic convention to temporal convention:

> We are accustomed still to the convention of dramatic time by which we allow two hours to pass in ten minutes; or, in the act intervals, twenty years in a quarter of an hour. We have lost the very similar convention of dramatic distance, if one may coin a new term, which no more logically nor unreasonably, allowed two feet to represent as many miles, and annihilated space as the other does time.[53]

Though the Elizabethan platform could be conceived to represent the actuality of the event taking place, that event could not be conceived by many to have happened in an unlocalized or conventional space.[54]

The use of traverse curtains on Edwardian reconstructions of the Elizabethan stage did more than facilitate various forms of localization; it enabled Edwardians to mitigate the theatricality of the Elizabethan stage. The conjectured traverse curtain could be used not only to indicate changes in scenic locality, and to make localities pictorially specific through the use of props, furniture and painted cloths, but could be used to conceal the process of setting the stage. While one scene was being enacted before the traverse curtains, the stagehands could be setting the heavier furniture for the rear stage or full stage scene which followed. Elizabethanists encountered one difficulty with their model, however: if the rear stage was concealed solely by the traverse curtains at the level of the stage pillars, then the audience seated or standing to the side of the platform stage would still be able to see the stagehands at work. To amend this problem, Brodmeier ran a solid wall from the tiring house to the pillars, enabling the actors to enter an "inner" scene from either the tiring house doors or from the corridors formed along the inner edge of the projecting walls, which bore a significant resemblance to the wing space of a conventional proscenium stage (see illustration 15). Baker rejected these side walls but, still afraid lest the audience at the sides saw the stagehands at work, he ran two more traverse curtains along the same plane. These extra curtains were undoubtedly used in his Harvard reconstruction.[55]

The placement of a traverse curtain at the stage pillars in reconstructions of the Elizabethan stage was, then, an attempt to satisfy the prevailing Victorian and Edwardian belief in scenic localization and the conservatism of Elizabethanists regarding theatrical convention. These attitudes, combined with the belief in Shakespeare's scenic flexibility and continuity of action, gave rise to the "alternation theory" of Elizabethan staging in the scholarship of the Edwardian period. Even after the placement of the traverse curtains at the stage pillars ceased to be featured in Elizabethan reconstructions, the alternation theory persisted, and affected the idea of the Elizabethan "multiple stage" popularized by John Cranford Adams and his followers.

The alternation theory was first proposed as a coherent system in 1904 by Cecil Brodmeier. The theory was designed to explain how the Elizabethans achieved continuity of action on their stage without sacrificing scenic detail. The alternation theory called for the division of the stage into distinct "zones." Each zone was a separate playing area, which could be used separately or in conjunction with another zone. These included the outer stage, the rear stage (i.e., the area behind the mid-stage traverse curtains) and, in other models, the recessed inner stage between the tiring house doors and the above. Each zone, with the exception of the outer stage, could be concealed by a separate traverse curtain. While a scene was being played on an outer zone, stagehands could be setting the scene in any one of the concealed zones. By parting the appropriate curtains, the separate scenes could follow each other without interruption.

The alternation theory had to deal with many pieces of contradictory data, which were modified to eliminate contradictions. In order for an alternation system to work, no two consecutive scenes can require heavy properties or occupy the full stage. When Brodmeier and his followers found such instances, they posited that the action at the end of the first scene or at the beginning of the second was shifted downstage of the traverse curtains so that the curtains could be drawn and the scene changed upstage. We will see that the technique of using the so-called "split scenes" was derived independently by several theatrical practitioners: Antoine, Barker, Casson, Payne and Bridges-Adams.

The end result of these conjectural features of the model is a stage which bears striking similarities to the proscenium stage of the Victorian era, with hidden stagehands, painted cloths, and the alternation of front scenes and full, built-up scenes. But this is hardly a coincidence. Edwardian Elizabethanists merely recycled contemporary values and, in effect, reconstructed the Elizabethan stage in their own theatrical image. This seems to be characteristic of Edwardian historical theatre scholarship, as the same phenomenon occured within the Greek revival movement. The reconstructed Greek stage at Bradfield, though it had a circular orchestra and an amphitheatre, also featured a roofed proscenium with the "palace doors" of the facade set far upstage behind a row of pillars. The ground plan, which I derived from photographs (see illustrations 16 and 17), bears a striking resemblance to Brodmeier's untenable Elizabethan model.

The paradoxes of Edwardian conceptions of the Elizabethan stage can be illustrated by two further examples: one, an unfinished piece of scholarship by William Archer; the other, a telling parody of Elizabethan dramaturgy and stagecraft by Bernard Shaw.

Though Archer was an opponent of William Poel and the Elizabethan Stage Society, he was nevertheless an ardent scholar of the Elizabethan stage. He was the first person to introduce the Swan drawing to the English public, and he went to great lengths to reject the alternation theory and its unhistorical premises in his review of Brodmeier in *The Quarterly Review*. But Archer the scholar still needed to satisfy his own curiosity concerning the dynamics of the Elizabethan stage, and so he embarked upon a thorough study of Elizabethan stagecraft based, like the works of his contemporaries, on close readings of the entire dramatic literature of the period. He did not live to complete the book, but a typescript of his notes is preserved, with commentary by Lawrence, in the Columbia University Library. Though his tentative conclusions appear to be the same as his 1908 review, we can see Archer testing preconceptions, and at times almost wishing to find himself wrong. For example, he rejects both the pillar traverses of Brodmeier and the strict alternation of front and full scenes, but he does hope to find a similar unbroken flow of scenes using the "inner" stage beneath the balcony. The platform of Archer's model of the Fortune Theatre, developed with Walter H. Godfrey in 1908, is neatly divided into "front," "middle," and "rear" zones (see illustration 18). On the flimsy argument that processions could not "pass over" the stage using two doors in the same plane (as in the Swan drawing), he conjectures a concave upstage space with oblique doors, and is tempted, on the basis of Prospero's placement of the gorgeous clothing to tempt Caliban and his cronies, to run a rod or curtain rope between the two "middle stage corners." He worries over the likelihood of a hearth placed on the stage in Aufidius's house, and in Peter Quince fashion, questions whether the moon was represented onstage in Enobarbus's death scene. After fully cataloguing the incidence of corpses being borne off the stage, he also makes note of plays which feature tableau scene endings, with the hope of discovering that this device was used on the Elizabethan stage. Surely Archer's conclusions would have been rational and educated, without many of the misconceptions of his contemporaries. But even he was tied to notions of dramaturgy and stagecraft of his own period, and particularly to conceptions of the Elizabethan stage, such as an unbroken continuity of action, which were derivative of the stagecraft of his recent past.

The limitations in the Edwardian understanding of the Elizabethan stage are best exemplified in a tongue-in-cheek parody of Elizabethan stagecraft: the first performance of Shaw's *The Admirable Bashville* by the Stage Society in 1903. When Shaw adapted his novel, *Cashel Byron's Profession*, into a stage play, he took the opportunity to parody, in the text, Elizabethan blank verse tragedy, and in the staging, the techniques of the Elizabethan stage. Shaw recollects:

> Two beefeaters carried on placards denoting the scene. When Mellish was left lying on stage, they were in a difficulty, but, on consideration, they went off and returned with a large Union Jack and held it in front of him while he crawled off. At the beginning they brought on the placard and whistled to the flymen to start the birds singing and turn up the lights. . . . All the indoor scenes except the Agricultural Hall were played on the inner stage.[56]

Here we see the exact localization of scenes, the discrimination between indoor and outdoor locales, the naive but extensive use of title and place placards, and an uneasy use of convention: while the beefeaters can break the fictive frame of the play, they could only deal with the non-Elizabethan dilemma of a body left onstage by comically hiding the mechanics of the stage illusion, just as Brodmeier's curtains hid the stagehands setting the full scene. Shaw was having his fun at the expense of the Elizabethanists; but his humor depended upon the limited perspective of his audience, their need for theatrical illusion and verisimilitude, and their reluctance to accept theatrical conventions unless these help to create, rather than destroy, a sense of stage reality.

Edwardian Elizabethanism was, then, for the most part a projection of the needs and values of the Edwardian theatre onto the shape and dynamics of the Elizabethan stage. We have seen how the traditionalist stage of the Edwardian period, with its increasing interest in built-up decor, was finding new ways to deal with the demands of continuity generated by Shakespeare's texts. The older Victorian methods of scenic alternation, which survived through the Edwardian period more in transpontine melodramas than in West End productions of Shakespeare, appealed to Elizabethanists more than did the textual alterations and scene changes on darkened stages of their traditionalist contemporaries. In seeking a flexible, alternating stage, the Edwardian Elizabethanists were reacting, not to the principles of pictorialism and representationalism, but to the recent departures in traditional stagecraft from the swift alternation of early Victorian scenery. And so, while claiming to return to the stage of 300 years earlier, the Elizabethanists were in fact calling for a return to the theatrical values of less than half a century before.

Perception

If there were genuine conceptual differences between the Elizabethanists and their traditionalist Edwardian contemporaries, these involved the much debated issue of pictorial representationalism. Here again the ostensible subject of debate obscures the deeper similarities and differences in the conception of the dramatic event and the conventional nature of the theatre. While the Elizabethanists believed that stagings of Shakespeare suffered from excessive pictorial elaboration, this belief was based on several assumptions regarding theatrical perception. Elizabethanism raised many questions about the ways by which the audience perceives the theatre event, the means the playwright employs to create his drama, and the ways in which the conventions of the theatre could be coordinated with the playwright's effects.

Elizabethanism was based on the assumption that the various faculties by which the audience perceived the theatre event were separate and mutually exclusive. The notion that Shakespeare actually pictured specific localities for his dramatic action and wished for these localities to be somehow, directly or indirectly, conveyed to the audience was not seriously questioned during the Edwardian period. What was debated was the question of whether these localities were best depicted on the stage or else suggested through Shakespeare's word pictures, and the corollary question of how the spectator perceived the thoughts and emotions of the theatre event: through his eyes or through his imagination.

Shaw and Poel were among those who believed that the illusion of the theatre simply could not compete with the far greater powers of the imagination. Shaw analyzed his own response to Poel's 1897 *Tempest:*

> A rag doll is fondly nursed by a child who can only stare at a simulacrum of infancy. A superstitious person left to himself will see a ghost in every ray of moonlight on the wall and every old coat hanging on a nail; but make up a really careful, elaborate, plausible, picturesque, bloodcurdling ghost for him, and his cunning grin will proclaim that he sees through it at a glance. The reason is, not that a man can *always* imagine things more vividly than art can present them to him, but that it takes an altogether extraordinary degree of art to compete with the pictures which the imagination makes when it is stimulated by such potent forces as the maternal instinct, superstitious awe, or the poetry of Shakespeare.[57]

Implicit in this analysis is the notion that Shakespeare desired his audience to imagine the scenes described in his poetry, the scenes that Shaw, as a reader, could conjure for himself and, within the scenic tradition, hoped could be realized. Poel and Shaw agreed on several points: that the imaginative response added to the appreciation of the drama, and the visual response distracted from it. Once the appeal to the imagination was made by the poet, any attempt to realize the scene visually would break the spell; "the attention of the audience," wrote Poel, "should not be taken off the mental picture that the poet's words create."[58]

At issue here is the question of how Shakespeare chose to appeal to his audience. Sidney Lee found that "no one would seriously deny that Shakespearean drama appeals primarily to the head and heart. Whoever seeks, therefore, by the production of Shakespearean drama chiefly to please the spectator's eyes shows scant respect both for the dramatist, whom he misrepresents, and for the spectator, whom he misleads."[59] According to this notion, the mind and the eye cannot work simultaneously. Poel believed that Shakespeare's "dramatic art . . . is ruined if the eye rests on any picture during the action of a whole scene."[60] Underlying this statement was his belief that "when a spectator is watching a theatrical performance the eye and the ear do not receive its impression simultaneously. . . . In a theatre there exists a conflict in the mind of every onlooker as to whether it shall watch or listen, and in proportion as the playgoer derives most pleasure from seeing the 'setting' he will become less inclined to listen."[61] Even Tree, when it suited him to promote his "draped" production of *Hamlet* (1905), distinguished between Shakespeare's appeal to the mind and to the various senses: "*Hamlet* is essentially a work of the imagination, and, indeed, the less the scenic treatment obtrudes itself on the retina of the physical eye, the more freedom is given to that other eye of the mind."[62] Martin Harvey, in promotion of the first of his nontraditional productions, drew his example from human perception, not only in the theatre, but in real life:

> The crowd at once fixes its attention on the victims of a railway accident rather than on the attendant spectacle of sinister-looking debris; but reproduce the accident on the stage, and the wreckage will, in nine cases out of ten, assume the first importance. The reason is plain. In reality human nature is immediately responsive to the needs of human nature, and the spectator is aware only of the urgent requirements of the wounded and dying. Surroundings are not considered. But in the stage accident, however realistic the acting, the spectator is not touched in the same inward and agonising way, and the eye, rather than the mind or heart, is the more deeply impressed.[63]

By implication, the demands of the eye can be superseded if the human element, created by the drama of the situation, becomes more real; Harvey thought that this was impossible in the theatre, but his premise was that the mind and the heart must be reached, if they are to be reached at all, without intervention or distraction.

The idea that the senses perceive theatrical impressions individually and unequally, and distinct from the emotional and intellectual faculties, was not supported universally. Archer, for one, asked: "are the ear and the imagination, then, more effectually stimulated because the eye is starved or even offended? Not a bit of it! The ideal presentation should be one in which ear and eye should take consentaneous delight, each in its due degree."[64] Furthermore, if the Elizabethan audiences did indeed actively imagine the scenes conjured up by the poetry, it was not necessarily true that modern audiences could regain this skill: "A modern audience is more or less accustomed to eke out with its imagination the imperfections of painted scenery; the habit of supplying scenery entirely from imagination, with no aid from the painter's brush, if it ever really existed in the generality of the public, would have to be laboriously re-acquired."[65] Max Beerbohm similarly maintained:

> that Shakespeare's masterpieces are not at all degraded by a setting of beauty, that they deserve such setting, and by it are made more beautiful, and that anyone who by it is distracted from their own intrinsic beauty betrays in himself a lack of visual sense. Visual beauty is complementary to beauty of sound and thought. Some people have no taste for it, just as others have no ear for music.[66]

Beerbohm further questioned whether the imaginative facility, which according to Sidney Lee and other Elizabethanists enabled Shakespeare's audience to picture the scenes of the play without the aid of pictorial representation, existed at all: Beerbohm asked, "must not there have been, even in those spacious days, a certain strain of the visual organs, the making of which must have distracted their attention from the play?"[67] Beerbohm went on to explain that the distraction of scenery was only a matter of the conventions of the day:

> good modern scenery would be distracting (at first) to a resurrected Elizabethan, because he would never have seen anything like it. Hansom cabs and bicycles would also puzzle him. But it does not follow that, because modes of locomotion were few and primitive in his day, hansom cabs and bicycles ought to be abolished. They save us a great deal of time and trouble. Nor have they produced decay in our faculty of walking, though there are many occasions when they are more useful to us than our unaided feet. Even so the developments in modern scenery, which are but a means of quickening dramatic illusion, do not signify that the imagination of the race has been decaying. When the average Victorian reads the *Midsummer Night's Dream* he sees, I am sure, quite as much of a wood as was seen by the average Elizabethan.

Beerbohm concluded by dismissing the notion that Elizabethans imagined anything at all: "You must imagine either everything or nothing. The only justification for no scenery would be invisible mimes [i.e., actors]. If the Elizabethans were so imaginative as Mr Lee supposes, why did they want to see their mimes? The fact that they did want to see them suggests that they did not see scenery which was not there." One can recognize the progressive fallacy of the "modern," i.e., traditionalist, school of scenography in Beerbohm's equation of pictorial representationalism with mechanized transportation. But within Beerbohm's anti-reconstructionist argument is a belief in the arbitrary conventionality of the theatre event which virtually exceeds that of the Elizabethanists. Only Beerbohm's faith in the superior power of theatrical illusion prevented him from accepting the suitability of Elizabethan stage convention for the production of Shakespeare. And he accurately pointed out that the Elizabethanists' preference for these conventions was only as valid as their root assumption that imaginatively visualized word pictures were more effective than represented ones. The Elizabethanists' persistent Edwardian belief in localization and the sympathetic relation of scene to action forced them into the bookish belief in the power of words and the capabilities of the imagination. And so the least tenable of the Elizabethanists' premises was the direct result of the Elizabethanists' failure to free themselves from traditional Edwardian assumptions, and these premises prevented them from freely exercising the conventional freedom that their revivalist stages afforded them.

Practice

As we have seen, Elizabethanism, during the Edwardian period, was shaped and limited by Edwardian assumptions about localization, the reality of the stage event and the unity of the theatrical presentation, and these assumptions affected scholarship in the reconstruction of stages, and caused a recalcitrance on the part of stage practitioners to take full advantage of the theatricality of the Elizabethan stage. We can now survey the range and extent of Elizabethanist production during the period to see how the limitations and freedoms of Elizabethanist theory manifested themselves on the stage.

William Poel's experiments in Elizabethanism have been described in great detail by Robert Speaight and others.[68] Only one aspect of Poel's productions need concern us here. The greatest dilemma in the actual theatre work of Poel and his followers was the translation of the theoretical principles of the platform stage, particularly Poel's concept of the added reality of the actor and the event, into the spaces available for performance, which were invariably proscenium theatres. The experience of the three-dimensional actor in the same space as his audience was, according to Poel, fundamentally different from that of the character within a separate scenic environment. Working within conventional playhouses, Poel could not place his actors amidst his audience; his only alternative was to reduce the visual sense of separation between actor and audience created by the proscenium arch. On the stage of the proscenium theatre Poel placed a replica of an Elizabethan playhouse. This replica included not just the platform stage, the above, and the heavens, but the galleries and Lord's rooms to either side, extending across the line of the proscenium to merge with the rings of the modern theatre. In the boxes on the stage sat, not members of the modern audience, but extras dressed as members of the Elizabethan audience. The pillars, the architectural accessories of the boxes, and the tiring house facade itself were all obviously *trompe l'oeil*. In short, Poel placed on the stage, not a verisimilar picture of the play's locale, as did traditional stagings, nor a neutral conventional playing space, but a verisimilar picture of the theatre in which the plays were originally performed. Audiences could be made to accept a new convention of staging only in the belief that they were witnessing an archaeological picture of a past age.

Arthur J. Harris has shown through a detailed study of the photographs of Poel's first Elizabethanist production (*Measure for Measure* at the Royalty Theatre, 1893) that Poel did not stay within the proscenium for this first production.[69] The square platform of the stage extended half its depth into the auditorium, with a new row of masked footlights at the front edge. Harris notes that the decorations on the proscenium arch, barely noticeable in the photographs, were incorporated into the design of the stage boxes, and that an

Elizabethan facing was placed over the first set of auditorium boxes, extending the Elizabethan playhouse as far into the house as the forward edge of the platform. But breaking through the proscenium arch did not change the essentially frontal nature of spectacle. No doubt it changed the sightlines from the rings, if they were even occupied at an ill-attended private performance; but no member of the real audience experienced the supposed "contact" of the platform stage in quite the way that either the Elizabethan audience or the fancy-dress stage audience experienced it.

Furthermore, if Harris's conclusions are correct, and the platform did extend several feet into the auditorium, the stage pillars were placed on exactly the plane of the proscenium arch. As Poel employed a traverse curtain between the pillars, the pillars themselves became a proscenium, replacing the one masked by the stage boxes. In effect, Poel was transforming the stage of Shakespeare into another version of the stage of his contemporaries (see illustrations 19 and 20). A "front" curtain between the pillars was similarly employed by Baker in his 1905 Harvard reconstruction, and by B. Iden Payne years later at Carnegie Institute of Technology.[70]

Poel tried to overcome the spatial limitation of his auditorium by an eccentric use of space. House entrances and exits were used in *The Comedy of Errors* (1895), *Much Ado About Nothing* (on tour) and *Samson Agonistes* (1900). Poel's use of space on stage was often inexplicable; Archer was not alone in criticizing the use of the above for the shipwreck in *The Tempest* (1897), which he likened to "a balloon . . . run ashore upon a steeple."[71]

It was Poel's tragedy that he was never able to duplicate the spatial conditions of the Elizabethan playhouse until his postwar productions at the Holborn Empire, which were marred by non-Elizabethan eccentricities documented by Speaight. Poel was aware of the advantages of the Elizabethan auditorium, and based his theories of verse delivery upon the premise that the proximity of the audience in the Elizabethan playhouse enabled the actor to convey "the faintest modulation of the performer's voice, and at the same time demanded no inartistic effort in more sonorous utterances."[72] Poel urged the Shakespeare Memorial Committee and the S.M.N.T. to built a playhouse which duplicated this rapport. By 1905, even his Fortune fit-up was lost to him, auctioned for £100 when the E.S.S. dissolved. The Elizabethan Stage Trust was established by the Rev. Stewart Headlam, Israel Gollancz, Mrs. G. L. Gomme and Poel to utilize the accessories of the defunct society, but Poel did not return to this model.[73] His stages at His Majesty's Theatre and for the Manchester Repertory Company will be discussed in a later context.

William Poel was not, of course, the only man to produce plays in the Elizabethan style, nor was he the first. While the majority of Edwardian experiments in Elizabethanism were derived directly from Poel's work, the trend towards simplicity and the use of curtains developed independently. Among Poel's precursors was the Ben Webster/J. R. Planché *Taming of the Shrew* at the Haymarket in 1844, which developed an Elizabethan performance frame from an archaeological approach to the Induction.[74] According to Alfred Darbyshire, Tom Taylor and Steele McKaye produced *Hamlet* in Manchester in 1873 "after the fashion in which it was played in Shakespeare's time."[75] On March 19, 1888, during his American tour, Henry Irving performed *The Merchant of Venice* at West Point on a bare fit-up twenty-foot stage against neutral curtains, under a Union Jack and the Stars and Stripes joined together by a palm branch; not surprisingly, Irving had recourse to placards announcing the location of the action as "A Street in Venice" or "Belmont."[76] And in the early 1890s, Elizabeth Robins and Marion Lea attempted to stage *Twelfth Night* in Middle Temple Hall, the site of its first recorded performance, but were denied permission by the authorities.[77] Poel produced the play there in 1897.

Of Poel's contemporaries, Ben Greet often turned to the simplified stagings which he learned to use from his collaboration with Poel on *Henry V* in 1901 and *Everyman* in 1902. Greet's major organizational talent was packaging and touring ready-made productions of musical comedies, with his Shakespearean work as a private sideline. Co-producing *Henry V* and *Everyman* with Poel enabled him to "develop" the theatrical properties and tour with them as his own productions; under Greet's auspices, Poel's work reached a greater audience than it had through any of the private E.S.S. ventures. Poel, however, resented the collaboration, and as the stage director's rights to his theatrical product had not yet been formally codified, Poel rightly felt that Greet's exploitation of the Poel productions was tantamount to theft; Poel prevented any photographs from being taken of his 1908 Manchester *Measure for Measure* for fear that Greet's spies would use them to steal the production.[78]

Greet was not, by disposition, an Elizabethanist. His Shakespeare seasons at the Olympic Theatre and the Metropole, Camberwell, in the late nineties were fully scenic, and were criticized by William Archer for being merely scaled down versions of Lyceum productions, replete with stage extras providing local color, rather than aesthetic alternatives fitting Greet's more modest financial resources.[79] When he first presented a non-scenic production, his 1902 provincial tour with Poel's *Henry V,* Greet found audiences less than enthusiastic; he reported that the audiences in Cambridge distinctly preferred the fully mounted productions in his repertoire.[80]

Poel's *Henry V* did provide Greet with a mode of production which has given him the reputation of being an Elizabethanist. Playing in the open air at Stratford-upon-Avon, Greet was able to simplify his scenic presentation without losing several opportunities for pictorial spectacle: Henry's armor glistened in the light of the open camp-fire, and before the battle of Agincourt he was given a dramatic entrance mounted on a white charger.[81] Greet had played "pastorals" as early as 1886, and the Elizabethan principles of continuity, occasional unlocalized scenes, and palpably three-dimensional actors outside of the proscenium frame, proved eminently suited to Greet's favorite summer pastime. Greet's company appeared for a season of eight Shakespeare plays in Regent's Park in 1902, and appeared in several other locations, including the Crystal Palace, through the decade. Outdoor productions were the backbone of his repeated American tours, and Elizabethan techniques simplified Greet's task in touring small towns and college campuses; as he could travel without the full portable proscenium of the standard English fit-up company. According to Sybil Thorndike, the Greet company "never performed in a proscenium at all. We played in the open air and in halls. And if we played in the theatres, we never had the curtain down."[82]

Pastoral productions of Shakespeare, most often *As You Like It* and *A Midsummer Night's Dream,* were a convenient form of low-budget management, particularly for actors "resting" between engagements, or for junior members of companies on vacation in the late summer. Among the actors who toured with Pastoral Shakespeare were Harcourt Williams, Philip Carr, and Patrick Kirwan, the latter's 1909 season being under the surprising patronage of Beerbohm Tree, in whose company Kirwan was an actor. Kirwan defined the difference between these pastoral experiments and conventional productions, explaining the link between pastorals and Elizabethanist experiments: "The chief difference between open-air playing and that within a theatre seems to me to lay in the abolition of the proscenium and in the constant freedom of action."[83]

Elizabethan simplicity could be found in many early Edwardian productions, if only in vaguely recognizable forms. Simplicity and suggestion were noted in two *Tempest* productions. The opening scene calls for either extreme elaboration or completely skeletal treatment. In Benson's staging of the play, a lantern swung back and forth on an otherwise dark and bare stage, while the actors tumbled about. In J. H. Leigh's 1903 production at the Court Theatre, the scene was played in total darkness, occasionally illuminated by flashes of lightning, with the dialogue underscored by the sounds of the bosun's whistle and the breaking of the ship. The stage lights then slowly rose on a picture of the island, with built-up ground cloths and clumps of seaweed.[84] Beerbohm carefully corrected the supposition of his critical colleagues that Leigh's method was Elizabethan: "The method is not the less spectacular because the spectacle has to be on a small scale."[85] What Beerbohm failed to note was the pictorialism of the production's nonrepresentational treatment of the scene: the lightning flashes reduced the scene to a series of tableaux, a sequence of

Shakespeare and Elizabethan Revival 73

pictures to replace a continuous movement which, if staged according to the scenic tradition of the rest of the play, would have been too costly to produce.

The form in which Elizabethanism was most clearly assimilated into standard theatrical practice was in the introduction of curtains or imitation tapestries in place of painted scenery, a device which became virtually a production cliché of the Edwardian period. Antecedents for the technique predate the Elizabethan revival, and include the screens of the Webster/ Planché 1844 *Shrew* and the tapestries strung between the pillars used by E. W. Godwin for the closet scene in Wilson Barrett's *Hamlet* (1884). One Edwardian who worked extensively with a simplified, draped style of production was Charles Fry. When Tree first performed his "Hamlet without scenery" in 1905, Fry promptly reminded the public that he had already produced 18 of Shakespeare's plays at the Court, the Royalty and several theatres in the East End on a similarly draped stage.[86] In 1904 Fry boasted his eleventh Court season, and in 1907 was the first to revive *Troilus and Cressida* in several centuries. Fry performed mostly matinees on the suburban circuit, and received little attention from the press, though alumni of his company included Lillian Braithwaite, Nora Kerin, Margaret Halston and Lewis Casson.[87]

Tree's tapestried *Hamlet* was the first full-scale commercial venture in Elizabethanism in the West End. Tree was by no means converted to Elizabethanism, and his motivations for producing *Hamlet* in the Elizabethan mode were largely practical and financial. He had produced it earlier that year in Oxford, where the scholasticism of the community and the economic determinants of the "flying matinee" inspired the gimmickry of Elizabethan simplicity. Tree had never been popular in his impersonation of Hamlet, so perhaps he hoped that the novelty of Elizabethanism would add to the audience draw of the performance scheduled for the spring Shakespeare Festival at His Majesty's. Furthermore, *Hamlet* was not in Tree's active repertoire; as we have seen, later Festival performances of the play in the traditional mode employed recycled scenery and little special production planning.

Maud Tree's appraisal of Tree's use of curtains was that he "hung them to prejudice, not to conviction."[88] The curtains themselves did not break substantial ground in nonrepresentationalism. Interior scenes were played in box sets walled with tapestries, alternated with front scenes of tapestry, affording a visual continuity without radically breaking from a scenic logic of castle interiors; certainly the murder of Polonius while he is hiding behind the arras, and the eavesdropping of the nunnery scene, suggested curtains to Tree, as they had to Barrett and Godwin years before. For exterior scenes, Tree effected a compromise between representationalism and Elizabethanism which actually resembled scenic conventionalism: he created a scenic picture of trees extending out of sight above the proscenium arch, which, to remain consistent with the drapery of the rest of the production, were painted on backcloths in imitation of woven tapestries.[89] Tree was making his audience aware both of the picture and of the theatrical means of creating the picture, a device later employed by Wilkinson and Rutherston for the front cloths of Barker's Savoy Shakespeare productions. In any event, Tree's *Hamlet,* though ideologically significant to him, did not require a great creative investment on Tree's part. The Tree Collection at Bristol, otherwise complete in production materials, has few records of the draped revivals, which were apparently thrown together when required with little attention and few technical demands.

Draped productions were soon recognized as an economical and artistically respected means of production, and so served for speculative managements, and for the normal plethora of matinees marking the debuts of young actors. Leah Bateman Hunter, later Olivia in Barker's *Twelfth Night,* made her debut as Juliet to Harcourt Williams's Romeo on a draped stage in 1908. Arthur Bourchier and Violet Vanbrugh reproduced their Garrick Theatre *Merchant of Venice* (1905) for the 1909 Stratford Festival, using the drapery and set pieces they devised for a command performance at Windsor. This was largely an expedient, as the backdrops of the Garrick production could not easily fit into the other theatres. They decided to place the practical set pieces of the original production against a neutral background of gold drapery, a solution which, within Edwardian scenic tradition, is difficult to imagine. Fay Davis and Gerald Lawrence attempted a joint Shakespearean management at the Court in 1909 using a draped stage: sixteenth-century Flemish tapestries "enclosed," i.e., boxed in, the stage, and set pieces included not only chairs and benches but shrubs for *As You Like It* and trees for *Romeo and Juliet.* Though scenically Elizabethan in style, the productions were apparently designed to be archaelogical in atmosphere, as they boasted orchestral music "of the period of each piece."[90] Louis Calvert staged *The Winter's Tale* in New York in 1910 "in the Elizabethan manner," and in 1913 produced and starred in *Hamlet* for the Pilgrim Players against curtains and tapestries.[91] Laurence Irving's First Quarto *Hamlet* for the Edinburgh B.E.S.S. was performed in Elizabethan costumes against a draped stage.[92] Henry Herbert, formerly a leading man for one of Benson's companies, toured on his own with productions utilizing neutral green velvet curtains for front scenes in lieu of painted front-cloths.[93] Fred Terry's 1911 production of *Romeo and Juliet* for his daughter's debut featured tab curtains painted in imitation of tapestry.[94] This otherwise traditional production, designed by Percy Macquoid and Joseph Harker, was revived by Tree at His Majesty's in 1913.

The prevalence of the draped production soon prompted disavowals from more serious theatre spokesmen and practitioners. Percy Fitzgerald confessed his "repulsion" for them, suggesting instead a conventional architectural stage on the Greek model.[95] Gordon Craig corrected Shaw's association of curtains with his name: "I know nothing about any curtains... and I possess none.... I made an experiment or two with some draped stuff instead of scenery, but that was because the theatre was not rich enough to run to wood and canvas."[96] He elsewhere attributed the idea of using curtains "to the thinkers, and not to the artists," and he clearly admired the latter more than the former.[97] And even Poel criticized productions in which Elizabethanism was limited to the use of curtains. People who go to these productions, Poel said, "will much prefer the addition of pictures and music," adding that, given the present state of Shakespearean acting, "it is impossible to advise giving up scenery."[98]

The *reductio ad absurdum* of Edwardian Elizabethanism was the 1914 season at the Stratford Festival, under the direction of Patrick Kirwan while Benson and his company were touring America. Kirwan had toured pastorals with a company called the Idyllic Players intermittently from 1904. In 1912 Kirwan was invited to head a company at the replica of the Globe Theatre designed by Sir Edwin Lutyens for the "Shakespeare's England" exhibition at Earls Court for the benefit of the S.M.N.T. I have been unable to locate a plan or a description of Lutyen's design, but the theatrical performances consisted of short extracts, with most of the show composed of atmospheric period touches in the audience, such as mischievous apprentices, orange girls, and stool salesmen. William Poel produced "a Shakespearian play" at the exhibition, though only a program survives.[99] J. Fisher White, a member of Tree's company and an instructor at the Academy of Dramatic Art, brought his students to the replica for a series of public performances of scenes. While acknowledging the value of the experience of acting in the open air for the young actor, White added that "Shakespeare would prefer the modern stage and would have welcomed any adjunct which assists the imagination."[100] Kirwan's repertoire at Earls Court included seven plays by Shakespeare and *The Chaste Maid of Cheapside,* presumably pieces already in the repertoire of the Idyllic Players.

The selection of Kirwan as director of the 1914 Stratford Festival was curious, and the productions under his direction were more curious still. Kirwan boasted of the Elizabethan authenticity which he had learned at Earls Court, and yet combined this with the latest "post-impressionist" devices of the Savoy Shakespeare, and with the star-actor egotism of his collaborator, Arthur Bourchier, who asserted his presence at Stratford in 1914 as Tree failed to do in 1905. In addition to playing Shylock, long familiar to Stratford audiences in his own semi-draped travelling production, Bourchier played one of the servants in *The Comedy of Errors,* interpolating the gag line, on meeting his brother, "Dromio, wherefore art thou Dromio."[101]

Kirwan extended an apron, abolished the footlights, and lit the stage from the back of the gallery. Full scenes were played in front of gold curtains, perhaps borrowed from Bourchier's *Merchant of Venice,* and apron "front" scenes were played in front of a plain grey curtain. While Kirwan hoped for Elizabethan continuity, promising *A Midsummer Night's Dream* with neither intervals nor Mendelssohn's score, local critics reported that intervals were frequent and waits long for both *The Merchant of Venice* and, surprisingly, *The Comedy of Errors.* Perhaps the most Elizabethan aspects of the Festival were in the semi-theatrical trappings: three trumpet blasts outside the theatre before the play began, a small ensemble of antique instruments in lieu of an orchestra, and Elizabethan costuming throughout. Margaret Halston, playing Beatrice, objected to the costumes, not on principle, which she could respect if not advocate, but because of their weight and discomfort: "I should like to play Beatrice as Ellen Terry used to play her—soft, floating draperies, everything made for ease of movement and grace of action."[102]

Kirwan's Elizabethanism broke down with his production of *The Dream.* The visual excesses of this production were not noteworthy in themselves, but because they were promoted by the director as being embodiments of his Elizabethanist principles. For example, Kirwan boasted of the Elizabethan accuracy of his costumes, yet critics noted that the material for Oberon's costume had been imported from Paris and was therefore "the latest thing out."[103] It was in the fantasy characters that Kirwan took the greatest liberties, but did so according to what he believed were Elizabethan notions of fantasy. Kirwan's promotional material reads:

> Following an old authority, Mr. Kirwan has arranged that Oberon shall have the guise of a splended iridescent beetle, with luminous jerkin of blue and green and shod with "ladybirds' wings"—that is with boots of scarlet, speckled with black—while on his head rises the horned crest of a beetle. Titania is likened to a star, so over her snow-white robe will be cast a star-shaped mantle, or tunic of silver, while silver stars will crown her hair.... Puck, in Elizabethan days, was likened to a mischievous little pony, so at Stratford he will wear a rough coat of pearl grey and an equine-like headpiece.[104]

The fairies were "pearl-grey shadow;" according to the *Era,* "Mr. Kirwan is relying on an ancient authority which states that these elves of the forest were, in the mind of the Bard of Avon, the ghosts of Elizabethan boys and girls, who flitted about during the 'witching hours,' and teased poor mortals who roamed abroad."[105] With the ponderous authority of Elizabethan authenticity, Kirwan selected what he believed to be the playwright's image for character or incident, and froze it into the design. And so Elizabethanism merged with the excesses of the New Stagecraft, the liberties of interpretation of which would become the trademark of the director's and the designer's theatre. As one harsh critic of Kirwan's *Dream* phrased it, "The sin of the impressionists is in fixing impressions."[106]

Of all Poel's followers and debtors, the only one to evolve a vital form of production was Martin Harvey, though he applied Elizabethan principles directly to only two productions and evolved a separate style for each. These two productions represent, in several ways, the best and worst of Edwardian experiments in Elizabethanism. The first, *The Taming of the Shrew* (1913) exercised a greater conventional freedom, integrating features of the New Stagecraft into an Elizabethanist frame; the second, *Henry V* (1916), represented a return to archaeologism through the transformation of the Elizabethan stage into a pictorial showcase.

The Elizabethanism of *The Taming of the Shrew* was inspired, as it was for Webster and Planché, by the performance frame offset by the Induction. As with the production seventy years before, the later production was actually an exercise in archaeology, here enhanced with features of the New Stagecraft learned from Reinhardt.

Harvey claimed that the inspiration for the production was independent of contemporary trends in Elizabethanism: "I had watched my own children give scenes from Shakespeare in the drawing-room, and had seen how little scenery was missed;" and he furthermore claimed that Poel's assistance, solicited for the production, was limited "to the necessary 'cuts' to be made in the play rather than the decoration of it."[107] However, Poel's contribution appears to have been greater than this, to judge by the preparation/rehearsal copy housed in the London Museum: the margins contain a running dialogue of suggestion, response and counter-suggestion between the collaborators, the principle aim of which was the development and elaboration of the performance format of the players, and a means of including the theatre audience into the frame of Christopher Sly and the arbitrary 1490 setting of the Induction.

The production was Elizabethanist insofar as it was set in a permanent neutral locale according to the scenic resources of a group of itinerant players, dressed in motley, and carrying with them properties, screens and curtains in a wagon. The neutral locale was a hall in a summer house of the Lord, opening up, past a terrace, onto a garden. This was depicted by a series of arches framing the stage, a balustraded rostrum upstage with two conventionalized trees, and a view of a landscape on the backcloth with a wide road receding into the distance. The players entered along the rostrum and played their scenes upon it and upon the stage proper, with Sly watching the play throughout from a bench placed at the forwardmost edge of the apron, built into the orchestra pit several steps down so that sight-lines were not obscured for the theatre audience. The screens were moved by hand by extras and stagehands dressed either as members of the travelling company or as servants in the Lord's house. Through these means Harvey was able to present a fluid and continuous production, and to steer clear of the disturbing social implications of the play by emphasizing the romping, athletic *commedia* aspects of the performance.

But in many ways Harvey's *Shrew* had more in common with the New Stagecraft than with Elizabethanism. Harvey had acted for Max Reinhardt in *Oedipus* at Covent Garden in 1912, and was touring with the production when he first rehearsed and produced *The Shrew*. He therefore had, as part of his touring equipment, a portable apron stage, proscenium masking, and equipment for front-of-house lighting. The servant/stagehands are recognizable Reinhardt devices. But more significant is the way Harvey chose to integrate the style of the staging of the Induction with that of the play proper. Rather than having a naturalistic setting into which the players would bring a purely theatrical display, Harvey used decorative front curtains reminiscent of most Edwardian experiments in Elizabethan staging.[108] The act drop parted at the beginning of the induction to reveal an imitation tapestry depicting an Italianate landscape: the device of using a tapestry which is at once decorative and pictorial is reminiscent of Tree's use of them for outdoor scenes in his 1905 *Hamlet*. For the scene in the Lord's chamber, the tapestries parted, revealing another set of decorative curtains, of white Roman satin with large decorative medallions; these medallions were indicated in reference to the Lord's "wanton pictures." The full set was revealed only just before the entrance of the players.

In staging the play itself, Harvey also blurred the line between the modern performance and the semi-improvisational piece performed within it. Huntly Carter described one scenic effect: "In the second half of the play a large canopied seat with a table in front occupied the center of the stage whenever a scene was supposed to be taking place in Petruchio's house. These properties were so arranged that they could be hoisted into the flies while a screen scene was being played."[109] The suggestion here is that the technical machinery of the stage was used in ways which would be impossible in a Lord's country house. Harvey's own retrospective description illustrates how he tried to excuse this under the guise of the enframed Elizabethan performance:

> Any change of scene was suggested by the actors themselves, who moved into this Hall either such screens as could be found in the house of their Princely host crudely to represent a street, or else some trellis-work covered with leaves cut from the neighbouring garden to represent a leafy lane; or again, some of the Lord's own hangings were let down from the ceiling of the hall for interior scenes.[110]

So Harvey explained even the Lord's curious fly system according to the archaism of the performance. He also revealed the characteristic Edwardian obsession with pictorial appropriateness (trellises and leaves for gardens, curtains for interiors, etc.). The promptbook further reveals Harvey's traditional use of Edwardian alternation: although changes were effected by visible stagehands, he did use downstage "street" scenes, formed by a configuration of curtains and potted hedges, to mask the placement of heavier pieces of furniture, such as a fifteen-foot long table for the last scene.

Harvey returned to an Elizabethan mode of performance for his production of *Henry V* in 1916, part of his tercentenary season at His Majesty's Theatre. His belief in the Elizabethanism of this production rested in the use of stage space and picture, rather than in the costumes, which resembled, in heraldry and historical authenticity, the costumes of his production of *Richard III*, performed during the same season.[111] For his model of the stage, he drew on a piece of popular Shakespeare scholarship by Darrell Figgis. Figgis's chapter on the Elizabethan stage reveals a belief in alternation, a rejection of Gaedertz's traverses at the pillars, and the fairly accepted belief that the whole stage could be localized by the setting discovered on the "inner" stage. This last feature appealed to Harvey, for he called the back stage "the crowning excellence of the Elizabethan stage," and described it in Edwardian terms: "Behind the curtains which conceal this back stage is a 'set' scene. It may be an interior or an exterior. The curtains are drawn back exposing this scene, and whatever this represents immediately becomes the keynote of the whole stage in front of it—main stage and apron stage."[112] Harvey transformed Figgis's model (see illustration 21) of a three-part stage into, effectively, a two-part one:

> The front consisted, in Shakespeare's day, of that portion of the stage which ran out into the Pit, about a half to a third of the stage proper. Of course, we could not sacrifice so many of the stalls as would be necessary to extend the stage as forward as in the Elizabethan playhouse, but we secured much the same result by erecting a false proscenium ... about half-way up and over the stage proper. This structure was permanent. Behind the false proscenium we hung a variety of curtains—decorative, neutral, of homely material, and of gold tissue. When these curtains were closed, the front area of the stage suggested either an exterior or an interior. For instance, landscape tapestry or neutral cloths serve for an exterior; for a rich interior use gold tissue; for a simple one, a homely material—perhaps burlap or felt, and so on. While the action is proceeding in front of these closed curtains, stage-hands can be setting a scene behind them. This may represent any locality which the situation demands—a tent, a bedchamber, a ship floating by the quay-side, anything you require. The curtains which have concealed this scene are drawn apart as the change of locality demands, and immediately the entire area of the stage becomes part of this locality—suggested by the small set at the back—which thus serves as a key-note to the whole. This is the theory of Darrell Figgis.[113]

Or rather, this was the model of Darrell Figgis transformed by Harvey into a vehicle for localization and modified pictorialism. Harvey excused the pictorialism of his stage by citing Elizabethan precedence for scenic realism, in the manner of Albright and Lawrence: Elizabethan stagecraft, claimed Harvey, had "advanced sufficiently during Shakespeare's day to include the use of painted cloths—the igniting of one of them, as we all know, caused the destruction of the Globe Theatre."[114] Harvey used his rear stage for spectacular scenic effects, not unlike the interpolated tableaux of Tree and others. The gate of Harfleur was shattered by cannon fire, and English soldiers poured through in response to Henry's battle-cry; and, at Southampton, the curtains, depicting the gate of embarkation, were drawn apart at the final couplet of the scene to reveal the English fleet ready to sail for France, an effect which Harvey's biographer likens to the transformation scene of the Christmas Pantomime "put to legitimate dramatic effect. Shakespeare had never thought of it. If he turned in his grave it would have been to wish he had."[115]

In spite of these non-Elizabethan additions, and the variety of scenic modes he employed in his other productions, Harvey did strongly believe in Elizabethan techniques; he later claimed that he had long considered touring with a complete fit-up Globe replica, and when, in the twenties, he was the object of a labor action, he missed the chance to perform *Richard III* without either scenery and costumes only because the strike was settled before he could do so.

Harvey's eclecticism made him at once exceptional among his contemporaries and strangely typical of his times, for he was able to forge, with varying degrees of success, new modes of productions from disparate schools and styles; varied productions coexisted in his repertoire just as the several schools of scenography coexisted during the Edwardian period, sharing certain aesthetic premises and appealing to varied audiences. I will show in the next chapter that several compromises in the Elizabethan style generated a mode of production which, utilizing features of the New Stagecraft, emerged as the dominant style of the following generation.

Limitations and Contradictions

While the Elizabethan revival movement met with modest success during the Edwardian period, there were several intrinsic contradictions in the movement's attitude toward theatre convention vis-à-vis the theatre audience. The Elizabethan revival was based upon the premise that the stagecraft of Shakespeare's plays could only be discerned and fully employed in a theatre reproducing the essentials of the stage for which they were originally written. But the movement generally skirted the fact that the theatre is only effective when performed for an audience receptive to the conventional language of the play and its staging. As we shall see, Granville Barker rejected a strictly Elizabethan approach on the grounds that the modern audience could not transform itself into an Elizabethan one. William Archer suggested that the productions of the E.S.S. could only succeed if the audience were to appear in costume, making of the occasion an "Elizabethan gaudy-night."[116]

Most experimenters in Elizabethan staging tried either to bridge the gap in audience perception or to obscure the issue. The latter was achieved, not by reproducing a truly Elizabethan rapport between audience and performance, but by creating a picture of that rapport for the appreciation of a largely disengaged modern audience. Poel's 1893 *Measure for Measure* employed a number of costumed extras as a stage audience: Elizabethan gallants sitting on the stage and in the stage boxes to the side; George Pierce Baker filled his stage boxes (with inadequate sight-lines to the stage) and his pit with Harvard undergraduates dressed in Elizabethan costume, reproducing Elizabethan daily life for the benefit of the paying audience during the half-hour before the *Hamlet* performance began (see illustration 22); Elizabethan extras were the most prominent feature of the Globe replica at the Earls Court exhibition; and B. Iden Payne attempted to archaeologize the audience of his 1908 Manchester *Knight of the Burning Pestle* (advertised as "A Pantomime of Three Hundred Years Ago") by planting actors in Elizabethan costume in the audience, preparing the way for the required involvement of Ralph, the Citizen, and his Wife.[117] Edward Mumford Moore is accurate in describing this aspect of the Elizabethan Revival as "a by-product of the historical accuracy school."[118]

The one example of an attempt to bridge the gap between the modern audience and the implied Elizabethan audience of a revivalist production can be found in Harvey's *Shrew*. Christopher Sly, placed on a bench at the front edge of the sunken apron stage, served as an intermediary between the modern audience and the Renaissance travelling players enacting the play. The promptbook in the London Museum contains the following note for the interval:

> Suggestion: all guests follow *Pet.* & *Kath.* off the terrace leaving the stage empty—save for *Lord.* Sly climbs from his seat [in] the orchestra (Kath. and Pet.) to be brought before him in pantomime of course. They are brought back & Sly congratulates them & offers them drink. Kath. refuses of course—Pet. can laughingly accept. They all retire together. Stage is left empty. Music or partsinging during interval.

While it is unclear whether this business was indeed used, we can nevertheless see in this clever curtain call a reminder to the audience that they could directly share in the response of a drunken tinker to a skeletal performance employing nonrepresentational decor, as well as an encouragement to the audience to patronize the bars in the foyers.

At the same time, there were some Edwardians who believed that a modern audience could be made to become receptive to unfamiliar and antiquated theatrical conventions. This belief underlies Max Beerbohm's criticism of Barker's productions of Greek plays at the Court: "An overt theatre, built on the Greek model, seems to me indispensible. Not otherwise than by becoming in spirit somewhat as the Greeks were, can we really enjoy a

Greek play; and, without the scenic conditions by which Greek Tragedy was shaped, we must fail in the effort to assimilate ourselves to a Greek audience."[119] Beerbohm assumed that not only is this assimilation, or transformation, possible, but that it could be induced by the incidental conditions of stage and playhouse. Granville Barker, who often talked of a sense of community forged from a diverse audience, also believed in the almost mystical ability of certain antiquated conventions to make an audience receptive to a different set of stimuli and responses. In the published score of his music for Barker's 1914 *Midsummer Night's Dream,* Cecil Sharp came out against the use of Elizabethan music in modern productions of Elizabethan plays.[120] Barker used his 1924 Preface to the play to oppose this view, favoring Elizabethan music over a modern score:

> Here, precisely, was an opportunity for leading an audience back, and all unconsciously, into that medium of sound, of emotion even, in which the play was first meant to make its effect. It is just because Elizabethan music *is* somewhat unfamiliar to the ear that I advocate it.... Music affects most of us without our well knowing why. Moreover, there is no art that can so readily, by suggestion, and even by its very unfamiliarity, transport us over time and space, though the destination be barely known.... Music, truly, is of its time; and there is innate in it something of the spirit and behavior of its time, which could never perhaps find expression in words. Words are for thoughts, and emotion must be framed in terms of thoughts before words will convey it. But music may express something, now as simple as set movements of a body, now as subtle as those moods of the mind and the measures to which emotion learns to beat. By reasoning about it we may make it more strange than it ever need be if we simply listen. For the emotional self is apter at shifting ground than the intellectual, apter to explode [sic] unknown ground. I am sure at least that you can sing and dance a man back into the seventeenth century far more easily than you can argue him there. And I cannot think that any approach to listening with Shakespeare's ears is other than a gain.[121]

An audience, listening with Shakespeare's ears, may indeed be able to see with Shakespeare's eyes and to respond according to Shakespeare's Elizabethan theatrical sensibilities.

Edwardian Elizabethanists never seriously considered one means of bridging the gap between the conventions of the plays and the responsiveness of the audience: the use of modern dress. Elizabethan costume was valued by the Elizabethanists, not only because of its archaeological accuracy to the period of the play's composition, but because the details of costuming carried with them varieties of associations perceptible to an Elizabethan audience. Such associations were often lost to the modern audience. Mario Borsa pointed out in 1908 that Poel's experiments in Elizabethan staging carried with them the theoretical seeds of modern-dress productions: as if the Elizabethans made all historical periods contemporary in manner and detail to their own day and age, the performances for modern audiences must make the historical periods contemporary to the present.[122] Borsa dismissed this notion as ludicrous, as did many of his contemporaries: J.A. Hammerton, considering Victorian archaeological accuracy superior to Garrick's use of modern dress, cites the absurdity of conceiving Irving as Hamlet "in an evening dress and an opera hat," just as Sarah Bernhardt laughed at the picture of Arthur Bourchier as Henry VIII in a silk hat.[123]

Poel was a firm believer in the value of costume appropriate to character and situation, arguing at great length minor details such as Isabella's dress as a novice (he felt that she should still wear the elegant dress of the upper classes) and Hamlet's appearance in the graveyard scene (which Poel felt should be that of a sailor). But many of Poel's decisions regarding costume, though illuminating, may have proved meaningless to modern audiences, e.g., his costuming of the Greeks as Elizabethan adventurers and the Trojans as court Masquers in *Troilus and Cressida* (1912). It is interesting that one of Poel's statements regarding consistency of character would contain within it the germs of modern-dress theory: "Everyone at a dress rehearsal must have noticed how, when a stage-manager walks on to the stage in his modern clothes, all the costumed figures upon it at once appear, by contrast, to be masqueraders at a fancy-dress ball."[124] It only occurred to Poel later that the costume of the stage-manager might be as telling as that of the masqueraders. And Poel's post-war productions took advantage of this realization: an *All's Well that Ends Well* featuring the King in a wheelchair with a modern nurse in attendance, and *Coriolanus* in the twenties with the title character shifting from leopard skin to modern military costume.

Edwardian Elizabethanism, then, contained within it the seeds of modern-dress theory, which would come into play in several adventurous productions in the succeeding decades. It may be surprising that the concept was not put into practice in theatrical production before the first World War, but the fact that it did not is significant: Elizabethanism, in its purest form, was as elitist as the membership of the private societies which supported it. Elizabethanism held that Shakespeare's art and craft belonged to the theatre and society of Shakespeare's own day. Translating the plays into terms and techniques comprehensible to the modern theatre-goer was held to be impossible and undesirable. Yet it is questionable whether the modern audience is capable of translating itself into an audience receptive to Elizabethan perceptions and values. On the one hand, Elizabethanists believed in the inherent power of theatrical convention. On the other, they undoubtedly felt that only one with specialized knowledge and sharpened historical sensibilities could truly perceive all the Elizabethan subtleties of the dramatic event. Elizabethanism, in its purest form, became a club of cognoscenti congratulating themselves on their historical insight; or it became, not a theatre form, but a picture of a theatre form, with the picture of an audience responding in ways the modern audiences could not.

Only in the hands of theatre practitioners who believed in the infinite receptivity of the audience, or in the absolute flexibility of theatrical convention, could Elizabethan principles be used to create a newer form of theatre, true to the Elizabethan texts in hand, and equal to the capabilities of the modern audience. Elizabethanism, with its coyness toward theatricality and its adherence to traditionalist premises of reality and localization, remained a coterie movement with strictly limited impact. What it did provide was a tentative scenic vocabulary which would contribute to the production styles that were to emerge after the first World War.

3

Shakespeare and the New Stagecraft

Traditionalist methods of producing Shakespeare were challenged, during the Edwardian period, not just by the principles of Elizabethanism but by an entirely new and different scenic vocabulary, which we can call "the New Stagecraft." The New Stagecraft, like Elizabethanism, was rooted in a great many traditionalist assumptions; the resulting productions in the new style were typically Edwardian in their exploration of theatrical idioms toward the creation of a dramatic product.

The designation "new stagecraft" is perforce a catch-all. No single term for such a theatrical movement existed during the Edwardian period; nor was there one single movement that deserves the designation more than another. There was, however, a flurry of activity, both formalized in "movements" and independent. Each of these movements appeared to be calling for a revision of the language of pictorial realism, using a variety of aesthetic idioms and employing a variety of new technical means. The "new stagecraft" was just one of many terms that the Edwardians used to describe these movements, and to distinguish them from the so-called "modern" methods of Beerbohm Tree. The term "new" conjures Edward Gordon Craig's desire to move "Towards a New Theatre" and Huntly Carter's perception of the "New Spirit in Drama and Art." I use the term "stagecraft" to distinguish this theatrical activity from the various new schools of dramaturgy, which in England were more likely to suggest the ideological realism of Shaw, Barker and Galsworthy than the non-representational neo-romanticism of Craig and his followers.

It is, moreover, important to group the various movements of the New Stagecraft together under that one banner because the breadth and depth of such activity was recognized by Edwardians as a collective redefinition of theatre art, a phenomenon which was occurring across Europe. Huntly Carter's attempt in 1912 to make a comprehensive survey of the movement indicates what was then recognized as the international scope of the New Stagecraft. Carter believed that the most vibrant theatrical advances were being made on the Continent, and advised England to open its doors to them:

> At the outset we are faced by the fact that England can no longer be regarded as insular in the matter of ideas. Ideas know no boundaries, and those of the reform of the European theatre and drama are at our doors. This involves us in the necessity of opening our stage to what may be called European influences: influences which we have to employ for our own purposes in the erection of a truly national theatre.[1]

Carter identified the new forces in the various European capitals; his list includes: the Théâtre des Arts in Paris, The Russian Ballet, Max Reinhardt, the Fortuny lighting system, Jaques-Dalcroze, the New Munich Shakespeare Stage, Jeno Kemendy of Budapest, Wyspianski in Cracow, The Moscow Art Theatre, and the Komisarzhevsky company in St. Petersburg. The list includes directors, designers, playwrights, producers, technicians and theorists, working with extreme realism, painterly pictorialism, and overt theatricalism, considered collectively as part of a single sweeping movement of modernism.

Since the New Stagecraft was an international movement, the English often dated their participation in the movement from the importation of Continental innovations. Several dates in particular stand out: Pavlova's first appearance in London with the Russian Imperial Ballet at the Palace (as part of a music hall turn) in April 1910; the first Post-Impressionist Exhibition from 8 November 1910; Max Reinhardt's production of *Sumurun* at the London Coliseum, 30 January 1911; the first appearance of Daighilev's Russian Ballet, with designs by Leon Bakst, at Covent Garden on 21 June 1911; Reinhardt's *The Miracle* at the Olympia exhibition centre, 23 December 1911; his *Oedipus* at Covent Garden, 13 January 1912; and the second Post-Impressionist Exhibition on 5 October 1912. So striking were the events of such a brief span of time that Virginia Woolf could state, in reference to the era if not to these specific events: "On or about December 1910 human character changed."[2]

Certainly human nature did not change, and despite the enormous influence of these and other events, neither did English theatrical art, for the aesthetic ideas and practices were already in the air well before the Continental invasion. Many of the new principles of the theatrical imports from the continent were inspired by Gordon Craig, as Craig himself often reminds us. The success of Reinhardt and Diaghilev's Russian Ballet in London at this time was itself proof that English audiences were ready to understand and appreciate the new visual language. And the fact that the Continental invasion was sponsored by a new breed of theatrical impresarios (Oswald Stoll, C. B. Cochran, et al.) connected with metropolitan Music Hall empires indicates that only with the beginning of the second decade of the new century was there an organizational framework for the commercial exploitation of the New Stagecraft. English experiments in the New Stagecraft prior to the Continental invasion failed in part through lack of such a framework. Craig's collaboration with Ellen Terry in her Imperial Theatre management only served to prove the incompatibility of such experimentation with what was then the prevailing organizational system of commercial management. Through the middle years of the first decade, certain experiments in alternate forms of management were attempted. While the Vedrenne-Barker management of the Court theatre focussed more on play writing and acting than on scenic reform, it did employ the talents of Charles Ricketts (for *Don Juan in Hell*); and in Barker's productions of the Greeks and Maeterlinck can be found the seeds of the scenic style used for Shakespeare at the Savoy. Ricketts began his work in the theatre by designing for private societies, and only began to work in the West End through the intervention of a financial patron. It was not until the endowed managements at the end of the decade, and in particular the Trench-Harrison management of the Haymarket, that designs of the New Stagecraft began to be commercially exploited. And by this time, the Continental invasion had begun. The coincidence of these events—the commercial exploitation of the New Stagecraft, and the importation of Continental reforms—reflects the organizational shift which allowed for the flourishing of the New Stagecraft at the beginning of the 1910s. It also explains the reception given to the Germans and Russians when their work was first seen in London.

The apparent domination of the New Stagecraft by continental artists at the beginning of the second decade of the century is misleading for two reasons. First, it has obscured the evolution of a particularly English school of the New Stagecraft during the first decade of the century. The contributors to this school resented the popular association of their work with the Continental imports.[3] The second problem is the result of the fracturing of the New Stagecraft into a myriad of "isms" which resulted from the public and critical affection for the "Russian Ballet style." The differences between these faddish "isms" were often superficial, and distinct from theatrical issues. And while fads gain supporters, they also fuel epithets from detractors.[4] The staging reforms of the New Stagecraft must be considered independent of stylistic sub-movements. Gordon Craig recognized the dangers of misinterpretation, objecting to the reduction of his work to a school, or the assignment of a code of signification to his designs. He wrote to the compiler of an edition of his designs:

> ... most particularly I want no *deep* (shallow) *psycological* (cant spell) *pre Raphaelitic, prehistoric, peritonitic* **meanings** read into these scenes. My aim is to be as simple as direct & as un Wagner, un Richard Strauss un Nietsche [sic] as possible—when they say *Blake there* I agree with 'em—& Blake's aim was *simplicity*.[5]

The New Stagecraft, as it was applied to English Shakespeare productions, was not a stylistic fad at all, but an attempt at finding a simple, evocative, and aesthetic pictorial language suitable to the dramatic demands of the material.

It is necessary, then, to consider the specific theatrical challenges of Shakespeare's texts which, according to the advocates of the New Stagecraft, the traditional scenography was incapable of meeting. The New Stagecraft shared a significant number of assumptions about the stage event and the nature of theatrical convention with the contemporary Edwardian schools of production, traditionalism and Elizabethanism; these shared assumptions informed the use of the New Stagecraft in the production of Shakespeare throughout the period.

Theory

The Special Demands of Shakespeare's Plays

Advocates of the New Stagecraft, like their traditionalist and Elizabethanist contemporaries, believed that Shakespeare's texts demanded swiftness and continuity in performance. As we have seen, the quest for continuity was impeded in the traditional stagecraft by departures from traditional mid-Victorian scenic alternation. The Elizabethanists proposed a neutral conventional space, where vestigial attempts at localization and scenic realism were incorporated into the apocryphal principle of alternation, modelled on Victorian stage practice. The New Stagecraft did not, like Elizabethanism, call for the neutralization of stage space. Instead, it suggested two interrelated solutions to the problem of stage continuity for Shakespeare. The first was a redefinition of the means used to create the illusion of stage reality, a preference for evocation and suggestion over direct statement, and the use of new visual and technological methods to change the scene. This solution owed its origin and methods to a reform movement within Edwardian traditionalism, and as a result inherited the traditionalist ambivalence toward theatrical convention, which it was able to transcend by embracing a more transparent theatricality; it also shared with traditionalism many assumptions concerning the relation of the stage environment to dramatic action and character. These phenomena can be traced through the productions of Gordon Craig and Charles Ricketts. The second solution involved the redefinition of stage space, changing the relationship of stage to auditorium and incorporating several aspects of Elizabethanist theory and practice. As the zone theory and the alteration theory were derivative of traditionalist attitudes, we will see how these same attitudes carried over into this branch of the New Stagecraft. The use of both branches of the New Stagecraft can be seen in a series of experimental productions of *Hamlet* by Martin Harvey.

The first of these solutions called for a new plasticity of the scenic picture. As both Adolph Appia and Gordon Craig conceived the theatre, three-dimensional scenery, making no attempt to portray three-dimensional phenomena on two-dimensional surfaces, could be made plastic employing the new dimension of light. A single three-dimensional setting could portray a variety of real or psychological localities through changes in lighting; for example, according to Appia's scheme, lighting could transform the forest of the Grail into the Grail Temple or Tristan and Isolde's parapet into their symbolic trysting place in the psychosexual realm of their love. Craig further believed that the solid configuration of stage space could itself be made mutable and plastic, and that this plasticity could be applied to Shakespeare. Craig's "Scene," a theoretical model for flexible scenery employing large mobile prisms and planes, was conceived independently of any consideration of the demands of Shakespeare; the inspiration came from a misreading of a drawing by Serlio illustrating perspective on the stage. Craig, however, saw the applicability of the "screens" to the special demands of Shakespeare's plays:

> Shakespeare and most poetic Drama to be performed has the utmost need of a scene of a special nature . . . a scene with a mobile face.
> If careful inquiry is made it will be seen that Shakespeare has not yet had a special scene made for his plays.
> I have attempted to supply one—a scene for the poetic Drama, deal it with what it may.[6]

Craig hoped to use his screens for Shakespearean productions: he had a model prepared with the hopes of persuading his mother to use them for a projected revival of The *Merchant of Venice,* and demonstrated to her their use throughout the play; the screens were used in the 1910 Moscow Art Theatre *Hamlet,* though without their flexibility, and with long waits during scene changes with the tab curtains down.

Craig's experiments demanded a new technology of stagecraft as well as a new aesthetic, and it is not surprising that the theoretical assertions of advocates of the New Stagecraft often included the call for technical invention and reform, particularly in the area of scene changing. Few productions in England during the Edwardian period actually utilized new technology. But one technical solution to the problem of scene changes appears in an unrealized production early in the period. Eleanor Calhoun was an American who had acted for Benson and who was part of a circle of high society aesthetes whose theatrical activities included E. W. Godwin's production of *As You Like It* in Coombe Wood in 1884. Calhoun had found backing from her friends for a commercial production of *Romeo and Juliet,* which she had already begun promoting in the trade papers when she married an eastern European prince and retired from the stage:

> I originated a plan for giving "Romeo and Juliet" in the spirit and environment of the golden youth and splendour of the Italian Renaissance, the rich after-glow of which was all about when Shakespeare wrote his version of the great love-tale from Southern climes. The

design was to adapt to the play's setting the full-pulsed convention of Veronese, not shrinking from any freedom of that convention. This background and frame were to be, however, only interpretive of luminous atmosphere and in order to liberate, rather than confine, both story and passion and the author's own most gloriously wrought-out convention in the telling of it. I invented and submitted to several friends, persons of authority in the land, a model for stage and style of scenery that would change almost like a dissolving view, so that the play could proceed without being split into acts.... All modern resource was to be employed to produce this splendor in simplicity.[7]

How these effects were to be achieved is unclear; her press releases only mention "a set of scenes which appear and melt one into the other, no time being lost in setting. The costume and scenery will be in the style of the Italian Renaissance."[8] The "dissolving view" was a common device of theatrical and para-theatrical spectacle in the Victorian period; its proposed application here to a play by Shakespeare was an attempt to redefine the technical nature of scenic pictorial reality and to create a new plasticity of stage picture suitable to the demands of the text.

A Continental technical innovation which was suggested for the staging of Shakespeare was the turntable. At the 1905 Guildhall debate on the Staging of Shakespeare, F. J. Furnivall suggested the use of a revolving stage to facilitate quick scene changes in Shakespeare productions.[9] A revolve was installed in the Coliseum (built in 1904), one of the centrally located Music Halls, where it was used to change heavy scenery used by consecutive Variety turns. The Coliseum was the site of Reinhardt's first London production, *Sumurun* (1911). Reinhardt's application of existing English technology to the legitimate drama, as it had already been applied in Germany, is an example of continental artists demonstrating to England principles which they already had at their disposal at home.

Traditionalism and Convention

It will be noted that, both in the case of Calhoun's proposed *Romeo and Juliet* and in many of Max Reinhardt's German productions utilizing the revolve, the use of new technology for changing scenes did not alter the essential pictorial representationalism of the décor. Calhoun's scenes would undoubtedly have been presented employing traditional means, and Reinhardt most often used his revolve to present a three-dimensionally "real" space fully elaborated, e.g., the Venice of *The Merchant of Venice* with houses, piazzas, and bridges, and the forest of *A Midsummer Night's Dream* with hillocks, streams, and tree trunks. While Appia called for the use of plastic light for Wagner's operas, the composer/director had been content to effect the scene changes in *Parsifal* and *Götterdämmerung* with traditional panoramas. The work of Appia and Craig did indeed challenge many premises of pictorial representationalism: but their most radical reforms were direct offshoots of several scenic movements which were designed not to eliminate but to perfect the verisimilitude of representationalism. The relation of non- and anti-illusionistic reform movements to the extreme visual realism of the progenitors of these movements reveals much about the realistic premises of the New Stagecraft.

We have seen that the traditional stagecraft was developing its realistic premises to the point that inherent contradictions arose between the dramatic ends of realism and the theatrical means used to achieve them. The result of this development was the partial acceptance of the conventionality of the theatre. At least one traditionalist could not accept the failure of the stage picture to create, truly and completely, the requisite illusion of reality. This arch traditionalist was, paradoxically, the progenitor of the New Stagecraft in England: Hubert Herkomer, R. A., who published an article expounding his ideas in *The Magazine of Art* in 1892.[10] As a successful realist painter and Royal Academician, Herkomer was frustrated by the inability of the traditional stagecraft to fulfill its realistic promises. Rather than accept the conventionality of the theatre event, Herkomer sought instead to perfect the illusion of realism in the theatre and to conceal the conventional means employed to create this illusion. Herkomer criticized the imperfect conventions of the traditional stagecraft: the problems stemming from the scale and proportions of the proscenium arch, the conventions of wing and border, the effect of footlights, the premises of two-dimensional *trompe l'oeil* scene-painting, and the inconsistent effects of light and shadow. Each of these problems he solved both in theory and in practical experiments, using models or full-scale stagings in his own home. To correct the discrepancy between small-scale localities presented on enormous stages, and the problem of irregularly shaped scenes, Herkomer developed a movable proscenium which could be altered both in size and shape during the course of a production. Herkomer was particularly critical of sky effects in the traditional stagecraft, wherein the upper edge of the vista was marked by blue sky-borders designed to mask the fly-rigging above the stage. To preserve the illusion of a limitless sky, he developed a system of oblique gauzes which both created the illusion of depth and extended without borders into the fly-loft. Herkomer deplored the distortions created by the footlights, and suggested lighting the stage from overhead or side sources to duplicate the effects of natural daylight or interior lighting.[11] Criticizing the use of two-dimensional scenery, Herkomer advocated built-up decor; shadow effects would be created by lighting, not by shadows painted on the surfaces. And to create the illusion of real surfaces, he advocated texturing the ground-cloth and wall surfaces to catch the light as the real object would in nature.

Note that Herkomer in no way questioned the illusionistic premise of the traditional stagecraft; he only rejected those devices that attempted to achieve complete verisimilitude through a simplistic conventionality. Most traditionalists, however, did not go to such lengths to conceal the conventional means of creating their effects, and consequently did not accept many of Herkomer's suggestions. William Archer, impressed by a demonstration of Herkomer's lighting effects and changeable proscenium in London in 1892, publicly urged Henry Irving to adopt his principles at the Lyceum, a suggestion which went unheeded.[12] And William Telbin rejected Herkomer's reforms at length in *The Magazine of Art*.[13] Nevertheless, several of his suggestions were ultimately incorporated into the traditional stagecraft, not because of their verisimilitude or for their concealment of theatrical means, but for their very conventionality. An example of this was the support given to Herkomer's attack on the use of sky borders. Shaw criticized the convention in his columns in 1896, and suggested a semicircular proscenium, inspired by the frescoes of Florence, to Barker in 1907.[14] In 1913, Harvey used broad semicircular arches for his *Taming of the Shrew* production, doubling as wings and borders, and creating the suggestion of architecture through an extension in depth of the proscenium frame. And in 1914 Oscar Asche and Joseph Harker used a series of receding key-hole arabesque arches for *Chu Chin Chow,* providing a neutral frame for realistic set pieces, and serving for interior and exterior scenes alike.[15] Thus, a device designed to strengthen the illusionism of a pictorial convention was used in support of conventionalism and theatricality.

If traditionalists ultimately adopted several of Herkomer's reforms for the sake of their conventional freedom, Gordon Craig incorporated a good number of Herkomer's discoveries despite their naturalistic premises. Gordon Craig attended the lecture, and the extent to which he assimilated Herkomer's techniques and principles has been documented by Edward Craig.[16] If Herkomer's cycloramas were designed to create a greater realistic effect, Craig could use them to create a sky for its own sake, as an unlimited neutral background for an abstracted or universal action. Craig adopted Herkomer's sky gauzes and front lighting for his *Dido and Aeneas* in Hampstead in 1901, and rebuilt the fly-system of the Imperial Theatre in 1903 in order to introduce a light bridge and to extend the height of his sky-cloth. Craig's obsession with sky-effects parallels the Edwardian interest in open-air theatricals: pastoral productions of Shakespeare, the open-air Greek productions beloved of Max Beerbohm, and even the civic pageants of Louis N. Parker. Craig linked the open, universal effects of the sky with the cosmic demands of his drama: "For a perfect drama, should it be possible some day to write one, the sky must be used as the only worthy background. The manager or producer reveals his estimate of the value of Shakespeare by the elaboration or simplicity of his background."[17] Herkomer's naturalistic device became a means of abstraction and non-representationalism.

The New Stagecraft shared in the same conventional freedom with which the traditional stagecraft was experimenting during the Edwardian period: while assimilating the ultra-realist reforms of Herkomer and his followers, practitioners of the New Stagecraft abandoned Herkomer's concealment of his theatrical means and used the techniques for their own sakes. One example was the assimilation of Herkomer's advocacy of three-dimensional scenery. Advocates of the New Stagecraft similarly rejected two-dimensional scenery painted to create the illusion of a third dimension; but in accepting real forms, with their areas of light and shadow, they were able to abandon altogether the representationalism of traditionalist two-dimensionality and could return to two dimensions for mere decorative, non-illusionistic effect.

The relation of the New Stagecraft to traditional scenography on the issue of two- or three-dimensionality is widely misunderstood. It is generally assumed that the antipathy between the old school and the new was fought over the issue of dimensions, the old school, with its *trompe l'oeil* painted canvas, supplanted by the New, with its built-up scenes and sculpted spaces. Certainly one of the most dramatic head-on collisions of scenic ideology in the Edwardian period was between Joseph Harker and Gordon Craig, on the subject of Craig's designs for Tree's projected *Macbeth*. Though Harker convinced Tree of their impracticability on the basis of scale (to realize the relationship in scale between actor and scenery the scenes would have had to pierce the roof of His Majesty's Theatre), Harker's principal motivation in criticizing the scenes was to perpetuate the scene-painter's theatre and to prevent the employment of scenery which would not require the scene-painter's services. As Harker describes the outcome of the argument: "I need hardly add that these over-vigorous and yet strangely dyspeptic creations were promptly scrapped, the scenic productions at His Majesty's thereafter being left to scene-painters of less revolutionary principles;" note Harker's persistence in labelling designers "scene-painters."[18]

And yet the struggle between two- and three-dimensionality of scenery did not fall so neatly along traditional versus New Stagecraft lines. We have already seen that, within the traditional stagecraft, the question of painted versus built-up scenery was a perennial issue, representative of the traditionalists' cautious acceptance of the theatricality of their scenic convention. Within the New Stagecraft, the debate concerning two- and three-dimensionality is proof of the complete acceptance of this theatricality, the willingness to reveal the theatrical means by which the dramatic effects are created. Craig did, indeed, reject the *trompe l'oeil* effects of the traditional stagecraft. He ridiculed Craven's famous garden set for Tree's *Twelfth Night* (1901):

> There was a garden scene in a certain production of "Twelfth Night" that I once saw which contained a long flight of green grass steps, and it gave no sense of illusion to the spectator,

for no one ever went up more than six or ten out of the hundred steps. Then they all turned off sharply to the right or the left—six or ten were real steps, the rest all painted.[19]

Craig's objection does not seem to be based on a blanket rejection of painted effects, however; it is based instead on the false pretences of the scene, the attempt to pretend that two- and three-dimensional scenery can be combined to create the genuine illusion of real space. Yet Craig was prepared to use two-dimensional and painted effects in his own designs when it suited his theatrical purposes, and he was one of several practitioners of the New Stagecraft who employed scene-painters of the old school to realize his designs: W. J. Helmsley received special praise from Craig for his execution of the scenery for *Acis and Galatea* in 1902; Ricketts frequently employed the assistance of Harker; and William Telbin executed the non-illusionistic designs of Martin Harvey.[20]

The debate regarding the use of two- and three-dimensionality in the New Stagecraft was by no means the same as the debate among traditionalists. Traditionalists were concerned with effective techniques for creating the illusion of something real and concrete. Practitioners of the New Stagecraft were more interested in creating an evocative theatrical effect. While the two-dimensionality of much traditionalist decor brought out the artifice of their scenic conventions, the explicit artificiality of the New Stagecraft embraced the use of both two- and three-dimensional techniques. The issue of dimensions was an issue of style and utility, and not of fundamental technique or philosophy. Even Max Reinhardt, master of variable scenic space and staunch advocate of three-dimensional scenery revealed in its many planes and facets on a revolve, could be made to see by Ernst Stern "how much more effective the painted canvas was than the three-dimensional decor of the revolving stage."[21] The New Stagecraft at the beginning of the century contained within its international movement the solid structures of Craig and Appia and the painted frontal decor of Bakst, and was also free to incorporate devices of the traditionalist stage toward the creation of nonrepresentational effects.

Fantasy and Reality

Although the New Stagecraft was free from the confines of exact pictorial representation of the natural world, and although it freely accepted the theatricality of the conventional medium, it was in many ways bound by the realistic assumptions about the stage world and the dramatic event of contemporary traditionalism. Gordon Craig's complaints to the contrary, the early work of the practitioners of the New Stagecraft did in fact receive significant critical acceptance during the Edwardian period. The willingness of the more traditional Edwardians to accept the work of the New Stagecraft was determined by the degree to which the designs satisfied the demands of environment and the definitions of the dramatic event encoded within the traditional stagecraft. The degree of compatibility between the New Stagecraft and the premises of the traditional stagecraft accounts for the relative success of only a certain type of theatrical work, and further points to the way in which certain techniques of the New Stagecraft could be adopted by more traditionalist practitioners later in the Edwardian period.

On first inspection, there appear to be many essential contradictions between the environmental premises of the traditional stagecraft and the New Stagecraft. As we have seen, the traditional stagecraft saw the stage environment as the means of verifying the fictive reality of the stage event; it provided a context for behavior and action, and visually reflected and supported the nature of the dramatic activity, the tone of each dramatic moment, the sociological context of the character, the psychological state of the character, and the character's perception of his world. By contrast, the New Stagecraft saw the stage environment as less specific and more abstract. Instead of providing an historical or sociological context for the characters and the dramatic activity, the New Stagecraft sought to present an abstracted, cosmic context. By removing the character from an archaeological context, the theatre presented a picture not of a specific, particular psychological problem, but of a universal, shared experience. Gordon Craig's preference for broad expanses of sky, looming monoliths and geometrical configurations of planes seems to support this universalizing intention.

On some levels, this apparent incompatibility stood in the way of traditionalist assimilation of the New Stagecraft. The inability of several traditionalists to accept nonrepresentationalism reflects, in part, their persistent belief in highly articulated specified contexts for dramatic action and character. Martin Harvey, who often acknowledged Craig's influence on his own work, nonetheless ridiculed Craig for not being able to meet the demands of representationalism. Harvey recalls his dissatisfaction when Craig showed him the model for "Scene":

> "Yes, but Teddy," I said, "what will you do for a tree?" He ignored the trifling difficulty and proceeded with a new and more interesting change of blocks.
> "Splendid," I said, "but what about a *tree?*"[22]

As we shall see, Harvey imitated Craig in his powerful axes, striking colors, and evocative effects, but he never abandoned the evocation of real architecture or natural effects for pure abstraction. Craig was aware of the fact that he could not convince many traditionalists to use his designs unless he assigned to them an arbitrary representationalism. He recalls Tree's reaction when shown the designs he had commissioned of Craig for *Macbeth* (though Craig facetiously denies that Tree was intended in the anecdote):

"Would you mind telling me," he said, "what that is supposed to represent?" Of course such a courteous question deserves a courteous answer, so I replied that my whole reason for placing the pillar there was that it should stand for the stone at Scone at which the Kings of Scotland were crowned. "Most interesting," he replied. Now had I been unable to furnish him with some historical fact to back up a purely fantastical imaginative design made for a purely fantastical imaginative scene, he would have been dissatisfied. I am used to this sort of thing, and so I am generally ready with a stupid reply to a stupid question.[23]

Yet, despite the differences between the traditional stagecraft and the New Stagecraft in the definition of the relation of the scenic environment to dramatic action and character, there are a great many conceptual points shared by both schools. After all, Tree was willing and eager to use Craig as a designer for *Macbeth,* and when he eventually staged the play without Craig's designs (1911), he attempted, within the representational idiom, to create a nightmarish and subjectively distorted stage environment. Though they differed with regard to the temporal and geographical specificity of the stage environment, both schools agreed that the scenic environment could and must reflect dramatic action and character in some way. The theory and techniques of the New Stagecraft proved acceptable, indeed welcome, to Edwardian traditionalists when the specific environmental context they wished to depict could only be depicted in fantastic or abstract terms. In such cases, the services of the New Stagecraft were actively recruited by traditionalist actors and managers.

Edwardians recognized several dramatic genres that carried their own demands of relative environmental realism and probability. In discussing the question of dramatic probability, William Archer recognized that several orders of plausibility exist beyond the "first order" of realism, and that these are determined by the expectations established by the dramatic genre. He identified one class of plays, "romances, farces, a certain order of light comedies and semi-comic melodramas," in which the author, "without altogether despising and abjuring truth, makes it on principle subsidary to delightfulness;" this Archer calls "plausibility of the second order." "Plausibility of the third order" pertained to "sheer fantasies, like *A Midsummer Night's Dream,* or *Peter Pan,* or *The Blue Bird.*"[24] Edwardians took an extreme interest in this third class. Legitimate theatres presented fantasy plays, aimed both at juvenile and adult audiences, in competition with the Pantomimes during Christmas season.[25] Many productions of Shakespeare were produced during Christmas season and geared to similar audiences.[26]

There is much evidence that Edwardians saw in these plays the opportunity to experiment with new pictorial subjects, new visual idioms and innovative technical means of production. The *Times's* review of Irving's *Cymbeline* reveals how fantasy could be preferred to archaeology:

> It is obvious that any attempt to obtain archaeological consistency in such a hotch-potch of history, fiction and period must fail, and the question suggests itself whether ... for such plays as *Cymbeline* ... it would not be well to adopt on the stage a more or less fantastic setting, with something of the indefiniteness of place, period, and costume, which the modern stage-manager for some reason will only allow for comic opera.[27]

Shakespeare's plays with fantasy settings called for some scenic dimension of fantasy: as realistic scenery created the illusion of reality for natural localities, fantastic scenery had to be used to create the illusion of a fantastic reality appropriate to the world of the fantasy plays. As Beerbohm wrote of *A Midsummer Night's Dream,* "there must be the illusion of fairies, illusion of a true dream."[28] Beerbohm criticized Harker's realistic sets for Asche's *As You Like It* (1907) according to the same criteria:

> Arden, as shown under his auspices, is a very beautiful place. But it is not, like Shakespeare's Arden, an enchanted place. It is "a lovely spot." ... Things have come to a pretty pass when we bother our heads about verisimilitude for such a dream as "As You Like It."[29]

And yet, the critic for the *Illustrated London News* praised this very production:

> We need this sort of excursion in the playhouse—this stay by proxy under the greenwood tree, this transference to an ideal world, the denizens of which pass their time in light-hearted disregard of the cares and troubles of so-called reality, and move ... in an atmosphere of love.[30]

The two reviews were not contradictory; though the tastes of the critics differed, their critical criteria were identical: fantasy had to be presented in a fantastic setting. This aspect of traditionalist thinking opened the doors to the New Stagecraft during the early years of the new century, and particularly paved the way for the favorable critical reception in artistic circles of Gordon Craig's early work.

Practice

Pictorial Experiments: Craig and Ricketts

Gordon Craig's first four theatrical productions were fundamentally compatible with Edwardian prejudices regarding the suitability of the stage environment to the dramatic action. These productions were designed for the Purcell Society, a musical group headed by Craig's friend Martin Fallas Shaw, and included *Dido and Aeneas* (1901); *Acis and Galatea* (1902); *The Masque of Love* (1902); and Laurence Housman's *Bethlehem* (1903). It was to

Craig's advantage to introduce his stagecraft in musical vehicles with amateur casts in pieces requiring a "fantastic" treatment. Patterned composition, atmosphere and environment suggested by movement, were all aided by the musical idiom of the entire event, and attracted the attention of Yeats, Arthur Symons, and Will Rothenstein on those terms. Symons in particular noted Craig's use of pose, movement, and axis for harmonic effect, e.g., perpendicularity achieved by ribbons falling from outstretched arms, garlands about a maypole, and the angularity of the kneeling figure.[31] Symons also praised Craig for the evocation of the Pastoral setting of *Acis*, which employed "no trickle of real water in a trough, no sheaves of real corn among painted trees, no imitation of a flushed sky on canvas," but used instead nymphs laughing on the ground and children in straw hats tossing up colored balloons to evoke the breezes of a spring day.[32] The key to the beauty of the resulting picture was the subjugation of character, action and movement to a harmonic effect in keeping with the music. Craig created something altogether new, and undoubtedly dramatic; and his greatest achievement was the visualization of the fantastic, music made pictorially memorable.

The rarefied world of music and dance, and the formal pastoral settings of these pieces, were recognized as singularly appropriate for Craig's new style of production. The visual style effectively prepared the audience for the formal idiom of the musical dramas being presented. As Yeats said in praise of *Dido and Aeneas:* "He created an ideal country where everything was possible, even speaking in verse, or speaking in music, or the expression of the whole of life in a dance."[33] And so long as the world being represented on the stage was just such an ideal country, Craig's scenic style could be used to verify the dramatic reality of the stage event, perfectly in keeping with Edwardian traditionalist principles. Traditionalists were therefore prepared to accept Craig's style of production only insofar as it was appropriate to the nature of the dramatic material. As Craig's mother, Ellen Terry, said, quoting from his father, E. W. Godwin, scenery should be "entirely accurate or entirely fanciful."[34] The *Review of the Week* suggested that Craig's work could be applied to "Shakespeare and Maeterlinck in all their poetry."[35] After seeing *Acis and Galatea* (1902), Max Beerbohm suggested that Craig's designs would be suited to the fantasy of Christmas Pantomimes or Maeterlinck plays, and in 1907 Beerbohm expressed his regret that Granville Barker had not retained Craig to design a revival of *Prunella*.[36]

This categorization of Craig's work had its disadvantages. William Poel, no supporter of Craig, while recalling the latter's early productions, differentiated between the dramatic material to which they were applied and the demands of Shakespeare:

> Some years ago I saw Mr. Craig's production of "Acis and Galatea," followed by a masque. It was a stagery of great beauty, and seemed to initiate new possibilities. But then both were

musical entertainments which gained appreciably by picturesque background. The action never clashed with the quaint setting. Unlike the demands of tragedy, the representation made no direct appeal to the reason, and no obvious attempt to purify the emotions. Its main business was to delight the eye.[37]

Beerbohm, in an otherwise favorable review of *The Vikings* (1903), reached similar conclusions:

> For a modern play, in which the aim is to produce the nearest possible illusion of actuality, Mr. Craig's system would be manifestly impossible. Further, it would be inappropriate to any poetic plays in which we are meant to accept the characters primarily as human beings. It could not be applied, for instance, to the plays of Shakespeare, except to those which Shakespeare wrote as fantasies. For his fantasies it would be as much more right than the present system as it were less right for his human plays. It would strike a proper keynote, reminding the audience that here they are translated from the plane of what actually does exist to the plane of what actually doesn't and couldn't.[38]

Traditionalists could accept Craig's designs only when they confirmed the realistic premises of their own scenographic system.

The production of *The Vikings* was, in fact, part of a programmatic attempt on Craig's part to supersede the limitations of this critical assumption. In 1903, Craig embarked on a commercial managerial venture with his mother at the Imperial Theatre. Though only two plays were produced, *The Vikings* by Ibsen and *Much Ado About Nothing,* it is clear that Craig intended a full series of productions, selected to illustrate the variety of forms his designs could take in support of a variety of dramatic genres. Craig wrote Will Rothenstein, in response to Beerbohm's review of *The Vikings:* "Max didn't quite manage it. Tell him when next you see him that if possible I shall put my next production around a realistic play. *Much Ado* will please the others a bit. . . . I don't think any will be able to giggle about it."[39] *The Vikings* and *Much Ado,* along with the rejected and unproduced realistic play (perhaps Heijermans' *The Good Hope,* produced by Terry without Craig on tour the following year), were programmatic assertions on Craig's part of the applicability of his work to non-operatic and non-fantastic forms of drama. Writing of these productions retrospectively, Craig complained that "everyone remembers their performances; my *mise en scène* is forgotten."[40] Certainly this is not true, nor was it intended to be. But if Craig's designs are memorable, it is for their assimilation and adaptation of the theatrical traditions associated with the genres of the plays in question.

Craig's first reform, once embarked upon commercial management with his mother and with a theatre lease in hand, was the renovation of the technical resources of the theatre. There is some disagreement about the amount of renovation which took place, varying from Marguerite Steen's description of Craig "virtually disembowelling the theatre" to Craig's recollection that he was "quite content with the stage, and even its inadequate lighting equipment would do."[41] The work involved the installation of a lighting bridge across the inside of the proscenium arch (a feature then unknown in English theatres), the removal of borders, and the raising of the fly system well out of sight above the proscenium. Ellen Terry defended these renovations, despite the expense involved: "When I worked with him I found him far from impractical. It was the modern theatre which was unpractical when he was in it! It was wrongly designed, wrongly built."[42] Terry further states that "the great height of the proscenium made his lighting lose all its value." Craig, behind the visor of one of his *Mask* pseudonyms, challenged this statement, however; he acknowledged that the light, from high above the proscenium rather than from perches to the sides and from the footlights, lacked "force" and "glare," and dismissed his mother's criticism as the work of her autobiographical collaborator, Christopher St. John.[43] The use of lighting from above did, in *The Vikings,* create a new and different effect, to which the Edwardian theatregoer was not accustomed; not only were the eyes and mouth overshadowed, but, with the large headgear of the Viking warriors, the entire face was sometimes cast in shadow.[44]

No doubt this defect encouraged Craig's use of limelight for Hiordis. However, the use of limelight was related to Craig's intention in staging the play. The features of his staging which were most successful were those most clearly linked to the play's genre—romantic costume melodrama—and to the traditional means of staging such plays: the creation of a dramatically and emotionally charged environment, with heightened histrionic moments and striking visual pictures. The most memorable moments of the production were produced by the congruence of Ibsen's stage directions, Ellen Terry's magnetic acting (her temperamental unsuitability notwithstanding) and Craig's ability to underscore the drama pictorially:Hiordis' knotting of the bow-string with her hair, and sharpening the arrowheads, pantomine moments which Craig and Terry introduced. Craig's use of limelight at such moments was not a betrayal of his principles but the deliberate employment of traditional scenic conventions in support of important dramatic moments.

It is interesting to see how Craig's attempt at producing a romantic costume melodrama made his work subject to traditionalist standards, the realism of the environment and its relation to the dramatic action, that had been ignored in consideration of his operatic productions. One of the strongest critics of the production, in the privacy of personal correspondence, was Bernard Shaw. We have seen how Shaw was a traditionalist with regard to his belief in integrating details of the physical environment with the tone of the dramatic event. Shaw's quarrel with Craig had no bearing on questions of scenic representationalism, nor the technical means by which Craig created his pictorial effects; it dealt merely with Craig's effective correlation of the environment with the drama. Shaw wrote Ellen Terry about how the first scene of *The Vikings* should have been treated:

> Now, the first act of The Vikings should be a most lovely morning scene, all rosy mists, fresh air, virgin light, and diamond dewdrops. The men should be glowing from their baths, robust, solid, with no nonsense about them. Into this cheerful and real scene there should come a woman like the shadow of death—a woman in black, with white face and snakes in her hair, so to speak, a messenger of death to every man in the play.
>
> Instead of which, Signor Tedvardo, not being able to manage full light and local color, turns the dawn into night; makes the warriors fantastic and unreal; and finally introduces comfort and color in the shape of a fine figure of a woman in a particularly cosy bearskin mantle which heaps her shoulders up to her ears and gives her an air of jollity which positively radiates goodnature in spite of the unfortunate lady's efforts to make mischief.[45]

Years later, Craig rebutted Shaw in print, claiming that he had merely followed the authorial stage directions in depicting "a stormy, snow-grey winter day." Craig added in defense of the darkness of his scene that "in Helgoland the sky on a stormy winter day is lead-colour."[46] It is important to note that Craig did not challenge Shaw's critical premises. While the two disagreed about the dramatic shape of the scene in question, they seem to have agreed that the physical environment depicted on the stage must reflect the emotional and symbolic tenor of the dramatic action. Craig demonstrates here that he himself worked from traditionalist premises about the environment and the dramatic event. Although he employed different technical means to create his stage pictures, the pictures themselves functioned in relation to the drama as they would have in the productions of his acknowledged master, Henry Irving.

If *The Vikings* was an attempt to demonstrate the applicability of his production idiom to romantic costume melodrama, Craig had the opportunity to apply his work to Shakespearean comedy in *Much Ado About Nothing*, his sole production of Shakespeare in England. Craig and Terry turned to *Much Ado* as a corrective to *The Vikings*: as a means of exploiting the actress's reputation in a play, role and metier more suitable to her special talents. Terry's letter to Craig reveals her motives:

> —but what about Much Ado? I've only £ 500 to spend on it—and if I had 5000 it would be impossible to *scene & dress* the Play in three weeks in your way, let alone drill supers and rehearse everybody. Then again, I believe in the *old* play, and the *old me* in it, would not be acceptable to the Public in a *different style* to the one they know—Lose no time dear, please, in telling me if you see yr way to stage managing the thing with *existing scenery & dresses* (wherever we may be able to pick them up)—as slight as possible and with nice lighting—to make it all look as beautiful as may be.[47]

Due to the commercial failure of *The Vikings*, Craig had to make do with costumes designed by his sister in collaboration with a firm, and a very short rehearsal period. The designs for the production were not the old play in the old style, however, but a way of reconceiving the play according to his new scenic principles. Had he had the time and money, he might have forged a new style of Shakespearean production. As he had not, the resulting compromise reveals how compatible his scenic style was with the histrionic and dramatic style of the Lyceum.

The Vikings and Much Ado made distinctly different demands upon the scenic designer, particularly in regard to the number and sequence of the scenes: Ibsen's play called for a single set for each scene, with intervals between them, while Shakespeare's comedy demanded the flexibility and continuity recognized by the Edwardians. The Vikings was, consequently, more suitable to a particular type of scenic elaboration. The press release for The Vikings describes the scenes: "each will fill the entire stage of the Imperial. They are called respectively, The Rock, The Banquet, The Bow, and The Storm."[48] Not needing to worry about rapid changes, Craig was able to build up and surface the stage floor: the first and last scenes were so steeply raked as to render the combat by broadsword nearly impossible, though it made for dramatic upstage entrances of warriors, spear first, over the high crags. And Craig was able to alter the lighting throughout the course of each scene, according to changes in weather and time of day, thereby transforming the appearance and tone of the scene.

By contrast, the sets for Much Ado had to be simple and flexible. Terry's instructions to Craig, while the production was in preparation, reveal her scenic priorities:

> *Now* whilst there is still time to simplify the scenery and lighting for Much Ado, I want to impress upon you that *everything* depends upon the *quick change of the scenes on the first night*—it's no use afterwards, for the newspapers speak of the *first night*.[49]

Craig's solution to this demand was the familiar solution of the traditionalists: the alternation of built scenes with simpler front scenes, and whenever possible, the rearrangement of the text and the placement of intervals so that a single set could occupy the stage for an entire act. As Craig and Terry were using a modified Lyceum version of the play, this traditional arrangement was ready-made. Act 1 (of a four-act arrangement) consisted, scenically, of a single set: Leonato's house; act 2 featured a built-up garden set for three of the four scenes, the remaining scene (the third) being a street, presumably a front scene; act 3 contained only the church scene; and act 4 alternated between a Prison, Leonato's garden (as in act 2), the monument, and the garden again. The first scene, Leonato's house, afforded scenic opportunities similar to the work Craig staged for the Purcell Society: Terry specified in a letter to Craig "a dance, in which I dance too, during the scene with Benedick, and all going very merrily."[50] The Masque gave Craig the opportunity to employ familiar decorative devices: masquers in "uniformed gowns of silver lozenges, with diadems of mistletoe on their heads," dancing in patterns dictated by their manipulation of large arched garlands, which visually extended the rhythms of their costumes and movements.[51] This scene was restaged with Craig's designs for the 1906 Drury Lane Jubilee performance for Ellen Terry; it is most representative of Craig's early operatic style, and accordingly is the subject of two pictorial documents: a photograph of the Jubilee performance, and a drawing by Byam Shaw in the Jubilee program (See illustration 23).[52]

Most of the scenes in the production exemplified a compromise between Craig's greater reforms of space and lighting with the special demands of a production staged along vaguely traditional lines. Beerbohm's complaints about human scale and the open expanses of borderless stage space in *The Vikings* were answered through the use of false prosceniums, decoratively related to the particular scene, or, as Beerbohm described it, by making "the scenery itself . . . a sort of inner proscenium."[53] So, in the set for Leonato's house, the room was created by panels of tapestries at the back and to the sides; and while Craig, in his renovation of the theatre, had removed the masking between the top of the set and the proscenium arch, he replaced it, in this scene, with a "vast expanse of tapestry, . . . hung on a wall descending to that side of the hall's ceiling which is nearest to the foot-lights," i.e., in the plane of the proscenium frame.[54] The garden set consisted of a series of arched hedges (see illustration 24); like the interior set, it had side walls as well as a wall along the rear of the stage; and a "second proscenium" was created by lattice work, with "a gigantic treillage of vine" in place of the tapestried panel of the first set.[55] The backcloth for the scene was a sky, with no painted embellishment, lit in "Reckitts blue," and while the *Illustrated London News* thought that this set "lacked all sense of distance." The contrast in lighting between the cloth and the set, and the symmetrical severity of the hedges, could allow for striking visual effects, not uncoincidentally associated with music: Balthazar's song was accompanied by minstrels in long robes who stood, silhouetted against the sky, in the arches of the hedge.[56] This set was, according to Edward Craig, inspired by Taddeo Gaddi. Craig found similar inspiration from Serlio: the cloth for the front scene in act 2 was copied directly from him; and the five "Tuscan pillars," between which were hung tapestries of the first scene, and which were rearranged throughout the play for additional sets, found similar inspiration in Serlio, who was later to provide the germ for Craig's "Scene."

The most striking and impressive scene in the production was the Church scene (act 3 in the production), which was at once the most *Craigische* and, at the same time, represented the closest ties with the principles of the traditional stagecraft. Ellen Terry compared the scene with E. W. Godwin's design for the

104   *Shakespeare and New Stagecraft*

Temple of Artemis in Tennyson's *The Cup* (1881) at the Lyceum, in which "a great deal of effect was due to the lighting. The gigantic figure of the many-breasted Artemis, placed far back in the scene-dock, loomed through a blue mist, while the foreground of the picture was in yellow light."[57] Instead of exploiting the depth of the stage, Craig exploited its height, now without inner framing or borders: a giant crucifix, in the style of Cimabue, loomed up beyond the upper edge of the picture, disappearing into the darkness. Craig used large spaces and unlit dark expanses to create the illusion of a Byzantine cathedral. The figures of the characters gradually appeared out of the gloom, illuminated only by a circle of multicolored light on the floor, coming from an unseen stained-glass window.[58]

Craig's goal in this scene, and the means by which he achieved it, is most indicative of the relation of his work to the school of scenic realism. Craig sets up a contrast between the two methods:

> We didn't reproduce the interior of a Palace in Messina, because that would have been a very costly affair; we should have had to travel to Messina to measure the place up and bring back the plans of part of it, and then struggle to get it on to the stage, and so forth. This sort of labour was beginning to strike some of us in the theatre as rather ridiculous. It was very pleasant to come and see the interior of a Cathedral at Messina, almost in facsimile, and to hear a lovely organ booming or purring out the beautiful sounds which sacred music can breathe forth. But somehow all this made the younger people of 1902-3—and I was one of them—a little impatient.[59]

While Craig did not reproduce a cathedral in plan and elevation on the stage, however, he did employ just the techniques he ridicules, and several others, to create his effect. Before the lights of the unseen window were brought up, while the stage was in complete darkness, "the music of an organ swells out from the gloom of the stage."[60] Craig was depending on the evocative powers of synaesthesia, a device well used by Irving to set the imagination going in support of the visual sense. Craig's use of the unseen window reflects another traditional device: the suggestion of three-dimensional space beyond the viewer's range of vision. Edward Craig describes the suggested location of this window as "above the proscenium arch"; by implication, this space could be revealed to the audience only by rotating the set 180 degrees. Edward Craig also notes the use of gathered curtaining to create the illusion of immense pillars, disappearing upwards into darkness: these pillars were decorated in "a *varnished* pattern that sparkled in the dim light."[61] The suggestion of a surface through the skillful use of materials and the creative use of light echoes Herkomer's quite naturalistic experimentations in the same techniques. In short, Craig employed rather stunning and individual devices to achieve an effect in keeping with the principles of traditional theatre: localization, environmental evocation, synaesthesia, the implication of unseen space, the illusion of 360 degree reality, and the play of light against surface. And while the means which Craig employed to create this effect were rather unconventional, his use of materials was always secondary to the effect he wished to create. In fact, early sketches for this scene reveal Craig's original plan to create the effect of a cathedral, with its pillars and vaulting, through the use of traditional cut cloths.[62] Percy Fitzgerald was dissatisfied with the conservative nature of Craig's reforms. After describing the illusion of the pillars in the Church scene, he noted: "This was most effective at first, until we saw that these were deceptive draperies. . . . so it comes to this—that loose clothes [sic], hung about more or less gracefully, have taken the place of canvas, stretched upon screens. It will not do, I fear, for the improvement is not on the lines of principle."[63] Fitzgerald distinguished between Craig's reforms in means with his reforms in overall scenic suggestion; in doing so, he rightly perceived that many of the fundamental principles of scenic representationalism, if not pictorial verisimilitude, were not only accepted but redoubled in importance by Craig in this, his only English production of Shakespeare.

Craig's later solutions to the issues of Shakespearean staging were more advanced. As has already been noted, Craig's development of his screens model greatly affected his ideas about the staging of Shakespeare. He did not employ the screens in his unproduced designs for Tree's *Macbeth,* but he did urge Ellen Terry to use them for *The Merchant of Venice,* and he used them, without their intended flexibility, for *Hamlet* at the Moscow Art Theatre.[64] He justified this use, and his choice of play, in the catalogue of an exhibition of his models in Manchester in 1912:

> I chose *Hamlet* as it is of all modern plays the most inspired, the most literary, the most dramatic, the most picturesque. . . . Added to these reasons, I chose it because I had long known the figure of Hamlet, had acted the role myself, and wished once more to test my theory that the Shakespearean play does not naturally belong to our art of the theatre.[65]

Craig's goal, then, was to promote his own art of the theatre by putting it to the test of Shakespeare. Edward Craig felt that this was actually a prostitution of the principle of the screens, the use of scenery designed for purely abstract movement in a play which required specified locales.[66] Yet in applying his screens to a production of Shakespeare, Craig was able both to explore a new technology and aesthetic of scenechanging, and to exploit the more traditional conceptions of Shakespearean staging which he had inherited from his Victorian predecessors and Edwardian contemporaries. The continuous staging provided by the screens did not work in performance due to an accident at the final rehearsal, and so Craig never fully tested his concept of movable scenery against a text of Shakespeare. Still the traditionalism of the production deserves some attention.

The traditionalism of Craig's Moscow *Hamlet* lies in its employment of subjective vision, based on the focus of the production on the character and psychology of the title character.[67] Craig conceived the character "almost motionless, standing secure, firm like a snowcapped mountain, at whose base many small figures of mean men and their women creep or scramble."[68] This conception could be translated into scenic terms by the translation of the physical world of the play into an embodiment of Hamlet's psychological perception of it. Craig elaborated upon his visual conception of the court scenes in a conversation with Stanislavsky:

> All the tragedy of Hamlet is his isolation. And the background of this isolation is the court, a world of pretense. . . . And in this golden court, this world of show, there must not be different individualities as there would be in a realistic play. No, here everything melts into a single mass. Separate faces as in the old masters of painting must be coloured with one brush, one paint.[69]

Physically, the scene represents Hamlet's own perception of the court: "You see the stage divided by a barrier. On the one side sits Hamlet, fallen, as it were, into a dream, on the other side you see his dream. You see it, as it were, through the mind's eye of Hamlet."[70]

Stanislavsky understood and appreciated this "monodrama" conception, but questioned how the scenes in which the title character did not appear would be treated. Craig replied: "I should like Hamlet to be on stage always, in every scene, all through the play."[71] This was not carried through completely in production. But the transformation of the physical world into a view of a particular character was done in at least one which Hamlet did not appear: according to Stanislavsky, Craig wanted the Ghost's appearance in the first scene of the play to be presented as "an hallucination of the frightened soldiers."[72]

Notwithstanding the many stunning visual effects of the production and the breakthroughs he made in the nonrepresentationalism of the decor, Craig seems to have accepted the traditionalist view of the limited uses of his scenic system: that it worked best in the depiction of fantasy and distorted reality. No doubt Craig's *Macbeth* designs for Tree sought the same effects. Craig's initial choice of plays, in response to Stanislavsky's invitation to work at the Moscow Art Theatre, reveals that Craig placed his own work in such categories: in addition to *Hamlet*, he proposed *Macbeth, The Tempest, A Midsummer's Night Dream* [sic], all of which employ fantasy or the supernatural, *The Vikings* (which he had already produced), *Peer Gynt* (also a fantasy), and *Ghosts*, in which the title metaphor could be represented in visual terms, as the supernatural elements in *Rosmersholm* were emphasized in his production for Duse in 1905.[73]

In conclusion, while Craig experimented with new forms of abstraction, he consciously and deliberately accepted, in his Shakespearean work, the pictorial premises of his traditionalist contemporaries. His most important contribution to English scenography was not his massive cubes and doorways, but the new vocabulary of aesthetic means for creating such poetic, evocative and simplified scenery. Within the limitations of the pictorial tradition of Shakespeare, a tradition which Craig inherited and implicitly accepted, his ideas were suported and imitated by advocates of the New Stagecraft.

If Craig's own work falls within the traditionalist scenic aesthetic in respect to both his implicit surrender to the concept of dramatic genre and his practical use of their environmental principles, it is not surprising that his less doctrinaire fellow practitioners of the New Stagecraft produced results well within scenic traditionalism. The most revealing of the productions of Shakespeare using the New Stagecraft was one of the most publicized and one of the least successful: the 1909 *King Lear* at the Haymarket, under the management of Herbert Trench, with designs by Charles Ricketts. *Lear* inaugurated Trench's management, and signalled an immediate departure from his original plans to run several productions in repertory. Trench was a man of little theatrical experience, and yet his notions of scenery in relation to the drama reveal much about the scenography of the productions under his management.

Trench prefaced his management's manifesto with a thinly veiled attack on the traditional methods of Tree, and in particular Tree's forthcoming production of *Henry VIII:*

> Presently we shall have upon us an avalanche of Shakespearian upholstery. There will be the familiar glitter of stage-crowds, betinselled cavalcades, "built-up" palaces and chapels; of coronations modelled upon fancy balls. The cloth of gold in these will cost fabulous sums, and the lace and velvet robes of the cardinals will later furnish forth valuable dining-room curtains for illustrious actor-managers.[74]

This breach of professional etiquette cost Trench a public explanation and apology.

When Trench first proposed to produce *Lear* as the inaugural production of his management, he inspired Gordon Craig, under one of his many *Mask* pseudonyms, to define his principles of dramatic genre and the appropriateness of particular styles of decor to each genre:

> Mr. Trench probably thinks that by dispensing with Romantic scenery he has made the task easier. . . . as if scenery or no scenery made any difference to the stupendous undertaking.
> I feel inclined to agree with Mr Gordon Craig, who holds that it is impossible to produce these plays upon the stage, yet who also holds that, *if* you produce them at all you must do so in as Romantic a manner as possible. Shakespeare is not an Aeschylus; no, nor so hard a playwright as the author of "Everyman"; nor so cold a master as those early Chinese writers. Shakespeare is distinctly Romantic; often vulgar in colour, breaking all laws; and I hold that when we produce him on the stage we should try to match his Romance and his lawlessness as well as we can. . . .

The manner of Shakespeare is what is called the grand Romantic manner, not the classic manner.[75]

Here Craig accepted both Edwardian traditionalist notions of dramatic genre and the possible appropriateness of the New Stagecraft to certain types of drama, and he linked his own work to the romantic traditionalism of his master, Henry Irving. Trench, in his theoretical pronouncement regarding the policy of his Haymarket management, fully adopted Craig's categorization of Shakespeare as a Romantic, and not a classic, playwright, and called for "symbolic" scenery in the staging of romantic plays:

> In the first place we will imagine that plays are finely sifted by the stage-manager into two groups that will receive handlings of scenery wholly distinct in style: the Realistic and the Symbolic. For instance, in modern realistic comedy you may often prudently aim at a real if modest illusion of picture. But in romantic comedy or tragedy the scene-land should be symbolic, and its painted cloths merely fragmentary and suggestive: the latter style aiming not at deceiving you by completeness of representation, but at another virtue, the freer virtue of a suggested spaciousness and universality. In this symbolic kind there is a special advantage. The scenery not only may be, but should be, imperfect, in order that the living persons may stand vivider in their due proportions before the eye. Drown an actress in jewels, and how shall she avail herself of the passion that breathes from her eyes? Encumber the boards with massive and gnarled forest-trees or cathedrals, and how shall the uncertainties, the tortuosities and ironies and submeanings of *man* stand out against them? You have wasted money on the material, the earthy and the expensive, and stinted it on rare human instruments of expression, who are harder to get although easier to buy.[76]

Note Trench's adoption of Craig's belief that a spiritual drama should be shifted onto a universal, unparticularized, cosmic plane. In discussing Shakespeare's position in this spectrum, Trench adopted the Elizabethanist notion that the verbal component of Shakespeare's art precluded a visual spectacle:

> Now all Shakespeare's plays lend themselves of course to this treatment by *Symbolic* scenery; his own particular virtue lying in a supreme poetry or felicity of expression, which carries (as it were) the scenery half-implicit in the language, plainly all true Shakespeare-lovers will adopt the style of stage-management in which the poetry and beauty of the language is thrown into sharpest salience and relief. To that all other virtues of staging, however puissant and legitimate in themselves, must, in his case, be subordinated.... In a word, the Shakespearian stage should lend itself, by a studious sobriety and reserve in colours, to the higher delights of the ear and the intelligence.[77]

Trench did have specific ideas about how to create this "imperfect," i.e., simplified and abstracted scenery: he advocated the use of an apron stage, which he called the "debateable land"; lighting isolating the important events or characters in a scene from the rest of the picture, which would "halo away into obscurity" at the edges "like an impressionist picture"; make-up "from within" (?); crowd scenes created by the employment of only "modest numbers" of supernumeraries, or preferably a whole army "suggested by a group of spears behind a wall"; and the use of a single designer for each production, temperamentally matched to the mood of the particular piece.[78]

Certainly Trench's ideas were half-baked and inconsistent. But his desire to set Shakespeare's play apart from the realistic drama was an attempt to release the plays from the pictorial representationalism demanded of modern realistic plays. With Craig, he underscored the romanticism of the plays in order to resurrect the chiaroscura techniques of Henry Irving in place of the "fierce blaze of evenly shed, unflickering and merciless electric light."[79] And, like Craig, he sought a way of retaining the pictorialism of the older romantic traditions while adding to it a level of "universality" through the use of abstracted avant-garde stage techniques.

Trench's selection of Ricketts was in many ways appropriate to this ideal. Their collaboration was, to some extent, a package deal, since both had gained their current position through the support and patronage of Lord Howard de Walden. Ricketts had designed *Attila* (1907) for Oscar Asche, a production in which Lord Howard had a financial interest, and had produced Lord Howard's own play, *Lanval,* in 1908. Ricketts's art represented the several directions of the New Stagecraft. In terms of sheer beauty, he was able to create striking pictures with vibrantly contrasting colors, as in *Salome* (1906, for the Literary Theatre Society) and *Don Juan in Hell* (1907, for the Court). He was interested in flexible, conventional decor, such as he used for *The Death of Tintagiles* (1912) for Barker at the St. James's, another venture in which Lord Howard was financially interested.[80]

Unlike many of his contemporaries, Ricketts was vehemently non-ideological in his designs with regard to aesthetic movements; in a presentation copy of his *Pages on Art* to Martin Harvey, he noted that the essays were: "written against over-dogmatism of a Craig kind."[81] And he questioned the common avant-garde view that scenery should simplify the drama into merely descriptive visual images: when Trench and he were discussing a contemplated revival of *The Dream,* Trench saw a bunch of flowers floating in a bowl of water and suggested that as the desirable effect for the fairies. Ricketts replied:

> They have often been prettified too long in that way. I do not see the fairies as flowers, in spite of Shakespeare's names; to me they are beings, yet not quite human ones—not dangerous to man, yet likely to make him uncomfortable and to disquiet him. I see them rather less than men and women; I shall give them green flesh, as something in nature, and green hair—or blue hair for some.[82]

Ricketts sought a design concept which would not merely telegraph a meaning but embody a dramatic idea; rather than create a stage image which would make the designer's definitive statement with regard to the play, he chose to establish a dramatic relationship which would then be elaborated in performance by the actors and the director.

Although Ricketts considered *Lear* "his most complete achievement in the theatre," there was little in the production that lay outside pictorial traditionalism.[83] He did boast of using Herkomer's contracting proscenium in the production, though I have found no critical notices which commented on its use.[84] Most of Ricketts's effects appear to have been temporal and atmospheric: one review mentions "the gaunt castle of Gloucester, with the sky lowering over its rude ramparts; the reminiscences of Stonehenge, where the huge monoliths tower in the foreground against the misty hillside, drenched by the midnight storm; [and] the forest, in which the snow-clad trunks of the bare trees break the light of the winter's day"[85] (See illustration 25). Note that almost all these pictures employed a creative use of different stage planes: looming monoliths or trees in the foreground or middleground against an artistically illuminated backcloth. Ricketts evidently relied upon lighting to evoke the heath; Beerbohm complained that he did not see the scene at all: "Lear raved in inky darkness, which the streaks of lightning strove vainly to illumine."[86]

Ricketts's effects were primarily painterly, and continued to be so in his works after the war. Trench's original manifesto called for individual artists to design each production, but it also dictated that "the rough designs should then be carried into execution by the excellent Hackers [sic], the Telbins, and the Stanfields of our day."[87] Harker executed Ricketts's *Lear* designs, as he did the *Attila* designs in 1907. The aesthetic contrast between the beauty of Ricketts's designs and their traditional execution and employment of two-dimensional devices was noted by Craig, who took issue with critical comparisons with his own theories:

> I am convinced that what the critics have mistaken for my method is Mr. Ricketts' own method, and that if Mr. Ricketts employs large blue sky-backgrounds, or towering trees in straight lines, or schemes instead of confusions of colours, or lights which lend a poetry to the scene, instead of lights blended by vulgarity, he is but following a "method" employed since time immemorial by all men of taste.
>
> For the artificial manner in which he treats all this he cannot be responsible. He is working inside a theatre under artificial conditions, and therefore everything he does becomes *theatrical*.[88]

Craig gave Ricketts the benefit of the doubt, blaming the conservatism of the scenic means on the technology and the traditions in which he worked. But, behind this, was the complaint of an artist who dealt increasingly with abstractions against a man who did not, and who could acknowledge and employ the frankly artificial dimension of theatre language. Ricketts, like the management of the theatre in which he worked, was part of a movement that was enhancing and supplementing an established theatrical method and tradition without supplanting it or changing its values. Commenting on Trench's quarrel with Tree (resulting from the former's slur against the latter's methods), Craig noted that Trench's financially successful production of *The Blue Bird* was theoretically as conservative as, and artistically inferior to, Tree's production of *Pinkie and the Fairies* across the street.[89] The "symbolic," suggestive style was becoming part of the standard scenic vocabulary, first through plays of fantasy, and then through the poetic drama, without the dogma of a new movement.

Spatial Experiments: Modified Elizabethanism

Both Craig and Ricketts belong to one set of reforms of the New Stagecraft designed, in part, to meet the demands of simplicity and continuity made by Shakespeare's texts. The simplification, abstraction and suggestiveness of the decor freed the production from the heavy encumbrances of strictly representational scenery, and allowed for the swift change of scenes demanded by the text. A completely different set of solutions was offered by other practitioners of the New Stagecraft, and these involved a new approach to the use of space, one which redefined the relation of acting space to scenic space and of stage to auditorium. If the pictorial branch of the New Stagecraft shared many attitudes and features of staging with the pictorialism of the traditional stagecraft, the spatial branch of the New Stagecraft bore many resemblances to contemporary Elizabethanism, which was in turn influenced by many theatrical premises of the traditional stagecraft. These spatial solutions represented an attempt to incorporate the theoretical advances of Elizabethanism without accepting the limitations of the historical attitudes of that school. The result was an arrangement of stage space which provided a dominant mode of staging for productions of Shakespeare in the 1920s.

As the new visual style of the Post-Impressionist exhibitions and the first visits of the Russian Ballet fueled English activity employing the New Stagecraft, the spatial experiments in England during the Edwardian period were stimulated by the London productions of Max Reinhardt. These productions included: *Sumurun* and *Venetian Nights* at the Coliseum under the sponsorship of Oswald Stoll; *Oedipus,* in Gilbert Murray's translation, at Covent Garden, featuring Martin Harvey, Lillah McCarthy and Louis Calvert; and *The Miracle* at the Olympia exhibition centre, under the sponsorship of C.B. Cochran. Several of these productions made direct contributions to the new visual style: the simplified decor of *Sumurun* and *Venetian Nights* employed bold colors, and broad expanses of white offset by brightly colored costumes. These productions also used the revolve built into the stage of the Coliseum, though the use of this innovation did not immediately affect English staging due to the lack of such equipment in the average theatre. The visual style of these productions generated English experiments. In 1913, George Alexander hired Ernest Stern, one of Reinhardt's designers, to produce *Turandot,* which he had designed in Germany for Reinhardt, at the St. James' Theatre. Carter believes that this production failed only because the lighting in the theatre, all of which came from within the proscenium frame, was insufficient for the designs.[90] After Basil Dean saw *Sumurun,* he followed Reinhardt back to Berlin to see his *Oedipus,* and copied the sky-dome of the Deutsches Theater in his Liverpool Repertory Theatre.

Reinhardt's English work is more noteworthy and ostensibly influential with regard to his use of theatrical space. As we have seen, the Elizabethanists were obsessed with the ideal of the platform stage, but failed to achieve this ideal within existing playhouses. Reinhardt's *Oedipus* and *The Miracle,* on the other hand, both transformed the spatial relationship between the theatrical event and the spectator, and changed the visual image of the playhouse itself. *Oedipus* was the less successful of the two; Reinhardt's German production had been performed in a circus, and he had hoped to use the Albert Hall as the closest English equivalent. In the end, he had to settle for Covent Garden, which he altered in a compromise attempt to recapture the openness of a truly circular space. Several rows of stalls were removed, the proscenium was masked in black drapery, and the first two sets of boxes, on either side of the playing space, were masked at the stage level but left practical on the upper levels. A *trompel'oeil* colonnade (which created enough illusion for Huntly Carter to call them "massive black columns") stood in front of a facade with a doorway, placed at the plane of the proscenium arch.[91] A flight of broad steps and platforms rose from the level of the stalls to the colonnade. The lower spaces, extending into the auditorium, were reserved almost exclusively for the enormous chorus of extras (see   illustrations 26 and 27).

The use of an apron stage, of which this was an extended variation, was not new to English audiences, but Reinhardt's boldness, and the attention drawn to the production, made even the Elizabethanists credit Reinhardt for popularizing the notion of an open stage and a neutral facade. William Poel, retrospectively asserting his own claim as an innovator, nevertheless recalls that "it was not until Reinhardt took up the continuous movement, and the acting in front of curtains, that the London stage became at all impressed," and as early as 1912, Poel wrote:

> But although, as an Englishman, I may claim that Shakespeare's country was the first to agitate for a return to the open platform, I do not overlook the fact that it was Professor Reinhardt's genius which gave practical shape on a larger scale to the principles of Elizabethan staging, and that he showed himself capable of understanding and adapting

these principles to modern conditions while at the same time he proved himself to be a genuine artist by his ability to subordinate the setting to the requirements of the drama.[92]

In fact, there was appropriately little that was Elizabethan about Reinhardt's *Oedipus;* and its use of space, a compromise of his original intentions, was unsatisfactory. The sight-lines of the theatre prevented his playing space from extending beyond a few rows of the stalls. Also his division of space, with the multitudes below and the principals above, forced him to put the audience in direct spatial contact with the chorus, a problem which had not occurred in the circus arena. Oedipus's final exit, through the rows of stalls occupied by patrons in evening dress, created illusionary problems which, as we have seen, the Edwardians were not capable of handling. The Edwardians did not follow Reinhardt's example in placing dramatic action in the auditorium, but they were inspired by these experiments to extend the stage proper beyond the limits of the proscenium arch and out onto an apron. And so, Reinhardt inspired a compromise of Elizabethanist ideals of the platform stage with the picture stage tradition of the advocates of the New Stagecraft, resulting in a stage which became the dominant form for later Shakespearean experiments.

The spatial compromise between the platform stage and the picture stage was in fact evolving independently of Reinhardt in England during the Edwardian period. Within the mainstream of Elizabethanism, a model for the stage was emerging which incorporated pictorial features of the Edwardian stage and remained compatible with the sight-lines and actor-audience relationship of the traditional Edwardian playhouse. One of the first productions to feature a hybrid Elizabethan stage of this type was William Poel's production of *Two Gentlemen of Verona* at Tree's 1910 Shakespeare Festival. For this production, Poel erected an apron stage covering the orchestra pit, and a tiring house facade upstage (see illustration 28). The one contemporary photograph of the production shows the relation of the facade to the rest of the stage at His Majesty's Theatre. One contemporary account reveals that the upstage area beneath the stage pillars was placed six yards from the normal curtain line, that the balcony lay directly underneath the heavens, and that the floor of this stage area was raised above the level of the stage proper.[93] Remembering Poel's preference for traverses at the pillars, we can conclude that the tiring house was a self-contained false proscenium with a raised floor. Poel had used a raised upstage area before: in his 1903 *Edward II* (with Granville Barker in the title role), in which the platform was used in lieu of an above, and in his production of Schiller's *Wallenstein* (1900).[94] An upstage rostrum was a regular feature of Charles Fry's draped productions, and the upstage "gallery" in Harvey's *Shrew* was raised three steps off of the level of the stage floor. Tree retained Poel's *Two Gentlemen* apron for his production of *Henry VIII,* and kept the front lighting that went with it. And the apron, a few steps below the level of the stage, was featured in Barker's

Savoy Shakespeare productions.

Poel's divided stage with an apron was, in fact, a practical version in a proscenium playhouse of the zone theory so dear to advocates of the alternation theory of the Elizabethan stage. The apron, main stage, and rostrum in effect replaced the three parts of the Elizabethan stage in Brodmeier's and Figgis's models. As we have seen, the alternation theory itself was an attempt to recapture the flexibility and continuity of the Victorian stage; it is small wonder, then, that the restoration of the stage apron proved so adaptable to existing Victorian playhouses.

Poel's work in the provinces led to another turn in Edwardian Elizabethanism. He produced *Measure for Measure* in 1908 for the Manchester Repertory Company on the invitation of B. Iden Payne, after which Payne turned to Shakespeare on his own and produced *Much Ado About Nothing* according to modified Poel principles, using "representational scenery, though very simple."[95] Continuity was assured through the alternation of built scenes and neutral front curtains.

The use of representational scenery within a modified Elizabethanist model had its Continental origins in Jocza Savits's Munich Shakespeare Stage of 1889 and the New Munich Stage of 1909.[96] These stages employed an architectural false proscenium with apron and proscenium doors, behind which could be placed vividly realistic representational vistas. Reinhardt used such a model for his production of *Julius Caesar* in 1920. The Munich stage bears some resemblance to the English Restoration stage, though the combination of architectural acting space and vistas of realistic scenic space seems more akin to the Teatro Olimpico of Palladio.

A similar stage was evolving in England based on revised Elizabethanist principles. In 1913 Lewis Casson at the Manchester Rep produced *Julius Caesar* in a manner designed "to retain some of the splendours of Tree whilst at the same time incorporating some of the ideas of Poel."[97] An architectural front stage area with a false proscenium was built, while architectural features with painted vistas behind them were discovered within the opening; the architecture remained throughout the production, but the vistas changed suiting the different locales. Casson credited the device to Andre Antoine, whose *King Lear* he had seen in 1910. Antoine used a curtain at center stage but, as Casson noted, used "the full stage depth of each set, with tableau curtains that closed before the end of the scene, leaving the action to be finished on the front stage while the new scene was set."[98] One recognizes in this device the "split scene" of Brodmeier, invented to explain how two consecutive heavy scenes could be played without pause; Antoine and Casson made the changes swifter by employing a wagon stage for the upstage vista.

So prevalent was this transformation of Elizabethan principles that Oscar Asche and Joseph Harker conceived a similar stage, specially designed for Asche's Australian tours. In place of the neutral middle stage and a changing rear stage, Harker devised "a more or less permanent foreground, with a fixed background, the alternation of the scenes being facilitated by means of interchangeable set-pieces and curtains."[99] A stage similar to Casson's was employed by W. Bridges-Adams throughout the 1920s, which fulfilled his differentiation of scenic space (the rear stage) and acting space (the foreground). Norman Marshall describes a similar stage designed by J.B. Fagan at the Oxford Playhouse to compensate for the limited stage space:

> There was a wide, deep apron stage; behind it a smaller inner stage with curtains drawing across in front of it. In fact it was not unlike an Elizabethan stage, but without the Elizabethan gallery at the back. Settings were suggested simply and economically by using scenery only on the inner stage. Scenes could be played on the apron while another scene was being got ready behind the curtains of the inner stage. It was difficult to see any other advantages. At the end of an act the cast had to be manoeuvred upstage off the apron so that the curtains could draw in front of them.[100]

It is interesting to note the ends to which Fagan went to retain the tableau act ending.

The Edwardian divided stage affected the scenic conception of at least one play during the 1920s. In 1923 Bernard Shaw conceived his epic chronicle *Saint Joan,* to designs by Charles Ricketts, for a two level set divided by a curtain. In the second act, the curtains parted to change the locale from the anteroom to the throne room, and the curtains themselves, parted slightly, provided the scenery for the tent scene. Such a scene can be seen as a direct descendant of the Edwardian modification of the Elizabethan stage: one which provided a degree of continuity through the division of the stage into separable areas, the use of curtains, and the use of different stage levels; at the same time the stage retained Victorian principles of localization and an environment appropriate to the action of each scene. Edwardian Elizabethanism resulted in a compromise stage which bridged the values of the traditional stage with the aesthetics of the New Stagecraft. Advanced productions of Shakespeare in the 1920s inherited their stagecraft from this Edwardian movement, rather than directly from the more renowned Savoy Shakespeare productions of Granville Barker, which were themselves the product of this movement.

Picture and Space: Harvey's Hamlet

There was one Edwardian producer of Shakespeare who availed himself of both the stylistic pictorial advances of the New Stagecraft and the innovations of the New Stagecraft regarding stage space. Of all of his contemporaries, Martin Harvey was most faithfully committed to the application of the principles of the New Stagecraft to Shakespeare; his commitment was reflected not only in his second, third, and fourth productions of *Hamlet,* all of which were dogmatically avant-garde, but in his direct acknowledgment of his debt to Gordon Craig and Max Reinhardt. And yet, Harvey's productions of *Hamlet* retained many essentials of traditional production values, and accordingly reflected typical Edwardian attitudes toward scenic issues. An examination of Harvey's *Hamlet* productions will reveal the full nature of the contribution of the New Stagecraft to Edwardian productions of Shakespeare, and will, at the same time, explain the compatibility of all the scenic schools with one another during the period.

Harvey's first, traditional production of *Hamlet* was in 1905; it was a failure, the acting and decor suffering from comparisons with the Asche/ Stuart *Hamlet,* with H.B. Irving, which was running concurrently at the Adelphi. The first of Harvey's avant-garde *Hamlets* dates from 1909 in the provinces, and was not seen in London. Harvey acknowledged that the production "owes its origins to the ideas of Gordon Craig."[101] (Craig, writing under a pseudonym in the *Mask,* thanked Harvey for his acknowledgment, and used the occasion to level an attack on others who had used his ideas without credit.)[102] The inspiration for the production, Harvey later claimed, came from the discovery at a rehearsal of the play that scenic embellishment was unnecessary in sustaining the effect of the drama:

> The ghost stalked across the floor of the empty hall where we were rehearsing, in his ulster, using an umbrella for his mace. Bernardo and Marcellus handled their walking-sticks as though they were spears, the King and Queen were royal enough seated on cane-bottomed chairs, Laertes and I used our canes for foils and I forced the poison down the throat of the King out of a glass rummer.[103]

Harvey, like the Elizabethanists, could not see in this the obvious implications of modern-dress production; such an observation required a different set of historical asssumptions than that of the Edwardian period. But he did see beyond the archaeological trappings to the drama itself:

> Watching the rehearsal of the play and engrossed with the music of the words and the rhythm of its movement as one scene followed another without the hateful pauses which changes of one scene required, I realised how unnecessary and distracting was all the equipment of scenery, heavy properties and strange costume with which we always encumber it.[104]

Harvey's reaction led him, for the purposes of this production, to a rejection of verisimilar scenic representationalism, though he would return to it in his 1910 *Richard III,* which remained in his repertoire for years.

While Harvey rejected archaeological accuracy in his *Hamlet* production, however, he did not reject one of the principles upon which archaeology is based; for while he desired to "suggest" rather than "represent" the locale of the action, he nonetheless desired to suggest the period of the play's action, with its attendant environmental qualities, as Ricketts had "suggested," though through pictorial means, the barbarism of pre-Christian Britain through his druidic monoliths in *Lear*. Though Harvey rejected the exact historical determinism of archaeological staging, he desired to retain, through non-archaeological means, what he considered to be the more important aspects of a particularized period or environment. In a promotional pamphlet in support of his 1910 tour, he wrote:

> In producing this tragedy originally [1905], I felt it my duty to present it as gorgeously as my resources would allow, to give an accurate picture of life in the 11th century. Now I wish to carry it a step further, and I hope, higher, by presenting it in such a manner as to *suggest* the half luxurious, half barbaric atmosphere of Denmark in the early middle ages, but to allow the mind, by a greater breadth and simplicity of decoration, to dwell with more concentration upon the noble structure of the story itself.[105]

This implies that, though the drama of Hamlet's mind is universal, it is not completely freed from considerations of fictive historical time and place. Harvey's 1909 promotional pamphlet phrases this more simply: the decor "suggests rather than realizes the details of 'period,'" i.e., period is there all the same, and retains its dominant role.[106] In fact, the critics of the productions, in response to its appearance in Stratford-upon-Avon at least, found the eleventh-century barbarism, albeit merely suggested, rather excessive.[107]

Harvey's plan for the decor featured large periaktoi, which he learned about in his preliminary research into Greek tragedy, and which were used in ancient times, according to Harvey, to "suggest various localities." He described their present use:

> The localities to be suggested are few in *Hamlet:* royal interiors, battlements and the graveyard scene. For the first, I had the side of the *periaktoi* visible to the audience, covered with large squares of gold, suggestive of barbaric splendour, for the second, ramparts and the outline perhaps of a castle wall, for the third a neutral expanse of grey. Of course, in their use by the Greeks, the background would always be the same, but in my case, I had to carry realism a little further and my back-cloths were painted to emphasise the character of the locality; in the case of interiors I used heavy gold curtains.[108]

No doubt Harvey's pillars had some illusion of solidity, and a degree of monumentality, and there seems to have been some abstraction of the picture, rather than direct, painted representation. But, in function, the use of periaktoi was merely a return to the principles of changeable scenery. If they were indeed turned within sight of the audience, which is unclear, they at best resembled the wing and groove system still vestigial in many provincial houses. Although the scenery was designed "to give much greater swiftness to the unfolding of the plot" by assuring that "the waits between the acts are of the shortest," Harvey does not appear to have departed from the dramatic rhythm of the picture stage, with its numerous tableaux; one review noted that "nothing was hurried, and each time the curtain came down it fell upon a finished picture."[109]

Harvey extended the idea of suggestion into the dramatic action of the play, making the various projections of Hamlet's mind imaginary and not visually represented: "Remember me" was spoken by the Ghost after he had already left the stage, as if it were an imaginative echo; the Ghost was invisible to the audience as well as Gertrude in the closet scene; and the two portraits were not depicted. Furthermore, on the Ghost's first two appearances, he entered "quickly and darkly"; only when the Ghost and Hamlet were left alone was he seen clearly, when "a ray of natural moonlight, falling also on the sea, illumined him faintly, and made him look so real that Hamlet would have thrown himself upon his breast."[110] Note that Harvey allowed for a verisimilar explanation for the lighting device, and that the locale was particularized sufficiently that the reviewer could notice the sea on the supposedly abstract and stylized backcloth.

Harvey's second avant-garde production of *Hamlet* was directly indebted to the influence of Max Reinhardt. Harvey worked with Reinhardt in 1912 in *Oedipus,* and carried the production, with a portable apron stage, on his provincial tour the following season. In 1911, Reinhardt and Harvey dined together in Paris and discussed the former's Deutsches Theater production of *Hamlet,* which had used a revolve, a plaster sky-dome, and a rostrum upstage, into which Ophelia's grave was placed, with the gravedigger standing on the floor of the stage proper when standing in the trap. In 1913, Harvey announced to the public his regrets that the services of Max Reinhardt were not available, as originally hoped, for a staging of *Hamlet* at the London Opera House according to the details of the Berlin production.[111] The cancellation was probably due to Harvey's deference to Forbes Robertson's Farewell season at Drury Lane, and his reluctance to compete with him in the role as he had with H.B. Irving in 1905, and with Tree in Stratford in 1909.

In any event, Harvey restaged *Hamlet,* according to Reinhardt's principles, for touring beginning in 1913, and brought the production to His Majesty's Theatre for his Shakespeare season in 1916. The rostrum suited touring purposes, where the location of traps in provincial theatres was variable and unreliable; and as he was already touring with *Oedipus* and *The Taming of the Shrew,* an apron was already part of his travelling equipment. The revolve was abandoned, and in place of the plaster horizon was one of white canvas stretched over semicircular iron tubing; "into this concave erection," Harvey recalls, "which went up into the flies some 60 feet in height, we dropped, with practically no waste of time, various curtains to represent the barbaric splendours of a castle in the early Middle Ages, and could at least speak the maximum amount of text in a minimum of time."[112] And so, Harvey continued his practice of evoking locale and suggesting a highly specific time and place. The backdrops were, according to a review, "a series of tableaux curtains of varied colours and materials, appropriate to the action taking place. The Queen's chamber, with a background of tapestry, Ophelia's room in cloth of gold, rich curtains for Court chambers, white back-cloths to indicate the sky, decorated with electric light 'stars,' in the battlement scenes."[113] The arrangement of colors against the curtains was striking:

> We get long draperies of royal blue, with an edging of gold plates in which disport queer black birds, making a glorious contrast to the purples and reds and golds of the costumes or deep cream draperies to throw black and red or curtains of dull purple and gold as background for the venetian blue of the Queen's robes and Hamlet's sable clothing.[114]

The battlement scenes were played in dim light, from above, with the watchmen largely in silhouette against the dome. As with *Oedipus* and *The Shrew,* the footlights were abandoned; the lighting came from the back of the upper circle, and patrons of that part of the house leaving early cast shadows on the stage in the final scene; presumably at His Majesty's Theatre Harvey used the front-of-house lighting installed in 1910 for Poel's *Two Gentlemen of Verona* and retained for Tree's *Henry VIII.*[115]

The graveyard scene consisted of a few twisted trees and tombstones placed about the rostrum, described by Arthur Machen:

> Again the great dim circle of sky, but now against it in black vagueness rose very old tomb and ancient crosses; these marked the sepulchres of kings and warriors who had died so long ago that their monuments had sunken and were bending to the earth. And against the sky rose black, twisted trees, contorted by the great winds of the sea into grim misshapen shapes.[116]

Disher properly identifies this last item: a "fate tree," the characteristic stage symbol of Harvey's mentor, Henry Irving.[117] Into the evocative atmosphere of his new staging Harvey placed one of the few consistently symbolic naturalistic details of the one of the greatest of the traditionalists; within the stripped and rarefied decor, this charged naturalistic detail transcended naturalism and became an isolated symbol. And so, Harvey's 1913-16 production of *Hamlet* retained the degree of stylization, the evocation of historical period, and the details of localization of the 1909 production. The substitution of cloths and curtains for periaktoi and drops made little difference, since the front curtains were still employed; and the sky-dome served merely to accentuate the typical differentiation of interior and exterior localities, and to allow for a greater elaboration of meteorological phenomena, all of which reflect the pictorial naturalism of Harvey's methods:

> Sometimes we are there at the solemn hour of midnight when the ghost of the old King stalks along the ramparts of the castle at Elsinore; at another time when the floor of heaven

is strewn with stars and, in the mysterious glimpses of the moon, Hamlet is seen waiting for the spirit of his father; and yet again when, in the sombre twilight, the corpse of the distracted Ophelia is laid to rest on what appears to be a lofty windswept eminence below which the sun is sinking in angry blood-red clouds.[118]

Such is Harvey's departure from archaeology; if he did not abandon evocations, he did open the play up to a celestial or cosmic dimension in his depiction of outdoor space; and in doing so, he returned to a naturalism of method which more than compensates for the abstraction or conventionalization of his interior spaces.

Harvey's 1919 *Hamlet* at Covent Garden retained many features of his previous version, including the strong vertical axis, the purple and blue drapery, and the fate trees of the graveyard scene; and it retained many features of blocking and business: the silhouettes in the first scene, the imaginary Ghost in the closet scene, etc. As in the 1913 version, the spatial organization of the play scene was unconventional: the players acted downstage in the sunken apron, and the court upstage looked at their backs. Scenically, the production had the highest aspirations of the three, but the product in many ways seems the most conservative. In his autobiography, Gordon Craig recalls that Harvey asked him to design the production, and that he declined, further blaming Harvey for having hesitated so long in asking him, and for having collaborated with Reinhardt in his place years before.[119] The resulting production owed its pictorial conservatism not to George Sherringham's designs, which are stunning, but to an increased use of curtain tableaux, conjoined with creative lighting effects. The *Observer* records:

> There are no built-up sets to waste time in changing; and the only time that is wasted is spent on tableaux, which have evidently taken Mr. Harvey's fancy . . . tableaux which end each scene and hold it before us until by one of many cunning devices in lighting it shall fade away. Possibly it is to make room for these tableaux that Mr. Harvey has been so drastic in his cuts.[120]

And so, scenery which was originally conceived for its flexibility and to assure the continuity of the play's action, was used to slow the rhythm down for the accommodation of pictorial statement. The 1919 production was a culmination of this tendency, not only in Harvey's work, but in the application of the New Stagecraft in general. And the production itself culminated in an appropriate image for this: for the first time Harvey restored the appearance of Fortinbras, whose cutting Yeats had regretted in 1909.[121] But the function of the restoration was the creation of yet another picture: Hamlet placed on the spears and shields of Fortinbras's army, and borne upstage to the rostrum. This was, indeed, Shakespeare's effect; but it was also the effect of an illustration by Arthur Rackham of Siegried's funeral procession in Wagner's *Ring*, an allusion noticed by more than one critic and no doubt intended by Harvey. It further alluded to a common traditionalist type of curtain tableau (described above, pp. 23-25). And so, the apotheosis of Hamlet, as depicted at the end of Harvey's 1919 production, was also the apotheosis of the pictorialism of the Edwardian scenic avant-garde: the techniques of the New Stagecraft employed for the elaboration and elevation of the pictorial principles of the traditional stagecraft.

In it purest form, the New Stagecraft was not a single stagecraft at all, despite the attempts by Carter and others to consider the broad range of activities as a single movement. It remained a tool, a visual and physical idiom. And since the attitudes toward the theatre underlying the various aspects of the movement were rooted in the more conservative and more highly articulated scenographic schools of the period, the vocabulary of the New Stagecraft could be freely adapted to suit less doctrinaire but more immediate theatrical purposes. The ultimate influence of the movement on succeeding decades of Shakespeare production was the result, not of any one particular "ism," or of a single designer or director, but of the compatibility of the Stagecraft with the other contemporary schools of Shakespeare production of which the Edwardian period was comprised.

4

Shakespeare and Granville Barker

If any single individual, single production or set of productions has been singled out as initiating a new era in Shakespeare production, transcending the limitations of the times, and directly inspiring and influencing later generations, it is Harley Granville Barker and his three Shakespeare productions at the Savoy theatre (*The Winter's Tale* and *Twelfth Night,* 1912, and *A Midsummer Night's Dream,* 1914). Nevertheless, Barker would be the first to admit that he was very much a man of his time, an Edwardian producing Shakespeare for Edwardian audiences. Barker's true significance can be more accurately determined if he is considered, not as an inspired innovator rejecting accepted methods of staging and inventing his own, but as a man of his period, developing the attitudes and techniques of his own day. Barker's Shakespeare productions were inspired and ambitious, and yet they were often miscalculated and selfcontradictory, more so than adulatory theatre historians, the present writer included, have been willing to admit. Barker and his productions remain noteworthy because he distilled in them all the issues and concerns of Edwardian scenic theory and practice. And, more than any other Edwardian producer of Shakespeare, he forged theatrical products which were at once true to text, accessible to audiences, and theatrically possible.

In reconstructing Barker's theoretical views and the ways in which these views were embodied in his theatrical work, it is important to balance the evidence of his critical and scholarly works, executed for the most part long after he had retired from active work in the theatre, with his actual work as a Shakespeare producer. In many of his later writings we find a confirmation and reassertion of the ideas which had informed his theatre work years before; in others, we find a cautious rethinking of earlier notions, revised extensively in the wake of practical experience. But it is clear that Barker had, at the time of his Shakespeare productions, a meticulously worked out system of ideas regarding the nature of the theatrical experience, the relation of text and audience to performance, and the nature of the theatrical space. It is necessary to reconstruct this system of ideas, on the evidence of Barker's critical writings and stage practice; only then can the specific details of his productions be set in the context of the theatrical ideas of his time.

Theory

Convention

Barker derived his first premise from the Elizabethanists: that Shakespeare wrote for the theatre of his day, and that the mechanics of that theatre had changed in the 300 years since. To produce a play of three centuries past, or any play for that matter, requires an act of translation: the translation of Shakespeare's text to conform with modern stagecraft and audience expectations, or the translation of modern values to conform with the art of the past. "The very advantages of the modern theatre," Barker wrote, "make it a round hole into which the square peg of Shakespeare's plays will not fit. We abjure rounding the peg. Very well . . . the question that remains is what can be done towards squaring the hole."[1] "As he [Shakespeare] cannot now come to us, the nearer we can get to him the closer understanding we shall have of him."[2] Barker seems to have been in favor of transforming the modern theatre, and the theatrical sensibilities of the audience that attended it, in order to accommodate Shakespeare's art: "It all comes to this: what degree of translation will the plays bear—much is inevitable—and of what degree of translation of mind is the audience capable?"[3]

Barker seems to have had his doubts about the latter's capability however. He excused the "translations" of the plays made by Garrick and his contemporaries, on the grounds that "the essence of it was living drama to them, and they meant to keep it alive for their public. They wanted to avoid whatever would provoke question and so check the spontaneity of response upon which acted drama depends."[4] Spontaneity of response was a cardinal law of Barker's theatre: "Self-consciousness in the theatre, whether on the part of actors or audience, is stultifying. Self-surrender, of the actors to the characters they play, and of the audience to the immediate emotional impact—this is the capital factor in the illusion, the make-believe, which underlies our natural enjoyment of dramatic art."[5] It was because of the loss of spontaneity that Barker rejected the strict Elizabethanism of Poel and his disciples:

> We cannot quite discard the present, and, even could we, entering into the past would be a harder matter still. We should need to sit in an Elizabethan theatre as Elizabethans and be able as unconsciously, as spontaneously to enjoy the play. For spontaneity of enjoyment is the very life of the theatre and its art. This cannot be. Some half-way house of meeting must be found.[6]

Barker recognized the fallacy of the Elizabethanist school, which bothered both Archer and Beerbohm though they were not quite able precisely to pinpoint why: it was not that the process of transforming oneself into an Elizabethan with Elizabethan responses was undersirable or counter-productive; it was merely impossible. Barker recognized that we cannot turn ourselves into Elizabethans, "and every mental effort to do so will subtract from our enjoyment of [the plays]. This is the case against the circumstantial reproduction of Shakespeare's staging."[7]

Barker's doubts led him to some inconsistencies with regard to the relation of Shakespeare's art to his own age: while he was anxious to recognize the purely Elizabethan features of Shakespeare's art and stagecraft, his own hopes for staging Shakespeare for modern audiences depended upon the playwright's temporally transcendent universality.

> Let us admit [he writes] that while Shakespeare was an Elizabethan playwright he was—and now is to us—predominantly something much more. Therefore we had better not too unquestioningly thrust him back within the confines his genius has escaped, nor presume him to have felt the pettier circumstances of his theatre sacrosanct.[8]

Any yet Barker never fully let himself forget the work of the Elizabethanists which helped him to recognize the instrinsic relationship of Shakespeare and his theatre, and specifically the theatre of his time: "It may be that his genius quite transcends the medium in which it worked—though surely at one moment to praise his stagecraft and in the next to contend that in the problem of producing his plays it may safely be ignored is something more than paradoxical."[9] Accordingly, Barker recognized the need "to distinguish between the artistic essentials and the merely incidental features of the stage for which Shakespeare designed his plays."[10] The essentials were those features which must be carried forward into any translation of the scripts into modern performance, and without which the productions would not replicate the essence of Shakespeare's understanding of character and action. The incidentals were the trappings of Elizabethanism: deliberate archaisms, or quaint obscurities. So, in production, Barker, an arch defender of Shakespeare's texts, nonetheless made a few cuts in *Twelfth Night* on the grounds that certain obscurities of humor are inessential, or at least untranslatable in theatrical terms:

> To have one's full laugh at the play's comedy is no longer possible, even for an audience of Elizabethan experts. Though the humour that is set in character is humour still, so much of the salt of it, its play upon time and place, can have no savour for us.... I would cut nothing else, but I think I am justified in cutting these pathetic survivals.[11]

There was a paradox, then, in Barker's faith in Shakespeare's stagecraft, his integrity as an artist in his own day and according to the physical conditions of his art, and Barker's equal belief in the crucial importance of a freely responsive modern audience. He asked:

> Are we here upon the horns of a dilemma; must we deform Shakespeare to the shape of our modern theatre, or restore for him a theatre to which we can now only make a self-conscious and sophisticated approach? The question resolves to this: can we come to responding, spontaneously enough, to more than one kind of dramatic convention, to accepting more than one medium of illusion?[12]

Barker's answer to this question was an optimistic affirmative.

Part of the gap between modern audience expectations and the antiquated craft of Shakespeare can be closed by the cultivation of what Barker called "an historical sense of Shakespeare's art."[13] The rest depends upon the key word in the preceding passage, "convention." While the drama is inextricably linked to the conventions of the theatre for which it was written, these conventions are universally comprehensible because they comprise a compact between actor and audience. While a convention in a given period is so prevalent that it is rarely articulated or recognized by contemporary audiences, it, like any other compact, can be renegotiated when necessary. Barker's whole system of production and method of textual criticism was founded upon his definition of theatrical convention and how it operates:

> There is no escape from convention in the theatre, and all conventions can be made acceptable, though they cannot all be used indiscriminately, for they are founded in the physical conditions of the stage of their origin, and are often interdependent one with another. Together they form a code, and they are as a treaty made with the audience. No article of it is to be abrogated unless we can be persuaded to consent, and upon its basis we surrender our imaginations to the playwright.[14]

To make Shakespeare comprehensible to a modern audience, it is necessary to define the conventions at work, deeply rooted in the text and related to the theatre for which the plays were written, and to make these conventions somehow acceptable. The ideal condition is when the convention of the play and the perceptual conventions of the audience are identical: "Here is the advantage of an accepted convention: it provides common ground on which dramatist and audience are mutually at ease. Without knowing what he is about to do they know within a little how he is about to do it, and their attention can be concentrated on the 'what' with much of the 'how' taken for granted."[15] Accordingly, dramatic form, as a convention, is not a limitation but a freedom. "Form is the equivalent of a code of manners by which performer and audience are at once put on terms with each other. In rigidity it may equally become a nuisance. But as manners are the framework of a free society, so is a friendly agreement upon form a necessary basis for the social arts."[16] Barker imagined the theatre as "a game of make-believe, and the rules of any game may be varied by use and acceptance."[17]

Clearly, Barker's belief in the freeing power of theatrical convention was a direct product of the theatrical awareness of his day. Traditionalists were prepared to accept a certain degree of conventional freedom in their productions, due to the inherent contradictions between their realist aspirations and the artificiality of their illusory theatrical means. Elizabethanists adhered to what they believed to be a nonnegotiable set of conventions geared specifically towards Shakespeare's plays, conventions which, as they perceived them, actually tried to conceal their own illusionary mechanism. And the advocates of the New Stagecraft were occasionally prepared to acknowledge the open theatricality of their work, provided that theatrical devices were employed to suggest or evoke the illusion of a fantastic or universal "reality." For Barker, convention was a means to an end, a way of establishing a language system by which the drama could communicate, in theatrical terms, with an audience.

The secret for producing the classics is to discover the means of training the audience to accept a new and fresh set of theatrical conventions. One way is to convince the audience that, indeed, the conventions of the present are not hard and fast rules but merely an arbitrary code, made acceptable through popular usage. In Barker's ideal universe, audiences would be retrained in theatrical perception in a drama school attached to an "exemplary" theatre. In the real world, it is up to each production to state to the audience immediately that standard conventions are being relaced by new ones. These new ones can be accepted if the production has sufficient inner consistency, and its conventions are intrinsically true to the text and to the space. There are other means of making an audience receptive to an unfamiliar set of conventions. As we have seen (in chapter 2), Barker felt that the use of the music of Shakespeare's day could subliminally increase the audience's ability to respond to Elizabethan convention. Another means of educating modern audiences to Elizabethan convention is to find modern analogues for otherwise obsolete conventions. For example, Barker restored the direct address to the audience in soliloquy and asides, a device which had faded with the advent of fourth-wall naturalism and the Robertsonian school. Barker's courage in restoring the convention was based upon his recognition that it was still alive in a different form of contemporary theatre, the music hall: "We may measure the response to Burbage's 'O, that this too too solid flesh would melt . . .' by recalling—those of us that happily can—Dan Leno as a washerwoman, confiding domestic troubles to a theatre full of friends, and taken unhindered to their hearts."[18]

Like the Elizabethanists, Barker believed that the craft of Shakespeare's plays was deeply affected by the theatre for which they were written. But, unlike them, he felt that the precise relationship between the plays and the

Elizabethan theatre carried a different set of implications with regard to modern performance. For one thing, the Elizabethan stage was not a rigid and predetermined entity: "Even while Shakespeare was at work," wrote Barker, "the stage to which he fitted his plays underwent constant and perhaps radical change."[19] Furthermore, Barker felt that the revolution in Shakespeare's own craft surpassed the changes in the theatre itself: "Of any revolution in his stagecraft there could be little question. Though the theatre for which he has learned to work is grown richer, its mechanical and pictorial aspects remain fundamentally and unaccommodatingly the same."[20] Barker believed that the physical conventions of the stage inform, but do not necessarily predetermine, the conventions of stagecraft which the playwright will choose in writing for it; Shakespeare's art grew within the limitations of the theatre for which he wrote, but transcended the less sophisticated forms achieved in the works of his contemporaries, and in his own early work:

> Shakespeare's work shows such principles as the growth of a tree shows. It is not haphazard merely because it is not formal; it is shaped by inner strength. The theatre, as he found it, allowed him and encouraged him to a great freedom of development. Because the material resources of a stage are simple, it does not follow that the technique of its playwriting will stay so. . . . The advance and the not less amazing gulf which divides its best from its worst may be ascribed to the simplicity of the machinery it employed.[21]

The first step in rediscovering a convention for staging Shakespeare acceptable to modern audiences was to rediscover the essentials of this machinery, and in so doing, to free the works of the playwright to find their own convention, linked to this machinery, but pertaining more to the individual art of the playwright himself.

Barker's understanding of Elizabethan stage convention, and the relation of Shakespeare's art to it, changed a good deal over time, and was revised continually during his later years as a scholar, demonstrating how time and theatrical experience can temper and transform earlier notions. One of the first of his Prefaces for *The Player's Shakespeare,* which he did not revise for the collected edition, was his Preface to *Macbeth*, in which he argued that "the direct alternation of inner and outer scenes is arguably complete."[22] Barker sent the proofs of an earlier draft of this essay to William Archer, with a proposed illustration by Rutherston (which was not used) of a plan for the Globe Theatre. Archer, who was hard at work on his own study of Elizabethan stagecraft at the time, was horrified by some of Barker's conclusions. Among the preconceptions for which he took Barker to task were the notion that the inner stage was used primarily for "intimate" or interior scenes, and the idea that the rear stage curtain was used to denote a lapse of time. Archer's main point was: "The Elizabethans had not three stages which they could easily employ separately, but one stage with a small extension at the back & a larger extension above."[23] Barker acknowledged many of his errors and disowned Rutherston's drawing. Indeed, Barker, after having been temporarily bogged down in the incidentals of the stage, returned to the essentials, arguing for the flexibility of the stage space and the degree to which the stagecraft of the play was independent of the particulars of the stage; he wrote Archer: "I dare say . . . they did use the rear stage less than I allow for, but I feel that their playing was probably so elastic and so little stage-managed, in our present sense of meticulous arrangement, that they easily adapted themselves to whatever stage they found themselves on."[24] Barker's revised views appear throughout the later Prefaces, and owe much to Archer's criticisms. Barker abandoned the strict zone theory, and adopted Archer's notion of a single space with extensions:

> I think that scenes were more often played "in relation to" the inner stage than consistently with its boundaries . . . one need not suppose that the Elizabethan actor ever saw the division between inner stage and main stage as a fixed boundary, nor that the Elizabethan audiences had cultivated a sense of locality that they questioned its crossing and recrossing or even asked themselves at certain ambiguous moments where exactly the characters were meant to be.[25]

It is interesting, though, to note the grounds upon which Barker rejected the use of the inner stage as a playing space: he remarked that "it is idle . . . to imagine scenes upon inner and upper stage without evidence that they will be audible or visible there."[26] And yet Barker countered Archer's use of the same argument:

> There is one point about the Elisabethan [sic] stage which I fancy we're apt to forget. Our demands to be able to see the entire action of the play and see it all the time is a very modern one. In hardly any old theatre is it possible for the people at the sides to see more than half the stage. When I took the Savoy I found that from a large number of places in the gallery it was practically impossible to see the stage at all.[27]

It would seem that Barker, eager to reproduce the spatial machinery of the Elizabethan stage, was prepared to accept, and to augment, the poor sightlines of conventional playhouses. So we find in Barker's stage practice virtually all his later, more consistent theories; and yet there always remain vestigial Edwardian ideas which make his work distinctly of its time, however great his desire to alter contemporary conventions.

This same phenomenon is observable in Barker's understanding of Elizabethan scenic convention, and the question of localization. Regardless of Archer's criticism, Barker was, in his later writings, quite consistent in his rejection of Edwardian localization of scenes, the disease which plagued even the staunchest Elizabethanists. To Barker, Elizabethan audiences had little or no conception of specific fictive locale: "if they stopped to ask themselves where such and such a character, under their eyes at the minute, was supposed to be, 'On the stage' might well have served for an immediate answer."[28] One useful analogue Barker made to describe the difference between the pictorial theatre and the Elizabethan conventional theatre was the difference between scenery and properties: "Scenery is something to look at; a property is something to use."[29] Consistent with his view of Elizabethan stage space was the notion that the stage is a machine to be used, not a frame in which a picture, or a particular stagecraft, is placed. Barker's understanding of Elizabethan scenic localization was strongly related to his belief in the centrality of the actor; as he wrote Jacques Copeau, "The art of the theatre is the art of the actor, first, last, and all the time."[30] The actor became the determinant of locale on the Elizabethan stage; "with Shakespeare the locality of the scene has dramatic importance, or it has none," and the decisive factor in determining locality was its effect upon the characters.[31] Actors "carry place and time with them as they move," e.g., Juliet brings her bedroom and Cleopatra her monument down from the above to the main stage as they move.[32] Realistic scenery destroyed this relationship by interposing the spectator's direct sensory response to the locale between the scene and the character; realistic scenery will "set up a direct relation between the beauties of Inverness Castle or the cold of the night of Elsinore in place of the indirect relation through the channel of the feelings of Banquo and Duncan, Hamlet and Horatio."[33] Barker rejected realistic scenery on other grounds as well. It did not allow for the simultaneity of the Elizabethan stage, i.e., the property by which the morning farewell of Romeo and Juliet (played on the upper stage, according to Barker) scenically persists while the following scene, of Capulet's wedding preparation, goes on below.[34] And realistic scenery and acute localization created verisimilar inconsistencies, such as Bianca's interview with Cassio taking place in the middle of Desdemona's bedroom; "If we insist on placing and picturing the play's action now definitely here, now exactly there, we shall only be making complex what he has left simple, and find ourselves set to answer riddles which he never asked."[35]

Nevertheless, Barker's attitudes toward the dramatic importance of the stage locality, and the theatrical means which may be employed to realize the stage environment, fall within Edwardian traditions of environmental realism. While Shaw believed that only romantic desolation could provide the proper background for the headless corpse scene in *Cymbeline,* Barker felt that the corpse "is really not much more to us than a dummy and a pretext for [Imogen's] aria of agony," and that therefore only a stylized, fantastic environment can make such an elaborately contrived scene seem true to life: "There is one sort of realism to be gained on a bare stage and another in scenic illusion; but before a decoratively conventional cave we shall not take things too literally. The right interpretation of all this will depend upon a style of production and acting fitted to the play."³⁶ Shaw asked for harsh scenic realism to make the horror of the scene more immediate; Barker called for fantastic decoration to mitigate the horror with the benignity of the fairy tale. Barker's conclusions were different from Shaw's but the principles upon which they based their judgments were identical. Barker further advocated an "atmospheric sort of background" for *King Lear* to insure that "the prevailing atmosphere and accent is barbaric and remote."³⁷ For *Macbeth*, Barker advocated a decorative effect which

> can give us something of the barbaric grandeur with which we may suppose Macbeth would emphasize his regality. It can no doubt sharpen the contrast—though the play itself provided this by one stroke after another—between the court, the sights that the weird sisters show, the simplicity of Macduff's home, the kindly security of England and the unnatural strain of that scene of tragic twilight through which Lady Macbeth's tortured spirit drifts towards death.³⁸

Barker suggested that the resources of modern lighting could help to indicate what Shakespeare described in poetic passages, for example the contrast in *Hamlet* between Horatio's description of the dawn in act 1, scene 1 and the Ghost's in, act 1, scene 5.³⁹ Barker wished to create a context of stage reality consistent with character, situation and dramatic mood. This context could be created by scenery, or by the relation of an implied environment to a concrete stage action; for example, Barker pictured the scene of Banquo's murder in *Macbeth* in the context of offstage action: "The lights of the banquetting chamber have been visible, or snatches of music or talk heard coming from it" while the murder takes place.⁴⁰ The assumption that the location of a scene on the stage connects tangibly and concretely to a dramatically charged location off-stage was yet another assertion of the overall fictive reality of the events on the stage, which could be established through the creation of a visually real stage picture.

Barker's traditionalist adherence to the belief in localized stage environments was evident in his Savoy productions. In the promotional material for *The Winter's Tale*, Norman Wilkinson described the curtains to be used for scenes played on the apron: "The designs with which they are adorned forming as it were the subject of the pictures represented. For instance, the sea-shore of a 'desolate place,' where the infant Perdita is saved from a bear by the Shepherd, shows a shadowy sea-view."⁴¹ This localized compromise was similar to Tree's tapestry depicting the trees of the graveyard scene in *Hamlet*, and Harvey's tapestry front cloth of an Italianate landscape in *The Taming of the Shrew*. Nor was Barker's persistence in defining locality confined to his stage practice. In his acting text to *Twelfth Night,* available, with preface, to first-night audiences, he carefully avoided act and scene numbers in order to emphasize the continuity of the text, and yet retained locality designations, a practice for which Poel took him to task.⁴²

It is interesting to see where Granville Barker stood in relation to his contemporaries regarding the issue of theatrical perception, and how his position remained fairly consistent into his years as a literary critic. Firstly, Barker categorically rejected the notion that Elizabethan audiences actively pictured with their imagination the locality suggested by the action or the poetry. "Shakespeare did not ask his audience," concludes Barker, "to pretend to themselves that the doors" of the tiring house "were not there."[43] Barker never ceased to be surprised that the modern reader, however well informed about conjectural Elizabethan stage convention, continued to picture that Elizabethan audience "busily conjuring . . . up" the locational stage directions of later editors "before the eye of faith. The Elizabethan audience was at no such pains."[44]

And yet Barker did share the belief of many that visual sensations work counter to, and not supportive of, the overall dramatic effect. Without scenery, on the Elizabethan stage, "there was no distracting of mind or eye," and consequently "a unity of effect was kept."[45] This concept of unity of effect persists throughout Barker's criticism. Barker distrusted the notion that the senses work in conjunction with one another: "If our *eyes* are distracted by a painted picture of the castle and its nests [in *Macbeth* act 1, sc. 6] the nine lines will have been spoken before our *ears* have begun to listen, and Shakespeare's whole effect will be lost."[46] Barker seems to have regretted even the decorative alternatives of the Savoy productions, asking, "Have they thereby eliminated the competition too?"[47] Barker's distrust of decor, as expressed in the 1920s, is profound:

> May not the beauty of a setting belittle the actor who is seen in it? Is the ear not cheated by delighting the eye? For the eye responds more easily, people look before they listen, we are naturally lazy, and our total faculty of attention is limited. "Dark night that from the eye his function takes / The ear more quick of apprehension makes "[*A Midsummer Night's Dream* act 3, sc. 2, lines 177-78]. [Note][48]

To this analysis Barker appended a further suspicion: "There may even be a deep disharmony in an attempt to respond with sight and hearing simultaneously to any purely *emotional* appeal."[49] Here Barker suspected not only a disunity between the sensatory media at the artist's disposal, but between the very means of the theatre and the effect it wished to induce in the audience.

Barker was deeply aware of the capabilities of his contemporary audience, and feared that this audience might no longer be able to accept the visual conventions of Shakespeare on his own terms. For the contemporary audience, "The eye must be occupied and satisfied. It has been taught how to add its gains to the sum of the emotion of a play can excite, and it has grown exigent. It is not satisfied, it will turn traitor and frustrate the other senses."[50] It was in satisfying what he called "that still hungry eye" that Barker questioned our ability to truly capture an Elizabethan response to the plays:

> In this play [*A Midsummer Night's Dream*] he asks attention for his verse, for a little music, and allows for the eye only some simple costumed action and a little dancing on a palpable stage. With these materials, within these bounds, his faculties at full strength, he produces his play. Using these materials, kept within those bounds, and stretching our faculties of interpretation and appreciation to their full, we still—it is barely possible—may not be able to compass his vision and achieve his purposes, limited as they were.[51]

The solution for Barker, the means of "meeting Shakespeare half-way," lay in "the illusion lodged in the actor himself":

> Set him in our midst, make him one of ourselves, fix our attention wholly on him, and we shall come to feel so at one with him that not only will the barrier between our actual world and his imagined world the more easily vanish, but the innermost of the character he plays will be just what it will be easiest for him to reveal and for us to respond to.... All illusion upon the platform stage inevitably centred in the actor.[52]

While many theorists posed a conflict between the unquestionable reality of the actor and the scene behind him, Barker noted that our perception of the dramatically real environment depends wholly upon the conventional premises behind our perception of the actor:

> There is no illusion, so there is every illusion. Nothing very strange about this man, not even the dress he wears, leaning forward a little we could touch him; we are as intimate and familiar with him as it is possible to be. We agree to call him "Hamlet," to suppose that he is where he says he is, we admit that he thinks aloud and in blank verse too. It is possible that the more we are asked to imagine the easier we find it to do. It is certain that, once our imagination is working, visual illusion will count for little in the stimulating of emotion beside this intimacy that allows the magnetism of personality full sway.[53]

In presenting the actor and the character on the stage, Barker believed in many of the principles of the traditional stagecraft: that every theatrical means should be employed to verify the reality of the actor: "Every producer of a play must aim for what we may call 'the constant credibility of the actor.' It weakens the illusion in which an audience must be held if the play's clear intentions are not fulfilled, if the actors must say one thing, even a trifling thing, and do another."[54] For example, a Cleopatra who refers to lace and doesn't have any would, for Barker, destroy that illusion. And so Barker returned to a premise which the actor's theatre of the late nineteenth century would have been pleased to accept: that the focus of stage reality is on the actor; find a convention by which the reality of the actor can be transmitted and appreciated, and the imagination is set free to take care of everything else.

Space

Barker actively sought just such a convention for the presentation of the Shakespearean actor on the modern stage, and here again the Savoy productions represented a laboratory experiment through which Barker was able to reach more sound and consistent critical theories. Establishing an Elizabethan relationship solved many corollary problems of Elizabethan conventions; for example, soliloquy was no longer a problem for Barker once the essentials of an Elizabethan spatial rapport between actor and audience was established.[55] We have already seen how Barker believed in the Elizabethan actor's complete identification with his role; this identification, aided by the physical relationship between the actor and audience on the platform stage, effectively solves any problem of scenic illusion:

> With the actors forgetting themselves in their character the spectators the more easily forget their own world for the world of the play. The illusion so created, we should note, is lodged in the actors and characters alone. Shakespeare's theatre does not lend itself to the visual illusion, which, by the aid of realistic scenery and lighting, seems physically to isolate them in that other world. But he can, helped by the ubiquity of his platform stage, preserve the intimacy which this sacrifices. His aim is to keep the actor, now identified with the character, in as close a relation to the spectators—as that by which the clown, in his own right, exercises his sway over them.[56]

The platform stage affords, for Barker, another feature impossible on the picture stage: an actor's spatial prominence and three-dimensionality effectively changes with his location on the platform stage. Barker cited two examples: Polonius and the musicians in contrast to Hamlet at the end of the recorder sequence, and Desdemona and company during Iago's brief aside in act 2, scene 1 of *Othello;* Barker described the pictorial effect as that of "a fully rounded statue placed before a bas-relief."[57]

This last observation in particular, along with Barker's firm belief in the existence of an inner stage and his implicit belief in the zone theory that goes with it, was a direct product of his experiments with the apron stage at the Savoy. We have already seen how the apron, as a compromise, was used by Poel at the Royalty Theatre in 1893 and at His Majesty's Theatre in 1910; and we have seen how the use of an apron was the product of Edwardian avant-garde experimentation. Barker first used an apron at a special performance of *Iphigenia in Tauris* during the 1912 Shakespeare Festival at His Majesty's Theatre; no doubt it was the very same apron used by Poel and by Tree for *Two Gentlemen of Verona* and *Henry VIII* two years before. Barker's use of the apron at the Savoy, and of the main stage behind it, was described in detail by Albert Rutherston; from this description can be ascertained many features in common with the traditional Victorian stage, and the Elizabethanists of the alternationist school which such staging inspired:

> When Mr. Wilkinson and myself were called in to help produce what are known as the *Barker* Shakespeare productions at the Savoy Theatre, we used in our respective plays what may be described as two forms of decorative scene, namely, front curtains and built scenes, the latter occupying the whole of the existing stage proper, the former acting as backgrounds for the short front stage scenes; a double stage after the manner of the Elizabethan Theatre was used, thus making it possible to give a Shakespeare play, with its many changes of scene and action, without pause, and without cutting down the text.
>
> These curtains were meant to be suggestive only of the time, place and mood of the action that took place in front of them. There was no attempt at scenic illusion, only such colour and form as were sufficient and appropriate both to the material used, and the suggestion which had to be implied. The curtains fell in broad folds, and the designs were painted on with dyes.
>
> The built scenes on the stage proper, which constituted the main decoration, were solid, built in three dimensions, having plan and elevation, not flat pieces of canvas painted to look like what they were not, and attempting to give the design and plan that was demanded by the play, the charm of light and shade, line, form, and colour, which resulted from that and the mimes in front, and that alone.[58]

The only thing to distinguish this decor from traditionalist scenery was the deliberate rejection of the verisimilar, extended to the nature of the materials used in creating linear designs on the curtains and spatial designs in the built scenes. This scheme allowed Barker to demonstrate two essentials of the Elizabethan stage, as he understood it: the rapport between audience and actor on the platform stage, and the spatial difference in the actor's presence on the apron and on the main stage.

Such were Barker's intentions in devising this scenic model; but his results were not completely successful. Concerning the intimacy of the audience with the actor, Barker did achieve a degree of success: soliloquies and asides were made directly to the audience; and the few drawings of photographs of the productions which capture the spatial relationship of stage to auditorium do suggest a novel sense of contact (see illustrations 29 and 30) Nevertheless a critic for the *Outlook* called Barker's use of the apron a "wrong dramatic principle," claiming that Barker got his actors closer to the audience but did not make the audience feel that they were indeed any closer to the action of the play.[59] Another problem was that Barker, like Poel, never departed from the frontality of the proscenium stage. Norman Marshall erroneously calls Barker the first to use front-of-house lighting in England, a mistake repeated by many scholars including Styan; but, in addition to two box lights at the front of the first circle, six cylinder lights at the front of the dress circle, and four white arc lamps directly above the mainstage, he used two side lamps, one in each "stage" box, i.e., the boxes closest to the stage which overlooked the extended apron stage.[60] In taking away these spaces from spectators, Barker increased the frontality of the production. Furthermore, the Victorian playhouse did not offer universally good sight-lines for this frontality, and several astute observers questioned the value of Barker's backstage reforms without corresponding major changes in the front of house. C. B. Purdom, later Barker's biographer, noted in 1912 that "the existing theatre, with its audience partly below the level of the stage, partly at the side of it, and partly right over it, is unsuitable for this new art" and that "for the purposes of the stage decoration Mr. Barker is introducing it is hopelessly bad."[61] Gordon Craig, criticizing Barker's refusal to head the New Theatre in New York because of its excessively large size, countered that the size of the theatre is not as crucial as the shape of the auditorium.[62] And, as we have seen, Barker himself was resigned to the fact that many gallery seats had no view whatever of the twelve-foot apron stage. Barker was attempting to reform the relation of the players to the audience without considering the vantage of the audience within the rigid architecture of the traditional theatre.

As to Barker's notion of the sculptural appearance of the actor on the platform stage, his Savoy double stage was a dismal failure, perhaps the result of a confusion of goals. For instead of creating the effect of sculpture on the forestage and of bas-relief within, Barker achieved quite the opposite. Barker's forestage did provide ample space for complicated movement (and it was used for scenes of complex blocking, such as the duel scene in *Twelfth Night* and the lovers' quarrel in *The Dream*); and space on the apron was increased by the placement of a false proscenium a few feet upstage of the real one, which increased the depth and allowed for two different stage levels on the apron. But the effect of the front scenes was that of a frieze, and Barker often exploited this effect, as in the scene between Cleomenes and Dion returning from the oracle in *The Winter's Tale,* passing over the stage in strict profile, and at various times in the duel scene in *Twelfth Night.* By contrast, the three-dimensionality of the main stage created the effect of sculpture. According to Cathleen Nesbitt, who played Perdita, Barker told his actors, "There's never going to be much to sit on except a bench or gilded stool. You must decorate the stage yourselves"; and Nesbitt recalls that she "revelled in the feeling of *space*" on the set.[63] Indeed, Barker seems to have intended to keep the actors on the main stage spatially independent of the decor. The set for the sheep-shearing scene in *The Winter's Tale* consisted of a three-dimensional cottage upstage with a fence running across the center of the stage, effectively dividing the actor from the architecture. It appears, then, that the built-up scenes were intended to heighten the three-dimensionality of the actor, without allowing him to become merely a unit in the pictorial context. Perhaps, in flattening the sculptural quality of the front scenes and increasing it on the full stage, Barker intended to unify the two spaces of his double stage. But it appears that the result merely undercut his own theories about the function of the Elizabethan platform stage, and created a perpetual conflict between the audience's perception of what Norman Marshall describes as "two utterly different kinds of stage conventions."[64]

Barker's later criticism bears out his disappointment with the apron stage as a compromise solution. In the 1920s he stated that spatial issues should be explored experimentally, in actual theatre work, but added: "The thrusting of the plays within a proscenium, or the attempt to drag them half out again on to a platform stage which has been added as a structural afterthought in defiance of lines of sight and other such practical considerations, is quite too empirical to be enlightening."[65] This statement can be considered his final word on his own spatial experiments at the Savoy. Barker considered other solutions to the problem of scenic space in relation to Shakespeare's plays, and later rejected all but a modern version of Shakespeare's own full platform. In a report for the *Times* on the Theatre Exhibition in Berlin in 1910, Barker revealed that he had become enamored of the revolve, which he thought could "quite revolutionize the playing of many-scened Elizabethan classics—may, it is to be hoped, shortly do so in England."[66] But by the 1920s Barker came to think of the revolve as "mainly a nuisance," claiming that Shakespeare's plays demanded "a forthrightness and uniformity of action which is not occasioned by a twisted, tricky background."[67] He further rejected the staging of the plays in the round, believing that "the spectators would be dominantly in touch with each other but distracted from the play."[68] And so the experiments at the Savoy, though they created, or at least encouraged, a trend for divided stages with aprons, were, for the director, merely an indication that an Elizabethan spatial arrangement could not be approximated within the conventional modern playhouse.

Decor

In producing Shakespeare at the Savoy according to experimental scenic principles, Barker had to deal with an important consideration quite apart from considerations of Elizabethan stage space. He had consciously to choose a visual idiom of design in which to work, at a time when London was alive with the various currents of the New Stagecraft. Whatever Barker's choice, it was bound to draw audience attention and dominate critical debate; and unquestionably his choices have dominated historical criticism since then. It is therefore necessary to examine Barker's relationship to the various contemporary scenic movements, and to consider how his final choices in the Savoy productions were affected by these considerations.

Barker was acutely aware of the movements about him at the time, and undoubtedly knew that critics were bound to associate his work with any or all of them. When the *Daily Mail* asserted that Barker "has probably taken the wind out of the sails of other stage reformers," Gordon Craig wrote a letter in defense of the many practitioners of the New Stagecraft across Europe whose success did not depend on Barker's.[69] This gave Barker the chance to state publicly, as he had privately ten years before, that Craig "was an excellent man to steal from," and that he was indebted to him and to "that other destructive idealist" William Poel, who together had pioneered a "freedom of spirit and fearlessness of purpose" which could easily be "stolen."[70] From this statement, one can conclude, as did Bridges-Adams, that Barker deliberately "caught the Reinhardt tide, and whatever other tides were running his way, at the flood."[71]

And yet Barker's isolated statements about the various movements in modern stage design reveal that he was little enamored of any of them for their own sakes. It was his belief that "to exalt the theatre," as the heresy of "creative scenery" does, "at the expense of the drama is a retrograde step."[72] He described the "egotism of the apostles" of the New Stagecraft:

> They are not content to play the humble part of interpreter. For them the play must be a pipe upon which they may sound what stop they please; not the music itself, in whose beauty they and their pipe should be quite forgotten. They do not make their case better by talking high-falutin nonsense about the "absolute art" of the theatre, in which the play itself must take a secondary place.[73]

Barker ridiculed the "megalomaniac projects for vast stages, dotted with strange symbolic structures, weird lights flashing and weird music sounding, and a few actors crawling dejectedly around," and was thankful that England, at least, was spared the main force of the movement, with Shakespeare staged "according to this or that even more irrelevant theory or presentationalism, symbolism, constructivism or what not."[74] As for the merely beautiful designs of the New Stagecraft, Barker seems to have had little patience; about the Russian Ballet, he remarked, "The beautiful scenery distracted my attention from the action of the dance."[75]

Barker seems to have been equally uncomplimentary about the Elizabethanists. While he considered the shipwreck scene in Poel's *Tempest* (1897) "one of the most effective things I have ever seen done," and wrote an introductory letter for Poel to Max Reinhardt, claiming that "he taught us all (by his great devotion) more about the staging of Shakespeare and the spirit of playing it, I think, than anyone else in Europe," he could not fully accept Poel's strict Elizabethanism.[76] He wrote Gilbert Murray, "Poel is one of these limpid-eyed enthusiasts who sacrifices himself body, soul and pocket to his cause and expects and is absolutely unscrupulous in making everyone else do the same thing."[77]

Given these prejudices, one would think that Barker could not easily find collaborators sympathetic with his approach. Yet Barker was aware of the fact that the collaborative director, who, unlike Craig's seven-headed director, could not design his own scenes, depended upon the artistic talents of other men. Barker himself did not have either the taste or the artistic discretion to make design decisions for himself. With regard to costumes, he confessed that he "neither knew green from pink nor cared."[78] But he did not wish to curb the designer's creativity. The designer, Barker believed, should approach the play with the same understanding with which the actors approach it: he should "interpret it to the full extent of his—and of its own—capacity for individual expression," limited only by the considerations of convention and economy.[79] Barker recognized the dangers of the creative designer competing with the actors, "the sole interpreters Shakespeare has licensed," or with Shakespeare himself.[80] The designer "must first make sure that his work will fuse with Shakespeare's. What Shakespeare's purposes will not accept, he must reject."[81] Much of Barker's scenic art can be determined by the work he personally sanctioned from his designers; as his work stood or fell with contemporary audiences by their contributions, so his intentions must stand or fall by our interpretation of their work.

The primary feature of the Savoy designs was a systematic departure from realistic imitation, a feature which it had in common with other examples of the New Stagecraft. Barker was quick to distinguish between "scenery, as scenery is mostly understood—canvas, realistically painted" and "decoration," which he declined to define and preferred to let Norman Wilkinson and Albert Rutherston demonstrate.[82] Rutherston's credo was unequivocal: "I consider any form of exact realism in the theatre wrong;" but he later qualified this statement, allowing for realism "granting only that 'realism' be not a form but a result of expression."[83] In fact, a particular form of realism was the result of Rutherston and Wilkinson's expression, the realism of solid form, without the deceit of false impressions. Rutherston described his method:

> In making a scene which represents, let us say, a solid building, the important thing is to suggest a solid thing, and unless this effect is obtained no mere decoration of the surface of it can have meaning. No painting of bricks and mortar is needed. The thing must be reduced to a simple background for your living and moving figures to live and move against, and the impression to be given is that behind and around them is a solid thing.[84]

Note the difference in the relation of surface to volume here as compared to the theories and techniques of Hubert Herkomer. Wilkinson similarly described the built-up scenes, which he claimed "were treated in a real manner, that is, in that everything was solid, of those dimensions—tangible, not a piece of canvas painted to look like what it was not."[85] In practice, Barker's built-up scenes fell into two categories: those of items simple and architectural enough to be chiefly, and effortlessly, verisimilar, and those which were complete abstractions. In the first category were the pillars and curtains of the Palace in

Sicilia and the fence and cottage in Bohemia in *The Winter's Tale*; the tapestried room of the "caterwauling" scene, the grates of the prison, and the gates of Olivia's Palace in *Twelfth Night*; and the Palace of Theseus in *The Dream*. In the second were the strange conical trees of Olivia's garden, which provided the dominant visual effect in *Twelfth Night*; and Titania's bower, in which Rutherston relied on dyed fabric hung in folds, commonly used for the front scenes in all three productions, and here used in lieu of the rigorous architectural three-dimensionality of the other built-up scenes. While Wilkinson and Rutherston rejected *trompe l'oeil* and false realism, they nevertheless created specific localities, with architectural solidity, or with a geometrical suggestion of natural or architectural forms. The originality of the designers was in their unashamedly theatrical means of achieving their effects, but the effects themselves were by no means unconventional, however visually striking.

A similar paradox resulted from their treatment of period "style." Just as they rejected painted canvas but still replicated simplified architecture to create the suggestion of locality, they rejected archaeological accuracy and yet strove for the suggestion of specific time and place. Wilkinson claimed that the decoration was "free from 'style' and 'period'—simply something that is the result of a thorough investigation of the play as it stands—alone."[86] But Rutherston described the process by which a sense of period could be achieved in the theatre:

> I hold that it is wrong simply to attempt to copy from the past . . . if we take to the fashion-plate for our inspiration—a fashion-plate, dead and lifeless, will be the only result. . . . When we design clothes for it [the Theatre] we must use inventiveness, building on a foundation of knowledge of a particular moment or period, but re-creating it, making it a living thing—avoiding the lifeless dummy. It is necessary to convey an *impression* of a particular moment or period: if we successfully convey this, then the moment or period will exist for the audience.[87]

In practice, while Barker rejected the period archaeology of productions of *The Winter's Tale* from Charles Kean through Beerbohm Tree (1906), he did want to create a particular period of flavor of Renaissance classical fantasy. He did draw on archaeological sources: a throne in the judgment scene was copied exactly from a Minoan throne in the British Museum, and Barker was unashamed enough to boast of this to the press.[88] And he turned to the one artist mentioned in the play for creative inspiration, though he later claimed that the similarity of Rutherston's costumes to the designs of Giulio Romano was purely coincidental:

> Renaissance-classic, that is, classic dress as Shakespeare saw it, would be the thing. And when we had quite made up our minds to this I suddenly thought and said to Rothenstein, "Giulio Romano! There's our pattern designer recommended by the play itself." It's little I

know of Giulio Romano. Ought I to confess that Rothenstein could remember little more? But Giulio Romano was looked up, and there the costumes were much as we had forethought them."[89]

As we shall see, a similar method, with quite a different inspiration, was used for *Twelfth Night.*

Another dimension of the designs for the Savoy Shakespeare productions was the immediate visual impression they created for the audience. While Barker himself did not design the productions, he had an implicit faith in his designers; it remains to be seen how well they served him, and to what degree he may be held responsible for the eccentricities and shocking excesses of the designs. Our present day understanding of the productions is, to a great degree, limited to the fact that the texts were relatively uncut and that the designs were stunning; the fact that contemporary audiences found them arrestingly shocking only confirms our superior historical sense of their modernity. It is unclear, however, whether the shock effect was an incidental side effect of Barker's quest for an ideal form, or was a strategy crucially linked to the abolition of false Shakespearean traditions. Shock seems to have been, to a great extent, a part of Rutherston's program: it was "only by shouting out very loudly and very clearly from our housetops that we in this world stand any chance of being heard. If we insist much, we get perhaps a little; if we insist little we probably get nothing."[90] The *Era*'s promotional statement for *The Dream* mentions that "in the case of 'A Midsummer Night's Dream,' Mr. Barker wishes it to be known that the play was specially selected by him as one which his most adverse critics would consider least suited to his much-discussed methods of staging."[91] While this statement is not a direct quotation, it remained uncontradicted by Barker in the following weeks. A year earlier, with the opening of *The Winter's Tale,* Barker stated in print: "I absolutely deny that the Savoy production is wilfully eccentric," though he also remarked, in the same interview, that "the English public wants kicking into life about once a year."[92] No doubt Barker could claim the one while practicing the other, knowing full well that it takes much more than wilful eccentricity to shock the public into life. Certainly many of his critics thought the attack on public sensibilities quite deliberate, or, if uncalculated, the fault of his collaborators.[93] Bridges-Adams had the firmest belief that Barker's primary strategy was shock, to capture adherents by a synthetic trendiness and to aggravate detractors by a deliberate abuse of traditional expectations; he claimed that "even the fantastic draperies, that took the place of Tree's front cloths and Poel's traverse curtains, came down with a defiant flop, as if Barker himself had hurled them at us from the flies, saying 'There! What do you think of that?' "[94] This description is interpretive conjecture on Bridges-Adams's part, but he is on more solid ground in his citation of Hermione's huge umbrella in the first scene of *The Winter's Tale* and Malvolio's cloak after his appearance in yellow stockings in *Twelfth Night*, both of which stunned audiences with their bright colors.[95] Bridges-Adams complained that many of these visual effects actually distracted from the audience perception of character and acting, a criticism which Barker would have been sorry to hear:

> The first appearance of Miss Lillah McCarthy under a tremendous gold umbrella was so stunning that I cannot remember as much of her Hermione as I would like to. Ainley's Leontes came as near great acting as can be when one man's performance is dominated by another man's brain. I shall always remember the thunder of his voice and the nightmare splendour of his jealousy as he paced up and down beside the brazier, with madness in his eyes—the finest spectacle of the evening. But I cannot for the life of me remember whether that madness was on him when the play began, or whether he pounced on him in a flash: and that is the kind of thing Irving would have made you remember to your dying day.[96]

Bridges-Adams further asserted that Barker's use of strong white light, which "swept shadows from the stage as if they harboured germs," was a deliberate, antitraditional attempt to shock the public.[97] Surely it was a departure from the chiaroscuro techniques of Irving; Bridges-Adams uses it as evidence of Barker's distrust of the magic of the stage, or of the world of fantasy depicted on it: Barker's witches in his projected *Macbeth* "might have proved to be the Witches of a man who didn't hold with Witches."[98] But Bridges-Adams's observation perhaps reveals Barker's true intention in his visual unconventionality. Barker chose, not to deny the magic of the stage, but to demystify the trappings of the stage which are usually used to create the magic. Indeed, Barker's choice of *The Winter's Tale* for his first production contains a metaphor for the demands he was making upon his audiences. As Leontes must perform an act of faith to restore Hermione to life, so the modern audience, denied the smudgepots and gauzes and limelights of traditional romantic staging, needed to perform an act of faith to complete the theatrical illusion. And just as Hermione's death was merely a trick of Paulina's contrivance, so the magic of the Savoy productions was the result of the manipulation of theatrical convention by Barker and his collaborators.

An important feature of Barker's scenic work was the degree to which it was organically related to the ongoing exploration of the play in the theatre, rather than the predetermined chessboard precision ascribed to it by Bridges-Adams. As Barker later phrased it in his introduction to *The Player's Shakespeare*, the goal of production is "the setting out to discover what, as plays, they essentially are," which can only be achieved "by experimenting upon the living body of the play."[99] With regard to *The Winter's Tale*, Barker remarked to an interviewer in the *Evening News*: "If you had any conception of the experiments, the changes, the modifications which have been necessary to get us where we are, you would be less inclined to suspect Mr. Rothenstein, for instance, of philistine baiting. There's simply no time for it. And what in heaven's name are we to gain by it?"[100] The statement was in part a response to the review of the play printed the day before, which included a reaction to the scene (act 3, sc. 3) in which the infant Perdita is abandoned to Antigonus on the seacoast of Bohemia. The critic complained:

> It seems a lapse of consistency . . . to give us the reticent Japanese treatment of the backcloth, with the seemly absence of stage snow, and at the same time and the whole time to produce the rumble of thunder to the manifest confusion of the text, to say nothing of the bear, too difficult a character to sustain except in way of comic relief.[101]

The criticism of the lack of snow merely ignores the gestural simplicity of Barker's scenic statement, but the noise of the drums is a production detail which troubled Barker in rehearsals:

> We made many experiments. I wanted to get the effect of people shouting through a storm. We tried having the drums intermittently, and all I can say is that the effect was killed. So we restored them. . . . We have a palette of effects at our command, and we try to arrange them so that the emotional elements of the play as its action is unfolded may be heightened.[102]

No doubt there were many other examples of scenic or dramatic effects altered through experimentation throughout rehearsals: the use of masks for Polixenes and Camillo in the fourth act, and their manner of holding them toward the audience rather than placing them over their faces, is perhaps an example. (Barker had used masks only once before in *Iphigenia in Tauris*, 1912, in which one was worn by Athena.) All such experiments represent Barker's manipulation of existing theatrical means, and experimentation with new and unknown ones, to create particular dramatic effects.

Practice

Now that we have examined Barker's theories of theatrical convention, stage space, and modern decor, we can examine in greater detail certain aspects of his three Savoy Shakespeare productions. As each production as a whole has been frequently described, by Purdom, Byrne, Speaight, Griffiths, Styan, Hunt, Kelly, Williams and myself among others, the broader details need not be recapitulated.[103] Each production posed specific problems, however, and inspired particular treatments, which are revealing of Barker's scenic methods.

In *The Winter's Tale*, it is important to understand the nature of Barker's new pictorial style, as he was first experimenting with it. The brightness of the production has already been noted. The set, like that of *Twelfth Night*, was completely boxed in upstage by white walls, one at the back and one each along the wings. Not only did this forcibly put an end to the problem of wings, solved by many avant-garde designers through the use of a curving cyclorama, but it eliminated any verisimilitude of daylight and sky, either in color, depth, or meteorological effect.

The palace set, which served for virtually every interior scene in the first half of the play, consisted of a rectangular colonnade of pillars, between which were hung curtains. The curtains were rearranged, and the furniture was changed or reset, to suggest a variety of locales within the palace. One may recognize in this use of pillars and curtaining the same device as Tree's interiors in his draped *Hamlet,* and Leonato's house in Craig's *Much Ado About Nothing.* If Barker ran into difficulties with this decor, it was in his attempt to employ an architectural unit for a variety of specific localities. The pillars and curtains were not a neutral unlocalized facade; but Barker asked his audiences to imagine that they could define both a generalized palace and several specific localities within it. Barker could not decide whether he was creating a space or a room, and so created contradictory results.

Compositionally, Barker introduced many striking features in *The Winter's Tale.* I have noted the use of profile, and of conversational processions in profile crossing the stage. To this may be added the grouping of actors in one plane, particularly in front scenes before the decorative curtains. An example in *The Winter's Tale* is in act 5, scene 2, noteworthy for its very survival from the blue pencil: the three gentlemen, in black, silver and touches of red, were grouped left, while Autolycus stood in the corresponding place in the same plane at the right, with the broad expanse of the middle stage left open.[104] In *Twelfth Night* a similar compositional moment is in the duel scene: Viola and Andrew leaned against the proscenium at opposite ends while Fabian and Toby stood in the center.[105]

With regard to the lighting, there appears to have been much more variation in its brightness than Bridges-Adams would have us believe; the lighting was changed to suit the drama as the speed of the verse was changed to suit important dramatic statements. The prison scene was played in half-darkness, and in one scene, presumably act 2, scene 1, Leontes seethed in his self-induced jealousy illuminated only by the light of a brazier, a scene which Wilkinson described as "one of the darkest on record."[106] It is also important to note the Elizabethanist trappings of the production: the three trumpet blasts before the play began, the abolition of the pit orchestra, and the use of a quartet of costumed antique-instrumentalists to accompany the traditionally dressed Morris dancers in the sheepshearing scene.

Barker's production of *Twelfth Night* was more critically and popularly successful, a result, the critics claimed, of Barker having taken their advice and toned down the juvenile eccentricities of his earlier production. But much of Barker's success was due to the fact that his task in the later play was simply more congenial. *Twelfth Night* was, for Barker, "the last play of Shakespeare's golden age. I feel happy ease in the writing, and find happy carelessness in the putting together."[107] The locale was not as problematically fantastic, nor the structure of the play as reputedly broken-backed, as *The Winter's Tale*. The critics and audience alike were more accustomed to the general tenor of his production methods. He was able to effectively limit the use of his one major built-up scene to a single locale, the same ubiquitous "Olivia's Garden" for which Tree had built his unstrikable terraced garden. Barker's set was equally permanent; the other built scenes were placed before it or inserted into it. The "kitchen" scene was a small tapestried room, complete with ceiling, and without doors; the characters parted the tapestries to enter or exit. The prison was a simple grate with curtains on either side, parallel to the front of the stage. And the final scene was placed before a gate to Olivia's property, also frontal and appropriate to the action of the scene, both public and semiprivate in feeling. The decor for the prison and the gate resemble the set pieces which, Barker maintained in his critical writing, were used on the inner stage at the Globe, e.g., the barred gate of Juliet's tomb, which would be opened by Romeo so that the following scene could be placed within. In the kitchen scene, the use of furniture and a realistically confining space made one critic remark, surprisingly, that "it might have come straight across from His Majesty's Theatre, where the aim is to make everything look so real that 'you can touch it.' "[108](See illustration 31).

Wilkinson's costume designs display an interesting facet of the production. While *The Winter's Tale* was evocatively Renaissance-classical in the style of Veronese and Giulio Romano, *Twelfth Night* was more specifically Elizabethan-cosmopolitan-fashionable. Wilkinson described his intentions in various press interviews:

> The costumes . . . I have endeavoured to make as supremely courtly and elegant as possible. You see "Twelfth Night" is a comedy of manners, and I have tried to suggest the very essence of foppishness, both in the men and the women. Mr. Barker has taken the end of the Elizabethan era, about 1603, as the period, and upon that I have moulded a sort of suggestion of Renaissance stiffness with oriental veneer. . . . I have not been pedantically "Elizabethan" in my treatment, but I have tried to give the atmosphere of well-bred stylishness, and modishness to types of people who undoubtedly represented the "high-life" of that particular era. . . . I imagine . . . that to the Elizabethan gallants "Twelfth Night" ranked as would a very smartly-dressed comedy at a fashionable West End theatre in our day. My aim, therefore, has been to produce cloths of a particularly good cut of the Elizabethan type, combined with the romance of the Persian type of dressing. Romance and smartness are what I am aiming for.[109]

A case could be made in support of the conjecture that Barker thoroughly intended, in his production of *Twelfth Night*, to ape the success of Edwardian fashionable drawing-room comedy, such as was playing elsewhere in the West End. This would practically explain the production's popularity with critics and the public, to which the fashion-plate ethic of Wilkinson's Elizabethan style no doubt contributed.

Barker did not always eschew the traditional device of the curtain tableau, although in one instance of his use of it he relied upon what he believed was Elizabethan precedents. The "kitchen" scene was in an inset, which Barker believed corresponded to the Elizabethan inner stage; and so he could lower his curtains as the Elizabethans, he believed, would have drawn their traverses: on a completed picture. In the production, the curtain fell on the picture of Toby and Andrew vainly trying to blow out the candles in the candelabrum on stage.[110]

A very different set of problems was posed by *A Midsummer Night's Dream*, and the main problem, the depiction of the fairies, haunted Barker through the rest of his critical career. In seeking to make the fairies unhuman and otherworldly, he devised the most outrageous and trendy effect of his career, his metal-curled gold faced automata.

His preface to the acting edition of the play, on sale in the theatre, made it clear how seriously Barker considered the challenge of the fairies: "The fairies are the producer's test. Let me confess that, though mainly love of the play, yet partly, too, a hope of passing that test has inspired the present production. Foolhardy one feels facing it. But if a method of staging can compass the difficulties of *A Midsummer Night's Dream*, surely its cause is won."[111] Barker puzzled over an adequate solution, rejecting realistic adults or children. "They must be not too startling. But one wishes people weren't so easily startled. I won't have them dowdy. They musn't warp your imagination—stepping too boldly between Shakespeare's spirit and yours."[112] Barker's solution was unquestionable startling, and perhaps he had intended that this would be so, beyond what he would admit in print.

Barker avoided symbolic statement in his conception of his fairies, and he rejected William Archer's attempt to read symbols into them. Puck was dressed in red with a blond tangle of hair studded with berries; "a blast of scarlet shooting through a blue curtain of stars," as Graham Robertson described him.[113] Archer was puzzled by this mop of hair, musing in a letter to Barker that perhaps it had been meant to symbolize the *ignis fatuus:* "But I am quite uncertain & even if I have guessed right, I wonder how many people in the audience rose to it?"[114] Barker had no such symbolism in mind: he only sought a visual image which at once set the character apart from the other fairies and freed him for his unfettered mischief; Barker elaborated his image to Archer: Puck "is as English as he can be, and though sometimes he is invisible, sometimes he goes and lives among the village folk as a grown up person at that. Still perhaps in trying to get the point we exaggerated it."[115]

Barker's problem was not the exaggeration, but the lack of consistency in his immortals. In his later *Player's Shakespeare* preface, he defined the primary task: "Here is the designer's problem, if one exists. He will further have to contrive some unity of effect."[116] And yet Barker felt the strong need to differentiate between the various types of fairies, and to find theatrical means of portraying them in keeping with the inspirations Shakespeare drew upon in creating them: "Oberon and Titania are romantic creations: sprung from Huron of Bordeaux, etc., say the commentators; come from the farthest steppe of India, says Shakespeare. But Puck is English folklore."[117] Accordingly, the fairies were gilded and metallic; many observers noted the allusion to their supposed Indian inspiration, seeing them as brazen idols. Oberon and Titania received more conventional, though stylized, treatment. And Puck, as we have seen, was a thing apart. But the one thing Barker perhaps failed to create out of this potpourri of styles was a "unity of effect." And so, his startling image for the fairies could not be seen as a concept of the production, but as a case-by-case physicalization of a poetic image appropriate for each character. It is unfair to Barker to judge his results by those of his imitators, but one can see how this phenomenon led to the absurdities of Kirwan's Stratford production of *The Dream* later the same year.

Another stylistic departure in Barker's *Dream* was the use of curtaining for both the full scenes and the front scenes in the forest. Hitherto curtains had only been used in the front scenes, and, with architectural verisimilitude, between the pillars in the Palace scenes in *The Winter's Tale*. The use of curtains here did not increase or decrease the representationalism of the full scene, though G. C. D. Odell, who had not seen either *The Winter's Tale* or *Twelfth Night,* could not accept the curtains as decor at all: "No human being . . . can be expected to be anything but worried or annoyed by pink silk curtains that are supposed to be the roofs of houses [in act 1, sc. 2, a front scene], or green silk curtains that are supposed to be forest trees; especially when they blow and stream out in the gales of the stage."[118] Odell equates the scenic effects of a front scene and a full scene. In either of the earlier productions, those two scenes would have been treated very differently. In Barker's *Dream*, there was a fundamental scenic unity unlike either of the other productions. Unlike the Forest set, the Palace of Theseus, in the first and last acts of the play, followed the example of *The Winter's Tale* in its architectural solidity, though here it was unambiguously localized. Norman Marshall and Trevor Griffiths both conjecture that the shift from the three-dimensionality of Athens to the curtaining of the forests might have been a scenic analogue for the differences between the two localities as they are sensed by the characters.[119]

A staging device used in all three plays involved the use of what Brodmeier called the split scene, the shift from full stage to the front stage during the course of a single textual scene to allow for the resetting of the next full scene. Barker's direct inspiration for this technique was a production he saw in Germany in 1910; he wrote to Archer:

> I have, by the way, and I expect you have, seen a performance of Götz von Berlichingen given with a rear stage constantly reset with scenery, the characters beginning the scenes there, coming out of it when need be and the curtains closing on them while the scene was carried on to its end and the next scene set meanwhile.[120]

One recognizes Antoine's *Lear* set, admired by Casson and incorporated into his own Shakespeare stagings. In general Barker did not resort to this technique, but in certain instances (such as in act 2, scene 4 of *Twelfth Night*), the use of a split scene, the action shifting to the apron while a decorative curtain was lowered, was unremarkable. In one case in *A Midsummer Night's Dream,* however, the result was more significant. In act 3, scene 2 the action had shifted to the front stage in order to clear the action of the lovers from the locale of Bottom and Titania's lovemaking. In preparation for Puck's putting the mortal lovers to sleep, the scene shifted to the full stage. Barker took advantage of this moment to introduce a piece of extra-theatrical awareness on the part of Puck; the Harvard promptbook reads: "Obe turns and exits quickly through the curtains C. followed by train [.] Puck then down C lower stage [,] motions for lights to go down [on the apron] then [crosses] up to cloth, bends down & raises curtain as it ascends." In other words, Puck asserts his awareness of the dramatic artifice of the stage machinery, and becomes a mediator between the audience and the theatrical event.

Styan enthusiastically lauds this moment: "The spectator had in part become an immortal himself, granted the power to control and observe the antics of the earthly lovers. By this simple device, the theatre of Bertolt Brecht, Peter Brook and perhaps the real Shakespeare came a step closer."[121] The wonder of the moment deserves Styan's enthusiasm. But, on a simpler level, Barker was restoring to his stage the principles of the Elizabethan theatre which had been lost in the Edwardian Theatre to the Music Halls; as Barker described it, the genius of Burbage now embodied in the artistry of Dan Leno. *The Winter's Tale* had lacked a truly Shakespearean clown, capable of breaking through the boundaries of the theatre (though Barker had the second gentleman in act 5, scene 2 played for comedy); and Feste in *Twelfth Night* was transformed into a dramatically consistent character within the frame of the play. Here, in Puck, Barker attempted to reestablish the link between actor and audience by creating a special sense of extradramatic awareness.

But even the novel application of this technique to the classical drama was not original: it had been used three seasons before in Tree's *Henry VIII* (1910). A favorite non-textual silent character who appeared in the cast of characters in several of Tree's Shakespeare productions (*Hamlet, King John, Richard II,* and *Henry VIII*) was a court jester who, within the naturalistic frame of the play, could serve as a silent commentator, adding punctuation to the events of the play. In *Henry VIII*, Tree was still using the apron stage which William Poel had erected for his *Two Gentlemen of Verona*. Perhaps inspired by the opening lines of the play ("I come no more to make you laugh"), Tree assigned the prologue to Wolsey's Jester, who peeked out from behind the curtains at the opening of the play and came through them onto the apron for the speech. At the end of the prologue, the following direction appears in the promptbook; "Lights up in front D[o]m[e lights] down as curtain rises.... On hearing organ Jester goes to curtains returns down extension [i.e., apron] & makes gesture for curtains to rise. Curtain up. Jester goes to Church door listens." The Jester's business needs little explanation, for in it we can see the same action that Barker employed with Puck in *The Dream*.[122] The Jester continued as a silent commentator on the action in Tree's *Henry VIII*, following Wolsey into the cloisters, thus symbolizing his final withdrawal from public and political life; and, before he decided to cut the Christening scene, Tree had the fool return, in black, weeping, as a contrapuntal reminder of Wolsey long after his last appearance on the stage.

I cite this business, not to challenge Barker's originality, but to question the importance of originality in the work of Barker or any other Edwardian innovator. That he attempted, in one small instance, to reestablish a magical bond between spectator and performer need hardly be original to be commendable. That Tree had employed a similar device is of significance only when we consider the conditions under which he did so: only with an apron stage, however inessential to the staging of the play, could Tree transform his traditional within-frame commentator into a special ambassador between actor and audience. Barker's device, like the rest of his theories and practices, was a conscious attempt to maximize the dramatic effect of his material, using means currently available, to reach a contemporary audience. The most conservative of Barker's contemporaries attempted no less. That Barker found new scenic means to do so attests to his ingenuity. But these were only available to him because of the recognition by his Edwardian contemporaries of the conventional freedom afforded by any language of scenography. Shakespeare producers of the Edwardian period were free to exploit this conventional freedom independent of the degree to which they qualified the realistic premises of pictorial representationalism. Tree and Barker represent opposite ends of the spectrum, not in the recognition of theatricality, but only in their willingness to let this theatricality modify the rest of their scenic vocabulary. Regardless of this polar dichotomy, Barker and Tree were, by virtue of their theatrical self-awareness, equally men of their times.

The style of the Savoy Shakespeare productions most closely resembles the style which would come to dominate stagings of Shakespeare after the war. But the Savoy style was not Barker's creation, however creative Barker was in employing it. Barker's virtue lay not in his power of invention, but in his ability to integrate the varied and disparate features of the stagecraft of his day into a coherent system of staging. Tree and his traditionalist colleagues ushered in new techniques through the developments in their own school of stagecraft. Poel and Craig created new aesthetics out of elements they inherited from their conservative predecessors, and each broke new ground in their respective schools. Harvey rejoiced in several schools, employing one and then another, defending all of them. Only Barker integrated the developments, experiments and discoveries of his day into a single, effective system of staging. The attitudes embodied in the Savoy Shakespeare productions, the new techniques which were practiced, the system of conventions which Barker advocated, and the freedom with which these conventions were employed, were all present in the works of Barker's many contemporaries. Conservatives and innovators together brought about the evolution of a theatrical style which the Edwardian period willed to later generations. Only by understanding the work of all the Edwardians can the work of any individual theatre artist be appreciated.

5

Epilogue: Shakespeare and the Director

Thus far this book has concentrated on the changes in scenography in the production of Shakespeare's plays during the Edwardian period. Many of the aesthetic assumptions behind these scenic changes contributed to the emergence of the stage director and ultimately to the rise of the Director's Theatre. As I have shown, the scenographic reforms detailed in the previous chapters were not merely the results of individual directorial innovations. Similarly, the articulation of the director's role and his rise to power in the theatrical process were not the results of individual assertion, but the natural extension of several attitudes about the dramatic text and the theatrical product. These attitudes reflect the relationship of the artist to his age, the belief that the playwright's intentions are embodied in his dramatic work and are discernible to the modern interpreter, and the concept of "unity of effect" linked to Edwardian definitions of the stage environment. All of these issues came into play in the production of Shakespeare during the Edwardian period.

Well before the Edwardian period, Shakespeare had served as the vehicle for eccentric experimentation, flagrant revision and travesty. The plays were in the public domain, and the playwright could not quarrel with the treatment given to his scripts. As Shaw said of Tree and Irving, the actor, manager or director "turn[s] to Shakespeare as to a forest out of which . . . scaffolding could be hewn without remonstrance from the landlord."[1] But Shakespeare does not merely allow for individual interpretation; he virtually demands it. So great are the potentialities of the scripts and so difficult is the task of realizing any one aspect of the plays that the theatre artist is forced to select a single facet of the text which can be compassed in performance. Gordon Craig turned this difficulty into a paradox, asserting that "to represent *Hamlet* rightly is an impossibility" because "*Hamlet* and the other plays of Shakespeare have so vast and so complete a form when read, that they can but lose heavily when presented to us after having undergone stage treatment."[2]

Another difficulty in producing Shakespeare is that the stagecraft and dramaturgy of the plays are shaped by the conditions of the playwright's time and playhouse. The Elizabethanist belief that Shakespeare's art belonged to the Elizabethan period was best phrased by William Poel. Poel cited Ruskin's statement, "It is a constant law that the greatest poets ... live entirely in their own age, and the greatest fruits of their work are gathered out of their own age," and applied it to the staging of Shakespeare: "Shakespeare and his companions," wrote Poel, "wrote about what they knew, and about nothing else. Their material was their own and their neighbour's experiences; and their plays were shaped to suit the theatre of the day and no other."[3]

The inverse of this statement is Ben Jonson's assertion that Shakespeare "was not of an age, but for all time" by virtue of the continued life of his dramatic work.[4] Here lies the paradox of theatrical activity, for the theatrical practitioner belongs to his own age as strongly as does the playwright whose text he is preparing for production; he must appeal directly to an audience of his contemporaries for the duration of the theatre event. If Elizabethanists asserted that the playwright belonged to his time, other Edwardians were making the same claims for themselves. As Beerbohm Tree stated,

> Every man should avail himself of the aids which his generation affords him. It is only the weakling who harks back echoically to the methods of a bygone generation. ... No man is great in any walk of life unless he is, in the best sense, of his time.[5]

This attitude was not confined to the "modern" traditionalists of the Edwardian period. Bernard Shaw advised Ellen Terry

> to be a mother to Shakespeare—to cover his foolishness and barrennesses, and to make the most of his little scattered glimpses of divinity. If you cannot believe in the greatness of your own age & time & inheritance, you will fall into the most horrible confusion of mind and contrariety of spirit like a noble little child looking up to foolish, mean & selfish parents.[6]

And Granville Barker conceded that "while poetry, painting, sculpture can exist for a little in the cloister or the desert, as a reflection of the past or a promise for the future, the drama ... simple, democratic, crude if you will ... must be of its age."[7] Barker built upon the paradox of the temporality of the playscript and the immediacy of the theatre event when he created his theory of theatrical convention which, as we have seen, is the cornerstone of his theory and practice. Shakespeare's plays "are like music written to be performed upon an instrument now broken almost beyond repair."[8] For Barker, "the literature of the past is a foreign literature. We must either learn its language or suffer it to be translated."[9] Dramatic literature demanded translation; plays are "subject from the first to interpretation and its betrayals."[10] The need for the dramatic script to be "translated" in performance, and the delicate balance between an accurate translation and the betrayal of the playwright's intentions, were fundamental premises of the Director's Theatre.

One crucial assumption of the Director's Theatre was widespread during the Edwardian period: the belief that the intention of the playwright is built into the dramatic script and is discernible to the modern theatrical interpreter. Edwardian theatre artists perceived that each play by Shakespeare demanded its own characteristic treatment. To some extent, even the work of William Poel reflects this notion. Although Poel's assertion was that one style of staging, namely that of the Elizabethan period, was essential for the faithful production of any and all of Shakespeare's plays, Poel covered his tracks by not producing certain plays which, perhaps, he felt would not support this assertion. Of the Roman plays, Poel did not produce *Julius Caesar* or *Antony and Cleopatra*, and produced *Coriolanus* only in the 1920s; the only Shakespearean history he produced was *Henry V*; he avoided plays particularly associated with outdoor settings, such as *As You Like It* and *A Midsummer Night's Dream*; and, except for *The Tempest*, for which there are legitimate historical grounds for introducing elements of the Masque, he avoided plays with lyrical fantasy. *Troilus and Cressida* was the only play he produced calling for a sense of cultural difference if not historical accuracy, and he achieved this only through a happy visual metaphor of Jacobean theatrical costuming. Poel's critics and supporters alike noticed his selectivity in finding vehicles for his Elizabethanist experiments, and some would support him only as far as they felt the play in hand was appropriate to Elizabethan treatment. Even Shaw was lukewarm in one of his supportive reviews:

> There is no general rule, not even for any particular author. You can do best without scenery in *The Tempest* and *A Midsummer Night's Dream*, because the best scenery you can get will only destroy the illusion created by the poetry; but it does not at all follow that scenery will not improve a representation of *Othello*.[11]

Ellen Terry, no strong advocate of Poel's methods, makes a similar distinction: "I saw his production of 'Two Gentlemen of Verona,' and it delighted me, but I should not like to see 'Romeo and Juliet' in that Elizabethan setting, much less 'Julius Caesar.' "[12]

Edwardian theatre practitioners who produced Shakespeare in a wide variety of differing production styles were quick to assert that the design of a production is directly related to the intrinsic nature of the play. Beerbohm Tree distinguished between "symbolic" and "realistic" plays in defense of the historical pictorialism of his *Henry VIII* (1910):

> Probably no English author is less "symbolic" than Shakespeare. *Hamlet* is a play which, to my mind, does not suffer bvy the simplest setting; indeed, a severe simplicity of treatment seems to me to assist rather than to detract from the imaginative development of that masterpiece. But I hold that, with the exception of certain scenes in *The Tempest*, no plays

by Shakespeare are susceptible to what is called "symbolic" treatment. To attempt to present *Henry VIII* in other than a realistic manner would ensure absolute failure.[13]

In a later publication of the same essay, Tree appended an "afterthought" taking into consideration the increasing number of "symbolic" productions:

> In our recent production of *Macbeth* [1911, for which Gordon Craig was originally retained to provide designs] . . . the scenery was characterized by simple grandeur rather than by magnificence of detail. Rugged simplicity was the note of an admirable production of *King Lear* at the Haymarket Theatre. It would, of course, be an artistic mistake to apply this treatment to such plays as *Julius Caesar* or *Richard II* or *Henry VIII*, or indeed to any of the history plays.[14]

We have seen that Gordon Craig was limited in his choice of plays to which he could apply his "symbolic" scenic technique, both by the attitudes of his contemporaries, and by his own silent compliance with their beliefs.

Theatre artists who worked in several different scenic schools simultaneously had to justify their choices in similar ways. Martin Harvey, for example, had to explain the consistency of his artistic policy when his repertory included two productions in different Elizabethan styles (*The Taming of the Shrew* and *Henry V*), one in the manner of Reinhardt or Craig (*Hamlet*) and one employing traditional pictorial realism (*Richard III*); in a speech opening the Theatre Exhibit in Manchester in 1926, Harvey claimed that he "thought it would be interesting to the public to see examples of these four different methods of producing plays," and then defended the variety aesthetically:

> A criticism of those four different methods was made by Mr. Littlewood in—I think—the *Pall Mall Gazette*. He said, in substance, "Mr. Martin Harvey has shown us by these productions that the *method* of producing a Shakespearean play does not matter, so long as the spirit of the play is the producer's first consideration." That is the truth. Everything must be subordinated to the play itself. It does not matter whether your style is the realistic, the academic, the archaeological, whether it is old-fashioned or whether it is reformed—the words of Shakespeare come back again. "The play's the thing." It is the spirit in which a play is produced that matters, and not the form. To design a new, ingenious, eccentric setting is nothing, unless the design arises naturally and inevitably from the play itself, and is conceived, too, in a spirit that subordinates decoration to the illustration and the expression of the play. In other words, the setting of the play must be studied from the inside-out, and not from the outside-in.[15]

Elsewhere Harvey defined the task in similar terms:

> If you are out to express the play itself, to work from the inside out and not from the outside in, if you are to stir the imagination of an audience to such a pitch as shall leave them, by suggestion, to their own mental picture of such an environment as is fitting and becoming to the play which you are producing, the task is not so easy.[16]

And so Harvey envisioned the producer's goal as generating in the audience their own imaginative reconstruction of a distinct environment suitable to the particular play. It is interesting that Charles Ricketts, a scenic "reformer," should express a similar opinion in quite the same way:

> The idea has been forcing itself upon me that there are as many possible styles of theatre decoration as there are plays, varying from the processional action of Marlowe's *Faust* [sic], which could be acted against a tapestry, to the horizons and immensities required to stage *Macbeth*.[17]

Like Harvey, Ricketts went on to link the different needs of each play to the need for different environments and visual tones:

> As the curtain goes up a shattered tree or cromlech will prepare the spectator for the desolation of *Lear*. . . . *Macbeth* might fall in a solitude where a forest has once been swept away by fire; but magical seas, fantastic rocks and trees are needed to give illusion to *The Tempest*.[18]

We can see that the increasingly prevalent Edwardian belief in an appropriate theatrical style for each play corresponds to the belief in an appropriate scenic environment for each play, a fundamental premise of traditional stagecraft. The designer and the director sought the scenic *mot juste*, a visual correlative for the special quality which they believed was envisioned by the playwright and implanted by him into the script.

Granville Barker certainly believed in the existence of a discernible authorial intention in the plays of Shakespeare, and made the existence of such an intention a prominent feature of his philosophy of scholarship and directing. In the introduction to his *Prefaces*, he stated that

> For a golden rule, whether staging or costuming or cutting is in question, and a comprehensive creed, a producer might well pin this on his wall: Gain Shakespeare's effects by Shakespeare's means when you can; for, plainly, this will be the better way. But gain Shakespeare's effects; and it is your business to discern them.[19]

Barker not only assumed that it is within the reach of the director to discern these effects, but that authorial intentions are concrete and discernible. This attitude informs Barker's rather perceptive criticism in the *Prefaces*, when he described as an examination of the plays "in the light of the interpretation he designed for them, so far as this can be deduced; to discover, if possible, the production he would have desired for them, all merely incidental circumstances apart."[20] Barker claimed to have been able to deduce the interpretation which Shakespeare intended for his plays as early as 1912. He wrote in the preface to the acting edition of the Savoy *Twelfth Night* that "the plan of the play was altered in the writing of it," i.e., that the playwright's intentions changed in mid-play; and he believed that the play's "scandalously ill-arranged and ill-written last scene" could be staged properly if the director/scholar could "discover . . . amid the chaos scraps of the play he [Shakespeare] meant to write."[21] The director, Barker claimed, is entitled to presuppose authorial intentions which the author himself failed to actualize in his script.

Barker's definition of the director corresponds to the golden rule quoted above: the director is the deputy of the playwright, and must not assert his individual creativity unless it serves to realize the playwright's intended effects. Barker judged other directors by this standard: in 1910 he paused to consider whether Reinhardt was a megalomaniac because he was "as much a creator as an interpreter"; Barker judged Reinhardt's Berlin production of *The Comedy of Errors* on the basis of its fidelity to Shakespeare's intentions: "Has he kept and illuminated the spirit of the play? I think he is entitled to an aquittal. Such an aquittal must carry with it triumph and admiration."[22]

Other Edwardian theatre artists did not accept Barker's criteria so readily. If the scope of Shakespeare's text is so vast, then the filtration of the text through the interpretation of the individual is crucially necessary. The contribution of the interpreter is consequently more creative, for he must choose and select aspects of the text which are amenable to his own talents, perceptions, and disposition. This was the view of Beerbohm Tree, who eloquently summarized the claims of the Director's Theatre in 1910 in a defense of his "modern" method of staging:

> No Shakespeare play will succeed unless it is informed by imaginative acting, and treatment. It is, in fact, the treatment of the artist which is essential, for without such treatment Shakespeare is far better read than seen. I am sorry to have to make this obvious claim for the artist—it is only the artist or the potential artist who understands.[23]

One year later, Tree added that "the greatest value of Shakespeare production lies in the point of view of those who present his works. But for this creative or re-creative work it would be infinitely preferable to read them in the study."[24] Here, in the words of an Edwardian traditionalist, is the rationale for the Director's Theatre: the script must be interpretively recreated by a man who stands in the same relation to his own art and times that the playwright did to his.

These same premises were shared by Gordon Craig, who similarly felt that the director must recreate the play according to his own artistic sensibilities. If a "man of the theatre" wishes to produce Shakespeare, wrote Craig in 1910, "he must first of all woo the spirits in those plays; for unless he understands them with his whole being he shall but produce a thing of rags and tatters."[25] So far Craig would concur with Barker, who called for a similar understanding of Shakespeare's effects. But Craig went a step further, praising the "actor producers" of Irving's generation for asserting themselves more actively in the recreative process:

> The idea of the play as a theatre piece strikes him... This *idea* which strikes him may be a right or a wrong one from the dramatist's point of view..., but, right or wrong, this is how it strikes him, and it is this impression that he decides to put over the footlights, so that it shall strike the spectators in the way and amaze their very faculties of eyes and ears.[26]

The "idea" of the creative director corresponds to what we now call the directorial "concept."

Another aspect of the Director's Theatre corresponds to a premise of Edwardian scenography. According to Edwardian environmental theory, the world of the stage is created and verified by the coordination of all illusionary elements according to the principle of unity. Likewise, the "treatment" given to the play by the creative artist must pervade all artistic aspects of the production according to principles of unity. Gordon Craig developed his ideal of the seven-headed director so that every creative element of the production could be controlled by a single individual, and he based his theories of the mask and the übermarionette on the need to control the more uncertain elements of the actor's personality, physiognomy, and movement. Craig's opinions were echoed by many of his more conservative Edwardian contemporaries. His mother, for example, advocated the idea of an "artist-stage-manager" who should "be able to produce a play without calling in the outside assistance of a scenic designer, an artistic advisor, a ballet master, a costume designer, or any other 'feeder.'"[27] Craig's objections to Max Reinhardt were based on his belief that Reinhardt's success was due, not to his own creativity, but to the distribution of artistic responsibility among too many individuals.[28]

The principle of artistic unity points to another essential difference between Gordon Craig and Granville Barker, for while Craig fulfilled his own ideal of the seven-headed director, Barker, like Reinhardt, delegated artistic responsibility to his collaborators. When asked the relation his own work bears with that of Barker at the Savoy, Craig responded:

> I cannot see my way to drawing any comparison. I am essentially a producer. I do not place the dressing in the hands of one person, the scenic design in the hands of another, &c., &c. I invent and superintend everything myself.[29]

Craig even questioned the validity of calling the Savoy Shakespeare productions Barker's; "the production is not Mr. Barker's but is the product of several men"; Craig clearly preferred "men of conviction, ... men with methods of their own."[30]

But while Barker was not his own designer, nor anything resembling the seven-headed director Craig fancied himself, his designers did, in keeping with the principles of the New Stagecraft, advocate a unity of artistic conception which usually entailed the dominance of a single director-designer. Wilkinson emphasized the importance of a consistent design, and accepted Barker's designation of his work as "decoration," as it entailed the supervision of the manufacture as well as the design of the set, costumes, and scenery.[31] As to workmanship, Wilkinson in particular boasted of his interest in the in-house construction of all the designs, unusual in a day when costumes were executed if not also designed by firms and scenery was painted in independent workshops. Wilkinson felt that "the bringing into being of the actual scenery, dresses, etc. is the work where art is needed, and it should be applied by one man who grasps the central idea of the work," and after *The Winter's Tale* he announced that he was going "to have a factory, which I shall supervise, where everything—scenery, properties, dresses, etc.—will be prepared."[32] *The Winter's Tale* was the only one of the three productions in which the design of the set and costumes were assigned to different people. Rutherston rather belligerently believed that only one man should be responsible for designs: "It is impossible that a dozen or six or three men working separately to produce a single idea *should* succeed; and they *must* fail before they even begin. To begin with, then, the decoration of a play, in every detail must be the conception and work of one mind alone."[33] Rutherston further believed that the "ideal state of things" would feature one man serving as "author, producer and decorator, in himself all in all," adding that only Craig was capable of filling such an office.[34] It is interesting to see how Rutherston exercised his own creativity while working in collaboration; his designs for the costumes in *The Winter's Tale* (now in the Harvard Theatre Collection) do reveal a creative mind at work, imposing its own creative insights, even with regard to a character's emotional visage and expression (see illustration 33); *The Standard,* reviewing an exhibition of the designs at the end of the run of the play, remarked that Rutherston "was trying hard to suit his own conceptions of the characters."[35] One assumes that these conceptions matched Barker's. In any event, Barker was prepared to accept the collaborative nature of his theatrical enterprise. For him, "performance and preparation are, almost from the beginning, a work of collaboration," and it is the responsibility of the director "to create unity *in* diversity."[36]

Barker's faith in committee work and Craig's belief in the central control of a single theatre artist were at the opposite ends of the directorial spectrum which grew out of the Edwardian period. But this dichotomy was characteristic of many aspects of theatre art and industry during the Edwardian period. For example, the actor-manager system was defended on the basis of its emphasis on the individual, just as the National Theatre scheme was supported on the basis of its reliance on institutional structures and committee control.

Epilogue: Shakespeare and Director

The actor-manager system, a vestige of Victorianism, and the Director's Theatre, the system of the future, shared, during the Edwardian period, a belief in the centrality of the individual, the "great man" theory of history and of artistic innovation. Gordon Craig legitimately used a quotation from his *bête noire* Beerbohm Tree as an epigraph for an issue of *The Mask*: "The Welfare of the Drama as of all institutions depends on men and not on systems."[37] During the Edwardian period, men and institutions vied for power; institutional structures competed with actor-centered or director-centered structures. The diversity in scenic styles was mirrored by the diversity of organizational structures. But just as the avant-garde scenic styles retained the aesthetic premises of traditional scenography, the more radical organizational system, the Director's Theatre, inherited a belief in the Great Man from the waning Actor-Manager system. And as the scenic diversity of the Edwardian period generated a more uniform language of Shakespeare production in the years to follow, the organizational diversity of the Edwardian period gave way to the individual-centered Director's Theatre which has dominated ever since.

The Director's Theatre, and the Great Man theory which accompanies it, have informed and, to a great degree, limited our historical understanding of the Edwardian theatre. But we must not let ourselves be misled by the glorification of individual artistic initiative which emerged from the diverse theatrical activity of the Edwardian period. The scenic reforms of the period were brought about by minor artisans as well as major artists, by reactionaries as well as radicals, by institutions as well as individuals. Only by understanding the variety of forms and aesthetics of the period can we appreciate the "unity in diversity" which was the greatest achievement of Edwardian scenography.

1. A front scene from Tree's *Antony and Cleopatra* (1906): the exterior of the monument.

2. A full scene from Tree's *Antony and Cleopatra*: the interior of the monument.

3. Alma Tadema's designs for Irving's *Coriolanus* (1901): the proscenium arch

4. The single set for Tree's production of Phillips' *Herod* (1900)

5. Design by Alma Tadema for Irving's *Coriolanus* (1901): a street

6. Design by Alma Tadema for Irving's *Coriolanus* (1901): the Forum of Antium

7. Design by Alma Tadema for Irving's *Coriolanus* (1901): the exterior of Aufidius's house

8. Garden Scene of Tree's *Twelfth Night* (1901).

9. A rendering of the Garden Scene. (Malvolio could not have stood where the drawing places him.)

10. The Grand Tableau from Act I of Waller's *Henry V* (1901)

11. Current events illustrated: the relief of Ladysmith

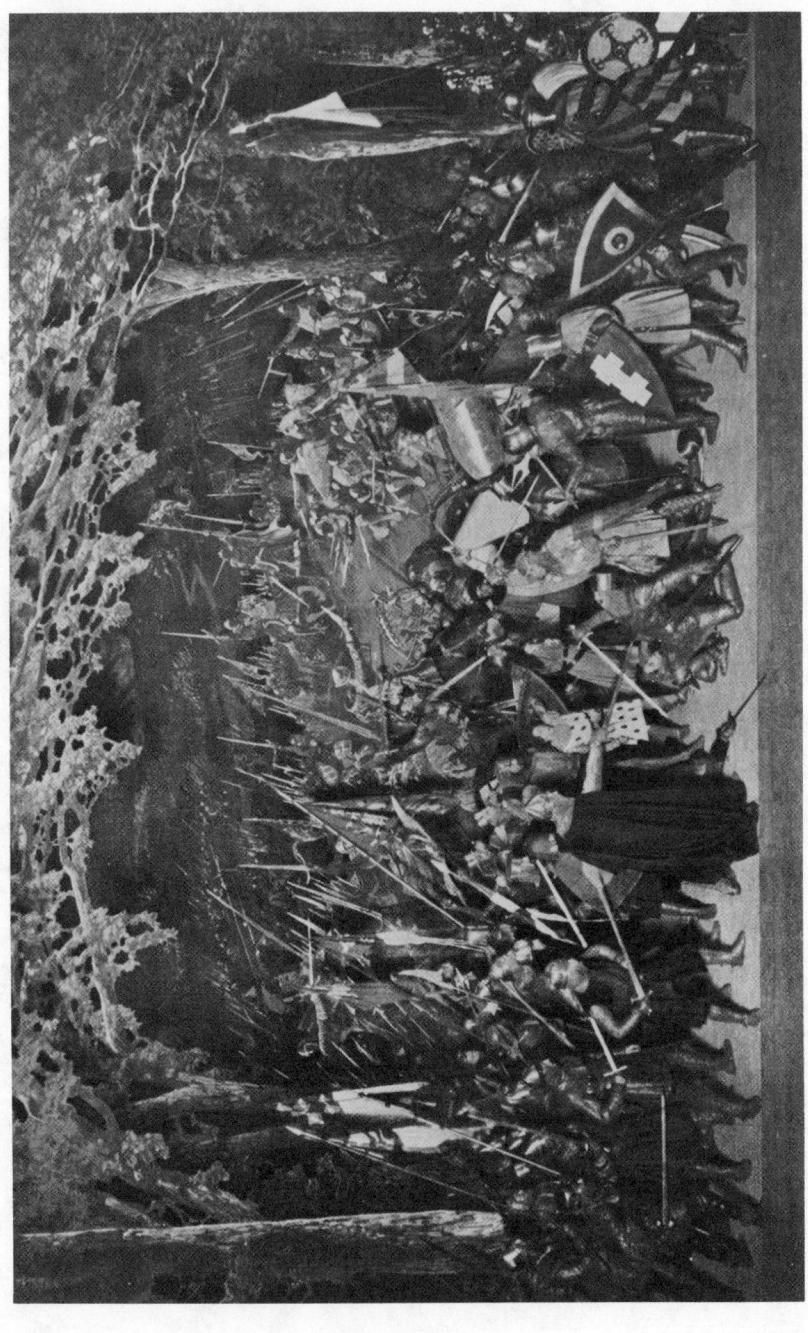

12. The Battle of Angiers: a tableau from Tree's *King John* (1899).

13. Poel's use of curtains: a scene from *Hamlet* (1900)

14. A cartoonist's view of Tree rehearsing *Hamlet*

15. Brodmeier's plan for the Elizabethan stage. (Note the front curtains and the enclosed wing space.)

16. The stage used by Granville Barker for *Iphigenia in Taurus* (1912) at the Greek Theatre, Bradfield

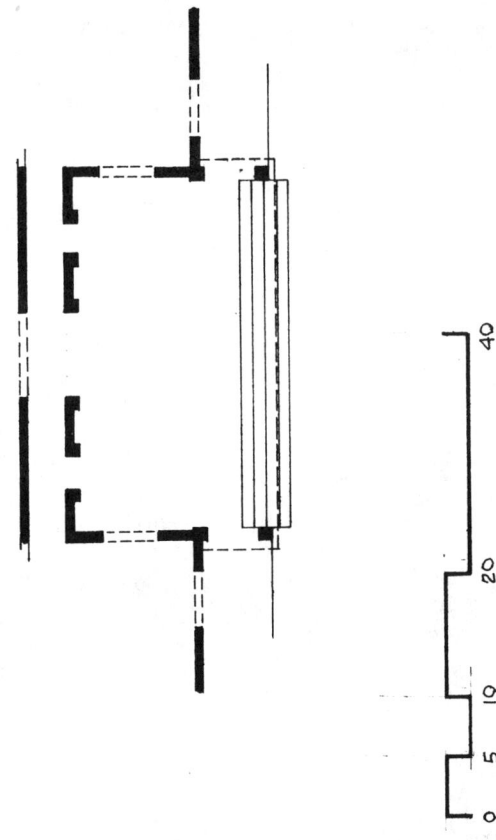

17. Plan of the stage area for Barker's *Iphigenia in Taurus*, derived from the photograph

18. Reconstruction by Walter H. Godfrey and William Archer of the Fortune Theatre

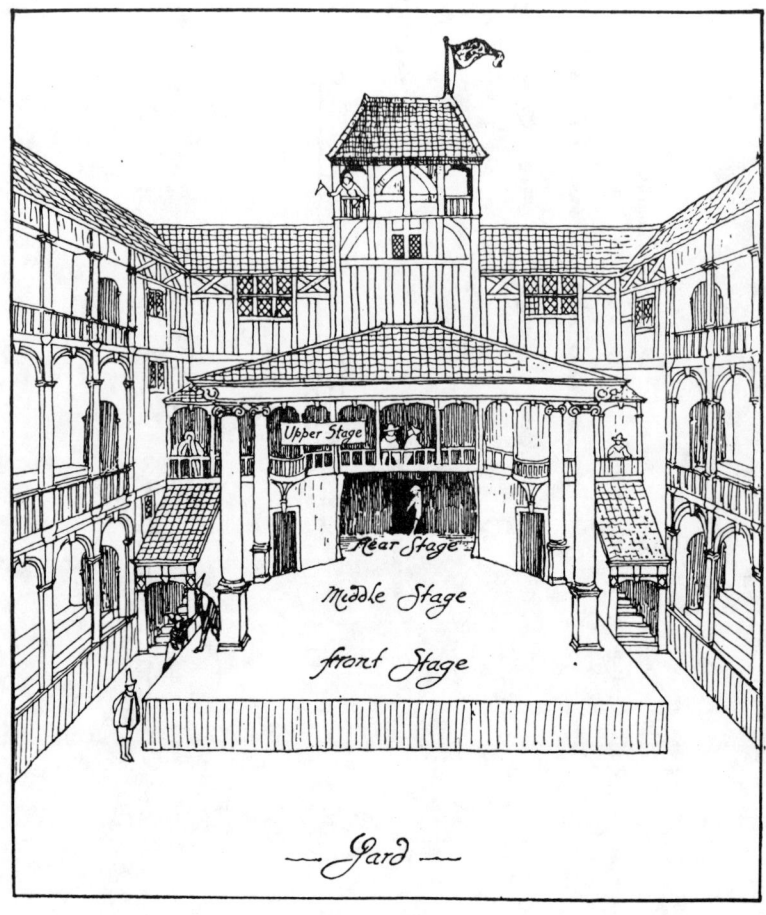

19. Probable placement of the fit-up stage for Poel's *Measure for Measure* (1893), based on Arthur J. Harris' analysis of photographs. Note: Auditorium features are conjectural

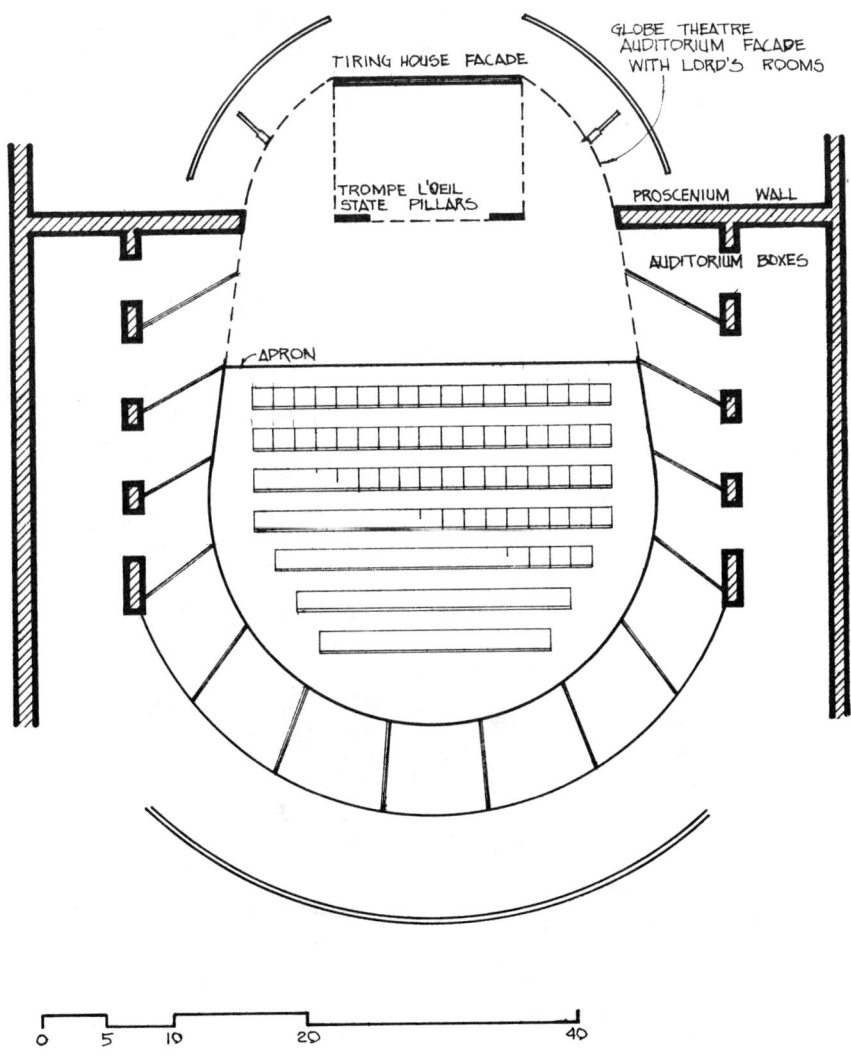

20. Poel's *Twelfth Night* (1897): the traverse curtains used for a "front" scene

21. Darrell Figgis's plan for an Elizabethan stage

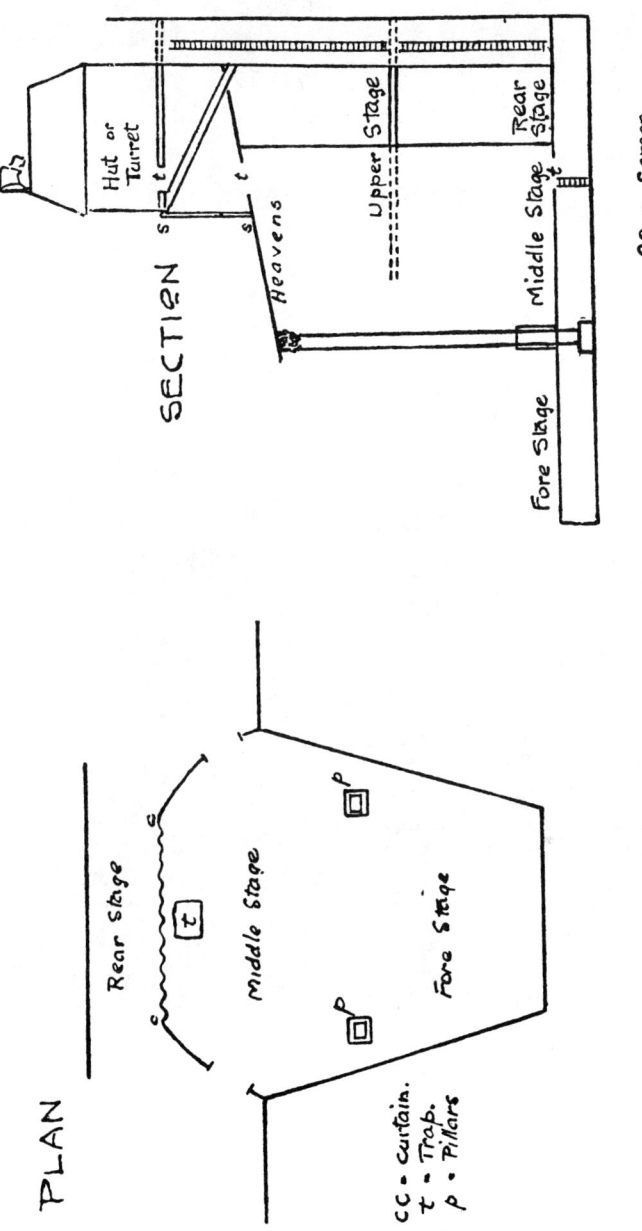

22. George Pierce Baker's Elizabethan Stage at Harvard

23. Byam Shaw's drawing of the Dance from Craig's *Much Ado About Nothing* (1903)

24. Designs for II.iii of Craig's *Much Ado About Nothing* (1903)

25. Design by Charles Ricketts for *King Lear* (1909)

26. The playing area for Max Reinhardt's *Oedipus* (1912) at Covent Garden

27. Plan of the playing area for Reinhardt's *Oedipus*, derived from the photograph

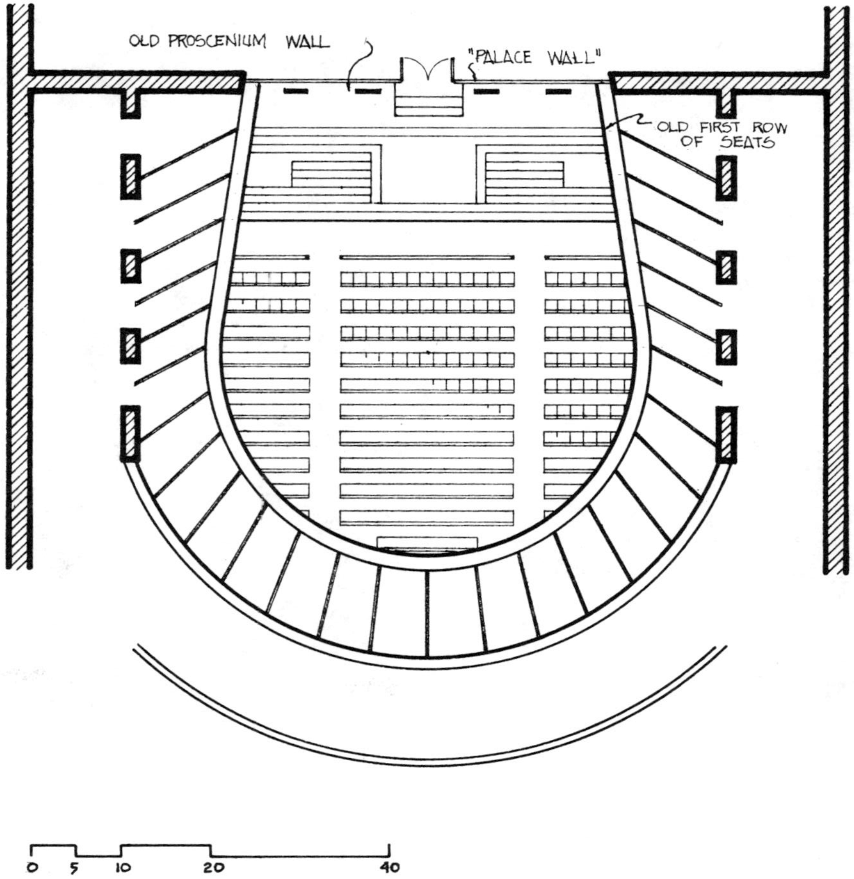

28. Photograph of the apron stage, under construction, for Poel's *Two Gentlemen of Verona* (1910), His Majesty's Theatre. (The white "X" identifies Poel)

29. Photographs of the Palace for *The Winter's Tale* and the Garden for *Twelfth Night* (1912)

30. A drawing of the Garden set, *Twelfth Night* (1912)

31. II.iii of Barker's *Twelfth Night* (1912)

32. Two forest scenes from Barker's *A Midsummer Night's Dream* (1914): the front scene (shown here for II.i) and the full scene (shown here for IV.i)

33. Albert Rutherston's costume design for Leontes in Barker's *The Winter's Tale* (1912)

Appendix

Shakespeare Productions in Greater London and Stratford, 1890-1916

The Productions

These are listed in chronological order, with Stratford festivals listed by month. Dates are either the opening nights of a run or the date of a single performance where specified. The names immediately following the title of the play indicate the actor-manager or company manager responsible for the production, or the lead actor if this more accurately describes the artistic integrity of the production; for example, Tree's *Winter's Tale* (150) is credited to Tree, even though he did not appear in the production, while *Romeo and Juliet* and *Hamlet* at the Lyceum in 1908 and 1909 (174 and 183) are credited to Matheson Lang, who "produced," i.e., stage directed, and starred in the productions, even though they were produced under the management of Smith and Carpenter. Guest appearances at the Stratford Festival are noted, and the distinction is made as to whether the actor was appearing with his own company and production or acting with Bensonians in Benson's production. Special matinees are noted. All of William Poel's productions are amateur, as was the reading of *Love's Labour's Lost* by the English Drama Society in 1906 (142). Playreadings by professional actors under the aegis of the British Empire Shakespeare Society (B. E. S. S.) are not listed, as these were too frequent to be documented here. Of Charles Fry's productions, only his 1907 *Troilus and Cressida* (166) is listed, as most of the others were in hired halls in the East End. Suburban theatres listed here include the Coronet Notting Hill, Fulham and Kennington. The Court theatre in Sloane square was, and remains, on the fringe between the West End and the suburbs, so the status of productions there is variable. Revivals of London productions, particularly during Shakespeare Festivals, are cross-indexed to early runs.

Documentation

The promptbooks enumerated in this list are those which have been consulted for this study. The numbers refer to the listings in Charles Shattuck's *The Shakespeare Promptbooks*, which includes information regarding location and availability. Additions or corrections to Shattuck are noted (e.g., 261, 278). The Beerbohm Tree promptbooks located by Shattuck in the Enthoven collection are now in the Beerbohm Tree Collection, University of Bristol Theatre Collection, and no longer require special permission. Several Benson promptbooks at the Shakespeare Centre Library in Stratford-upon-Avon have been consulted and are not noted in the production list; these include the following:

As You Like It 76-78.
Hamlet 152.
Julius Caesar 77.
Macbeth 127.
The Merchant of Venice 88.
A Midsummer Night's Dream 27.
Othello 89.
Romeo and Juliet 79, 80.
The Taming of the Shrew 42.
Twelfth Night 44.

Promptbooks for several Oscar Asche productions from his South African and Australian tours were consulted; these include:

Antony and Cleopatra 38.
Julius Caesar 73, 74.
The Merchant of Venice 111, 112.

Newspapers and reviews: Reviews consulted for each production are too numerous to list. The reviews in the *Era*, the *Times*, the *Saturday Review*, and the *Illustrated London News* have been consulted for virtually every production between 1895 and 1916. Several archives contain scrapbooks of press-clippings: The Tree Collection at Bristol provided virtually every press notice for the Haymarket and Her/His Majesty's Theatres throughout Tree's management; The Shakespeare Centre holds scrapbooks containing reviews of every production at the Shakespeare Memorial Theatre; and the Harvard Theatre Collection holds Lillah McCarthy's scrapbooks (useful for 244, 245, and 261) and press-clippings from Martin Harvey's later tours, useful for notices of earlier productions still in his repertoire. Harvard provided additional clippings for nos. 87, 139, and 199, and the Theatre Museum (formerly the Enthoven Collection) was consulted for clippings regarding nos. 79, 99, 103, 104, 106, 108 113, 115, 118, 129, 132, 136, 137, 147, 148, 152, 181 and 213.

1890

1.	24 Jan.	Globe	Shr.	Benson
2.	24 Feb.	St. James's	AYL	Lily Langtry, Arthur Bourchier
3.	6 March	Globe	Ham.	Benson
4.	29 March	Lyceum	1H4	Augustin Daly
5.	17 April	Globe	Oth.	Benson
6.	April	Stratford Festival		
			Jn.	Osmond Tearle
			TGV	Osmond Tearle
			Oth.	Osmond Tearle
			Lr.	Osmond Tearle
7.	17 June	Globe	Rom.	Otis Skinner
8.	15 July	Lyceum	AYL	Daly
9.	26 Oct.	Grand	Rom.	Bourchier, William Calvert, Miss Fortescue
10.	18 Nov.	Princess's	Ant.	Langtry

1891

11.	April	Stratford Festival		
			Tmp.	Benson
			Ham.	Benson
			Ado	Benson
12.	18 June	Shaftesbury	AYL	Ben Greet, with Mrs. Patrick Campbell Matinee only (?)

1892

13.	5 Jan.	Lyceum	H8	Irving
14.	21 Jan.	Haymarket	Ham.	Tree. Promptbooks: 118-125
15.	April	Stratford Festival		
			Tim.	Benson
			MND	Benson
			JC	Benson
			TN	Benson
16.	16 April	Olympic	JC	Edmund Tearle
17.	25 Aptil	Olympic	R3	Edmund Tearle
18.	21 May	Olympic	Oth.	Edmund Tearle
19.	10 Nov.	Lyceum	Lr.	Irving. Promptbooks: 95-97

1893

20.	April	Stratford Festival		
			Shr.	Benson
			Rom.	Benson
			Wiv.	Benson
			MV	Benson
			TN	Benson
		summer	Cor.	Benson
21.	27 June	Daly's	Shr.	Daly
22.	3 July	Drury Lane	Ham.	Mounet-Sully (in French)
23.	9, 10, 11 Nov.	Royalty	MM	Poel

1894

24.	8 Jan.	Daly's	TN	Daly
25.	April	Stratford Festival		
			Ado	Benson
			2H4	Benson
			AYL	Benson
			R3	Benson

1895

26.	April	Stratford Festival		
			WT	Greet, with H. B. Irving
			Ado	Greet, with H. B. Irving
			AYL	Greet, with H. B. Irving

198   Appendix

27.	21, 22 June	Burlington Hall	*TN*	Poel
	29 June	St. George's Hall		
28.	2 July	Daly's	*TGV*	Daly
29.	9 July	Daly's	*MND*	Daly
30.	22 July	Lyceum	*Mac.*	Irving, revival of 1888 production
31.	21 Sept.	Lyceum	*Rom.*	Forbes-Robertson
32.	6 Dec	Gray's Inn	*Err.*	Poel
	21 Dec.	St. George's Hall		

1896

33.	April	Stratford Festival		
			R2	Benson
			TN	Benson
			JC	Benson
			Mac.	Benson
			Shr.	Benson
			Ham.	Benson
34.	8 May	Haymarket	*1H4*	Tree. Promptbooks: 43-48
35.	15 May	Prince of Wales's	*Rom.*	Esme and Vera Beringer Charity matinee
36.	22 Sept.	Lyceum	*Cym.*	Irving. Run resumed 26 Dec. without Irving and Terry. Promptbook: 24
37.	28, 30 Nov.	Merchant Taylor's Hall		
	18 Jan.	Great Hall, Charterhouse	*TGV*	Poel
38.	2 Dec.	St. James's	*AYL*	Alexander
39.	19 Dec.	Lyceum	*R3*	Irving replaced after first night. Promptbook: 43

1897

40.	15 Feb.	Middle Temple	*TN*	Poel
41.	April	Stratford Festival		
			H5	Benson
			Wiv.	Benson
			AYL	Benson
			Rom.	Benson
			Tmp.	Benson
			Oth.	Benson
			MV	Benson
			Ado	Benson
			R3	Benson
		summer:	*AYL*	Daly
42.	10 May	Olympic	*Ham.*	Greet
43.	22 May	Lyric	*Oth.*	Wilson Barrett
44.	24 May	Olympic	*Ant.*	Louis Calvert and Janet Achurch. First produced in Manchester.

45.	26 May	Olympic	*MV*	Greet
46.	31 May	Olympic	*Mac.*	Greet
47.	11 August	Her Majesty's	*Ham.*	Tree (See 14)
48.	11 Sept.	Lyceum	*Ham.*	Forbes-Robertson
49.	1 Nov.	Her Majesty's	*Katherine and Petruchio* (Garrick)	Tree. Promptbooks: 36–39
50.	5 Nov.	Egyptian Hall, Mansion House	*Tmp.*	Poel
	13 Nov.	Goldsmith's Hall		
	20 Nov.	St. George's Hall		

1898

51.	22 Jan.	Her Majesty's	*JC*	Tree. Promptbooks: 56–60
52.	16 Feb.	St. James's	*Ado*	Alexander
53.	April	Stratford Festival		
			Ant.	Benson
			JC	Benson
			MV	Benson
			Ham.	Benson
			Shr.	Benson
			Cor.	Benson
			Wiv.	Benson
			TN	Benson
			2H4	Benson
54.	22 August	Fulham	*Oth.*	Frank Cooper, Calvert, Ellen Terry
55.	17 Sept.	Lyceum	*Mac.*	Forbes-Robertson
56.	29 Nov.	St. George's Hall	*MV*	Poel

1899

57.	27 March	Kennington	*MM*	Miss Wallis
58.	April	Stratford Festival		
			2H4	Benson
			Ham.	Benson, uncut
			R3	Benson
			Mac.	Benson
			TN	Benson
			H5	Benson
			MV	Benson
			Wiv.	Benson
			R2	Benson
		summer:	*Ham.*	Sarah Bernhardt (in French)
59.	12 June	Adelphi	*Ham.*	Sarah Bernhardt (in French)
60.	11 Sept.	Kennington	*R3*	Murray Carson
61.	20 Sept.	Her Majesty's	*Jn.*	Tree. Promptbooks: 49–55

200   Appendix

62.	11 Nov.	Lecture Theatre Univ. of London	R2	Poel, with Granville Barker
63.	2 Dec.	Lyric	Oth.	Barrett
64.	9 Dec.	Lyceum	Ham.	Barrett

1900

65.	10 Jan.	Her Majesty's	MND	Tree. Promptbooks: 28-34
66.	13 Feb.	Comedy	AYL	Greet
67.	15 Feb.	Lyceum	H5	Benson
68.	21 Feb.	Carpenter's Hall	Ham. (Q 1)	Poel
69.	22 Feb.	Lyceum	MND	Benson
70.	1 March	Lyceum	Ham.	Benson, uncut
71.	15 March	Lyceum	R2	Benson
72.	22 March	Lyceum	TN	Benson
73.	29 March	Lyceum	Ant.	Benson
74.	5 April	Lyceum	Tmp.	Benson
75.	April	Stratford Festival		
			Per.	Bensonians, without Benson
			AYL	Bensonians, without Benson
			Oth.	Bensonians, without Benson
			Mac.	Bensonians, without Benson
			MV	Bensonians, without Benson
76.	6 Sept.	Her Majesty's	JC	Tree (See 51)
77.	8 Nov.	Court	AYL	
78.	19 Dec.	Comedy	Wiv.	Benson
79.	22 Dec.	Lyceum	H5	Lewis Waller

1901

80.	2 Jan.	Comedy	Shr.	Benson
81.	16 Jan.	Comedy	MV	Benson
82.	5 Feb.	Her Majesty's	TN	Tree. Promptbooks: 46-52
83.	13 Feb.	Comedy	Cor.	Benson
84.	27 Feb.	Comedy	AYL	Benson
85.	13 March.	Comedy	R2	Benson
86.	27 March.	Comedy	Ham.	Benson
87.	15 April	Lyceum	Cor.	Irving. Promptbook: 24
88.	April	Stratford Festival		
			Jn.	Benson
			R2	Benson
			2H4	Benson
			H5	Benson
			2H6	Benson
			R3	Benson
			Ado	Benson
			Wiv.	Benson
			MV	Benson
			AYL	Benson

89.	21 Nov.	Lecture Theatre Univ. of London	H5	Poel

1902

90.	April	Stratford Festival		
			H8	Benson, with Ellen Terry
			TN	Benson
			Oth.	Benson
			Ham.	Benson
			Rom.	Benson
			Lr.	Benson
			Wiv.	Benson
			Shr.	Benson
			H5	Benson
91.	2 June	His Majesty's	TN	Tree (See 82)
92.	10 June	His Majesty's	Wiv.	Tree, with Ellen Terry and Mrs. Kendal. Promptbooks: 58-62
93.	?	His Majesty's	Ham.	Tree (See 14, 47)
94.	?	Lyric	Ham.	Forbes-Robertson, six matinees (See 48)
95.	?	Lyceum	MV	Irving, prior to tour
96.	15 Dec.	Lyric	Oth.	Forbes-Robertson

1903

97.	April	Stratford Festival		
			WT	Benson, with Ellen Terry
			Mac.	Benson
			Wiv.	Benson
			Ham.	Benson
			MND	Benson
98.	23 April	Lecture Theatre Univ. of London	TN	Poel
	16-20 June	Court		
99.	23 May	Imperial	Ado	Ellen Terry, Gordon Craig
100.	?	His Majesty's	Wiv.	Tree (See 92)
101.	14 July	Drury Lane	MV	Irving, Terry, "all star cast," charity matinee
102.	10 Sept.	His Majesty's	R2	Tree. Promptbooks: 26-34
103.	26 Oct.	Court	Tmp.	J. H. Leigh

1904

104.	17 Feb.	Court	Rom.	Leigh
105.	19 March	Court	Ado.	Poel
	22 April	Lecture Theatre Univ. of London		
106.	8 April	Court	TGV	Leigh, directed by Granville Barker

107.	April	Stratford Festival		
			Ham.	Benson
			MV	Benson
			R2	Benson
			WT	Benson
			Wiv.	Benson
			2H4	Benson
			H5	Benson
			Lr.	Benson
			JC	Benson
			AYL	Benson
			TN	Benson
			Shr.	Benson
			Tmp.	Benson
108.	18 May	Court	*Tim.*	Leigh
109.	6 June	His Majesty's	*Wiv.*	Tree (See 92, 100)
110.	7 June	His Majesty's	*TN*	Tree, special matinee. (See 82, 91)
111.	28 June	His Majesty's	*JC*	Tree's "Repertoire Company." (See 51-76)
112.	14 Sept.	His Majesty's	*Tmp.*	Tree. Promptbooks: 36-41
113.	29 Nov.	Adelphi	*Shr.*	Oscar Asche, Otho Stuart. Promptbook: 43
114.	December	Terry's	*Err.*	Poel

1905

115.	21 Jan.	Imperial	*H5*	Waller (See 79)
116.	24 Jan.	His Majesty's	*Ado*	Tree. Promptbooks: 65-72
117.	April	Stratford Festival		
			MV	Benson
			Ado	Benson
			Wiv.	Benson
			TN	Benson
			Err.	Benson
			AYL	Benson
			Shr.	Benson
			Rom.	Benson
			Ham.	Benson
			Oth.	Benson
			Mac.	Benson
			R2	Benson
			1H4	Benson
			2H4	Benson
			H5	Benson
118.	4 April	Adelphi	*Ham.*	Asche/Stuart, with H. B. Irving
119.	8 April	Shaftesbury	*Oth.*	Hubert Carter
120.	22 April	Imperial	*Rom.*	Waller, Promptbook: 83
121.	24 April	His Majesty's	*R2*	Tree (See 102)
122.	25 April	His Majesty's	*Wiv.*	Tree (See 92, 100, 109)

123.	26 April	His Majesty's	*TN*	Tree (See 82, 91, 110)
124.	27 April	His Majesty's	*Ham.*	Tree (See 14, 47, 93) (Matinee 24 March)
125.	28 April	His Majesty's	*Ado*	Tree (See 116)
126.	29 April	His Majesty's	*JC*	Tree (See 51, 76, 111)
127.	5, 6, 9, 11 April	Royalty	*Rom.*	Poel
128.	9, 11 May	Terry's	*MV*	Constance Stuart and Norman Forbes, special matinees
129.	22 May	Lyric	*Ham.*	Martin Harvey
130.	22 May	Drury Lane	*MV*	Irving
131.	4 July	Adelphi	*Err.*	Benson
132.	5 August	Adelphi	*Shr.*	Asche/Stuart, revival prior to tour (See 113)
133.	11 Oct.	Garrick	*MV*	Bourchier
134.	25 Nov.	Adelphi	*MND*	Asche/Stuart
135.	26 Dec.	His Majesty's	*Tmp.*	Tree (See 112)

1906

136.	9 Jan.	St. James's	*AYL*	William Mollison, matinees, then evening
137.	20 March	Adelphi	*MM*	Asche/Stuart. Ellen Terry as Francesca on 28 April. Promptbook: 15
138.	April	Stratford Festival		
			Ado	Benson
			R2	Benson
			2H4	Benson
			1, 2, 3H6	Benson
			R3	Benson
			Ham.	Benson
			JC	Benson
			Mac.	Benson
			MND	Benson
			AYL	Benson
			Lr.	Benson
			Shr.	Benson
		November:	*Mac.*	Bourchier
139.	14 April	Garrick	*MV*	Bourchier
140.	23 April	His Majesty's	*Tmp.*	Tree (See 112, 135)
141.	24 April	His Majesty's	*1H4*	Tree (See 34)
142.	24 April	Bloomsbury Hall	*LLL*	English Drama Society
143.	25 April	His Majesty's	*TN*	Tree (See 82, 91, 110, 123)
144.	26 April (mat. 28 April)	His Majesty's	*Ham.*	Tree (See 14, 47, 93, 124)
145.	27 April	His Majesty's	*Wiv.*	Tree (See 92, 100, 109, 122)
146.	28 April	His Majesty's	*JC*	Tree (See 51, 76, 111, 126)

204 Appendix

147.	17 May	Lyric	*Oth.*	Waller, matinees, then evening. Promptbook: 91
148.	2 June	Adelphi	*Shr.*	Asche/Steart (See 113, 132)
149.	12 June	Drury Lane		Ellen Terry's Jubilee, with a scene from *Ado*. (See 99)
150.	1 Sept.	His Majesty's	*WT*	Produced by Tree, with Ellen Terry. Promptbooks: 34-39
151.	19 Nov.	His Majesty's	*R2*	Tree (See 102, 121)
152.	1 Dec.	Adelphi	*MND*	Asche/Stuart. (See 134)
153.	11 Dec.	Garrick	*Mac.*	Bourchier
154.	27 Dec.	His Majesty's	*Ant.*	Tree. Promptbooks: 21-31

1907

155.	April	Stratford Festival	*LLL*	Benson
			Cor.	Benson
			MV	Bourchier
			H5	Benson
			AYL	Benson
			TN	Benson
			Oth.	Waller (See 147)
			Ado	Henry Ainley and Edith Wynne Matthison with Bensonians
			Shr.	Benson
			R2	Benson
			Ham.	Benson
			Wiv.	Benson
156.	22 April	His Majesty's	*Tmp.*	Tree (See 112, 135, 140)
157.	23 April	His Majesty's	*WT*	Tree (See 150)
158.	24 April 30 May	His Majesty's	*Ham.*	Tree (matinees) (See 14, 47, 93, 124, 144)
159.	24, 27 April	His Majesty's	*TN*	Tree (See 82, 91, 110, 123, 143)
160.	25 April	His Majesty's	*JC*	Tree (See 51, 76, 111, 126, 146)
161.	26 April	Waldorf	*TN*	E. H. Sothern and Julia Marlowe
162.	27 April	His Majesty's	*Wiv.*	Tree (See 92, 100, 109, 122, 145)
163.	29 April	Waldorf	*AYL*	Sothern and Marlowe
164.	1 May	Waldorf	*Ham.*	Sothern and Marlowe
165.	2 May	Waldorf	*Rom.*	Sothern and Marlowe
166.	1 June	Great Queen St.	*Tro.*	Charles Fry
167.	11-15 June	Fulham	*MV*	Poel
168.	7 Oct.	His Majesty's	*AYL*	Asche. Promptbook: 86
169.	7 Nov.	His Majesty's	*Oth.*	Asche (matinees only) Promptbooks: 92-93
170.	12, 19 Dec.	His Majesty's	*Shr.*	Asche (matinees only) (See 113, 132, 148)

1908

171.	10 Feb.	Royalty	*MV*	Ine Cameron
172.	13 Feb.	Royalty	*Rom.*	Cameron
173.	Feb.	Coronet, Notting Hill	*MA*	Benson
			R2	Benson
			2H4	Benson
			Shr.	Benson
174.	14 March	Lyceum	*Rom.*	Matheson Lang and Norah Kerin
175.	4 April	His Majesty's	*MV*	Tree. Promptbooks: 104-111
176.	April	Stratford Festival		
			MND	Benson
			WT	Benson
			R3	Benson
			H5	Waller, then Benson
			Rom.	Ainley, Constance Collier, Bensonians
			Ham.	Forbes-Robertson (See 48, 94)
			MM	Poel
			Ado	Benson
			R2	Benson
			Tmp.	Benson
			Wiv.	Benson
			JC	Benson
			Mac.	Benson
177.	20 April	His Majesty's	*Wiv.*	Tree (See 92, 100, 109, 122, 145, 162)
	30 May			
	21 June			
178.	22 April	His Majesty's	*TN*	Tree (See 82, 91, 110, 123, 143, 159)
179.	24, 25 April	His Majesty's	*Ham.*	Tree (See 14, 47, 93, 124, 144, 158)
180.	22 June	Aldwych	*Shr.*	Asche (See 113, 132, 148, 170)
180.	25 Nov.	Lyric	*H5*	Waller (See 79, 115)

1909

182.	8 Feb.	Shaftesbury	*Ham.*	H. B. Irving
183.	13 March	Lyceum	*Ham.*	Lang
184.	April	Stratford Festival		
			Cym.	Benson
			Ado	Robert Loraine and Bensonians
			Ham.	Lang and Bensonians
			H5	Benson
			R3	Benson
			MV	Ainley, then Benson, Collier
			R2	Benson

206   *Appendix*

			Jn.	Benson
			Wiv.	Benson
			1H4	Waller and Calvert
			TN	Benson
			2H6	Benson
			Shr.	Benson
185.	12 April	Court	AYL	Gerald Lawrence and Fay Davis
186.	19 April	Court	Rom.	Lawrence and Davis
187.	26 April	Court	MV	Lawrence and Davis
188.	3 May	Court	TN	Lawrence and Davis
189.	7 May	Garrick	Mac.	Bourchier (See 153)
190.	11 May	Lyric	1H4	Waller and Calvert
191.	17 May	Court	Ham.	Lawrence and Davis
192.	22-26 June	Fulham	Mac.	Poel
193.	25 June	His Majesty's	TN	Tree (See 82, 91, 110, 123, 143, 159, 178)
194.	26 June	His Majesty's	JC	Tree (See 51, 76, 111, 126, 146, 160)
195.	30 June	His Majesty's	R3	Benson
196.	30 June	His Majesty's	MV	Tree (See 175)
197.	3 July	His Majesty's	Mac.	Bourchier (See 153, 189)
198.	?	His Majesty's	Ham.	Tree (See 14, 47, 93, 124, 144, 158, 179)
199.	8 Sept.	Haymarket	Lr.	Herbert Trench

1910

200.	19 Feb.	Court	MV	Arthur Phillips
201.	21 March	Lyric	Oth.	Giovanni Grasso (in Italian)
202.	28 March	His Majesty's	Wiv.	Tree (See 92, 100, 109, 122, 145, 162, 177)
203.	April	Stratford Festival		
			TGV	Benson
			Ham.	Tree
			Ham.	Harvey
			WT	Benson
			R3	Benson
			TN	Benson
			Ado	Loraine, V. Vanbrugh and Bensonians
			Cor.	Benson
			MV	Ellen Terry and James Carew, with Bensonians
		summer season:	WT	Benson
			JC	Benson
			Mac.	Benson
			TN	Benson
			AYL	Benson
			R2	Benson
			Ham.	Benson, uncut
			H5	Benson
			Wiv.	Benson

204.	2 April	His Majesty's	JC	Tree (See 51, 76, 111, 126, 146, 160, 194)
205.	7 April	His Majesty's	TN	Tree (See 82, 91, 110, 123, 143, 159, 178, 193)
206.	11 April	His Majesty's	Ham.	Tree (See 14, 47, 93, 124, 144, 158, 179, 198)
207.	12 April	His Majesty's	Lr.	Trench (See 199)
208.	13 April	His Majesty's	MV	Bourchier (See 133, 139)
209.	14 April 4 May (matinees)	His Majesty's Queen's	Ham.	H.B. Irving (See 182)
210.	18 April	His Majesty's	Shr.	Benson
211.	19 April	His Majesty's	Cor.	Benson
212.	20 April	His Majesty's	TGV	Poel
213.	21 April	His Majesty's	H5	Waller (See 79, 115, 181)
214.	25 April	His Majesty's	MV	Tree (See 175, 196)
215.	27 April	His Majesty's	R2	Tree (See 102, 121, 151)
216.	29 April	His Majesty's	Gala,	including scenes from Mac. and Rom. (Bourchier) (Ainley and Collier)
217.	28 May	Lyceum	R3	Harvey
218.	1 Sept.	His Majesty's	H8	Tree. Promptbooks: 61-67
219.	23 Sept.	Court	Ado	Rehearsal Company
220.	25 Feb.	Garrick	Wiv.	Asche

1911

221.	April	Stratford Festival		
			Ado	V. Vanbrugh with Bensonians
			Wiv.	Benson
			MV	Nancy Price and Bensonians
			TN	Benson
			H5	Benson
			JC	Ainley and Bensonians
			Mac.	Lang and Bensonians
			Ado	Julia Neilson and Fred Terry
			AYL	Ainley, Lena Ashwell, Bensonians
			Rom.	Waller
			MND	Benson
			R3	Benson
			Ado	Benson
			Oth.	Asche
		summer season:	MND	Benson
			H5	Benson
			R2	Benson
			MV	Collier and Benson
			Rom.	Collier and Bensonians
			AYL	Phyllis Neilson-Terry and Bensonians

208 *Appendix*

			Shr.	Benson
			Ham.	Benson, uncut
			Tmp.	Benson
222.	17 April	His Majesty's	MND	Tree; remounting of 1900 production (See 65)
223.	11 May	New	AYL	Neilson and Terry, with Neilson-Terry. Matinees
224.	22 May	His Majesty's	JC	Tree (See 51, 76, 126, 146, 160, 194, 204)
225.	30 May	His Majesty's	AYL	Asche (See 168)
226.	1 June	His Majesty's	MV	Tree (See 175, 196, 214)
227.	5 June	His Majesty's	TN	Tree (See 82, 91, 110, 123, 143, 159, 178, 193, 205)
228.	6 June	His Majesty's	R3	Benson
229.	9 June	His Majesty's	Shr.	Benson
230.	12 June	His Majesty's	H8	Tree (See 218)
231.	16 June	His Majesty's	JC	Tree. "Coronation Gala," Forum Scene directed by Granville Barker. Promptbook: 64. (See 51, 76, 111, 126, 146, 160, 194, 204, 224)
232.	3 July	His Majesty's	Wiv.	Tree (See 92, 100, 109, 122, 145, 162, 177, 202)
233.	?	His Majesty's	Ham.	H.B. Irving (See 182, 209)
234.	2 Sept.	New	Rom.	Neilson-Terry
235.	5 Sept.	His Majesty's	Mac.	Tree. Promptbooks: 122-125

1912

236.	April	Stratford Festival		
			Ant.	Benson
			MV	Benson
			H5	Benson
			MND	Benson
			Ham.	Benson, uncut
			Rom.	Benson
			Cor.	Benson
			Shr.	Benson and V. Vanbrugh
			JC	Benson
			TN	Benson
			R3	Benson
		summer season:	Oth.	Benson
			H5	Benson
			Ant.	Benson
			MND	Benson
			Wiv.	Benson
237.	9 April	His Majesty's	Oth.	Tree. Promptbooks: 95-100
238.	20 May	His Majesty's	MV	Tree (See 175, 196, 214, 226)

239.	23 May	His Majesty's	*TN*	Tree (See 82, 91, 110, 123, 143, 159, 178, 193, 205, 227)
240.	27 May	His Majesty's	*H8*	Tree (See 218, 230)
241.	1 June	His Majesty's	*Oth.*	Tree (See 237)
242.	4 June	His Majesty's	*JC*	Tree (See 51, 76, 111, 126, 146, 160, 194, 204, 224, 231)
243.	6 June	His Majesty's	*Wiv.*	Tree (See 92, 100, 109, 122, 145, 162, 177, 202, 232)
244.	21 Sept.	Savoy	*WT*	Barker
245.	15 Nov.	Savoy	*TN*	Barker. Promptbook: 80
246.	10 Dec.	King's Hall, Covent Garden	*Tro.*	Poel

1913

247.	9 March	King's Hall Covent Garden	*Ham.*	Pioneer Players, Calvert
248.	22 March	Drury Lane	*Ham.*	Forbes-Robertson (See 48, 94)
249.	22 March	New Prince's	*Rom.*	
250.	April	Stratford Festival		
			2H4	Benson
			R2	Benson
			H5	Benson
			R3	Benson
			Ado	Benson and V. Vanbrugh
			AYL	Benson
			Ham.	Benson
			Tro.	Poel
		summer season:	*AYL*	Benson
			Ham.	Benson
			Jn.	Benson
			R2	Benson
			MV	Benson
			Wiv.	Benson
			Ado	Benson
			Rom.	Benson
			Shr.	Benson
			TN	Benson
			2H4	Benson
251.	29 April	Court	*JC*	Matinee
252.	5 May	Drury Lane	*MV*	Forbes-Robertson
253.	10 May	Prince of Wales's	*Shr.*	Harvey. Promptbook: 58
254.	19 May	Drury Lane	*Oth.*	Forbes-Robertson
255.	9 June	His Majesty's	*MV*	Tree (See 175, 196, 214, 226, 238)
256.	16 June	His Majesty's	*TN*	Tree (See 82, 91, 110, 123, 143, 159, 178, 193, 205, 227, 239)

210 Appendix

257.	23 June	His Majesty's	JC	Tree (See 51, 76, 111, 126, 146, 160, 194, 204, 224, 231, 242)
258.	30 June	His Majesty's	Rom.	Tree, using the Neilson and Terry production (see 234). Promptbooks: 85-86
259.	1 July	Coronet, Notting Hill	Err.	Henry Herbert

1914

260.	27, 29, 30 Jan.	Little	Ham.	Poel
261.	6 Feb.	Savoy	MND	Barker. Promptbook: 35, plus another copy in the Harvard Theatre Collection.
262.	April	Stratford Festival		
			Ado	Patrick Kirwan
			MND	Kirwan
			Err.	Kirwan
			TN	Kirwan
			Ham.	H.B. Irving
			AYL	Lawrence and Davis
			Wiv.	Kirwan
			MV	Bourchier
		summer season:	Ado	Benson
			Ham.	Benson
			R2	Benson
			2H4	Benson
			H5	Benson
			Wiv.	Benson
			MV	Benson
			TN	Benson
			JC	Benson
			AYL	Benson
			Shr.	Benson
			Rom.	Benson
263.	May	Royal Victoria Hall	First season,	including TN, AYL, Ado
264.	14 Nov.	His Majesty's	1H4	Tree (See 34, 141)
265.	16 Nov.	Prince's	MV	Frank Cellier, Florence Glossop-Harris
266.	26 Dec.	Shaftesbury	H5	Benson

1915

267.	April	Stratford Festival		
			JC	Benson
			Rom.	Benson
			Wiv.	Asche
			MV	Benson
			Shr.	Benson

Appendix 211

		summer season:	*Ham.*	Benson
			H5	Benson
			Cor.	Benson
			TN	Benson
			R3	Benson
			Shr.	Benson
			Wiv.	Benson
			Ham.	Benson
			2H4	Benson
			H5	Benson
			R3	Benson
			AYL	Benson
			TN	Benson
			Rom.	Benson
268.	5 July	His Majesty's	*H8*	Tree, charity benefit. (See 218, 230, 240)
269.	6 Dec.	St. James's	*MV*	Lang
270.	20 Dec.	Court	*MND*	Benson
271.	23 Dec.	Duke of York's	*Err.*	Miss Horniman's Company

1916

272.	29 Jan.	Apollo	*Shr.*	Asche (See 113, 132, 148, 170, 180)
273.	April	Stratford Festival		
			H5	Benson
			MV	Benson
			Shr.	Benson
			Jn.	Benson
			Wiv.	Benson
			AWW	Benson
			Ham.	Benson
			2H4	Benson
			MND	Benson
		Tercentenary Matinee: scenes from:	*Ado*	Alexander, I. Vanbrugh
			2H4	Benson
			WT	Ainley, McCarthy
			Ham.	H.B. Irving
			Mac.	Mary Anderson
			Shr.	Asche
		summer season:	*Err.*	Old Vic Company
			Oth.	Old Vic Company
			Ado	Old Vic Company
			Tmp.	Old Vic Compnay
			WT	Old Vic Company
			TGV	Old Vic Company
			Ham.	Old Vic Company
			Mac.	Old Vic Company
			H8	Ellen Terry
			Cor.	Benson

274.	2 May	Drury Lane	*JC*	Tercentenary Performance
275.	8 May	His Majesty's	*Ham.*	Harvey
276.	15 May	His Majesty's	*Shr.*	Harvey (see 253)
277.	22 May	His Majesty's	*R3*	Harvey
278.	29 May	His Majesty's	*H5*	Harvey. The promptbook listed in Shattuck (28) is no longer in the London Museum, but is in the private collection of Mr. Martin Holmes

Notes

Introduction

1. Samuel Hynes, *The Edwardian Turn of Mind* (Princeton: Princeton Univ. Press, 1968), p. vii.

2. See Samuel Hynes, *Edwardian Occasions* (New York: Oxford Univ. Press, 1972), pp. 1-12.

3. Standard accounts of the period include Muriel St. Clare Byrne, "Fifty Years of Shakespearean Production: 1898-1948," *Shakespeare Survey*, 2 (1949), 1-20; Robert Speaight, *Shakespeare on the Stage* (Boston: Little, Brown, 1973); J.L. Styan, *The Shakespeare Revolution* (Cambridge: Cambridge Univ. Press, 1977); and J. C. Trewin, *Shakespeare on the English Stage, 1900-1964* (London: Barrie and Rockliff, 1964).

4. See Robert Speaight, *William Poel and the Elizabethan Revival* (London: Heinemann, 1954); Edward Craig, *Edward Gordon Craig, The Story of His Life* (New York: Knopf, 1968); and C. B. Purdom, *Harley Granville Barker, Man of the Theatre, Dramatist and Scholar* (London: Rockliff, 1955).

5. See Laurence Irving, *Henry Irving, The Actor and His World* (New York: MacMillan, 1952); Roger Manvell, *Ellen Terry* (London: Heinemann, 1968); Hesketh Pearson, *Beerbohm Tree: His Life and Laughter* (London: Methuen, 1956); Madeleine Bingham, *Henry Irving, the Greatest Victorian Actor* (New York: Stein and Day, 1978) and *"The Great Lover," The Life and Art of Herbert Beerbohm Tree* (New York: Atheneum, 1979).

6. John Russell Brown, *Free Shakespeare* (London: Heinemann, 1974).

7. After 1895 he produced only *Cymbeline* (1896), *Richard III* (revival, 1896), and *Coriolanus* (1901).

8. William Archer, *The Theatrical "World" for 1895* (London: Walter Scott, 1896), p. 38 (31 Jan.), and *The Theatrical "World" for 1896* (London: Walter Scott, 1897), p. 204 (8 July). Archer's "ambition stops short of *Troilus and Cressida* . . . and of *Titus Andronicus."*

9. These figures are derived from the productions listed in the appendix. The 1890-1899 figures do not include special matinees and suburban runs of touring companies, nor do they include Tree's production of Garrick's *Katherine and Petruchio*. If one considers full-scale revivals of productions as separate productions, the number rises from 29 to 32. The figures for 1900-1909 do not include special matinees or suburban performances, but do include productions at the Court Theatre in Sloane Square. Counting major revivals (outside of the Shakespeare Festivals) as separate productions, the number rises from 63 to 79 productions.

10. In 1910, Tree expanded his festival even further to include a larger number of visiting productions by other managers.

11. *Two Gentlemen:* Augustin Daly (1895), J. H. Leigh (1904, Poel at Tree's Shakespeare Festival, 1910). *The Tempest:* Benson (1900), Leigh (1903), Tree (1904, revived 1905, 1906,

1907). *Coriolanus:* Benson (1901, 1910), Irving (1901). *Timon of Athens:* Leigh (1904). *Richard II:* Benson (1900, 1901), Tree (1903, revived 1905, 1906, 1907, 1910). *1 Henry IV:* Benson (1908). *The Comedy of Errors:* Benson (1905). *Love's Labour's Lost:* Amateur (1906). *Troilus and Cressida:* Fry (1907), Poel (1912).

Chapter 1

1. The traditional stagecraft has rarely been discussed as a coherent aesthetic system. J. L. Styan gives cursory treatment to it in a chapter entitled "Victorian Shakespeare" in *The Shakespeare Revolution* (Cambridge: Cambridge Univ. Press, 1977, pp. 11-29). Michael Booth's *The Victorian Spectacular Theatre, 1850-1910* (Boston: Routledge & Kegan Paul, 1981) was not available when this book went to press.

2. William Telbin, "Art in the Theatre: The Question of Reform," *The Magazine of Art,* 17 (1894), 48.

3. *Era,* 16 March 1912. Barnes's emphasis.

4. E. W. Godwin, in the *Western Daily Press,* 11 Oct. 1864, quoted in John Stokes, *Resistible Theatres: Enterprise and Experiment in the Late Nineteenth Century* (London: Paul Elek, 1972), p. 37.

5. See William Gillette, "The Illusion of the First Time in Acting," in *Papers on Acting,* ed. Brander Matthews (1915; rpt. New York: Hill and Wang, 1958), pp. 115-35.

6. Oscar Wilde, "The Truth of Masks" (1891), in *The Artist as Critic,* ed. Richard Ellmann (New York: Vintage, 1968), p. 420-21.

7. Henry Irving, "Four Great Actors," *The Drama* (New York: Tait, 1893), p. 131. Irving's emphasis.

8. Alfred Darbyshire, *The Art of the Victorian Stage* (London: Sherratt and Hughes, 1907), p. 8.

9. Ibid, p. 10.

10. William Archer, "Art in the Theatre: The Limitations of Scenery," *The Magazine of Art,* 19 (1896), 432; see also Georg Brandes, letter to Huntly Carter, 15 March 1911, Shakespeare Centre Library, Stratford-upon-Avon: "Shakespeare . . . always had the scene before his eyes."

11. Another early example of this device can be found in Mary Anderson's 1884 *Romeo and Juliet,* in New York at least, which employed "revolving sets" that "turned inside out" the Friar's cell and Juliet's chamber before the audience's eyes. (G. C. O. Odell, *Shakespeare from Betterton to Irving;* 1920 [rpt. New York: Dover, 1966], II, 399).

12. *Telegraph,* 28 Dec. 1906, quoted in Muriel St. Clare Byrne, Notes on the Illustrations to *Prefaces to Shakespeare,* by Harley Granville-Barker (1946; rpt. in 4 vols., Princeton: Princeton Univ. Press, 1965), III, 250.

13. Odell, II, 399.

14. Gordon Crosse, *Shakespearean Playgoing 1890-1952* (London: A. W. Mowbray, 1953), p. 40.

15. Sir Kenneth R. Barnes, *Welcome, Good Friends* (London: Peter Davies, 1958), p. 131.

16. W. Bridges-Adams, "The Irving Inheritance," in *A Bridges-Adams Letter Book,* ed. Robert Speaight (London: Society for Theatre Research, 1971), p. 104. Madeleine Bing-

ham describes a similar moment in Tree's *Oliver Twist* (1905), in which Fagin watches the offstage murder of Nancy, in *"The Great Lover," The Life and Art of Herbert Beerbohm Tree* (New York: Atheneum, 1979), p. 141.

17. In J. A. Hammerton, ed., *The Actor's Art* (London: George Redway, 1897), p. 213.
18. Herbert Beerbohm Tree, *Thoughts and Afterthoughts* (London: Cassell, 1915), p. 213.
19. Ibid., p. 58.
20. See, for example, Max Beerbohm, *More Theatres* (New York, Taplinger, 1969), pp. 230-31 (the review originally published 20 Jan. 1900).
21. George Bernard Shaw, *Our Theatres in the Nineties* (London: Constable, 1932), I, 189 (20 July 1895).
22. Odell, II, 421.
23. Percy Fitzgerald, *Shakespearean Representation, its Laws and Limits* (London: Elliot Stock, 1908), p. 65.
24. A. B. Walkley, *Playhouse Impressions* (London: T. Fisher Unwin, 1892), p. 16.
25. All references to programs and promptbooks for Tree productions are to material housed in the Beerbohm Tree Collection, Univ. of Bristol Theatre Collection, unless otherwise noted. All other programs are housed in the Theatre Museum. Other promptbooks consulted can be located in Charles Shattuck, *The Shakespeare Promptbooks: A Descriptive Bibliography* (Urbana: Univ. of Illinois Press, 1965), as noted in the Appendix.
26. *Era*, 29 Sept. 1915.
27. *Stage*, undated clipping in Harvard Theatre Collection.
28. *Referee*, 15 Oct. 1905. Gillette had planned to produce *Hamlet* in London, as described at length in Georg W. Schuttler, "Sherlock Holmes as Hamlet?" *Theatre Survey* 18 (1977), 72-85.
29. Interview in *Daily Telegraph*, 4 Oct. 1905.
30. *Era*, 13 Jan. 1906.
31. Letters from Shaw to Ellen Terry, 23 Sept. 1896, 25 Sept. 1896, *Collected Letters*, ed. Dan H. Laurence (New York: Dodd, Mead, 1972), II, 666-67.
32. Shaw, *Our Theatres in the Nineties*, II, (26 Sept. 1896).
33. Letters from Shaw to Terry, 27 July 1897, *Collected Letters*, II, 789.
34. Ibid. See also "The Religion of the Pianoforte," *Fortnightly Review*, 55 (1894), 256.
35. Shaw, *Our Theatres in the Nineties*, III, 207 (2 Oct. 1897).
36. *Era*, 4 April 1908.
37. See Joseph W. Donohue, Jr., *Dramatic Character in the English Romantic Age* (Princeton: Princeton Univ. Press, 1970), pp. 248-49.
38. Ellen Terry, "Stage Decoration," *Windsor Magazine*, 35, No. 204 (Dec. 1911), 90.
39. Sir George Arthur, *From Phelps to Gielgud* (London: Chapman and Hall, 1936), p. 85.
40. *Era*, 22 Oct. 1910.

41. Terry, "Stage Decoration," p. 89.
42. Percy Cross Standing, *Sir Lawrence Alma-Tadema, O.M., R.A.* (London: Cassell, 1905), pp. 93-94.
43. Sir John Martin-Harvey, *The Autobiography of Sir John Martin-Harvey* (London: Sampson, Low and Marston, n.d.), p. 309.
44. Tom Heslewood, "Some Memories of Irving," *Drama*, 10 (1938), 88.
45. Laurence Irving, *The Precarious Crust* (London: Chatto and Windus, 1971), p. 57. Graham Robertson, the actor, author and designer, describes Irving's effects: "At the Lyceum there was no heedless extravagance, no pomp and circumstance for their own sakes. All was suggestion, preparing the mind, through the eye, to receive the great actor's interpretation.... Everything at the Lyceum was *Maya*—illusion; the master spirit that had contrived all impressed its will upon us and made us see and hear what it pleased." (W. Graham Robertson, *Time Was* [London: Hamish Hamilton, 1931], p. 272).
46. Bram Stoker, "Irving and Stage Lighting," *Nineteenth Century*, 69 (1911), 903.
47. Gordon Craig writes: "I suppose few actors have acted in darker scenes than Irving. At the Lyceum the lights were often turned very low. It was from Irving that I learnt to plunge my scenes in a good deal too much gloom—but the fault must not be laid at his door."(Edward Gordon Craig, *Henry Irving* [London: J. M. Dent, 1930], p. 117).
48. Harvey, *Autobiography*, p. 466.
49. Johnston Forbes-Robertson, "The Theatre of Yesterday, To-Day and To-Morrow," *Century Magazine*, 87 (1914), 510.
50. Charles Ricketts, *Pages on Art* (London, Constable, 1913), p. 232.
51. Bridges-Adams, letter to John Moore, 31 Jan. 1962, in *The Bridges-Adams Letter Book*, p. 15.
52. Ibid. Perch limes were individually controlled spotlights mounted at an elevation within either side of the proscenium arch.
53. Darbyshire, *Art of the Victorian Stage*, p. 3-4. Darbyshire's emphasis.
54. Ibid., p. 74.
55. Ibid., p. 105.
56. Quoted in Robert Speaight, *William Poel and the Elizabethan Revival* (London: Heinemann, 1954), p. 107.
57. William Archer, *Play-Making, a Manual of Craftsmanship*, 2nd ed. (London: Chapman and Hall, 1913), p. 192.
58. See Beerbohm, *More Theatres*, p. 349.
59. The Forum scene of Frank Benson's *Julius Caesar* ended with a spectacular view of Caesar's corpse afire on a funeral pyre, a picture stolen by Tree in his 1898 production. In Tree's production, Caesar's body was solemnly carried off by soldiers after Antony's lamentation (act 3, sc. 1). Asche's touring production of the same play ends with Brutus, played by Asche, carried aloft on the shoulders of the Roman soldiers in a picture after the curtain has first fallen. And Benson's *Macbeth* ends, after the first curtain, with the picture of the victorious Malcolm borne aloft on the shields of his men.

Notes for Chapter 1   217

60. In Tree's *Julius Caesar* (1898), curtain business is used to increase the sense of impending doom: as Caesar exits to the Senate and his death after confronting the Soothsayer for the second time, some girls throw flowers before him, which startle him with their resemblance to blood (see the *Era,* 22 Jan. 1898). Before the third day of the battle in Asche's *Antony and Cleopatra,* Antony encounters the Soothsayer, hovering about the throne and glaring at him. Tree replaces the dialogue between the Lancastrian nobles after Gaunt's death in *Richard II* (1903) with an interpolated sequence: after the King exits, the curtains of an alcove upstage part to reveal the corpse laid out, arrayed with candles, with the nobles around it; as described in the promptbook:

> as [Percy] speaks the line "and living too," etc. Ross says enthusiastically "Bolingbroke". Northumberland, correcting him, says "Lancaster! Long live the Duke of Lancaster!" They all draw their swords, raising them over the bed as they shout in a fervent undertone [!] "Long live the Duke of Lancaster." As they stand the organ is heard, and monks chanting; they drop their swords and cross themselves. As they do so, the music swells out loudly and the curtain falls.
>
> For 2nd PICTURE, they are discovered shaking hands across the bed—organ swelling out still more.

And, in Benson's *Hamlet,* the curtain rises after the second act to reveal Hamlet busily writing the insertion into *The Murder of Gonzago.*

61. In Benson's *Richard II,* Bolingbroke and the court exit before Richard in the deposition to leave him alone for an indicative and memorable picture: "The orchestra asserts itself in some clearly defined rhythms, and Richard, who stands apart, self-absorbed and momentarily imbecile, vacantly beats time with his forefinger to the music as the curtain falls "(*Sketch,* 17 March 1897). An interpolation at the end of act 1, scene 3 of Tree's *Merchant of Venice* (1908) shows the character of Shylock as he normally does not let the Christians see him: "Shylock comes from his hiding place, to front of bridge wall, and in the red glow of the deep sunset is seen to spit out after Antonio, as the *Curtain Falls.*" In the Stratford version of Lewis Waller's *Othello* (1907), Iago remains onstage after the stage has been cleared following Roderigo's murder; the promptbook records that Iago "thrusts his dagger deep in Rod's body—draws it out—wipes it on Rod's vest—laughs loudly—*curtain.*" This business is identical to that of Benson, recorded on film, when Richard of Gloucester has murdered Henry VI in the tower.

62. Lucius, played by Mrs. Tree, was part of the crowd at the end of Tree's *Julius Caesar,* come to mourn for her former master. In Bourchier's *Macbeth* (1906), Fleance reentered to weep beside his father's body (*Era* 15 Dec. 1906). In Matheson Lang's *Hamlet* (1909), the Prince returned to Ophelia's graveside to shed an extra tear; and when Tree brought his production to Stratford the following year, Laertes, played by local favorite Henry Ainley, returned to the graveside instead and reverently kissed a handful of the dirt which was soon to cover his sister's remains (*Era,* 20 March 1909; *Birmingham Gazette,* 23 April 1910).

63. Max Beerbohm, *Last Theatres* (New York: Taplinger, 1970), p. 357 (21 March 1908).

64. Quoted in Fitzgerald, *Shakespearean Representation,* p. 79, note.

65. Crosse, *Shakespearean Playgoing,* p. 41.

66. *Era,* 30 July 1910.

67. Richard Foulkes, "Herbert Beerbohm Tree's *King Henry VIII:* Expenditure, Spectacle and Experiment," *Theatre Research International,* 3 (1977), 29-30.

68. Richard Flanagan, who filled the stages of his annual Manchester Shakespeare revivals with live animals, including deer in *As You Like It* and pigeons, goats and a live bear in *The Winter's Tale*, was particularly guilty of unjustified interpolations. The church scene in *Much Ado About Nothing* came to a halt to make way for a second church scene and the singing of a Palestrina mass; C. E. Montague objected, but conceded that "the managers probably know their business better than we, and as they seem to think that people will not have Shakespeare without these interruptions there is nothing for us but to suffer the interruptions as gladly as one can" (W. T. Arnold, *The Manchester Stage: 1880-1900* [Westminster: Constable, 1900], p. 109). Flanagan loved church scenes and their attendant ceremonies: *Twelfth Night* ended with a spectacular church tableau with the marriage of Viola and Orsino, and *Romeo and Juliet* ended with a tableau of San Zeno Maggiore with the lovers lying in state and their respective families ceremonially reconciled (*Era*, 21 Jan. 1905). Tree, needless to say, was one of the worst offenders within this tradition: the advance publicity for his 1899 *Midsummer Night's Dream* explained that "There will be no ballet in the ordinary sense of the word, for that, indeed, Mr. Tree holds would be a desecration of Shakespeare, but there will be certain gambols of the elves and fairies just as long as Mendelssohn's music demands" (*Era*, 23 Dec. 1899). Tree was not so coy in his 1911 restaging of the production, which boasted "a ballet danced by seventy-five children, and symbolising, the 'Triumph of Light over Darkness' " (*Era*, 8 April 1911). Similarly, the Masque in *The Tempest* (1904) was expanded into an allegory of Cupid and his dart.

69. The Masque in *The Tempest* had some Shakespearean license, as Tree was sure to remind his critics. When George Alexander produced *As You Like It* (1896), he shied away from Graham Robertson's suggestion that he restore the appearance of Hymen at the end, with crimsom robed cupids on peacock wings and Hymen dressed in gold. Alexander complained, "They'll say I've been monkeying with Shakespeare. . . . We ought not to risk it." Robertson pacified him by suggesting that they submit to the papers a notice saying that they were courageously restoring "The Masque of Hymen, usually omitted in representation" (Robertson, *Time Was*, p. 262). Archer nevertheless complained that the Masque had become "an elaborate Drury Lane ballet instead of the simplest piece of rustic mumming it ought to be" (William Archer, *The Theatrical "World" for 1896* [London: Walter Scott, 1897], p. 331, 9 Dec.). Tree was the greatest pageant master of his generation, and he cited authorial intention in his defense: "Shakespeare was a pageant master, as Ben Johnson was," said Tree in a speech in 1909 (*Era*, 3 July 1909). For *Henry VIII* (1910) he employed Louis N. Parker, a playwright in his stable who was also a popular Edwardian pageant master, to arrange the processions. Tree used his production of the play, employing the talents of his fellow actor-managers Arthur Bourchier and Violet Vanbrugh, as an assertion of his right to call His Majesty's Theatre a National Theatre. His selection of *Henry VIII* further suggests that he was asserting the importance of pageantry as a legitimate adjunct of the Shakespearean drama, and he cited Elizabethan precedent, including the burning of the Globe, in his favor. Always quick to turn incidentals into assertions, Tree claimed that the apron stage, which had been installed for Poel's *Two Gentlemen of Verona*, was an Elizabethan device particularly designed for the purpose: the promotional material speciously claimed that, " 'Henry VIII' being so much in the nature of a pageant, Sir Herbert has determined to adopt the olden-time arrangement of the 'apron' stage" (*Era*, 6 Aug. 1910).

70. Additional details can be found in Tree's rough draft for the note in the margins of his preparation copy of the play, listed in Charles Shattuck, *The Shakespeare Promptbooks* (Urbana: Univ. of Illinois Press, 1965), as *Richard II*, no. 26.

71. *Era*, 2 Dec. 1899.

72. Richard Dickins, *Forty Years of Shakespeare on the English Stage* (London: privately printed, 1907), p. 110.
73. Shaw, *Our Theatres in the Nineties,* III, 52 (20 Feb. 1897).
74. Beerbohm, *Last Theatres,* p. 520-21 (8 June 1910).
75. See Michael Mullin, "Strange Images of Death: Sir Herbert Beerbohm Tree's *Macbeth,* 1911," *Theatre Survey,* 17 (1976), p. 135.
76. Laurence Senelick, "The Craig-Stanislavsky *Hamlet* at the Moscow Art Theatre," *Theatre Quarterly,* 6 (1976), p. 121.
77. Viola Tree, "My Father," in *Herbert Beerbohm Tree; Some Memories of Him and of his Art,* ed. Max Beerbohm (London, 1920; rpt. New York: Benjamin Blom, 1969), p. 176.
78. Matheson Lang, *Mr. Wu Looks Back* (London: Stanley Paul, 1940), p. 82.
79. *Julius Caesar* program. Tree used a similar argument in defense of his arrangements of several other plays. His three-act division of *The Tempest* "comes much nearer to the system which prevailed in Shakespeare's own time, when scenes and acts followed each other in swift succession" (*Thoughts and Afterthoughts,* p. 214); *King John* was "full of action and movement, and the story will be told concisely and chronologically" (*Era,* 19 Aug. 1899); *Twelfth Night,* which he claimed to present with "no undue elaboration of scenery" (!), fulfilled his plan "to follow out Shakespeare's own intention, and to present this fantastic effort in as complete and natural a form as possible" (*Era,* 19 Jan. 1901); and *Macbeth,* when it was first announced in 1906, was to be presented with "absolute simplicity . . . and strength" (*Era,* 29 Sept. 1906).
80. Tree, *Thoughts and Afterthoughts,* p. 53.
81. Dickins, *Forty Years of Shakespeare on the English Stage,* p. 136.
82. Lou Warwick, *The Mackenzies Called Compton* (Northampton: self-published, 1977), p. 163.
83. From miscellaneous productions logs, Tree Collection, University of Bristol Theatre Collection.
84. List of "Scenery in Store, 1906," Shakespeare Centre Library, Stratford-upon-Avon.
85. Winifred F. E. C. Isaac, *Ben Greet and the Old Vic* (London: self-published, 1964), p. 132.
86. William Poel, *Monthly Letters,* ed. A. M. T[rethwey] (London: T. Werner Laurie, 1929), p. 81.
87. William Archer and Granville Barker, *A National Theatre: Schemes and Estimates* (London: Duckworth, 1907), pp. 72-73.
88. W. A. S. Benson, " 'Agamemnon' at Oxford," *Cornhill Magazine,* NS 46 (1919), 543.
89. See Shaw, *Our Theatres in the Nineties,* I, 170-77 (6 July 1895).
90. Dickins, *Forty Years of Shakespeare on the Enlgish Stage,* pp. 8, 91.
91. *Era,* 4 March 1911.
92. William Archer, "The Elizabethan Stage," *Quarterly Review,* 208 (1908), 448-49.
93. Ellen Terry, *Ellen Terry's Memoirs,* ed. Edith Craig and Christopher St. John (New York: Putnam, 1932), p. 134; Odell, II, 438.

94. W. J. Lawrence, "Art in the Theatre: Scenery on Tour," *The Magazine of Art*, 19 (1896), 479.
95. Ibid.
96. William Archer, *The Theatrical "World" for 1897* (London: Walter Scott, 1898), p. 186 (30 June).
97. B. Iden Payne, *A Life in a Wooden O* (New Haven: Yale Univ. Press, 1977), p. 103.
98. Archer, "The Elizabethan Stage," p. 449.
99. Stoker, "Irving and Stage Lighting," p. 907.
100. Lawrence, "Scenery on tour," p. 479.
101. *Era*, 24 Sept. 1898.
102. *Era*, 13 Jan. 1900.
103. Archer, *Playmaking*, p. 108, note.
104. Fitzgerald, *Shakespearean Representation*, p. 113.
105. Sybil Rosenfeld, "Alma Tadema's Designs for Henry Irving's *Coriolanus*," *Shakespeare Jahrbuch 1974*, p. 91.
106. *Era*, 29 Dec. 1900.
107. Most of Shaw's opinion on this production can be found in "The Dying Tongue of Great Elizabeth," *Saturday Review*, 11 Feb., 1905 (rpt. London: London Shakespeare League, 1920).
108. A. B. Walkley, *Drama and Life* (New York: Brentano's 1908), p. 173.
109. *Era*, 27 Jan. 1900.
110. Terry, "Stage Decoration," p. 80.
111. Shaw, *Our Theatres in the Nineties*, II, 184 (11 July 1896).
112. Ibid., 212-13 (10 Oct. 1896).
113. Albert Rutherston, "Decoration in the Art of the Theatre," *Monthly Chapbook*, 1, No. 2 (Aug. 1919), 18.
114. Harvey, *Autobiography*, p. 405. Harvey's emphasis.
115. Joseph Harker, *Studio and Stage* (London: Nisbet, 1924), pp. 196, 218.
116. Rutherston, "Decoration in the Art of the Theatre," p. 15.
117. William Poel, *Shakespeare in the Theatre* (London: Sidgwick and Jackson, 1913), p. 222.
118. In Harker, *Studio and Stage*, p. 186.
119. Terry, "Stage Decoration," p. 78.
120. Lawrence, "Scenery on Tour," p. 476.
121. R. Phené Spiers, "The Architecture of *Coriolanus* at the Lyceum Theatre," *Architectural Review*, 10, no. 56 (July 1901), 3-4.
122. In Harker, *Studio and Stage*, p. 209.

123. Ibid., p. 190.
124. Ibid., p. 208.
125. Odell, II, 438.
126. Terry, *Memoirs*, p. 134.
127. *Era*, 9 Feb. 1901.
128. Mario Borsa, *The English Theatre of To-day*, trans. Selwyn Brinton (London: John Lane, 1908), pp. 187-88.

Chapter 2

1. J.L. Styan, *The Shakespeare Revolution* (Cambridge: Cambridge Univ. Press. 1977), chaps. 2-4. See in particular pp. 40-75.
2. Herbert Beerbohm Tree, *Thoughts and Afterthoughts* (London: Cassell, 1915), p. 60.
3. Ibid., p. 305.
4. Arthur Bourchier, *Some Reflections on the Drama—and Shakespeare* (Oxford: B. H. Blackwell, 1911), p. 40.
5. William Archer, *About the Theatre* (London: T. Fisher Unwin, 1886), p. 244.
6. E. K. Chambers, "The Stage of the Globe," in *The Works of Shakespeare* (Stratford-upon-Avon: Shakespeare Head Press, 1907), 10, 353.
7. Henry Arthur Jones, "Dr. Pearson on the Modern Drama," *Nineteenth Century*, 34 (1893), 545-46.
8. Sidney Lee, *Shakespeare's Henry V, An Account and an Estimate* (London: Smith, Elder, 1900), n. pag.
9. Sidney Lee, "Shakespeare and the Modern Stage," *Nineteenth Century*, 47 (1900), 155; reprinted in revised form in *Shakespeare and the Modern Stage* (London: John Murray, 1906).
10. Harley Granville-Barker, "From *Henry V* to *Hamlet*" (1925), in *More Prefaces to Shakespeare*, ed. Edward M. Moore (Princeton: Princeton Univ. Press, 1974), p. 144.
11. Harley Granville-Barker, *Prefaces to Shakespeare* (1946; rpt. in 4 vols., Princeton: Princeton Univ. Press, 1965), I, 7.
12. Edward Gordon Craig, in "Modern Scenic Art," *The Stage Yearbook 1914*, p. 21.
13. Barker, "Introduction to *The Player's Shakespeare*" (1923), in *More Prefaces*, p. 58.
14. Barker, *Prefaces*, I, 2.
15. In Joseph Harker, *Studio and Stage* (London: Nisbet, 1924), p. 188.
16. Sir John Martin-Harvey, *The Autobiography of Sir John Martin-Harvey* (London: Sampson, Low and Marston, n.d.), p. 340.
17. William Poel, Letter, *Nation*, 12 July 1913, p. 571.
18. London Shakespeare League, *Report of a Public Discussion on the Best Method of Presenting Shakespeare's Plays, held at the Guildhall School of Music, London (by kind permission), on Tuesday, October 24th, 1905* (London: Chandos Press, 1905), p. 9.

19. Ibid., p. 5.
20. Max Beerbohm, *Around Theatres* (New York: Taplinger, 1969), p. 258 (20 June 1903).
21. Max Beerbohm, *More Theatres* (New York: Taplinger, 1969), p. 117 (25 Feb. 1899).
22. Ibid., p. 324 (24 November 1900); see also Max Beerbohm, *Last Theatres* (New York: Taplinger, 1970), p. 61 (4 June 1904).
23. William Archer, rev. of *Shakespeare in the Theatre*, by William Poel, *Nation*, 5 July 1913, p. 535.
24. William Archer, "A Sixteenth Century Playhouse," *Universal Review*, 1 (1888), 281-88.
25. William Archer, *The Theatrical "World" for 1894* (London: Walter Scott, 1895), p. 25 (17 Jan.).
26. William Archer, *The Theatrical "World" for 1895* (London: Walter Scott, 1896), p. 222 (27 June).
27. In Poel, "Shakespeare's Profession," *Journal of the Royal Society of Arts*, 63 (1915), 336.
28. Shakespeare League, *Report of Public Discussion*, p. 17.
29. William Poel, *Shakespeare in the Theatre* (London: Sidgwick and Jackson, 1913), p. 9.
30. William Poel, *Some Notes on Shakespeare's Stage and Plays* (Manchester: University Press, 1916), p. 11.
31. Styan, *The Shakespeare Revolution* pp. 50-51.
32. *Daily Chronicle*, 3 Sept. 1913, quoted in Robert Speaight, *William Poel and the Elizabethan Revival* (London: Heinemann, 1954), p. 90.
33. *Daily Telegraph*, quoted in Felix Felton, "Max Reinhardt in England," *Theatre Research*, 5 (1963), 137.
34. George Bernard Shaw, *Our Theatres in the Nineties* (London: Constable, 1932), III, 362 (16 April 1898).
35. William Poel, *Monthly Letters*, ed. A.M. T[rethwey] (London: T. Werner Laurie, 1929), p. 47.
36. Poel, *Shakespeare in the Theatre*, p. 179.
37. Veronica Turleigh, in Barry Jackson's file on William Poel in the Shakespeare Centre Library, Stratford-upon-Avon.
38. *Notes on Some of William Poel's Productions* (London: A.W. Patching, 1933), n. pag.
39. Ibid.
40. Poel, *Shakespeare in the Theatre*, p. 49.
41. William Poel, "Poetry in Drama," *The Mask*, 13 (1927), 705; Poel, *Shakespeare in the Theatre*, p. 59.
42. W.J. Lawrence, *The Elizabethan Playhouse and Other Studies*, II (1913; rpt. New York: Russell and Russell, 1963), pp. 151-52.
43. William Poel, "A Symposium on the Representation of Shakespeare," ed. Huntly Carter, *New Age*, 8 (1911), 250.

Notes for Chapter 2   223

44. William Poel, "Shakespeare's Prompt Copies. A Plea for Early Texts," *Times Literary Supplement,* 3 Feb. 1921.

45. William Poel, "Shakespeare's Prompt-Books," *Times Literary Supplement,* 4 Aug. 1921; William Poel, "The Stage in Shakespeare's Day," *National Review,* 15 (1890), 783.

46. William Poel, "Shakespeare's Promptbooks," *Times Literary Supplement,* 18 Aug. 1921.

47. Styan, *The Shakespeare Revolution* pp. 1-2.

48. Books and articles during the Edwardian period on the nature of the Elizabethan stage include: Victor Albright, *The Shaksperian Stage* (New York: Columbia Univ. Press, 1909); William Archer, "The Elizabethan Stage," *Quarterly Review,* 208 (1908), 442-74, "The Fortune Theatre, 1600," *Shakespeare Jahrbuch,* 44 (1908), 159-66, "A Sixteenth Century Playhouse," *Universal Review,* 1 (1888), 281-88, rev. of *Shakespeare in the Theatre,* by William Poel, *Nation,* 5 July 1913, pp. 535-36, and, with Walter H. Godfrey, "An Elizabethan Theatre," *Architectural Review,* 23 (1908), 239-44; George Pierce Baker, " 'Hamlet' on an Elizabethan Stage," *Shakespeare Jahrbuch,* 41 (1905), 296-301; Cecil Brodmeier, *Die Shakespeare-Bühne nach den alten Buhnenweisungen* (Weimar: Alexander Huschke, 1904); John Corbin, "Shakespeare and the Plastic Stage," *Atlantic Monthly,* 97 (1906), 364-83; Karl Theodor Gaedertz, *Zur Kenntniss der altenglische Bühne* (Bremen: C.E. Muller, 1888); W.J. Lawrence, "Some Characteristics of the Elizabethan-Stuart Stage," *Englische Studien,* 32 (1903), 36-51, *The Elizabethan Playhouse and Other Studies,* 2 vols. (1912 and 1913; rpt. New York: Russell and Russell, 1963); G.F. Reynolds, "What We Know of the Elizabethan Stage," *Modern Philology,* 9 (1911), 47-82. Richard Hosley was the first to trace the sources of apocryphal features of the Elizabethan stage to both "reconstruction origins," i.e. misconceptions inherited from earlier reconstructions, and "non-reconstruction origins," i.e. features of the contemporary theatre which shaped scholarly conceptions of the Elizabethan stage, in "The Origins of the So-called Elizabethan Multiple Stage," *The Drama Review,* 12, no. 2 (Winter, 1968), 28-50. Hosley does not identify the non-reconstruction origins as pertaining to a specifically late-Victorian and Edwardian theatrical framework.

49. Lawrence, *The Elizabethan Playhouse,* II, 67; Albright, *The Shaksperian Stage,* pp. 79 ff. Typical of Albright's methods is his description of the use of curtains on the Elizabethan stage: Albright argues that "we only need substitute the word 'curtain' for 'flats' " and then examine how flats are used on the contemporary melodrama stage. (See Albright, *The Shaksperian Stage,* p. 104). The supposed similarity between Elizabethan curtains and Victorian flats is behind one of Archer's rejections of the methods of the E.S.S.: why bother, Archer asks, to employ curtains at all when "it is as easy to change a scene as to draw a 'traverse' " (*The Theatrical "World" for 1895,* p. 224, 27 June).

50. William Poel, "The Elizabethan Stage," *The Theatre,* 31 (1893), 243.

51. Shaw, *Our Theatres in the Nineties,* I, 25 (2 Feb. 1895); "The Play of Ideas" (1950), in *Shaw on Theatre,* ed. E.J. West (New York, Hill and Wang, 1958), p. 293.

52. See Beerbohm, *More Theatres,* p. 232 (20 Jan. 1900).

53. Reynolds, *Some Principles of Elizabethan Staging,* II, 11.

54. More recently, scholars have been redefining the notion of localization with regard to the Elizabethan stage. For a discussion of the context to which the stage was neutral or localized, see Bernard Beckerman, *Shakespeare at the Globe* (New York, Collier, 1966), pp. 64-69.

Notes for Chapter 2

55. Of the several Elizabethan scholars of the period, only Reynolds appears to have challenged the assumptions underlying this use of the traverse curtains: "There is no indication that the Elizabethans were at all averse to the bringing on of furnishings before them ... the burden of proof is decidedly upon the alternationists when they assume that, because of the modern dislike for such a practice, properties were never used on the front stage" (*Some Principles of Elizabethan Staging*, I, 30). Reynolds is not only questioning the reluctance of his contemporaries to face the conventional theatricality of the Elizabethans, but he is challenging their method of historical argumentation as well.

56. Letter from Shaw to William Armstrong, 26 Sept., quoted in Raymond Mander and Joe Mitchenson, *Theatrical Companion to Shaw* (New York: Pitman, 1955), p. 81.

57. Shaw, *Our Theatres in the Nineties*, III, 242 (13 Nov. 1897). Shaw's emphasis.

58. William Poel, "The Theatre and its Needs," *Times Literary Supplement*, 6 April 1922.

59. Lee, "Shakespeare and the Modern Stage," p. 147.

60. Comments directed to Huntly Carter, quoted in Claris Glick, "William Poel: His Theories and Influence," *Shakespeare Survey*, 15 (1964), 22.

61. William Poel, "On Cutting Shakespeare," *Nation*, 23 Aug. 1919.

62. *Era*, 18 March 1905.

63. *Era*, 5 March 1910.

64. Archer, *The Theatrical "World" for 1895*, p. 114 (14 April).

65. William Archer, "The Limitations of Scenery," *The Magazine of Art*, 19 (1896), 434.

66. Beerbohm, *More Theatres*, p. 347-48 (9 Feb. 1901).

67. Ibid., p. 232 (20 Jan. 1900). Subsequent quotations are from the same source.

68. Articles on Poel include: Sir Lewis Casson, "William Poel and the Modern Theatre," *Listener*, 10 Jan. 1952, pp. 56-58; Claris Glick, "William Poel: His Theories and Influence," *Shakespeare Survey*, 15 (1964), 15-27; E.M. Moore, "William Poel," *Shakespeare Survey*, 23 (1972), 21-36; Stephen C. Schultz, "Two Notes on William Poel's Sources," *Nineteenth Century Theatre Research*, 2 (1974), 85-91, "William Poel on the Speaking of Shakespearean Verse: A Reevaluation," *Shakespeare Quarterly*, 28 (1977), 334-50; and J.A.B. Somerset, "William Poel's First Full Platform Stage," *Theatre Notebook*, 20 (1966), 118-21.

69. Arthur J. Harris, "William Poel's Elizabethan Stage: the First Experiment," *Theatre Notebook*, 17 (1963), 111-14.

70. See George Pierce Baker, "'Hamlet' on an Elizabethan Stage," and B. Iden Payne, *A Life in a Wooden O* (New Haven: Yale Univ. Press, 1977), p. 165.

71. William Archer, *Study and Stage* (London: Grant Richards, 1899), p. 232.

72. Poel, "The Elizabethan Stage," p. 245-46.

73. *Era*, 8 July 1905, 14 Oct. 1905.

74. See Jan MacDonald, "*The Taming of the Shrew* at the Haymarket Theatre, 1844 and 1847," in *Nineteenth Century British Theatre*, ed. Kenneth Richards and Peter Thompson (London: Methuen, 1971), pp. 157-70.

75. Alfred Darbyshire, *The Art of the Victorian Stage* (London: Sherratt and Hughes, 1907), p. 58.

76. Harvey, *Autobiography*, p. 97; Madeleine Bingham, *Henry Irving, The Greatest Victorian Actor* (New York: Stein and Day, 1978), p. 232.

77. Archer, *The Theatrical "World" for 1895*, p. 367; Elizabeth Robins, *Theatre and Friendship* (New York: Putnam, 1932), pp. 58, 61.

78. Payne, *A Life in a Wooden O*, p. 91.

79. William Archer, *The Theatrical "World" for 1897* (London: Walter Scott, 1898), pp. 152-53 (2 June).

80. *Era*, 4 Jan. 1902.

81. Winifred Loraine, *Robert Loraine, Soldier, Actor, Airman* (London: Collins, 1938).

82. Hal Burton, ed., *Great Acting* (London: BBC, 1967), p. 53.

83. In Huntly Carter's file on the staging of Shakespeare, Shakespeare Centre Library, Stratford-upon-Avon.

84. *Era*, 31 Oct. 1903.

85. Beerbohm, *Around Theatres*, p. 294 (7 Nov. 1903).

86. *Era*, 25 March 1905.

87. *Era*, 21 Sept. 1907.

88. Maud Tree, "Herbert and I," in *Herbert Beerbohm Tree; Some Memories of Him and his Art*, ed. Max Beerbohm (London, 1920; rpt. New York: Benjamin Blom, 1969), p. 124.

89. Huntly Carter, *The Theatre of Max Reinhardt* (London: 1914; rpt. New York: Benjamin Blom, 1964), p. 275.

90. *Era*, 27 March 1909.

91. *Era*, 16 April 1910, 15 March 1913.

92. Austin Brereton, *"H.B." and Laurence Irving* (London: Grant Richards, 1922), p. 189.

93. Letter from Andrew Leigh in Jackson's Poel file, Shakespeare Centre Library, Stratford-upon-Avon.

94. *Era*, 9 Sept. 1911.

95. Percy Fitzgerald, in "A Symposium on the Representation of Shakespeare," p. 250.

96. *The Mask*, 1, No. 12 (Feb. 1909).

97. Edward Gordon Craig, *Towards a New Theatre* (London: J.M. Dent, 1913), p. 83.

98. Poel, in "Symposium," p. 250.

99. According to Barry Jackson in his Poel file at the Shakespeare Centre Library, a program exists for this production at the Birmingham Reference Library.

100. *Era*, 22 June 1912.

101. *Birmingham Daily Post*, 23 April 1914.

102. *Standard*, 20 April 1914.

103. *Stratford-on-Avon Herald*, 17 April 1914.

104. *Sunday Times*, 12 April 1914.

105. *Era*, 15 April 1914.
106. *Daily Citizen*, 13 April 1914.
107. Harvey, *Autobiography*, p. 412.
108. These curtains are described by Huntly Carter in *Max Reinhardt*, pp. 260-63.
109. Carter, *Max Reinhardt*, p. 263.
110. Harvey, *Autobiography*, p. 413.
111. Charles Shattuck, in *The Shakespeare Promptbooks* (Urbana: Univ. of Illinois Press, 1965) notes that the promptbook for this production is "accompanied by [a] separate book of notes by Alfred Rodway containing also sketches, prints, watercolors of costumes, arms, etc." These materials are no longer in the London Museum, but are in the private collection of Mr. Martin Holmes.
112. R.N.G.-A., ed., *The Book of Martin Harvey* (London: Henry Walker, n.d.), pp. 59-61.
113. Harvey, *Autobiography*, pp. 467-68.
114. Ibid., p. 468. The fire actually started in the thatched roof.
115. Maurice W. Disher, *The Last Romantic* (London: Hutchinson, 1948), p. 230.
116. Archer, *The Theatrical "World" for 1895*, p. 373.
117. Payne, *A Life in a Wooden O*, p. 94.
118. Edward Mumford Moore, "Changes in Shakespearean Production from the Age of Irving to Granville-Barker," Diss. Harvard 1968, p. 81.
119. Beerbohm, *Last Theatres*, p. 214 (20 Jan. 1906).
120. Cecil J. Sharp, *The Songs and Incidental Music Arranged and Composed by Cecil J. Sharp for Granville Barker's Production of A Midsummer Night's Dream at the Savoy Theatre in January 1914* (London: Simpkin, Marshall, Hamilton, Kent, 1914).
121. Barker, *More Prefaces to Shakespeare*, p. 106-7.
122. Mario Borsa, *The English Theatre of To-day*, trans. Selwyn Brinton (London: John Lane, 1908), pp. 185-86.
123. J.A. Hammerton, ed., *The Actor's Art* (London: George Redway, 1897), p. 60.
124. William Poel, "Hamlet Retold," *Saturday Review*, 17 Jan. 1914, p. 74.

Chapter 3

1. Huntley Carter, *The New Spirit in Drama and Art* (London: Frank Palmer, 1912), p. v.
2. Virginia Woolf, "Mr. Bennett and Mrs. Brown," quoted in Samuel Hynes, *The Edwardian Turn of Mind* (Princeton: Princeton Univ. Press, 1968), p. 385.
3. Craig, for example, felt that the Russian Ballet "stole an idea or two from the only original dancer of the age, the American [i.e., Isadora Duncan], and another idea or two from the most advanced scene designers of Europe and superimposed all these upon the lively framework of the old French ballet,"(*The Mask*, 4[1911-1912], 98). And Albert Rutherston felt that their "employment of Leon Bakst . . . has struck a jarring note of plagiarism and sensational vulgarity," ("Decoration in the Art of the Theatre," *Monthly Chapbook*, 1, No. 2 [August 1919], 24).

Notes for Chapter 3

4. Constance Benson, for example, remarked, in response to the Nigel Playfair/Lovat Fraser *As You Like It* (1919): "Futurism has no beauties for me. I don't think I like any 'isms' in any form of art," *Mainly Players* (London: Thornton Butterworth, 1926), p. 302; Beerbohm Tree called post-impressionism "post-depressionism," echoing by Comyns Carr's remark that "post-impressionism is the temporary paradise of the charlatan," (*The Era*, 18 May 1912).

5. Gordon Craig, undated letter to an unknown correspondent, in the Folger Library. Craig's emphasis.

6. Edward Gordon Craig, *Scene* (Oxford, 1923; rpt. New York: Benjamin Blom, 1968), p. 19n.

7. Eleanor Calhoun, *Pleasures and Palaces* (New York: Century, 1915), p. 308-11.

8. *Era*, 8 Feb. 1902.

9. London Shakespeare League, *Report of a Public Discussion on the Best Method of Presenting Shakespeare's Plays, held at the Guildhall School of Music, London, (by kind permission), on Tuesday, October 24th, 1905* (London: Chandos Press, 1905), p. 21.

10. Hubert Herkomer, "Scenic Art," *The Magazine of Art*, 15 (1892), 259-64, 316-20; this article, and Herkomer's theories in general, are discussed by John Stokes in *Resistible Theatres* (London: Paul Elek, 1972); Edward Craig in "Gordon Craig and Hubert von Herkomer," *Theatre Research*, 10 (1969), 7-16, and in *Gordon Craig, The Story of His Life* (New York: Knopf, 1968); and Sybil Rosenfeld, in "Hubert Herkomer's Theatrical Theories and Practice and the New Stagecraft," in *The Triple Bond*, ed. Joseph Price (University Park: Pennsylvania State Univ. Press, 1975), pp. 274-79.

11. According to Frederick Penzel, J.E. Dove was the first Englishman to suggest frontal overhead lighting, and experimented with it in Edinburgh in 1847. See Penzel, *Theatre Lighting Before Electricity* (Middletown, Conn.: Wesleyan Univ. Press, 1978), pp. 62-63.

12. William Archer, *The Theatrical "World" for 1895* (London: Walter Scott, 1896), p. 27 (16 Jan.).

13. William Telbin, "Art in the Theatre: The Question of Reform," *The Magazine of Art*, 17 (1894), 44-48.

14. George Bernard Shaw, *Our Theatres in the Nineties* (London: Constable, 1932), II, 66 (7 March 1896); and *Bernard Shaw's Letters to Granville Barker* (New York: Theatre Arts Books, 1957), p. 79 (21 April 1907).

15. Oscar Asche, *Chu Chin Chow* (London: Samuel French, 1931), p. 58.

16. Edward Craig, "Gordon Craig and Hubert von Herkomer," pp. 7-16.

17. *The Mask*, 3 (1910), facing p. 14.

18. Joseph Harker, *Studio and Stage* (London: Nisbet, 1924), p. 176.

19. Edward Gordon Craig, *Towards a New Theatre* (London: J.M. Dent, 1913), p. 18.

20. Craig graciously acknowledged Helmsley's assistance, and attacked Harker anew, in *Index to the Story of My Days* (New York: Viking, 1957), p. 241.

21. Ernest Stern, *My Life My Stage* (London: Victor Gollancz, 1951), p. 120.

22. Sir John Martin-Harvey, *The Autobiography of Sir John Martin-Harvey* (London: Sampson, Low & Marston, n.d.), p. 136. Harvey's emphasis.

23. Craig, *Towards a New Theatre*, p. 77.

24. William Archer, *Playmaking*, 2nd ed. (London: Chapman & Hall, 1913), p. 216.

25. Such plays, in addition to the two mentioned, include Barker and Housman's *Prunella* (1904, revived 1905, 1906, 1910); Graham Robertson's *Pinkie and the Fairies* (His Majesty's Theatre, 1908); Gilbert's *The Fairy's Dilemma* (a parody of Pantomimes for adult audiences, Garrick Theatre, 1904); and Shaw's *Androcles and the Lion* (1913). In 1910, Shaw wrote to August Strindberg suggesting that he capitalize on the popularity of *The Blue Bird* (Haymarket Theatre, 1909, 1910) by persuading Tree to produce *Lucky Per's Pilgrimage* at His Majesty's Theatre in exchange for a production of a more serious play by him in the Afternoon Theatre series under the same management. See George Bernard Shaw, *Collected Letters*, ed. Dan H. Laurence (New York: Dodd, Mead, 1972), II, 906-09 (16 March 1910).

26. Examples include Alexander's *As You Like It* (1896); the Asche/Stuart *Midsummer Night's Dream* (1905); Tree's productions of the same play (1900 and 1911, both offering special souvenir programs for children); and *The Tempest* (1904, revived for Christmas 1905). An interesting comparative study might be made of the artistic inspirations behind Tree's *Tempest* and Barrie's *Peter Pan*, which was not produced until a year later but which Tree had already seen in manuscript, possibly before his Shakespeare production. Tree refused the play, and the opportunity to play Captain Hook.

27. Quoted in G.C.D. Odell, *Shakespeare from Betterton to Irving* (1920; rpt. New York: Dover, 1966), II, 448.

28. Max Beerbohm, *More Theatres* (New York: Taplinger, 1969), p. 230 (20 Jan. 1900).

29. Max Beerbohm, *Around Theatres* (New York: Taplinger, 1969), pp. 478-79 (12 Oct. 1907).

30. *Illustrated London News*, 12 Oct. 1907.

31. Arthur Symons, "A New Art of the Stage," *Monthly Review*, 7 (1902), 157-58.

32. Ibid., p. 159. See also Beerbohm, *Around Theatres*, p. 201 (5 April 1902).

33. W.B. Yeats, *Ideas of Good and Evil* (London: A.H. Bullen, 1903), p. 150.

34. Ellen Terry, "Stage Decoration," *Windsor Magazine*, 35, No. 204 (December 1911), 87.

35. 11 August 1900. Quoted in E. Craig, *Gordon Craig*, p. 123.

36. See *Around Theatres*, p. 201 (5 April 1902) and p. 467 (11 May 1907), and *More Theatres*, p. 528 (10 Jan. 1903).

37. William Poel, *Shakespeare in the Theatre* (London: Sidgwick & Jackson, 1913), p. 224.

38. Beerbohm, *More Theatres*, p. 563 (25 April 1903).

39. Quoted in William Rothenstein, *Men and Memories* (London: Faber, 1931), p. 54.

40. Edward Gordon Craig, *Woodcuts and Some Words* (London: J.M. Dent, 1924), p. 35.

41. Marguerite Steen, *A Pride of Terrys* (London: Longmans, Green, 1962), p. 291; Edward Gordon Craig, *Ellen Terry and Her Secret Self* (London: Sampson, Low & Marston, 1931), p. 132.

42. Ellen Terry, *Ellen Terry's Memoirs*, eds. Edith Craig and Christopher St. John (1908; rpt. New York: Putnam, 1932), p. 256.

43. See *The Mask*, 1 (1908), 180.

44. *Daily Telegraph*, 16 April 1903.

45. Shaw, *Collected Letters*, II, 324 (15 March 1903).

Notes for Chapter 3

46. Edward Gordon Craig, *Henry Irving* (London: J.M. Dent, 1930), p. 158.
47. Quoted in E. Craig, *Gordon Craig*, p. 174. Terry's emphases.
48. *Era*, 4 April 1903.
49. Quoted in E. Craig, *Gordon Craig*, p. 174-75. Terry's emphasis.
50. Ibid.
51. Beerbohm, *More Theatres*, p. 575 (30 May 1903).
52. The photograph is reproduced in Tom Prideaux, *Love or Nothing; The Life and Times of Ellen Terry* (New York: Scribner's, 1975), no. 34, between pages 180 and 181.
53. Beerbohm, *More Theatres*, p. 574 (30 May 1903).
54. Ibid.
55. Ibid.
56. *Era*, 30 May 1903; *Illustrated London News*, 30 May 1903.
57. Ellen Terry, *The Story of My Life* (New York: McClure, 1908), p. 196.
58. Described in detail by E. Craig in *Gordon Craig*, pp. 175-76.
59. Craig, *Index to the Story of My Days*, p. 249.
60. *Modern Society*, 30 May 1903, quoted in Denis Bablet, *Edward Gordon Craig*, trans. Daphne Woodward (New York: Theatre Arts Books, 1966), p. 62.
61. E. Craig, *Gordon Craig*, p. 175. E. Craig's emphasis.
62. One sketch is reproduced as plate 33 in George Nash, *Edward Gordon Craig, 1872-1966* (London: Her Majesty's Stationery Office, 1967).
63. Percy Fitzgerald, *Shakespearean Representation, its Laws and Limits* (London: Elliot Stock, 1908), p. 122.
64. The most thorough study of this production is Laurence Senelick, "The Craig-Stanislavsky *Hamlet* at the Moscow Art Theatre," *Theatre Quarterly*, 6 (1976), 56-122.
65. *City of Manchester Art Gallery. Exhibition of drawings and models for Hamlet, Macbeth, The Vikings and other plays by Edward Gordon Craig, 1912*, p. 22, quoted in Bablet, *Edward Gordon Craig*, p. 157.
66. E. Craig, *Gordon Craig*, p. 250.
67. See Laurence Senelick, "Moscow and Monodrama: The Meaning of the Craig-Stanislavsky *Hamlet*," *Theatre Research International* 6 (1981), 109-124.
68. Letter to Lilina, 13 Feb. 1909, quoted in Senelick, "The Craig-Stanislavsky Hamlet," p. 61.
69. 29 April 1909, quoted in Senelick, "The Craig-Stanislavsky Hamlet," p. 70.
70. Ibid.
71. Ibid.
72. Ibid., p. 64.
73. Letter from Craig to Stanislavsky, 27 July 1908, quoted in Senelick, p. 58.
74. Herbert Trench, "Shakespeare and Modern Staging," *Saturday Review*, 13 July 1910, p. 198.

75. *The Mask*, 2 (1909), 44.
76. Trench, "Shakespeare and Modern Staging," p. 198.
77. Ibid., p. 199.
78. Ibid., pp. 198-99.
79. Ibid., p. 199.
80. This set consisted of a semicircular colonnade with a variety of curtains in the openings. Norman Wilkinson used this device in the forest scenes of Barker's *A Midsummer Night's Dream* (1914), a borrowing which Ricketts recognized. See letter to R.N.R. Holst, Feb. 1914, quoted in Charles Ricketts, *Self-Portrait taken from the Letters and Journals of Charles Ricketts, R.A.,* ed. Cecil Lewis (London: Peter Davies, 1939), p. 188.
81. Quoted in Ifan Kyrle Fletcher, "Charles Ricketts and the Theatre," *Theatre Notebook*, 22 (1967), 14.
82. Gordon Bottomley, "Charles Ricketts, R.A.," *Theatre Arts Monthly*, 16 (1932), 391.
83. Ibid., p. 382
84. Charles Ricketts, *Pages on Art* (London: Constable, 1913), p. 234.
85. Unidentified clipping, Harvard Theatre Collection.
86. Max Beerbohm, *Last Theatres* (New York: Taplinger, 1970), p. 485 (18 Sept. 1909).
87. Trench, "Shakespeare and Modern Staging," p. 199.
88. Edward Gordon Craig, "The Scenery of King Lear," letter, *Saturday Review*, 25 Sept. 1909.
89. *The Mask*, 3 (1910), 95.
90. Huntly Carter, *The Theatre of Max Reinhardt* (London: 1914; rpt. New York: Benjamin Blom, 1964), p. 257.
91. Ibid., p. 218.
92. William Poel, "Shakespeare's Prompt Copies. A Plea for Early Texts," *Times Literary Supplement*, 3 Feb. 1921; and *Monthly Letters*, ed. A.M. T[rethwey] (London: T. Werner Lauries, 1929), p. 84.
93. *Yorkshire Post*, 21 April 1910.
94. Robert Speaight, *William Poel and the Elizabethan Revival* (London: Heinemann, 1954), p. 179.
95. B. Iden Payne, *A Life in a Wooden O* (New Haven: Yale Univ. Press, 1977), p. 174.
96. See Jocza Savits, *Shakespeare und die Bühne des Dramas* (Bonn: F. Cohen, 1917), and Hans Durian, *Jocza Savits und die Münchener Shakespearebühne* (Emsdetten: Lechte, 1937). Other continental origins for this model are described in George Altman, Ralph Freud, Kenneth Macgowan and William Melnitz, *Theater Pictorial* (Berkeley: Univ. of California Press, 1953), illustrations 269-83.
97. Rex Pogson, *Miss Horniman and the Gaiety Theatre, Manchester* (London: Rockliff, 1952), p. 159.
98. Sir Lewis Casson, "William Poel and the Modern Theatre," *Listener*, 10 Jan. 1952, p. 57.
99. Harker, *Studio and Stage*, p. 191.

Notes for Chapter 4 231

100. Norman Marshall, *The Other Theatre* (London: John Lehmann, 1947), p. 19.
101. Souvenir of Harvey's *Hamlet*, 1910, Shakespeare Centre Library, Stratford-upon-Avon.
102. *The Mask*, 2 (1909), 100.
103. Harvey, *Autobiography*, p. 376.
104. Ibid.
105. Souvenir of Harvey's *Hamlet*, 1910.
106. T.T., promotional pamphlet for Harvey's *Hamlet*, 1909, Shakespeare Centre Library, Stratford-upon-Avon.
107. Scrapbooks, Shakespeare Centre Library.
108. Harvey, *Autobiography*, p. 376.
109. *Leamington Spa Courrier*, undated clipping in Shakespeare Centre Library.
110. See *Birmingham Post*, 28 April 1910, and *Stratford-on-Avon Herald*, 29 April 1910.
111. *Era*, 4 Jan. 1913.
112. Harvey, *Autobiography*, p. 463.
113. *Era*, 12 April 1913.
114. Ibid., 10 May 1916.
115. Ibid., 12 April 1913.
116. Quoted in R.N.G.-A., *The Book of Martin Harvey* (London: Henry Walker, n.d.), p. 96.
117. Maurice W. Disher, *The Last Romantic* (London: Hutchinson, 1948), p. 226.
118. *The Book of Martin Harvey*, p. 63.
119. Craig, *Index to the Story of My Days*, p. 64.
120. *Observer*, 20 Dec. 1919.
121. Letter from Yeats to Harvey, 27 Oct. 1919, quoted in *The Book of Martin Harvey*, p. 86.

Chapter 4

1. Harley Granville-Barker, "Introduction to *The Player's Shakespeare*" (1923) in *More Prefaces to Shakespeare*, ed. Edward M. Moore (Princeton: Princeton Univ. Press, 1974), p. 47.
2. Harley Granville-Barker, *The Exemplary Theatre* (Boston: Little, Brown, 1922), pp. 194-95.
3. Ibid., p. 194.
4. Harley Granville-Barker, *Prefaces to Shakespeare* 1946; rpt. in 4 vols., Princeton: Princeton Univ. Press, 1965), I, 1.
5. Harley Granville-Barker, *Associating with Shakespeare* (London: Humphrey Milford, 1932), p. 18.
6. Barker, "Introduction to *The Player's Shakespeare*," *More Prefaces*, p. 55.
7. Barker, *Prefaces*, I, 3.

8. Ibid.
9. Barker, *The Exemplary Theatre*, p. 194.
10. Barker, "Introduction to *The Player's Shakespeare*," *More Prefaces*, p. 48.
11. Barker, "Preface to the Acting Edition of *Twelfth Night*" (1912), *More Prefaces*, p. 31.
12. Barker, *Associating with Shakespeare*, p. 22-23.
13. Ibid., p. 24.
14. Barker, *Prefaces*, I, 16.
15. Harley Granville-Barker, *On Dramatic Method* (1930; rpt. New York: Hill and Wang, 1956), p. 159.
16. Barker, *The Exemplary Theatre*, p. 65.
17. Barker, *Prefaces*, II, 218.
18. Ibid., I, 17.
19. Ibid., I, 4.
20. Ibid., IV, 256.
21. Ibid., I, 6-7.
22. Barker, "Preface to *Macbeth*" (1923), *More Prefaces*, p. 65.
23. Letter from Archer to Barker, 21 June 1923, British Library, Dept. of Manuscripts.
24. Letter from Barker to Archer, 22 June 1923, British Library, Dept. of Manuscripts.
25. Barker, *Prefaces*, II, 215, note.
26. Ibid., I, 5.
27. Letter from Barker to Archer, 22 June 1923, British Library, Dept. of Manuscripts.
28. Barker, "Introduction to *The Player's Shakespeare*," *More Prefaces*, p. 50.
29. Harley Granville-Barker, "A Note upon Chapters XX and XXI of *The Elizabethan Stage*," *Review of English Studies*, 1 (1925), 64.
30. Quoted in Norman Marshall, *The Producer and the Play* (London: MacDonald, 1962), p. 60.
31. Barker, *Prefaces*, I, 9.
32. Ibid., I, 11.
33. Barker, "Introduction to *The Player's Shakespeare*," *More Prefaces*, p. 49.
34. Barker, *Prefaces*, IV, 54.
35. Ibid., IV, 15.
36. Ibid., II, 92.
37. Ibid., IV, 15.
38. Barker, "Preface to *Macbeth*," *More Prefaces*, p. 67.
39. Barker, *Prefaces*, I, 40, note.

Notes for Chapter 4   233

40. Barker, "Preface to *Macbeth*," *More Prefaces*, p. 69.
41. Interview in the *Standard*, 21 Sept. 1912.
42. William Poel, "Shakespeare; a Standard Text," *Times Literary Supplement*, 3 Feb. 1921.
43. Barker, "Preface to *A Midsummer Night's Dream*" (1924), *More Prefaces*, p. 95.
44. Barker, *Prefaces*, I, 9.
45. Ibid., III, 9.
46. Harley Granville-Barker, "Shakespeare's Dramatic Art," *Companion to Shakespeare Studies*, ed. Harley Granville-Barker and G.B. Harrison (Cambridge, 1934; rpt. New York: Anchor, 1960), p. 74, note. Barker's emphases.
47. Barker, "Preface to *A Midsummer Night's Dream*," *More Prefaces*, p. 96.
48. Ibid., p. 97.
49. Ibid., p. 97, note. Barker's emphasis
50. Ibid., p. 95.
51. Ibid., pp. 96-97.
52. Barker, "Shakespeare's Dramatic Art," p. 68.
53. Barker, *Prefaces*, I, 16-17.
54. Harley Granville-Barker, "Shakespeare and Modern Stagecraft," *Yale Review*, 15 (1926), 708.
55. Barker, *Prefaces*, I, 17.
56. Ibid., I, 25.
57. Ibid., IV, 133, note.
58. Albert Rutherston, "Decoration in the Art of the Theatre," *Monthly Chapbook*, 1, No. 2 (Aug. 1919), 18-19.
59. *Outlook*, 2 May 1914.
60. Marshall, *The Producer and the Play*, p. 149. For an earlier use of frontal overhead lighting, see Chapter 3, Note 11, above. Huntly Carter, *The Theatre of Max Reinhardt* (London, 1914; rpt. New York: Benjamin Blom, 1964), p. 297.
61. *Everyman*, 29 Nov. 1912.
62. *The Mask*, 1 (1908), 90.
63. Cathleen Nesbitt, *A Little Love and Good Company* (London: Faber, 1975), p. 62.
64. Marshall, *The Producer and the Play*, p. 150.
65. Barker, *The Exemplary Theatre*, p. 204.
66. Harley Granville Barker, "The Theatre Exhibition in Berlin," *Times*, 7 Nov. 1910.
67. Barker, *The Exemplary Theatre*, p. 200-201.
68. Ibid., p. 203.
69. Letter, *Daily Mail*, 24 Sept. 1912.

70. Ibid., 26 Sept. 1912.
71. W. Bridges-Adams, in *Edwardian England, 1901-1914*, ed. Simon Nowell-Smith (London: Oxford Univ. Press, 1964), p. 405.
72. Harley Granville-Barker, *The Study of Drama* (Cambridge: Cambridge Univ. Press, 1934), p. 22.
73. Barker, *Associating with Shakespeare*, p. 18.
74. Ibid., p. 27; *Prefaces*, I, 2-3.
75. Interview in *Evening News*, 3 Dec. 1912.
76. Ibid.; letter from Barker to Max Reinhardt, 3 Sept. 1913, quoted in Robert Speaight, *William Poel and the Elizabethan Revival* (London: Heinemann, 1954), pp. 148-49.
77. Letter from Barker to Gilbert Murray, 5 June 1904, quoted in C.B. Purdom, *Harley Granville Barker: Man of the Theatre, Dramatist and Scholar* (London: Rickliff, 1955), p. 20.
78. Harley Granville Barker, Preface to 1907 edition of *A National Theatre: Schemes and Estimates*, by William Archer and H. Granville Barker (London: Duckworth, 1907), p. ix.
79. Barker, *The Exemplary Theatre*, p. 191.
80. Barker, *Prefaces*, III, 41.
81. Ibid., II, 219.
82. Barker, "Preface to the Acting Edition of *The Winter's Tale*" (1912), *More Prefaces*, pp. 24-25.
83. Rutherston, "Decoration in the Art of the Theatre," p. 20.
84. Albert Rothenstein (Rutherston), in "Modern Scenic Art," *The Stage Yearbook* 1914, p. 19.
85. Norman Wilkinson, in "Modern Scenic Art," p. 20.
86. Ibid.
87. Rutherston, "Decoration in the Art of the Theatre," p. 25. Rutherston's emphasis.
88. Interview in the *Standard*, 25 Sept. 1912.
89. Barker, "Preface to the Acting Edition of *The Winter's Tale*," *More Prefaces*, p. 24.
90. Rutherston, "Decoration in the Art of the Theatre," p. 27.
91. *Era*, 22 Feb. 1913.
92. Interview in the *Standard*, 25 Sept. 1912.
93. See the *Westminster Gazette*, 17 April 1914, and John Palmer, *The Future of the Theatre* (London: G. Bell, 1913), p. 117.
94. W. Bridges-Adams, "The Lost Leader," in *The Bridges-Adams Letter Book*, ed. Robert Speaight (London: Society for Theatre Research, 1971), p. 91.
95. A promotional photograph of Malvolio's upstage cross, displaying his cloak, was reproduced in several newspapers and magazines, which suggests that the photograph was distributed with the promotional materials.
96. Bridges-Adams, "The Lost Leader," p. 91.

97. Ibid., p. 92.
98. Bridges-Adams, letter to Robert Speaight, 25 Sept. 1952, quoted in Speaight, *William Poel and the Elizabethan Revival*, p. 201.
99. Barker, "Introduction to *The Player's Shakespeare*," *More Prefaces*, p. 46.
100. Interview in the *Evening News*, 24 Sept. 1912.
101. *Evening News*, 23 Sept. 1912.
102. Ibid., 24 Sept. 1912.
103. Purdom, *Granville Barker;* Muriel St. Clare Byrne, "Fifty Years of Shakespearean Production: 1898-1948," *Shakespeare Survey*, 2 (1949), 1-20; Trevor Griffiths, "Tradition and Innovation in Harley Granville Barker's *A Midsummer Night's Dream*," *Theatre Notebook*, 30 (1976), 78-86; J.L. Styan, *The Shakespeare Revolution* (Cambridge: Cambridge Univ. Press, 1977), pp. 82-104; Hugh Hunt, "Granville Barker's Shakespearean Productions," *Theatre Research*, 10 (1969), 44-59; Helen Marie Terese Kelly, "The Granville-Barker Shakespeare Productions. A Study Based on the Promptbooks," Diss. Michigan 1965; Gary J. Williams, "*A Midsummer Night's Dream*: The English and American Popular Traditions and Harley Granville-Barker's 'World Arbitrarily Made,' " *Theatre Studies*, 23 (1976-77), 40-52; Cary M. Mazer, "Harley Granville Barker's Production of *Twelfth Night* at the Savoy Theatre, November 15, 1912," Senior Thesis, Princeton University, 1974.
104. *Daily Graphic*, 2 Oct. 1912.
105. See photograph in *The Ladies' Field*, 30 Nov. 1912.
106. Interview in the *Daily Express*, 25 Sept. 1912.
107. Barker, "Preface to the Acting Edition of *Twelfth Night*," *More Prefaces*, p. 26-27.
108. *Tatler*, 27 Nov. 1912.
109. Interview in the *Standard*, 11 Nov. 1912; see also an interview in the *Evening News*, 12 Nov. 1912.
110. See *Oxford Times*, 3 Nov. 1912.
111. Barker, "Preface to the Acting Edition of *A Midsummer Night's Dream*" (1914), *More Prefaces*, p. 35.
112. Ibid., p. 38.
113. W. Graham Robertson, *Letters from Graham Robertson*, ed. Kerrison Preston (London: Hamish Hamilton, 1953), p. 16.
114. Letter from Archer to Barker, 11 Feb. 1914, British Library, Dept. of Manuscripts.
115. Letter from Barker to Archer, 14 Feb. 1914, British Library, Dept. of Manuscripts.
116. Barker, "Preface to *A Midsummer Night's Dream*," *More Prefaces*, p. 110.
117. Barker, "Preface to the Acting Edition of *A Midsummer Night's Dream*," *More Prefaces*, p. 38.
118. G.C.D. Odell, *Shakespeare from Betterton to Irving* (1920; rpt. New York: Dover, 1966), II, 468.
119. Marshall, *The Producer and the Play*, p. 156; Griffiths, "Tradition and Innovation," p. 80.

120. Letter from Barker to Archer, 22 June 1923, British Library, Dept. of Manuscripts.

121. Styan, *The Shakespeare Revolution*, p. 103.

122. Richard Foulkes notes the business, the use of the apron, and illumination by Dome lights in "Herbert Beerbohm Tree's *King Henry VIII*: Expenditure, Spectacle and Experiment," *Theatre Research International*, 3 (1977), but does not draw a connection between the business and Barker's later use of it, or relate Tree's use of the apron to Poel's installation of the apron for *The Two Gentlemen of Verona* the previous spring. Styan and Griffiths both note Barker's business for Puck, but neither of them relate it to Tree's similar business for the jester.

Chapter 5

1. George Bernard Shaw, "From the Point of View of a Playwright," in *Herbert Beerbohm Tree, Some Memories of Him and His Art*, ed. Max Beerbohm (1920; rpt. New York: Benjamin Blom, 1969), p. 241.

2. Edward Gordon Craig, *On the Art of the Theatre* (London: Heinemann, 1911), pp. 285, 143.

3. William Poel, "The Elizabethan Stage," *Theatre*, 31 (1893), 242.

4. Edwardians who based their arguments on this concept include Henry Irving, who noted that "Shakespeare was one of the most practical dramatists which the world has ever seen, and this notwithstanding that he lived in an age when the drawbacks which existed to the proper representation of stage plays were very many," ("Shakespeare as a Playwright," *The Henry Irving Shakespeare* [London: Blackie, 1888], p. xvii); William Archer "never ceased to regret the circumstance that Shakespeare was a man of his age, and in some respects the most far-seeing man of his age. That does not hinder him from being the greatest poet of all time, who has left us, in his plays, an inexhaustible reservoir of essential humanity," (*The Theatrical "World" for 1896* [London: Walter Scott, 1898], p. 163); Frank Benson noted that "the size and shape of the theatres alter, the patterns of scenery and the conventions of art-expression change, but the eternal truths of existence remain the same for all ages," (in *A Book of Homage to Shakespeare*, ed. Israel Gollancz [London: Humphrey Milford, Oxford Univ. Press, 1916], p. 39); Alan Mackinnon argued that "as Shakespeare was not for one age but for all time, a certain amount of license should be permitted in representation to suit the life of to-day," (London Shakespeare League, *Report of a Public Discussion*... [London: Chandos Press, 1905], p. 9); and Granville Barker notes that though Shakespeare was a man of his age, "Shakespeare was so much more than this, because the absolute dramatic value of his plays and his poetic power could break through so many barriers," (*Associating with Shakespeare* [London: Humphrey Milford, Oxford Univ. Press, 1932], p. 14).

5. Herbert Beerbohm Tree, *Thoughts and Afterthoughts* (London: Cassell, 1913), p. 56-57.

6. Letter from Shaw to Ellen Terry, 16 Sept. 1896, in *Collected Letters*, ed. Dan H. Laurence (New York: Dodd, Mead, 1972), I, 655-56.

7. Harley Granville-Barker, *The Exemplary Theatre* (Boston: Little, Brown, 1922), p. 23.

8. Barker, *Associating with Shakespeare*, p. 9.

9. Ibid., p. 7.

10. Ibid., p. 10.

11. George Bernard Shaw, *Our Theatre in the Nineties* (London: Constable, 1932), III, 243 (13 Nov. 1897).

Notes for Chapter 5

12. Ellen Terry, "Stage Decoration," *Windsor Magazine*, 35, No. 204 (1911), 72.
13. Tree, *Thoughts and Afterthoughts*, p. 293.
14. Ibid., p. 224.
15. In Joseph Harker, *Studio and Stage* (London: Nisbet, 1924), p. 201.
16. R.N.G.-A., ed., *The Book of Martin Harvey* (London: Henry Walker, n.d.), p. 63.
17. Charles Ricketts, *Pages on Art* (London: Constable, 1913), p. 239.
18. Ibid., p. 247.
19. Harley Granville-Barker, *Prefaces to Shakespeare* (1946; rpt. in 2 vols., Princeton: Princeton Univ. Press, 1963), I, 22-23.
20. Ibid., I, 4.
21. Harley Granville-Barker, Introduction to the Acting Edition of *Twelfth Night* (1912), *More Prefaces to Shakespeare* (Princeton: Princeton Univ. Press, 1974), pp. 27-28.
22. Harley Granville-Barker, "The Theatre in Berlin," *Times*, 19 Nov. 1910.
23. Letter to Huntly Carter, 1 Dec. 1910, Shakespeare Centre Library, Stratford-upon-Avon, printed in the "Symposium on the Representation of Shakespeare," *New Age*, 8 (1911).
24. Address to the Author's Club, 15 May 1911, *Era*, 20 May 1911.
25. Craig, *On the Art of the Theatre*, p. 266. Craig's emphasis.
26. Edward Gordon Craig, *Henry Irving* (London: J.M. Dent, 1930), p. 92. Craig's emphasis.
27. Terry, "Stage Decoration," p. 71. Tree similarly asserted that "the artist . . . must always have a substantial influence upon the situation; from his individuality springs effects which authors cannot invariably determine beforehand" (*Era*, 28 Sept. 1907). And Ernest Carpenter believed that "you cannot . . . get that strong dramatic effect which grips a [sic] audience unless you have the capable producer to supervise everybody and everything" (*Era*, 28 Sept. 1908).
28. For Craig's opinion of Reinhardt, see *The Mask*, 4, No. 3 (1912), 5, No. 4 (1913), and *Fourteen Notes on Eight Pages from The Story of the Theatre by Glenn Hughes* (Seattle: Univ. of Washington Bookstore, 1931), pp. 7, 19.
29. *Era*, 8 March 1913.
30. *The Mask*, 5 (1913), 281.
31. Norman Wilkinson, in "Modern Scenic Art," *Stage Yearbook 1914*, p. 19.
32. Ibid., p. 19; *Daily Express*, 25 Sept. 1912.
33. Albert Rutherston, "Decoration in the Art of the Theatre," *Monthly Chapbook*, 1, No. 2 (1919), 21. Rutherston's emphasis.
34. Ibid.
35. *Standard*, 16 Oct. 1912.
36. Barker, *Prefaces*, I, 5; *The Exemplary Theatre*, p. 119.
37. *The Mask*, 1 (1908), 90.

Bibliography

Primary Sources: Theory, Autobiography, Eyewitness Accounts

Albright, Victor E. *The Shaksperian Stage.* New York: Columbia Univ. Press, 1909.
Archer, William. *About the Theatre.* London: T. Fisher Unwin, 1886.
_____. "Art in the Theatre: The Limitations of Scenery." *Magazine of Art,* 19 (1896), 432-36.
_____. "The Elizabethan Stage." *Quarterly Review,* 208 (1908), 442-71.
_____. "The Fortune Theatre, 1600." *Shakespeare Jahrbuch,* 44 (1908), 159-66.
_____. "Notes, by William Archer, on Elizabethan Staging and Stage Conditions." Typescript, 1925, with explanatory notes by W.J. Lawrence. Columbia Univ. Library.
_____. *Play-Making: A Manual of Craftsmanship.* Rev. ed. 1913; rpt. London: Chapman & Hall, 1930.
_____. *Real Conversations.* London: Heinemann, 1904.
_____. Review of William Poel, *Shakespeare in the Theatre. Nation,* 5 July 1913, pp. 535-36.
_____. "A Sixteenth Century Playhouse." *Universal Review,* 1 (1888), 281-88.
_____. *Study and Stage.* London: Grant Richards, 1899.
_____. *The Theatrical "World" for 1893-1897.* 5 vols. London: Walter Scott, 1894-1898.
_____, and H. Granville Barker. *A National Theatre: Schemes and Estimates.* London: Duckworth, 1907.
_____, and Walter H. Godfrey, "An Elizabethan Theatre," *Architectural Review,* 23 (1908), 239-44.
Arnold, W.T. *The Manchester Stage: 1880-1900.* Westminster: Constable, 1900.
Asche, Oscar. *Oscar Asche: His Life.* London: Hurst & Blackett, 1929.
Baker, George Pierce. " 'Hamlet' on an Elizabethan Stage." *Shakespeare Jahrbuch,* 41 (1915), 296-301.
Barker, H. Granville. See Granville-Barker, Harley.
Beerbohm, Max. *Around Theatres.* New York: Taplinger, 1969.
_____, ed. *Herbert Beerbohm Tree: Some Memories of Him and of his Art.* London, 1920; rpt. New York: Benjamin Blom, 1969.
_____. *Last Theatres: 1904-1910.* New York: Taplinger, 1970.
_____. *More Theatres: 1898-1903.* New York: Taplinger, 1969.
Benson, W.A.S. " 'Agamemnon' at Oxford." *Cornhill Magazine,* NS 46 (1919), 534-46.
Borsa, Mario. *The English Theatre of To-day.* Trans. Selwyn Brinton. London: John Lane, 1908.
Bourchier, Arthur. *Some Reflections on the Drama—And Shakespeare.* Oxford: Blackwell, 1911.
Bransom, L.G., and M. Goodman, eds. *Press Cuttings on our Side.* London: London Shakespeare League, 1922.
Bridges-Adams, W. *A Bridges-Adams Letter Book.* Ed. Robert Speaight. London: Society for Theatre Research, 1971.

_____. "Shakespearean Tradition in the Theatre." *Quarterly Journal of Speech,* 16 (1930), 4-5, 414.
Brodmeier, Cecil. *Die Shakespeare-Bühne nach den alten Buhnenanweisungen.* Weimar: Alexander Huschke Nacht, 1904.
Carter, Huntly. *The Theatre of Max Reinhardt.* London: 1914; rpt. New York: Benjamin Blom, 1964.
Chambers, E.K. "The Stage of the Globe." In *The Works of Shakespeare,* 10: 351-62. Stratford-on-Avon: Shakespeare Head, 1907.
Corbin, John. "Shakespeare and the Plastic Stage." *Atlantic Monthly,* 97 (1906), 369-83.
Craig, Edward Gordon. *Ellen Terry and Her Secret Self.* London: Sampson, Low, Marston, 1931.
_____. "The First Time I Played Hamlet." *Listener,* 3 Jan. 1957, p. 19.
_____. *Fourteen Notes on Eight Pages from The Story of the Theatre by Glenn Hughes.* Seattle: Univ. of Washington Bookstore, 1931.
_____. *Henry Irving.* London: J.M. Dent, 1930.
_____. "Henry Irving, 1838-1938." *London Mercury,* 37 (1938), 400-05.
_____. "Henry Irving's Way." *Listener,* 26 July 1951, pp. 133-34.
_____. *Index to the Story of My Days.* New York: Viking, 1957.
_____. "Irving Seemingly Perplexed." *Drama,* No. 43 (1956), pp. 25-26.
_____. *On the Art of the Theatre.* London: Heinemann, 1911.
_____. "Reminiscences of Myself and Ellen Terry." *Listener,* 19 July 1951, pp. 97-98.
_____. *Scene.* Oxford, 1923; rpt. New York: Benjamin Blom, 1968.
_____. "The Scenery of King Lear." Letter. *Saturday Review,* 23 Sept. 1909.
_____. *The Theatre—Advancing.* Boston: Little, Brown, 1919.
_____. *Towards a New Theatre: Scenes with Critical Notes by the Inventor.* London: J.M. Dent, 1913.
_____. *Woodcuts and some Words.* London: J.M. Dent, 1924.
Craven, Arthur Scott, ed. "Modern Scenic Art: A Symposium." *Stage Yearbook of 1914,* pp. 17-26.
Crosse, Gordon. *Shakespearean Playgoing 1890-1952.* London: Mowbray, 1953.
Darbyshire, Alfred. *The Art of the Victorian Stage.* London: Sherratt & Hughes, 1907.
Dean, Basil. *Seven Ages: An Autobiography 1888-1927.* London: Hutchinson, 1970.
Dickins, Richard. *Forty Years of Shakespeare on the English Stage: August 1867-August 1907.* London: privately printed, 1907.
Figgis, Darrell. *Shakespeare: A Study.* London: J.M. Dent, 1911.
Fitzgerald, Percy. *Shakespearean Representation: Its Laws and Limits.* London: Elliot Stock, 1908.
Forbes-Robertson, Johnston. "Ellen Terry." *London Mercury,* 18 (1928), 492-96.
_____. *A Player under Three Reigns.* Boston: Little, Brown, 1925.
_____. "A Talk about the Theatre." *Outlook,* 96 (1910), 191-99.
_____. "The Theatre of Yesterday, To-day and To-morrow." *Century Magazine,* 87 (1913-1914), 505-10.
G.-A., R.N., ed. *The Book of Martin Harvey.* London: Henry Walker, n.d.
Gaedertz, Karl Theodor. *Zur Kenntniss der altenglische Bühne.* Bremen: W.E. Müller, 1888.
Granville-Barker, Harley. N.B. Works published before 1919 appeared under the name H. Granville Barker.
_____. *Associating with Shakespeare.* London: Oxford Univ. Press, 1932.
_____. "Alas, Poor Will!" *Listener,* 3 March 1937, pp. 387-89.
_____. "The Casting of *Hamlet:* A Fragment." *London Mercury,* 35 (Nov. 1936), 10-17.
_____. "The Coming of Ibsen." In *The Eighteen-Eighties.* Ed. Walter De la Mare. Cambridge: Cambridge Univ. Press, 1930.

———. *The Exemplary Theatre*. Boston: Little, Brown, 1922.
———. "Exit Planché—Enter Gilbert." In *The Eighteen-Sixties*. Ed. John Drinkwater. Cambridge: Cambridge Univ. Press, 1932.
———. "The Golden Thoughts of Granville Barker." *Play Pictorial*, 21, No. 126 (1912), iv.
———. "*Hamlet* in Plus Fours." *Yale Review*, 16 (1926), 205.
———. "The Heritage of the Actor." *Quarterly Review*, 240 (1923), 53-73.
———. *More Prefaces to Shakespeare*. Ed. Edward M. Moore. Princeton: Princeton Univ. Press, 1974.
———. *A National Theatre*. London: Sidgwick & Jackson, 1930.
———. "A Note on Chapters XX and XXI of *The Elizabethan Stage*." *Review of English Studies*, 1 (1925), 60-71.
———. "Notes on Rehearsing a Play." *Drama*, 1, No. 1 (1919), 2-5.
———. *On Dramatic Method*. 1930; rpt. New York: Hill & Wang, 1956.
———. "The Perennial Shakespeare." *Listener*, 20 Oct. 1937, pp. 823-26, 857-59.
———. Pref., *Little Plays of St. Francis*, by Laurence Housman, 1st ser. London: Sidgwick & Jackson, 1922.
———. *Prefaces to Shakespeare*. 1946; rpt. in 4 vols., Princeton: Princeton Univ. Press, 1965.
———. "Reconstruction in the Theatre." *The Times*, 20 Feb. 1919, p. 11.
———. Review of *Designs by Inigo Jones for Masques and Plays at Court*. *Review of English Studies*, 1 (1925), 231-35.
———. Review of *The Frontiers of Drama*, by Una Ellis-Fermor. *Review of English Studies*, 22 (1946), 144-47.
———. Review of *The Physical Conditions of the Elizabethan Public Playhouses* and *Pre-Restoration Studies*, by W.J. Lawrence. *Review of English Studies*, 4 (1928), 229-37.
———. "Shakespeare and Modern Stagecraft." *Yale Review*, 15 (1926), 703-24.
———. "Shakespeare's Dramatic Art." In *A Companion to Shakespeare Studies*. 1934; rpt. Garden City: Doubleday, 1960.
———. *The Study of Drama*. Cambridge: Cambridge Univ. Press, 1934.
———. "Tennyson, Swinburne, Meredith—and the Theatre." In *The Eighteen-Seventies*. Ed. Harley Granville-Barker. Cambridge: Cambridge Univ. Press, 1929.
———. "The Theatre Exhibition in Berlin." *The Times*, 7 Nov. 1910, p. 16.
———. "The Theatre in Berlin." *The Times*, 19 Nov. 1910, p. 6, 21 Nov. 1910, p. 12.
———. "The Theatre: the Next Phase." *The English Review*, 5 (1910), 631-48.
———. "Two German Theatres." *The Fortnightly Review*, NS 76 (1911), 60-70.
———. *The Use of the Drama*. Princeton: Princeton Univ. Press, 1945.
———. "Verse and Speech in *Coriolanus*." *Review of English Studies*, 23 (1947), 1-15.
Harker, Joseph. *Studio and Stage*. London: Nisbet, 1924.
Heighton, Joseph. "Actors as Artists." *Strand Magazine*, 38 (1909), 686-91.
" 'Henry V' at the Lyceum Theatre." *Architectural Review*, 9 (1901), 75-81.
Herkomer, Hubert. "Scenic Art." *Magazine of Art*, 15 (1892), 259-64, 316-20.
Heslewood, Tom. "Some Memories of Irving." *Drama*, 10 (1938), 87-89.
Kirwan, Patrick. *The Dawn of English Drama*. London: Harding & More, 1920.
Lang, Matheson. *Mr. Wu Looks Back*. London: Stanley Paul, 1940.
Lawrence, W.J. "Art in the Theatre: Scenery on Tour." *Magazine of Art*, 19 (1896), 476.
———. *The Elizabethan Playhouse and Other Studies*. Two series. 1912, 1913; rpt. New York: Russell & Russell, 1963.
———. "Some Characteristics of the Elizabethan-Stuart Stage." *Englische Studien*, 32 (1903), 36-51.
Lee, Sidney. "Shakespeare and the Modern Stage." *Nineteenth Century*, 47 (1900), 146-56.

_____. *Shakespeare and the Modern Stage, with Other Essays.* London: John Murray, 1906.
_____. *Shakespeare's Henry V, An Account and an Estimate.* London: Smith, Elder, 1900.
Le Gallienne, Richard. "Forbes-Robertson: An Appreciation." *Century Magazine,* 87 (1914), 511-15.
London Shakespeare League. *Report of a Public Discussion on the Best Method of Presenting Shakespeare's Plays, held at the Guildhall School of Music, London (by kind permission), on Tuesday, October 24th, 1905.* London: Chandos Press, 1905.
Martin-Harvey, Sir John. *The Autobiography of Sir John Martin-Harvey.* London: Sampson, Low, Marston, n.d.
The Mask. Ed. Edward Gordon Craig.
Nesbitt, Cathleen. "Cathleen Nesbitt talks to Michael Elliot about Harley Granville-Barker." *Listener,* 13 Jan. 1972, pp. 51-53.
_____. *A Little Love and Good Company.* London: Faber, 1975.
Notes on Some of William Poel's Productions. London: A.W. Patching, 1933.
Odell, G.C.D. *Shakespeare from Betterton to Irving.* 2 Vols. 1920; rpt. New York: Dover, 1966.
Payne, Ben Iden. *A Life in a Wooden O.* New Haven: Yale Univ. Press, 1977.
Poel, William. "Blasting the Heath." *Saturday Review,* 31 July 1909, p. 135.
_____. "The Elizabethan Stage." *Theatre,* 31 (1893), 241-47.
_____. "The First Quarto of *Hamlet.*" *Notes and Queries,* 12th series, 9 (1922), 301-03.
_____. "The Functions of a National Theatre." *Theatre,* 31 (1893), 162-66.
_____. "The Globe or the Swan." Letter. *Times,* 15 Oct. 1910.
_____. "Hamlet Retold." *Saturday Review,* 17 Jan. 1914, pp. 73-74.
_____. "Lectures on Drama." *New Age,* 9 (1911), 91-92.
_____. *Monthly Letters.* Ed. A.M.T.[rethwey]. London: T. Werner Laurie, 1929.
_____. "The National Theatre Question." *New Age,* 9 (1911), 174-77.
_____. "Poetry in Drama." *Contemporary Review,* 104 (1913), 699-707.
_____. "Poetry in Drama." *The Mask,* 13 (1927), 7-9.
_____. *Prominent Points in the Life and Writings of Shakespeare.* Manchester: Univ. Press, Longmans Green, 1919.
_____. "The Representation of Shakespeare." Letter. *Nation,* 12 July 1913, p. 571.
_____. "The Shakespeare Canon." Letters. *Times Literary Supplement,* 13, 27 April, 11 May, 1922, pp. 244, 276, 308.
_____. "Shakespeare Himself." Letter. *Saturday Review,* 27 June 1914, pp. 830-31.
_____. *Shakespeare in the Theatre.* London: Sidgwick & Jackson, 1913.
_____. "Shakespeare's Experience." Letter. *Times Literary Supplement,* 13 Jan. 1927, p. 28.
_____. "Shakespeare's Profession." *Journal of the Royal Society of Arts,* 63 (1915), 325-37.
_____. "Shakespeare's Prompt-Books." Letters. *Times Literary Supplement,* 4, 18 August, 8 Sept. 1921, pp. 500, 553, 580.
_____. "Shakespeare's Prompt-Copies. A Plea for Early Texts." Letter. *Times Literary Supplement,* 3 Feb. 1921, pp. 75-76.
_____. *Some Notes on Shakespeare's Stage and Plays.* Manchester: Univ. Press, Longmans Green, 1916.
_____. "The Stage in Shakespeare's Day." *National Review,* 15 (1890), 732-91.
_____. "The Theatre and its Needs." Letter. *Times Literary Supplement,* 6 April 1922, p. 228.
_____. "Was Isabella a Novice?" Letter. *Times Literary Supplement,* 16 July 1931, p. 564.
_____. *What is Wrong with the Stage? Some Notes on the English Theatre from the Earliest Times to the Present Day.* London: Allen & Unwin, 1920.
Reynolds, George F. *Some Principles of Elizabethan Staging.* Chicago: Univ. of Chicago Press, 1905.
_____. "What We Know of the Elizabethan Stage." *Modern Philology,* 9 (1911), 47-82.
Ricketts, Charles. *Pages on Art.* London: Constable, 1913.

———. *Self Portrait taken from the Letters and Journals of Charles Ricketts, R.A.* Eds. T. Sturge Moore and Cecil Lewis. London: Peter Davies, 1939.
———. "Stage Decoration." *Fortnightly Review*, NS 92 (1912), 1083-91.
Robertson, W. Graham. *Letters from Graham Robertson.* Ed. Kerrison Preston. London: Hamish Hamilton, 1953.
———. *Time Was.* London: Hamish Hamilton, 1931.
Rothenstein, William. Letter. *Saturday Review,* 9 May 1903, p. 588.
———. *Men and Memories.* London: Faber, 1931.
Rutherston, Albert. "Decoration in the Art of the Theatre." *Monthly Chapbook,* 1, no. 2 (1919).
———. *Sixteen Designs for the Theatre.* London: Oxford Univ. Press, 1928.
St. John, Christopher, ed. *Ellen Terry and Bernard Shaw: A Correspondence.* New York: Putnam, 1932.
Savits, Jocza. *Shakespeare und die Bühne des Dramas.* Bonn: F. Cohen, 1917.
Sharp, Cecil. *The Songs and Incidental Music Arranged and Composed by Cecil J. Sharp for Granville Barker's Production of A Midsummer Night's Dream at the Savoy Theatre in January, 1914.* London: Simpkin, Marshall, Hamilton, Kent, 1914.
Shaw, George Bernard. *Bernard Shaw's Letters to Granville Barker.* Ed. C.B. Purdom. New York: Theatre Arts Books, 1957.
———. *Collected Letters.* Ed. Dan H. Laurence. 2 Vols. (I: 1874-1897; II: 1898-1910). New York: Dodd, Mead, 1965-1972.
———. *"The Dying Tongue of Great Elizabeth," (a reprint from an article in The Saturday Review, February, 1905), To which is added a footnote by William Poel.* London: London Shakespeare League, 1920.
———. *Our Theatres in the Nineties.* 3 Vols. London: Constable, 1932.
———. *Pen Portraits and Review.* London: Constable, 1932.
———. *Shaw on Shakespeare.* Ed. Edwin Wilson. London: Penguin, 1969.
———. *Shaw on Theatre.* Ed. E.J. West. New York: Hill & Wang, 1958.
Shaw, Martin. *Up to Now.* London: Oxford Univ. Press, 1929.
Souvenir Programme given by the Theatrical and Musical Professions as a Tribute to Miss Ellen Terry on the Occasion of her Jubilee Tuesday Afternoon June 12th 1906.
Spiers, R. Phené. "The Architecture of *Coriolanus* at the Lyceum Theatre." *Architectural Review,* 10 (1901), 3-21.
———. " 'Herod' at Her Majesty's Theatre." *Architectural Review,* 9 (1901), 3-12.
Stephens, Walter. *"Hamlet" as Performed at His Majesty's Theatre, Friday, 24th March 1905.* N.p., n.p., 1905.
Stern, Ernest. *My Life My Stage.* London: Victor Gollancz, 1951.
Stoker, Bram. "Irving and Stage Lighting." *Nineteenth Century,* 64 (1911), 903-12.
Symons, Arthur. "A New Art of the Stage." *Monthly Review,* 7 (1902), 157-62.
"A Symposium on the Representation of Shakespeare." *New Age,* 8 (1911), 249-50, 558-60.
Telbin, William. "Art in the Theatre: Act Drops." *Magazine of Art,* 18 (1895), 335-41.
———. "Art in the Theatre: The Question of Reform." *Magazine of Art,* 17 (1894), 44-48.
———. "The Painting of Scenery." *Magazine of Art,* 12 (1889), 195-201.
———. "Reform in Stage Scenery." *Magazine of Art,* 17 (1894), 44-48.
———. "Scenery." *Magazine of Art,* 12 (1889), 91-103.
Terry, Ellen. *Ellen's Terry's Memoirs.* Eds. Edith Craig and Christopher St. John. New York: Putnam's, 1932.
———. "Stage Decoration." *Windsor Magazine,* 35, No. 204 (Dec. 1911), 71-90.
———. *The Story of My Life: Recollections and Reflections.* New York: McClure, 1908.
Tree, Herbert Beerbohm. *Thoughts and After-Thoughts.* London: Cassell, 1913.
———. "Shakespeare and Modern Staging." *Saturday Review,* 13 Aug. 1910, pp. 198-99.
" 'Twelfth Night' at Her Majesty's Theatre." *Architectural Review,* 9 (1901), 147-50.

Walkley, A.B. *Drama and Life.* New York: Brentano's, 1908.
_____. *Playhouse Impressions.* London: T. Fisher Unwin, 1892.
Wilde, Oscar. *The Artist as Critic: Critical Writings of Oscar Wilde.* Ed. Richard Ellmann. New York: Random House, 1968.

Secondary Sources: Biography, Scholarship, Criticism

Allard, Stephen. "William Poel in America." *Theatre Arts,* 1 (1916), 24-26.
Armstrong, William A. "Bernard Shaw and Forbes-Robertson's Hamlet." *Shakespeare Quarterly,* 15 (1964), 27-31.
_____. "George Bernard Shaw: the Playwright as Producer." *Modern Drama,* 8 (1966), 347-61.
Arrell, D.H. "The Old Drama and the New: Conceptions of the Nature of Theatrical Experience in the Work of William Archer, G.B. Shaw, W.B. Yeats, E.G. Craig and H. Granville-Barker." Diss. Warfield College, Univ. of London 1976.
Arthur, Sir George. *From Phelps to Gielgud.* London: Chapman & Hall, 1936.
Bablet, Denis. *Edward Gordon Craig.* Trans. Daphne Woodward. New York: Theatre Arts Books, 1966.
Ball, Robert Hamilton. "The Shakespeare Film as Record: Sir Herbert Beerbohm Tree." *Shakespeare Survey,* 2 (1952), 227-36.
Bandel, Betty. "Ellen Terry's Foul Papers." *Theatre Survey,* 10 (1969), 43-52.
Barshay, Bernard. "Gordon Craig's Theory of Acting." *Theatre Annual,* 1947, pp. 55-63.
Berry, Douglas M. "William Telbin's Theories of Scene-Painting: the Aesthetic of Romantic Realism." *Theatre Studies,* No. 21 (1974-1975), pp. 52-60.
Bingham, Madeleine. *'The Great Lover,' The Life and Art of Herbert Beerbohm Tree.* New York: Atheneum, 1979.
_____. *Henry Irving: The Greatest Victorian Actor.* New York: Stein & Day, 1978.
Booth, Michael R. "Ellen Terry's Rehearsal Copy of *King Lear.*" *Theatre Notebook,* 33 (1979), 23-49.
_____. "Shakespeare as Spectacle and History: The Victorian Period." *Theatre Research International,* NS 1 (1976), 99-113.
_____. "Spectacle as Production Style on the Victorian Stage." *Theatre Quarterly,* 8 (1979), 8-20.
_____. *The Victorian Spectacular Theatre, 1850-1910.* Boston: Routledge & Kegan Paul, 1981.
Bottomley, Gordon. "Charles Ricketts, R.A." *Theatre Arts,* 16 (1932), 377-95.
Brereton, Austin. *The Life of Henry Irving.* London: 1908; rpt. New York: Benjamin Blom, 1969.
_____. *"H.B." and Laurence Irving.* London: Grant Richards, 1922.
Brook, Peter. "The Influence of Gordon Craig in Theory and Practice." *Drama,* NS 37 (1955), 33-36.
Brown, Ivor. "Salute to William Poel." *Saturday Review,* 16 July 1927, pp. 90-91.
Brown, John Russell. *Free Shakespeare.* London: Heinemann, 1974.
Byrne, Muriel St. Clare. "Charles Kean and the Meininger Myth." *Theatre Research,* 6 (1964), 137-53.
_____. "Fifty Years of Shakespearean Production: 1898-1948." *Shakespeare Survey,* 2 (1949), 1-20.
Carlisle, Carol Jones. "The Nineteenth-Century Actors versus the Closet Critics of Shakespeare." *Studies in Philology,* 51 (1954), 599-615.
Carr, Philip. "A Great Actor-Manager: On Herbert Beerbohm Tree." *Listener,* 17 Dec. 1953, pp. 1050-51.
Casson, Lewis. "G.B.S. and the Court Theatre." *Listener,* 12 July 1951, pp. 53-54.
_____. "William Poel and the Modern Theater." *Listener,* 10 Jan. 1952, pp. 56-58.
Church, S.H. "Ben Greet and Shakespeare." *Carnegie Magazine,* 10 (1936), 92-93.

Collins, P.A.W. "Shaw on Shakespeare." *Shakespeare Survey,* 8 (1957), 1-13.
Craig, Edward. "E.W. Godwin and the Theatre." *Theatre Notebook,* 31 (1977), 3-33.
_____. "Gordon Craig and Hubert von Herkomer." *Theatre Research,* 10 (1969), 7-16.
_____. *Gordon Craig: The Story of His Life.* New York: Knopf, 1968.
Disher, Maurice W. *The Last Romantic: The Authorised Biography of Sir John Martin-Harvey.* London: Hutchinson, 1948.
Donohue, Joseph E., Jr., ed. *The Theatrical Manager in England and America.* Princeton: Princeton Univ. Press, 1971.
Dubois, Arthur E. "Shakespeare and 19th Century Drama." *Journal of English Literary History,* 1 (1934), 163-96.
Durian, Hans. *Jocza Savits und die Münchener Shakespearebühne.* Emsdetten: Henr. & J. Leichte, 1937.
Eliot, T.S. "Gordon Craig's Socratic Dialogues." *Drama,* NS 36 (1955), 16-21.
Felton, Felix. "Max Reinhardt in England." *Theatre Research,* 5 (1963), 134-42.
Fletcher, Ifan Kyrle. "Charles Ricketts and the Theatre." *Theatre Notebook,* 22 (1967), 6-23.
Foulkes, Richard. "Herbert Beerbohm Tree's *King Henry VIII*: Expenditure, Spectacle and Experiment." *Theatre Research International,* 3 (1977), 22-32.
Garnett, Edward. "Mr. Poel and the Theatre." *English Review,* 14 (1913), 589-95.
Glick, Claris. "William Poel: His Theories and Influence." *Shakespeare Survey,* 15 (1964), 15-27.
Gomme, Allan. "Honour to William Poel." *Drama,* 9 (1933), 147-48.
Grendon, Felix. "Shakespeare and Shaw." *Sewanee Review,* 16 (1908), 168-83.
Griffith, Trevor. "Tradition and Innovation in Harley Granville Barker's *A Midsummer Night's Dream.*" *Theatre Notebook,* 30 (1976), 78-86.
Harris, Arthur J. "William Poel's Elizabethan Stage: The First Experiment." *Theatre Notebook,* 17 (1963), 111-14.
Haywood, Charles. "George Bernard Shaw on Shakesperian Music." *Shakespeare Survey,* 20 (1969), 417-26.
Hewitt, Bernard. "Gordon Craig and Post-Impressionism." *Quarterly Journal of Speech,* 30 (1944), 75-80.
Hosley, Richard. "The Origins of the So-called Elizabethan Multiple Stage." *The Drama Review,* 12 no. 2 (Winter, 1968), 28-50.
Hunt, Hugh. "Granville-Barker's Shakespearean Productions." *Theatre Research,* 10 (1969), 44-59.
Ilyan, Eugene K. "Gordon Craig's Mission to Moscow." *Theatre Arts,* 38, No. 5 (1954), 78-79, 88-90.
_____. "How Stanislavsky and Gordon Craig Produced Hamlet." *Plays and Players,* March 1957, pp. 6-7, 21.
Irving, Laurence. *Henry Irving: The Actor and his World.* New York: Macmillan, 1952.
_____. *The Precarious Crust.* London: Chatto & Windus, 1971.
_____. *The Successors.* London: Rupert Harte-Davis, 1967.
Isaac, Winifred F.E.C. *Ben Greet and the Old Vic: A Biography of Sir Philip Ben Greet.* London: self-published, 1964.
Jackson, Russell. "E.W. Godwin and Wilson Barrett's *Hamlet* of 1884." *Shakespeare Jahrbuch 1974,* pp. 184-200.
_____. "The Lyceum in Irving's Absence: G.E. Terry's Letters to Bram Stoker." *Nineteenth Century Theatre Research,* 9 (1978), 25-34.
_____. "Shakespeare in Liverpool: Edward Saker's Revivals, 1876-81." *Theatre Notebook,* 32 (1978), 100-09.
Kelly, Helen Marie-Terese. "The Granville-Barker Shakespeare Productions: A Study Based on the Promptbooks." Diss. Michigan 1965.
Kleb, William E. "E. W. Godwin and the Bancrofts." *Theatre Notebook,* 30 (1976), 122-32.

———. "Shakespeare in Tottenham Street: An 'Aesthetic' *Merchant of Venice.*" *Theatre Survey,* 16 (1975), 97-120.
Knight, Leonard H. "Beerbohm Tree in America." *Theatre Survey,* 8 (1967), 37-52.
Krabbe, Henning. *Bernard Shaw on Shakespeare and English Shakespearean Acting.* Univ. of Aarhus, 1955.
Leeper, Janet. *Edward Gordon Craig: Designs for the Theatre.* Harmondsworth: Penguin, 1948.
Manvell, Roger. *Ellen Terry.* London: Heinemann, 1968.
Marshall, Norman. *The Producer and the Play.* London: MacDonald, 1962.
Mazer, Cary M. "Harley Granville Barker's Production of *Twelfth Night* at the Savoy Theatre, November 15, 1912." Senior Thesis Princeton 1974.
———. "Shaw on the American Stage." Seminar paper Berkeley 1975.
Moore, Edward Mumford. "Changes in Shakespearean Production from the Age of Irving to Granville-Barker." Diss. Harvard 1968.
———. "William Poel." *Shakespeare Survey,* 23 (1972), 21-36.
Mullin, Michael. "Strange Images of Death: Sir Herbert Beerbohm Tree's *Macbeth,* 1911." *Theatre Survey,* 17 (1976), 125-42.
Nash, George. *Edward Gordon Craig, 1872-1966.* London: Her Majesty's Stationery Office, 1967.
Pearson, Hesketh. *Beerbohm Tree: His Life and Laughter.* New York: Harper Bros., 1956.
Prideaux, Tom. *Love or Nothing: The Life and Times of Ellen Terry.* New York: Scribner's 1975.
Purdom, C.B. *Harley Granville Barker: Man of the Theatre, Dramatist and Scholar.* London: Rockliff, 1955.
Richards, Kenneth, and Peter Thompson, eds. *Essays on Nineteenth Century British Theatre.* London: Methuen, 1971.
Ripley, John. "'Imagination Holds Dominion': Stage Spectacle in Beerbohm Tree's Productions, 1897-1900." *Theatre Survey,* 9 (1968), 11-70.
Rosenfeld, Sybil. "Alma Tadema's Designs for Henry Irving's *Coriolanus.*" *Shakespeare Jahrbuch 1974,* pp. 84-95.
———. "Charles Ricketts's Designs for the Theatre." *Theatre Notebook,* 35 (1981), 12-17.
———. "Hubert Herkomer's Theatrical Theories and Practice and the New Stagecraft." In *The Triple Bond: Plays, Mainly Shakespearean, in Performance.* Ed. Joseph G. Price. University Park: Pennsylvania State Univ. Press, 1975.
———. "Some Experiments of Beerbohm Tree." *Nineteenth Century Theatre Research,* 2 (1974), 75-83.
Rostrow, David. "F.R. Benson's Early Productions of Shakespeare's Roman Plays at Stratford." *Theatre Notebook,* 25 (1970-71), 46-54.
Rowell, George. "A Lyceum Sketchbook." *Nineteenth Century Theatre Research,* 6 (1978),1-23.
———. "Tree's Shakespeare Festivals (1905-1913)." *Theatre Notebook,* 39 (1975), 74-81.
Sayler, Oliver M., ed. *Max Reinhardt and his Theatre.* New York: Brentano's, 1924.
Schmitt, Anthony B. "Herbert Beerbohm Tree produces *The Winter's Tale.*" *The Ohio State University Theatre Collection Bulletin,* No. 17 (1970), pp. 20-31.
Schultz, Stephen C. "Two Notes on William Poel's Source." *Nineteenth Century Theatre Research,* 2 (1974), 85-91.
———. "William Poel on the Speaking of Shakespearean Verse: A Reevaluation." *Shakespeare Quarterly,* 28 (1977), 334-50.
Schuttler, Georg W. "Sherlock Holmes as Hamlet?" *Theatre Survey,* (1977), 72-85.
Senelick, Laurence. "The Craig-Stanislavsky *Hamlet* at the Moscow Art Theatre." *Theatre Quarterly,* 6, No. 22 (1976), 56-122.
———. "Moscow and Monodrama: The Meaning of the Craig-Stanislavsky *Hamlet.*" *Theatre Research International,* 6 (1981), 109-124.
Shank, Theodore J. "Shakespeare and Nineteenth Century Realism." *Theatre Survey,* 4 (1963), 59-75.

Shattuck, Charles H. *The Shakespeare Promptbooks: A Descriptive Catalogue.*. Urbana: Univ. Of Illinois Press, 1965.
Silverman, Albert H. "Bernard Shaw's Shakespeare Criticism." *PMLA,* 72 (1957), 722-36.
Smith, J. Percy. "Superman v. Man: Bernard Shaw on Shakespeare." *Yale Review,* 42 (1952), 75-82.
Somerset, J.A.B. "William Poel's First Full Platform Stage." *Theatre Notebook,* 20 (1966), 118-21.
South, R.J. "Changes in the Interpretation of Shakespeare in the Second Half of the Nineteenth Century: The Treatment of the Plays by Theatres and Dramatic Critics." Diss. Queen Mary's College, Univ. of London 1951-52.
Speaight, Robert. *Shakespeare on the Stage.* Boston: Little, Brown, 1973.
_____ "William Poel, Innovator and Restorer." *Shakespeare Newsletter,* 4 (1954), 17.
_____. *William Poel and the Elizabethan Revival.* London: Heinemann, 1954.
Sprague, Arthur Colby. "Shakespeare and William Poel." *Univ. of Toronto Quarterly,* 17 (1947).
Steen, Marguerite. *A Pride of Terrys: Family Saga.* London: Longmans, Green 1962.
Stoker, Bram. *Personal Reminiscences of Henry Irving.* London: Macmillan, 1906.
Stokes, John. *Resistible Theatres: Enterprise and Experiment in the Late Nineteenth Century.* London: Paul Elek, 1972.
Strode, Scott Kreider. "Sir Johnston Forbes-Robertson (1853-1937): A Study and Assessment of His Theatrical Career." Diss. Indiana 1974.
Styan, J.L. *The Shakespeare Revolution: Criticism and Performance in the Twentieth Century.* Cambridge: Cambridge Univ. Press 1977.
Thomas, Noel K. "Harley Granville-Barker and the Greek Drama." *Educational Theatre Journal,* 7 (1955), 294-300.
_____. "A Study of Harley Granville-Barker as Producer and Dramatist." MA Thesis Bristol 1955-56.
Trewin, J.C. *Benson and the Bensonians.* London: Barrie & Rockliff, 1960.
_____. *Shakespeare on the English Stage 1900-1964.* London: Barrie & Rockliff, 1964.
Wells, Stanley. "Shakespeare in Max Beerbohm's Theatre Criticism." *Shakespeare Survey,* 29 (1976), 132-44.
Whitworth, Geoffrey. *Harley Granville-Barker, 1877-1946.* London: Sidgwick & Jackson, 1948.
William, David Terry. "An Analysis of Representative Productions of Sir Frank Benson." Diss. Indiana 1974.
Williams, Gary J. *"A Midsummer Night's Dream:* The English and American Popular Traditions and Harley Granville-Barker's 'World Arbitrarily Made.' " *Theatre Studies,* No. 23 (1976-77), pp. 40-52.

Additional Primary and Secondary Sources, Relating to Other Aspects of the Edwardian Theatre

"Actor-Managers." Articles by Bram Stoker, Henry Irving, and Charles Wyndham. *Nineteenth Century,* 27 (1890), 1040-51.
Adlard, Eleanor, ed. *Edy: Recollections of Edith Craig.* London: Frederick Muller, 1949.
Agate, James. "Irving as an Artist." *Listener,* 9 Feb. 1938, pp. 289-90.
Altman, George, and Ralph Freud, Kenneth Macgowan and William Melnitz. *Theater Pictorial.* Berkeley: Univ. of California Press, 1953.
Archer, William. "The Blight on the Drama." *Fortnightly Review,* NS 61 (1897), 21-32.
_____. *Masks or Faces?* 1888; rpt. New York: Hill & Wang, 1957.
_____. "A Plea for an Endowed Theatre." *Fortnightly Review,* NS 45 (1889), 610-26.
_____. "What can be done for the Drama." *Anglo-Saxon Review,* 4 (1900), 223-42.
Armstrong, Cecil Ferard. *The Actor's Companion.* London: Mills & Boon, 1912.
Asche, Oscar. *Chu Chin Chow.* London: Samuel French, 1931.
_____. *Acting Version of Measure for Measure Arranged by Oscar Asche for Otho Stuart's*

Production at the Adelphi Theatre March 1906 Together with Shakespeare's Full Text. London: J.J. Dent, 1906.
Ashwell, Lena. *Myself a Player*. London: Michael Joseph, 1936.
Aylmer, Felix. "The One That Got Away." *Drama,* NS, no. 86 (1967), 31-33.
Bancroft, Squire, and Marie Squire. *The Bancrofts: Recollections of Sixty Years.* 1909; rpt. New York: Benjamin Blom, 1969.
Baker, Michael. *The Rise of the Victorian Actor.* Totowa, N.J.: Rowman & Littlefield, 1978.
Barnes, J.H. *The Rise of the Victorian Actor.* London: Chapman & Hall, 1914.
―――. "Irving Days at the Lyceum." *Nineteenth Century,* 93 (1923), 99-106.
Barnes, Sir Kenneth R. *Welcome, Good Friends.* London: Peter Davies, 1958.
Beckerman, Bernard. *Shakespeare at the Globe: 1599-1609.* New York: Collier Books, 1966.
Benson, Constance. *Mainly Players: Bensonian Memories.* London: Thornton Butterworth, 1926.
Benson, Sir Frank. *I Want to Go on the Stage. Do! Don't! Why?* London: Ernest Benn, 1926.
―――. *My Memoirs.* London: Ernest Benn, 1930.
―――. "The National Theatre." *Nineteenth Century,* 49 (1901), 772-80.
Besier, Rudolph. *The Virgin Goddess.* London: J.M. Dent, 1907.
Bettany, W.A. Lewis. "The Strange Case of Mr. Forbes-Robertson." *Theatre,* 31 (1893), 155-61.
Binyon, Laurence. *Attila.* London: John Murray, 1907.
Booth, Michael R. "East End and West End: Class and Audience in Victorian London." *Theatre Research International,* 2 (1977), 98-103.
Brown, Ivor, and George Fearon. *Amazing Monument: A Short History of the Shakespeare Industry.* London: Heinemann, 1939.
Buckley, Reginald R. "F.R. Benson and the Stratford-on-Avon Festival." *World's Work,* April 1911.
―――. *The Shakespeare Revival and the Stratford-upon-Avon Movement.* London: George Allen, 1911.
Bryan, George B. "Dear Winston's Clever Mother: Lady Randolph Churchill and the National Theatre." *Theatre Survey,* 15 (1974), 143-70.
Burton, Hal, ed. *Great Acting.* London: British Broadcasting Corporation, 1967.
Burton, Percy. *Adventures among Immortals.* London: Hutchinson, 1938.
Calhoun, Eleanor. *Pleasures and Palaces: The Memoirs of Princess Lazarovitch-Hrebelianovich.* New York: Century Co., 1915.
Calvert, Louis. *Problems of the Actor.* New York: Henry Holt, 1918.
Calvert, Mrs. Charles. *Sixty-Eight Years on the Stage.* London: Mills & Boon, 1911.
Campbell, Mrs. Patrick. *My Life and Some Letters.* New York: Dodd, Mead, 1922.
Cannan, Gilbert. *The Joy of the Theatre.* New York: E.P. Dutton, 1913.
Carr, Alice Comyns. *Reminiscences.* London: Hutchinson, n.d.
Carr, J. Comyns. *Coasting Bohemia.* London: Macmillan, 1914.
―――. *Some Eminent Victorians.* London: Duckworth, 1908.
―――. *Tristram and Iseult.* London: Duckworth, 1906.
Carr, Philip. "The National Theatre Plan: Memories of the Early Struggle." *Manchester Guardian,* 13 July 1951, p. 6.
Carter, Huntly. *The New Spirit in Drama and Art.* London: Frank Palmer, 1912.
―――. *The New Spirit in the European Theatre, 1914-1924.* London: Ernest Benn, 1925.
Chapman-Huston, Major Desmond. *The Lamp of Memory.* London: Skeffington, 1949.
Clarence, O.B. *No Complaints.* London: Jonathan Cape, 1943.
Cochran, C.B. *Secrets of a Showman.* London: Heinemann, 1925.
Coffin, Hayden. *Hayden Coffin's Book.* London: Alston Rivers, 1930.
Cole, Marion. *Fogie: The Life of Elsie Fogarty, C.B.E.* London: Peter Davies, 1967.
Collier, Constance. *Harlequinade: The Story of My Life.* London: John Lane, 1929.
Complimentary Dinner to Mr. J.E. Vedrenne and Mr. H. Granville Barker at the Criterion Restaurant, 7th July, 1907.

Lyttelton, the Hon. Mrs. Alfred. "The National Memorial Theatre: The Work of the Shakespeare Memorial Committee." *World's Work,* April 1911.
MacCarthy, Desmond. *The Court Theatre 1904-1907.* London: A.H. Bullen, 1907.
McCarthy, Lillah. *Myself and My Friends.* New York: E.P. Dutton, 1933.
Mackinnon, Alan. *The Oxford Amateurs.* London: Chapman & Hall, 1910.
MacOwan, Michael. "Working with a Genius." *Plays and Players,* 1 no. 10 (1954), 7.
MacQueen-Pope, W. *Carriages at Eleven: The Story of the Edwardian Theatre.* London: Hutchinson, 1947.
Machen, Arthur. "The Benson Company: A Memory." *Theatre Arts,* 15 (1931), 735-38.
_____. *Far Off Things.* London: Martin Secker, 1922.
_____. *Things Near and Far.* London: Martin Secker, 1932.
Mander, Raymond, and Joe Mitchenson. *The Lost Theatres of London.* New York: Taplinger, 1968.
_____. *The Theatres of London.* New York: Hill & Wang, 1961.
_____. *Theatrical Companion to Shaw.* New York: Pitman, 1955.
Marshall, Norman. *The Other Theatre.* London: John Lehmann, 1947.
Mason, A.E.W. *Sir George Alexander and the St. James's Theatre.* London: Macmillan, 1935.
Mason, T. Redfern. "Forbes-Robertson's Coming Visit." *Theatre Magazine,* 3 (1903), 198-200.
Matthews, Brander, ed. *Papers on Acting.* New York: Hill & Wang, 1958.
"Mr. Granville Barker's Gramophones." *New Age,* 12 (1913), 225-26.
Morley, Malcolm. *Margate and its Theatres 1730-1965.* London: Museum Press, 1966.
Neilson, Julia. *This for Remembrance.* London: Hurst & Blackett, 1941.
Newton, H. Chance. *Cues and Curtain Calls.* London: John Lane, 1927.
Nicoll, Allardyce. *English Drama 1900-1930: The Beginnings of the Modern Period.* Cambridge: Cambridge Univ. Press, 1973.
Novick, Julius Lerner. "Henry Irving and 'Natural' Acting." Diss. Yale 1966.
Nowell-Smith, Simon, ed. *Edwardian England, 1901-1914.* London: Oxford Univ. Press, 1964.
"On Cutting Shakespeare." Letters. *Fortnightly Review* and *Nation: Fortnightly:* 112 (1919), 215-18 (Shaw): 479-80 (Poel). *Nation:* 25 (1919) 559-60 (Archer), 588-89, (Drinkwater); 617-18 (Poel, Archer, Drinkwater); 671-72 (Shaw); 700-01 (Archer); 756 (Bennett); 767 (Barker); 36 (1919), 38 (Archer).
Palmer, John. *The Future of the Theatre.* London: G. Bell, 1913.
Parker, John. *Who's Who in the Theatre.* 4th ed. London: Pitman, 1922.
Parker, Louis N. *Several of My Lives.* London: Chapman & Hall, 1928.
Parola, Gene J. "Walter Hampden's Career as Actor-Manager." Diss. Indiana 1970.
Parts I have Played: A Photographic and Descriptive Biography. Westminster: Abbey Press, 1909. [Lewis Waller, Cyril Maude, Martin Harvey, H.B. Irving and Dorothea Baird, Matheson Lang and Hutin Britton, George Alexander.]
Patterson, Ada. "An Interview with John Forbes-Robertson." *Theatre Magazine,* 7 (1907), 74-78.
Patterson, Marjorie. *The Dust of the Road.* London: Chatto & Windus, 1913.
Paulus, Gretchen. "Beerbohm Tree and 'The New Drama.' " *Univ. of Toronto Quarterly,* 27 (1957), 103-15.
Pearson, Hesketh. "G.B.S. in Rehearsal." *Listener,* 15 Aug. 1956, pp. 229-30.
_____. "A Great Theatrical Management." *Theatre Arts,* 39, No. 9 (1955), 76-77, 94-95.
_____. *Hesketh Pearson by Himself.* London: Heinemann, 1965.
_____. *The Last Actor-Managers.* New York: Harper, 1950.
_____. *The Life of Oscar Wilde.* London: Penguin, 1954.
_____. *Modern Men and Mummers.* New York: Harcourt, Brace, n.d.
Pemberton, T. Edgar. *The Kendals, a Biography.* London: C. Arthur Pearson, 1900.
Penzel, Frederick. *Theatre Lighting Before Electricity.* Middletown, Conn.: Wesleyan Univ. Press, 1978.
Phillips, Stephen. *Herod.* London: John Lane, 1901.
_____. *Nero.* London: Macmillan, 1906.
_____. *Paolo and Francesca.* London: John Lane, 1900.

———. *Ulysses*. London: John Lane, 1902.
———, and J. Comyns Carr. *Faust*. London: Macmillan, 1908.
Pinero, Sir Arthur. "The Theatre in the 'Seventies." In *The Eighteen-Seventies*. Ed. Harley Granville-Barker. Cambridge: Cambridge Univ. Press, 1929.
Pogson, Rex. *Miss Horniman and the Gaiety Theatre, Manchester*. London: Rockliff, 1952.
Pollock, Walter Herries. *Impressions of Henry Irving*. London: Longmans, Green, 1908.
Quartermaine, Leon. "Talking About Actors and Acting." *Shaw Review*, 3 (1960), 6-13.
Robins, Elizabeth. *Both Sides of the Curtain*. London: Heinemann, 1940.
———. *Theatre and Friendship: Some Henry James Letters*. New York: Putnam's, 1932.
Robinson, Lennox. *Curtain Up: An Autobiography*. London: Michael Joseph, 1942.
Rowell, George, ed. *Victorian Dramatic Criticism*. London: Methuen, 1971.
———. *The Victorian Theatre*. 2nd ed. Cambridge: Cambridge Univ. Press, 1978.
Schmidt, Karl. "How Barker Puts Plays On." *Harper's Weekly*, 60 (30 Jan. 1915), 115-16.
Schultz, Stephen C. "Towards an Irvingesque Theory of Shakespearean Acting." *Quarterly Journal of Speech*, 61 (1975), 428-38.
Scott, Clement. "Henry Irving: Actor, Manager and Diplomatist." *International Monthly*, 1 (1900), 323-39.
"Shakespeare: A Standard Text." Letters. *Times Literary Supplement:* 3 Feb. 1921 (Poel); 10 Feb. (Alfred W. Pollard, Richmond Noble); 17 Feb. (Barker, Percy Simpson); 24 Feb. (Poel); 3 March (Simpson); 17 March (Shaw); 24 March (Pollard); 31 March (Shaw); 7 April (Pollard, Marshall Montgomery, J. Dover Wilson, G.F. Abbott); 14 April (Shaw, Poel); 21 April (Pollard, Wilson).
Short, Ernest. *Theatrical Cavalcade*. London: Eyre & Spottiswoode, 1942.
Sparrow, W. Shaw. *Memories of Art and Life*. London: John Lane, 1925.
Speaight, Robert. *The Property Basket*. London: Collins & Harvill, 1970.
"The Stage as a Profession: an 1897 Controversy." *Shaw Review*, 11 (1968), 52-78.
Standing, Percy Cross. *Sir Lawrence Alma-Tadema, O.M., R.A.* London: Cassell, 1905.
Stephen, Walter. *A Plea for a National Repertory Theatre*. N.p.: n.p., 1905.
———. *The Proposed World's Tribute to Shakespeare, A Plea for the Erection of a Memorial Statue and a National Theatre*. London: Cassell, 1905.
Stier, Theodore. "Barker and Shaw at the Court Theatre: A View from the Pit." *Shaw Review*, 10 (1967), 18-33.
Stoker, Bram. "The Question of a National Theatre." *Nineteenth Century*, 63 (1908), 734-42.
Stratman, Carl J. *Britain's Theatrical Periodicals 1720-1967: A Bibliography*. New York: New York Public Library, 1972.
Stuart, Otho. *Memories of an Outsider*. Unpublished typescript, 126 pp., in the possession of Miss Betty Andraea, daughter of Otho Stuart Andraea.
Tree, Herbert Beerbohm. "The Actor-Manager. A Stage Reply." *Fortnightly Review*, NS 48 (1890), 16-19.
———. "The London Stage: A Reply." *Fortnightly Review*, NS 47 (1890), 922-31.
———. *Nothing Matters and Other Stories*. Boston: Houghton Mifflin, 1917.
Trench, Herbert. *The Collected Works of Herbert Trench*. London: Jonathan Cape, 1924.
Trewin, J.C. *The Edwardian Theatre*. Totowa, N.J.: Rowman & Littlefield, 1976.
———. *The Theatre Since 1900*. London: Andrew Dakers, 1951.
Vanbrugh, Irene. *To Tell My Story*. London: Hutchinson, 1948.
Vanbrugh, Violet. *Dare to be Wise*. London: Hodder & Stoughton, 1926.
———. "The Irving I Remember." *Listener*, 9 Feb. 1938, 290-91.
Vardac, Nicholas. *Stage to Screen: Theatrical Method from Garrick to Griffith*. Cambridge: Harvard Univ. Press, 1949.
Wall, Vincent. *Bernard Shaw: Pygmalion to Many Players*. Ann Arbor: Univ. of Michigan Press, 1973.

Waller, Lewis. "My Reminiscences." *Strand Magazine,* 38 (1909), 655-63.
Ward, Genevieve. *Both Sides of the Curtain.* London: Cassell, 1918.
Warwick, Lou. *The Mackenzies Called Compton.* Northampton: Self-published, 1977.
Watson, M.J. "The Growth of an Independent Theatre Movement in London, 1891-1914." M. Litt. Thesis Bristol 1969-1970.
West, E.J. "Irving in Shakespeare: Interpretation or Creation?" *Shakespeare Survey,* 6 (1955), 415-22.
Whitworth, Geoffrey. *The Making of a National Theatre.* London: Faber, n.d.
Wilde, Oscar. *The Letters of Oscar Wilde.* Ed. Rupert Harte-Davis. London: Rupert Harte-Davis, 1962.
Wills, Lt. Col. the Rev. Freeman, and The Rev. Canon Langbridge. *The Only Way.* London: Frederick Muller, 1942.
Wills, W.G. *Faust.* N.p.: n.p., 1886.
Wilson, A.E. *The Edwardian Theatre.* London: Barker, 1951.
Yeats, W.B. *Ideas of Good and Evil.* New York: Macmillan, 1903.

Index

Abstraction, 92, 94, 95, 106, 108, 109, 118, 120
Acis and Galatea (Purcell), 94, 97, 98
Actor: as determinant of locale, 130; rapport with audience, 70, 134, 135; relation to environment, 13, 19-22, 69
Actor-manager system, 2, 159
Actor's Theatre, 18, 19
Adams, John Cranford, 62
Admirable Bashville, The (Shaw), 64-65
Aeschylus, 107; *Agamemnon,* 33
Agamemnon (Aeschylus), 33
Aiglon, L' (Rostand), 19
Ainley, Henry: as Laertes, 217, n.62; as Leontes, 142
Albright, Victor, 60, 79; use of painted cloths, 61
Aldwych Theatre, 9
Alexander, George: on pageantry, 218, n.68; 218, n.69; PRODUCTIONS: *As You Like It,* 218, n.69; 228, n.26; *Turandot,* 112
All's Well That Ends Well, PRODUCTIONS: Amateur (1895), 4; Poel (postwar), 83
Alma Tadema, Lawrence: coaches Tree, 19; combines two- and three-dimensional scenery, 46; front scenes, 45-46; PRODUCTIONS: *Coriolanus,* 11, 35-36, 40, 45, 45-46, Illus. 3, 5, 6, 7; *Julius Caesar,* 46
Alternation system, 34-38, 39, 60, 65, 88, 102
Alternation theory, 58, 62-63, 79, 88, 128
Anderson, Mary, 35, 45
Androcles and the Lion (Shaw), 228, n.25
Anti-illusionism, 91
Antoine, Andre: use of split scenes, 63, 148; PRODUCTIONS: *King Lear,* 114, 148
Antony and Cleopatra, 4, 51, 64, 130, 133, 153; PRODUCTIONS: Asche, 14, 217, n.60, 31, 32, 41; Tree, 11, 31, 33, Illus. 1, 2
A posteriori argumentation, 60
Appia, Adolph, 88-89, 90, 94
Apology for Poetry (Sidney), 61
Apron stage, 8, 218, n.69; 76, 77, 78, 108, 113, 114, 120, 134-37, 137, 148, Illus. 28, 29, 30
Archaeology, 9-10, 14, 17, 18, 20, 69, 81, 82, 116-17, 120, 140, 154
Archer, William, 148: on alternation, 34-35; on *a posteriori* argumentation, 223, n.49; on Barker's fairies, 146; on costumed audiences, 80; exponent of Swan drawing, 54, 63; on Greet's Shakespeare seasons, 71; on localization, 11; manuscript notes on the Elizabethan stage, 63-64; on the masque in Alexander's *As You Like It,* 218, n.69; model of the Fortune stage, 64; on Poel's use of space, 70; on progress, 54; rejects alternation but uses zones, 64, Illus. 18; rejects Brodmeier, 63; rejects competition of sensory perception, 67; on reusable scenery, 32; on scene-changing in darkness, 37; on Shakespeare plays he had not seen, 4; on Shakespeare's supposed dissatisfaction with his theatre, 51; on Shakespeare's transcendence of his age, 236, n.4; supports Herkomer, 92; on tableaux, 22-23
Architectural stages, 74, 114, 115
Architectural Review, 45
Aristotelian form, 31
Artifice, 42, 43, 44, 48, 110
Artists, relation to their age, 151, 152, 156
Asche, Oscar: use of conventionalized borders, 92; use of narrative interpolations, 216, n.59, 217, n.60; stage for touring, 114-15; touring practices, 32; unnecessary scene-waits, 38; PRODUCTIONS:

Antony and Cleopatra, 14, 217, n.60, 31, 32, 41; *As You Like It,* 97; *Atilla,* 109, 110; *Chu Chin Chow,* 45, 92; *Hamlet,* 116; *Julius Caesar,* 216, n.59; 32; *Kismet,* 45; *Measure for Measure,* 14, 15; *The Merry Wives of Windsor,* 34; *A Midsummer Night's Dream,* 228, n.26; *Othello,* 32; *The Taming of the Shrew,* 34, 38; WORKS: *Chu Chin Chow,* 45, 92
As You Like It, 153; as pastoral, 72; PRODUCTIONS: Asche, 97; Alexander, 218, n.69, 228, n.26; Benson, 34; Courtneidge, 10; Davis/Lawrence, 74; Flanagan, 218, n.68; Godwin, 89; Playfair/Fraser, 227, n.4
Atilla (Binyon), 109, 110
Audience: dressed as Elizabethans, 69, 80-81, Illus. 22; as passive spectators, 9; receptivity to stage event, 80-81, 84, 124

Baker, George Piece: use of costumed audiences, 81; use of painted drops, 61; use of side curtains, 62; use of traverses, 60-61; PRODUCTIONS: *Hamlet,* 61, 70, 81, Illus. 22
Bakst, Leon, 86, 226, n.3, 94
Balzac, Honoré de, *For the Soul of the King,* 28
Bancroft, Squire and Marie, 4: on reality, 56; renovation of the Haymarket, 9; PRODUCTIONS: *The Merchant of Venice,* 16
Barker, Harley Granville, 2, 43, 54-55, 123-50: on actor as determinant of locale, 130; on actor/audience rapport, 134; on aprons, 137; use of aprons, 134-37; on audience as community, 82; on audience receptivity, 82, 124, 126, 127; on Berlin Theatre Exhibition, 137; use of built-up scenes, 139-40, 145; use of clowns, 148; on collaboration, 138-39, 158; on competition of sensory perception, 132; on convention, 124-31; on constructivism, 138; on continuity, 131; on Craig, 138; on *Cymbeline,* 130-31; use of decorative curtains, 131, 144, 147; use of drapery, 144; in *Edward II,* 113; on Elizabethanism, 80, 125-26, 144; on the environment as reflection of the drama, 130-31; on experimentation, 142-43; on fairies, 146-47; use of false proscenium, 136; on fantasy, 131; use of front scenes, 145; on Garrick, 124; on *Henry V* chorus, 52; on historical self-awareness, 52, 126, 127; on the illusion of the actor, 130, 133; on imaginative visualization of scenes, 132; on the inner stage, 134; use of insert scenes, 145, 146; use of lighting, 135, 142, 143-44; on localization, 129-30, 131, 144; manipulation of convention, 142; use of masks, 143; on masques, 52; on music, 82, 127; use of narrative interpolations, 146; on the New Stagecraft, 131; on offstage action, 131; on perception, 132-33; on the platform stage, 134; as playwright, 85; on the playwright's intentions, 155-56; on Poel, 138; on presentationalism, 138; use of profile groupings, 144; on proscenium stages, 137; on Reinhardt, 156; on relation of drama to the theatre for which it was written, 127-28; on reusable scenery, 32; use of rostrum, 136; on the Russian Ballet, 138; on Shakespeare's transcendence of his age, 236, n.4; use of shock, 141-42; on sight-lines, 129, 136, 137; on space, 134-37; use of split scenes, 63, 148; on spontaneity of response, 124, 126; on symbolism, 138; use of tableau scene endings, 146; on the temporality of drama, 152; on textual emendation, 125; on theatre in the round, 137; on training an audience, 127; on "translation," 124, 152; on the turntable, 137; urged by Shaw to use curved borders, 92; writes letter of introduction for Poel, 138; on the zone theory, 134; PRODUCTIONS: *The Death of Tintagiles,* 109; Greek productions, 53, 81-82, 87; *Iphigenia in Taurus,* 134, 143, Illus. 16, 17; *A Midsummer Night's Dream,* 82, 230, n.80, 123, 136, 140, 141, 146-49, Illus. 32; Maeterlinck plays, 87; *Macbeth* (projected), 142; Savoy Shakespeare, 74, 113-14, 115, 123, 129, 131, 134, 135, 136, 137, 139-150, Illus. 29, 30, 31, 32, 33; *Twelfth Night,* 74, 123, 131, 136, 140, 141, 142, 144-46, 147, 148, 155, Illus. 29, 30, 31; *The Winter's Tale,* 123, 131, 136, 140, 141-42, 143-44, 145, 147, 148, 158, Illus. 29, 33; WORKS: *Prunella,* 228, n.25, 98
Barnes, J. H., 9
Barrett, Wilson: PRODUCTIONS: *Hamlet,* 12, 73
Barrie, J. M., *Peter Pan,* 96, 228, n.26

Beaumont, Francis, *The Knight of the Burning Pestle,* 81
Beerbohm, Max: on Barker and the Greeks, 81-82; on Craig's opera designs, 98; on Craig's *Vikings,* 99, 103; on the Elizabethan Stage Society, 53; on environment as reflection of the drama, 19; on the Greek theatre, 53-54, 92; on Harker's designs for *As You Like It,* 97; on illusion, 13, 97; on H. B. Irving's *For the Soul of the King,* 28; on Lang's *Romeo and Juliet,* 25; on Leigh's *Tempest,* 72-73; rejection of the competition of sensory perception, 67-68; rejection of imaginative visualization of scenes, 67-68; on Sidney Lee, 68; on Shakespeare as a Romantic, 53-54; on Tree's *Twelfth Night,* 24
Bells, The (Lewis), 28
Benson, Constance, 227, n.4
Benson, Frank, 74: absent from Stratford, 75; and Alma Tadema, 19; use of alternation, 35; use of narrative interpolations, 216 n.59, 217, n.60, 217, n.61; purchase of Forbes Robertson's *Macbeth,* 32; use of scene-changes in darkness, 37; on Shakespeare's transcendence of his age, 236, n.4; touring practices, 32; PRODUCTIONS: *Agamemnon,* 33; *As You Like It,* 34; *The Comedy of Errors,* 214, n.11; *Coriolanus,* 214, n.11; *Hamlet,* 217, n.60; *Henry VI, part two,* 34; *Julius Caesar,* 216, n.59; *Macbeth,* 216, n.59, 35; *A Midsummer Night's Dream,* 33; *Richard II,* 214, n.11, 217, n.61; *Richard III,* 14, 217, n.61, 35; *The Tempest,* 214, n.11, 72
Berlin Theatre Exhibition, 137
Bernhardt, Sarah, 18-19, 83
Bethlehem (Housman), 97
Binyon, Laurence, *Attila,* 109, 110
Blake, William, 87
Blue Bird, The (Maeterlinck), 96, 111
Boer War, 47, Illus. 11
Borders, 91-92, 100
Borsa, Mario: on Poel's use of costumes, 82-83; on Tree's tableaux, 47-48
Boucicault, Dion, *The Corsican Brothers,* 28
Bourchier, Arthur: advocates Greek stage for Shakespeare, 53; as Henry VIII, 19, 218, n.69, 83; use of narrative interpolation, 217, n.62; on Shakespeare's dissatisfaction with his stage, 51; on two-dimensional scenery, 45; PRODUCTIONS: *Macbeth,* 217, n.62; 31; *The Merchant of Venice,* 15-16, 18, 74, 75-76

Box sets, 30. *See also* Fourth wall realism
Bradfield, Greek Theatre, 63, Illus. 16, 17
Bradley, A. C., 23-24
Braithwaite, Lillian, 73
Brandes, Georg, 11
Brecht, Bertolt, 148
Bridges-Adams, W.: on Baker and Reinhardt, 138; on Barker's lighting, 142; on Barker's shock tactics, 141-42; on Irving and stage lighting, 21; on H. B. Irving's *Markheim,* 12; productions, 115; use of split scenes, 63
British Empire Shakespeare Society (B. E. S. S.), 4, 74
Brodmeier, Cecil, 64, 114: use of side walls, 62, Illus. 15; split scenes, 114, 147-48; use of traverses, 60, 65; zone theory, 63
Brook, Peter, 148
Brown, John Russell, 2-3
Built-up scenes, 17, 30, 34-35, 36, 39, 44, 45, 48, 65, 72, 90, 91, 93, 102, 114, 120, 135, 139-40, 145, Illus. 2, 4
Burbage, Richard, 127, 148

Calhoun, Eleanor, 89-90
Calvert, Louis: in *Oedipus,* 111; PRODUCTIONS: *Henry V,* 74; *The Winter's Tale,* 74
Carr, Comyns, 227, n.4
Carr, Philip, 72
Carter, Huntly, 78, 85
Casson, Lewis: use of split scenes, 63, 148; work for Fry, 73; PRODUCTIONS: *Julius Caesar,* 114
Carpenter, Ernest, 25, 237, n.27; PRODUCTIONS: *Romeo and Juliet,* 31
Carpenter scenes, 34-35, 36
Cashel Byron's Profession (Shaw), 64
Chambers, E. K., 51
Changeable scenery, 88, 89
Character: alienation from environment, 26, 95-96; integration with environment, 26-29
Chaste Maid of Cheapside, The (Middleton), 75
Christmas Pantomime, 27, 80, 96, 98
Chu Chin Chow (Asche), 45, 92
Cimabue, 104
Clowns, 148-49
Cochran, C. B., 86
Coleman, George, 47
Coliseum, 90
Collaboration, 138-39, 158
Comedy of Errors, The, 4: PRODUCTIONS: Benson, 214, n.11; Kirwan, 75-76; Poel, 70; Reinhardt, 156

Competition of sensory percention. See Perception
Compositional values, 19-22
Compton Comedy Company, 32
Constructivism, 138
Continental invasion, 86-87
Continuity, 30-31, 34, 38, 47, 48, 58, 59, 65, 77-78, 88, 102, 105, 112, 114, 118, 120, 131
Conventions, 8, 34, 42-48, 50, 59, 62, 65, 68, 80, 82, 84, 88, 91, 92, 93, 94, 110, 124-31, 142, 149, 150
Conventional playing space, 88
Copeau, Jacques, 130
Corsican Brothers, The, 28
Courtneidge, Robert, 10
Coriolanus, 4, 64; PRODUCTIONS: Benson, 214, n.11; Irving, 214, n.11, 11, 35-36, 40, 41, 45-46, Illus. 3, 5, 6, 7; Poel, 83, 153
Costume, 18-19, 56-57, 82-83, 140-41, 145-56, 158, Illus. 33
Costume repertoire, 4
Cowden Clarke, Mary, *The Girlhood of Shakespeare's Heroines,* 23-24
Craig, Edward, 92, 105
Craig, Edward Gordon, 2, 42, 85, 86, 88, 150, 154, 158: on appropriate staging for each play, 154; on archaeology, 104; on Barker, 136, 137-38, 157; compatibility of early designs with music, 98; designs for Tree's *Macbeth,* 29, 93, 95-96, 105, 106; on draped stages, 75; incorporates Herkomer's ideas, 92; on individual v. institution, 159; influences Harvey, 116; on interpretive mandate, 156; on Irving and lighting, 216, n.47; invited to design Harvey's *Hamlet,* 120; on masks, 157; on masques, 52; on mutable scenery, 88-89; on the New Stagecraft, 87; praises W. J. Helmsley, 94; on Reinhardt, 157; renovation of the Imperial Theatre, 99-100; on Ricketts, 110; on Shakespeare's Romanticism, 107; on the Russian Ballet, 226, n.3; "Scene," 95, 103; screens, 89, 105; "seven-headed director," 138-39, 157; on sky effects, 92; on Tree's *Twelfth Night,* 46, 93-94; übermarionette, 157; on the unstageability of *Hamlet,* 151; PRODUCTIONS: *Acis and Galatea,* 94; *Dido and Aeneas,* 92, 97-98; *Hamlet,* 29, 89, 105-6; *The Merchant of Venice* (projected), 89, 105; *Much Ado About Nothing,* 99, 101-5, 144, Illus. 23, 24;
Rosmersholm, 106; *The Vikings,* 99-101, 102, 103
Craven, Hawes, 46-47, 93-94
Cup, The (Tennyson), 103-4
Cycloramas, 92, 144
Cymbeline, 130-31; PRODUCTIONS: Irving, 16, 96-97

Daly, Augustin, 214, n.11, 33-34
Darbyshire, Alfred, 10, 21-22, 25, 71
Davis, Fay, 74
Dean, Basil, 112
Death of Tintagiles, The (Maeterlinck), 109
Decorative front cloths, 73-74, 78, 114, 119, 131, 135, 144, 147
Demands of Interpretation. See Interpretation
De Witt, Johannes, Swan Drawing, 54, 60
Diaghilev, Sergei, 86
Dickens, Charles: *The Mystery of Edwin Drood,* 33; *Oliver Twist,* 215, n.16, 26
Dickins, Richard, 27, 31, 34
Dido and Aeneas (Purcell), 92, 97-98
Differentiation of interior and exterior space. See Space, differentiation of interior and exterior
Direct address to audience, 127, 135
Director's Theatre, 1, 2, 3, 6, 151, 152, 153, 156-57, 158-59
Dissolving view, 90
Doctor Faustus (Marlowe), 155
Don Juan in Hell (Shaw), 109
Dove, J. E., 227, n.11
D'Oyly Carte, 9
Drama, relation to the stage for which it was written, 58-59, 127-28, 151-52
Draped productions, 73-75, 113
Drawing-room drama, 4, 36, 44, 127, 145-46
Du Maurier, George, *Trilby,* 26
Duncan, Isadora, 226, n.3
Duse, Eleanora, 106

Earls Court, "Shakespeare's England" exhibit, 75, 81
Edward II (Marlowe), 113
Elizabethan costuming, 76
Elizabethanism, 42, 49-83, 85, 88, 125-26, 127, 138, 144, 154; modified, 111-15
Elizabethan stage, for touring, 32
Elizabethan Stage Society (E. S. S.), 13, 51, 52, 54, 63, 70, 71, 80
Elizabethan Stage Trust, 70
Endowed theatres, 4, 50
Environment: as a reflection of dramatic action, 13-14, 15-18, 29, 58, 59, 61, 68,

78, 95-97, 98, 100-101, 107, 115, 130-31, 151, 155, 157; as a reflection of psychological state, 26-29, 105-6
Episodic curtain, 41
Euripides, *Iphigenia in Taurus,* 134, 133, Illus. 16, 17
Everyman, 71, 107
Exemplary Theatre, 127
Experimentation, 143
"Expostulation with Inigo Jones" (Jonson), 52
Exterior scenes, 44, 47

Fable, 58
Fagan, J. B., 115
Fairies, in *A Midsummer Night's Dream,* 146-47
The Fairy's Dilemma (Gilbert), 228, n.25
False Proscenium. *See* Proscenium, false
Fantasy, 94-97, 111, 127, 131
Farce, 19, 96
Fate tree, 46, 119
Fictive reality of the stage event, 5, 8, 9-10, 12, 24, 26, 29, 36, 41, 48, 55-57, 59, 69, 95
Figgis, Darrell, 79, 114, Illus. 21
Fit-up Elizabethan stages, 69-70, 70-71, 80
Fitzgerald, Percy, 13-14, 37, 74, 105
Flanagan, Richard, 218, n.68, 218, n.69
Fly system, 100
Flying matinees, 73
Footlights, abolition of, 9, 91, 119
Forbes Robertson, Johnston: on actor and scenery, 21; advocates gas light, 20; advocates two-dimensional decor, 44; Benson uses *Macbeth* scenery, 32; as Buckingham, 19; as Hamlet, 61; uses scene-changes in darkness, 37; PRODUCTIONS: *Hamlet,* 16-17; *Macbeth,* 37
For the Soul of the King (after Balzac), 28
Fortune Theatre, 64, 69-70, Illus. 18
Fortuny lighting system, 86
Fourth Wall realism, 8, 11, 127
Fraser, Claude Lovat, 227, n.4
Free Shakespeare (Brown), 2-3
Front scenes, 34-35, 35-36, 36, 39, 45, 79, 102, 145, Illus. 1, 5, 6, 7, 20
Fry, Charles, 13, 113: PRODUCTIONS: *Troilus and Cressida,* 214, n.11
Furnivall, F. J., 90
Futurism, 227, n.4

Gaddi, Taddeo, 103
Gaedertz, Karl Theodor, 60-61, 79
Galsworthy, John, 85

Garrick, David, 124; *Katherine and Petruchio,* 213, n.9
Gas light, 20
Gauzes, 28-29, 91, 92
Ghosts (Ibsen), 106
Gilbert, W. S., 53; *The Fairy's Dilemma,* 228, n.25
Gillette, William, 15, 214, n.5
Giulio Romano, 140-41
The Girlhood of Shakespeare's Heroines (Cowden Clarke), 23-24
Globe Theatre: burning of, 218, n.69, 79-80; replica at Earls Court, 75, 81
Godfrey, W. H., 64, Illus. 18
Godwin, E. W., 10, 18, 98; PRODUCTIONS: *As You Like It,* 89; *The Cup,* 103-4; *Hamlet,* 73
Goethe, Johann Wolfgang von: *Götz von Berlichingen,* 148; *Werther,* 27; *Wilhelm Meister,* 27
Gollancz, Israel, 70
Gomme, Mrs. G. L., 70
Good Hope, The (Heijermans), 99
Götterdämmerung (Wagner), 90
Götz von Berlichingen (Goethe), 148
Gozzi, Carlo, *Turandot,* 112
Guildhall Symposium, 53, 90
Granville-Barker, Harley. *See* Barker, Harley Granville
Great Man theory, 159
Greek Theatre, 52, 53-54, 63, 74, 71-72, 81-82, 87, 92, 117, Illus. 16, 17
Greet, Ben, 71-72
Griffiths, Trevor, 147

Halston, Margaret, 73, 76
Hamlet, 25, 39, 127, 130, 131, 133, 134, 153; PRODUCTIONS: Asche/Stuart, 116; Baker, 61, 81; Barrett, 12, 73; Benson, 217, n.60; Craig, 29, 89, 105-6; Forbes Robertson, 16-17; Harvey, 88; Harvey (1906), 31, 116; Harvey (1909), 116-18, 119; Harvey (1913), 118-20; Harvey (1919), 120-21, 154; Irving, 13; L. Irving (Q1), 74; Lang, 217, n.62; Poel, Illus. 13; Reinhardt, 118; Taylor/McKaye, 71; Tree (traditional), 15, 217, n.62, 32, 33, 148; Tree (Elizabethan), 61, 66-67, 73-74, 131, 144, Illus. 14
Hammerton, J. A., 83
Handel, George Frederick, 94, 97, 98
Hare, John, 4, 53
Harker, Joseph, 52; against built-up scenes, 45; use of conventionalized borders, 92; on Craig's designs for *Macbeth,* 93; exe-

cutes Rickett's designs, 94, 110; on illusion of the actor, 43-44; stage for Asche's tours, 114-15; PRODUCTIONS: *As You Like It,* 97; *Romeo and Juliet,* 74
Harrison, Frederick, 87
Harvey, John Martin, 150; almost does *Richard III* without scenery, 86; on appropriateness of the Elizabethan stage for Shakespeare, 53; on appropriate staging for each play, 154-55; on Craig's "Scene," 95; debt to Craig, 116; debt to Reinhardt, 116; and Elizabethanism, 77-80; employs Telbin, 94; on illusion vested in the actor, 43; on Irving and composition, 20; and the New Stagecraft, 115-21; on perception, 67; plans to use fit-up Globe replica, 80; receives book from Ricketts, 109; in Reinhardt's *Oedipus,* 111; use of tapestry, 131; tours with *Oedipus,* 118, 119; PRODUCTIONS: *Hamlet,* 88; *Hamlet* (1906), 31, 116; *Hamlet* (1909), 116-18, 119; *Hamlet* (1913), 118-20; *Hamlet* (1919), 120-21, 154; *Henry V,* 77, 79-80, 154; *Richard III,* 20, 79, 154; *The Taming of the Shrew,* 77-79, 81, 92, 113, 118, 119, 131, 154
Haymarket Theatre, 9
Headlam, Rev. Stewart, 70
Heartbreak House (Shaw), 50
Heijermans, Herman, *The Good Hope,* 99
Helmsley, W. J., 94
Henry VIII, 154; PRODUCTIONS: Irving, 19; Tree, 18-19, 26, 218, n.69, 29, 38, 45, 107, 113, 119, 134, 148-49, 153
Henry V, 57; Chorus speech, 50-52; PRODUCTIONS: Calvert, 74; Coleman, 47; Harvey, 77, 79-80, 154; Poel/Greet, 71-72, 153; Waller, 38, 40, 47, Illus. 10
Henry IV, part one, PRODUCTIONS: Tree, 47
Henry IV, part two, 4
Henry VI, 4; *part two,* PRODUCTIONS: Benson, 34
Herbert, Henry, 74
Herkomer, Hubert, 91-92, 139; on abolition of footlights, 9; moveable proscenium, 110
Herod (Philips), 23-24, 40, 45, 47, Illus. 4
Heslewood, Tom, 20
History, attitudes towards, 49, 50-55, 126, 127
Histrionic art, equated with scenic art, 21-22

Home, Risden, *Nelson's Enchantress,* 28
Hosley, Richard, 223, n.48
Housman, Laurence, *Bethlehem,* 97; *Prunella,* 228, n.25, 98
Howard de Walden, Lord, 109
Hunter, Leah Bateman, 74

Ibsen, Henrik, *Ghosts,* 106; *Peer Gynt,* 106; *Rosmersholm,* 106; *The Vikings,* 99-101, 102, 103, 106
Idyllic Players, 75
Illude, to, 13
Illusion: limitations of, 51-52; of reality, 8, 12-13, 16, 26, 30, 38, 42, 44, 48, 65, 66, 68, 88, 91, 92, 94, 97, 127, 135, 157; of reality for fantasy, 97; of reality via costume, 18; of a separate world, 29; vested in the actor, 43-44, 130, 133
Illusion of the first time, 10, 56
Illustration, 12
Imaginative visualization of the scene, 66-68, 132
Imperial Theatre, renovations of, 92, 99-100
Inner stage, 61, 63, 79, 115, 128, 129, 134
Individual v. Institution, 158-59
Insert scenes, 145, 146, Illus. 31
Intentions, of the playwright, 151, 153, 155-56
Interpolated characters, 15, 18, 148-49
Interpretation, demands of, 151, 156-57
Iphigenia in Taurus (Euripides), 134, 143, Illus. 16, 17
Iris (Pinero), 41
Irving, Henry, 2, 3-4, 7, 101, 108, 151, 156; use of alternation, 35-36; use of combined two- and three-dimensional scenery, 46; on costume, 18; employs Alma Tadema, 19; use of fate trees, 46, 119; use of front scenes, 45-46; as Hamlet, 83; integration of actor and scenery, 20-21; and lighting, 20, 109; on localization, 10; use of narrative interpolations, 39; scene changes in darkness, 36-37; use of tableau curtains, 41; on Shakespeare's transcendence of his age, 236, n.4; touring repertoire, 32; use of two-dimensional scenery, 45; urged to use Herkomer's techniques, 92; PRODUCTIONS: *The Bells,* 28; *Coriolanus,* 214, n.11, 11, 35-36, 40, 41, 45-46, Illus. 3, 5, 6, 7; *The Corsican Brothers,* 28; *The Cup,* 103-4; *Cymbeline,* 16, 96-97; *Hamlet,* 13, 19; *The Merchant of Venice,* 39, 71; *Much Ado*

About Nothing, 13-14; *Romeo and Juliet,* 11, 45, 46
Irving, H. B., 12, 28, 116
Irving, Laurence (son of Henry Irving), 74
Irving, Laurence (grandson of Henry Irving), 20

Jacques-Dalcroze, 86
Jewish characters, 26
Jones, Henry Arthur, 52
Jones, Inigo, 52
Jonson, Ben, 218, n.69, 52, 152
Journalistic illustration, 47, Illus. 11
Jubilee for Ellen Terry, 103, Illus. 23
Julius Caesar, 12, 153, 154; PRODUCTIONS: Asche, 216, n.59, 32; Benson, 216, n.59; Casson, 114; Reinhardt, 114; Tree, 19, 216, n.59; 217, n.60; 217, n.62, 31, 46

Katherine and Petruchio (Garrick), 213, n.9
Kean, Charles, 9; PRODUCTIONS: *The Winter's Tale,* 10, 140
Kemendy, Jeno, 76
Kendal, W. H. and Madge, 4
Kerin, Nora, 73
King John, PRODUCTIONS: Tree, 23, 25-26, 219, n.79, 33, 47-48, 148, Illus. 12
King Lear, 131, 155; PRODUCTIONS: Antoine, 114, 148; Ricketts, 57, 107-10, 117, 154, Illus. 25
Kirwan, Patrick, 72, 75-76, 147
Kismet (Knoblauch), 45
Knight of the Burning Pestle, The (Beaumont), 81
Knoblauch, Edward, *Kismet,* 45

Lang, Matheson: touring scenery, 32; PRODUCTIONS: *Hamlet,* 217, n.62; *The Merchant of Venice,* 14; *Romeo and Juliet,* 25, 31
Lanval (Lord Howard de Walden), 109
Lawrence, Gerald, 74
Lawrence, W. J., on Benson, 35, 37, 44; on the Elizabethan stage, 60, 64, 79; on the Well-Made Play, 58
Lea, Marion, 71
Lee, Sidney, 51-52, 60, 66, 68
Leno, Dan, 127, 148
Leigh, J. H., PRODUCTIONS: *The Tempest,* 213, n.11, 72-73; *Timon of Athens,* 214, n.11; *Two Gentlemen of Verona,* 214, n.11
Lewis, Leopold, *The Bells,* 28
Liberalism, Victorian, 54-55
Light bridge, 92, 100

Lighting, 20, 142, 143-44; from the auditorium, 76, 78, 227, n.11, 119, 135, 149; electric, 109; gas, 20; from overhead, 91, 92, 100; plastic, 88-89, 90, 102
Limelight, 100
Limitations of theatrical illusion, 51-52
Liverpool Repertory Theatre, 112
Literary Theatre Society, 109
Littlewood, S. R., 154
Localization, 10-11, 33-34, 39, 58, 60, 61, 62, 65, 68, 79, 88, 104, 115, 118, 119, 129-30, 131, 144
Long-run system, 4
Lord's rooms, 69
Love's Labour's Lost, 4, 214, n.11
Lucky Per's Pilgrimage (Strindberg), 228, n.25
Lutyen, Edwin, 75

McCarthy, Lillah, 111, 142
McKaye, Steele, 71
Macquoid, Percy, 74
Macbeth, 106, 128, 130, 131, 132, 155; PRODUCTIONS: Barker (projected), 142; Benson, 216, n.59, 35; Bourchier, 217, n.62, 31; Forbes Robertson, 32, 37; Tree, 12, 29, 219, n.79, 93, 95-96, 105, 106, 154
Machen, Arthur, 119
Maeterlinck, Maurice, 87, 98; *The Blue Bird,* 96, 111; *Death of Tintagiles,* 109
Markheim (Stevenson), 12
Marlowe, Christopher, *Doctor Faustus,* 155; *Edward II,* 113
Marshall, Norman, 115, 135, 147
Martin Harvey, John. *See* Harvey, John Martin
Masks, 143, 157
Masques, 52, 83, 102-3, 153; in *The Tempest,* 218, n.68, 153
Masque of Love, The (Purcell), 97
Measure for Measure, 83; PRODUCTIONS: Asche/Stuart, 14, 15; Poel (E. S. S.), 69-70, 81, Illus. 19; Poel (Manchester), 71, 114
Meistersinger, Die (Wagner), 18
Melodrama, 60, 65, 96, 101
Mendelssohn, Felix, 76
Merchant of Venice, The, PRODUCTIONS: Asche, 32; Bancroft, 16; Bourchier, 15-16, 17, 74, 76; Craig/Terry (projected), 89, 105; Irving, 39, 71; Lang, 14; Reinhardt, 90; Tree, 17-18, 25, 217, n.61, 26, 33, 36, 39, 41

Merry Wives of Windsor, The, PRODUCTIONS: Asche, 34; Tree, 19, 32
Middleton, Thomas, *The Chaste Maid of Cheapside,* 75
Middle Temple, 71
Midsummer Night's Dream, A, 39, 68, 72, 96, 97, 106, 132, 133, 153; PRODUCTIONS: Asche/Stuart, 228, n.26; Barker, 82, 230, n.80, 123, 136, 140, 141, 146-49, Illus. 32; Benson, 33; Kirwan, 76, 147; Reinhardt, 90; Ricketts (projected), 109; Tree, 218, n.68, 27, 33, 37, 61-62, 228, n.26
Milton, John, *Samson Agonistes,* 70
The Miracle, 86, 11, 112
Modern dress, 83, 116
Modern dress repertoire, 4. *See also* Drawing-room comedy
Modernism, 86
"Modern" staging, 7, 53, 68, 85
Monodrama, 106
Montague, C. E., 218, n.68
Moore, Edward Mumford, 81
Morris, William, 43, 55
Moscow Art Theatre, 29, 86, 89, 105-6
Much Ado About Nothing, 13-14; PRODUCTIONS: Craig, 99, 101-5, 144, Illus. 23, 24; Irving, 13-14; Flanagan, 218, n.68; Payne, 36, 114; Poel, 70; Tree, 11, 14, 15, 33, 40-41
Munich Shakespeare Stage, 86, 114
Multiple Stage, 62, 79, 114, 128, 129
Murray, Gilbert, 53, 111, 138
Music, 82, 98, 127
Music Hall, 86, 127, 148
Mystery of Edwin Drood, The (after (Dickens), 33
Mystic gulf, 8-9

Narrative consistency, 57
Narrative interpolations, 22-26, 30, 39, 47, 48, 58, 59, 120-21, 137-39, 146, 149
National Theatre, 218, n.69, 32, 158. *See also* Shakespeare Memorial National Theatre
Naturalism, 8. *See also* Realism
Nelson's Enchantress (Home), 28
Nero (Philips), 33
New Drama, The, 85
New Stagecraft, The, 43, 76, 77, 78, 80, 85-121, 157
Nietzsche, Friedrich, 87
Non-illusionism, 5, 56, 91, 94
Non-representationalism, 2, 5, 59, 81, 94, 95, 106

Obligatory scenes, 23
Odell, G. C. D., 35, 45, 147
Oedipus (Sophocles), 9, 56, 86, 111-13, 118, 119, Illus. 26, 27
Offstage, in relation to onstage action and space, 12, 105, 131
Old Comedy, 32
Old Vic, 32
Oliver Twist (after Dickens), 215, n.16, 26
180 degree rotation, 11-12
One scene/one act, 30, 36, 41, 58, 102
Opera, 32, 92, 94, 97-98
Organizational determinants, 3, 31-33, 50, 87
Othello, 35, 130, 134, 134, 153; PRODUCTIONS: Asche, 32; Waller, 217, n.61, 34
Ours (Robertson), 53
Outlaw's Christmas, The, 60

Pageants, 22, 26, 218, n.69, 92
Pages on Art (Ricketts), 109
Painted scenery. *See* Trompe l'oeil
Palestrina, Giovanni Pierluigi, 218, n.68
Palladio, Andrea, 14
Pantomime, Christmas. *See* Christmas Pantomime
Pantomime sequences. *See* Narrative interpolation
Paolo and Francesca (Philips), 23
Parker, Louis N., 218, n.69, 92
Parsifal (Wagner), 89, 90
Pastoral, 72, 92
Pavlova, Anna, 86
Payne, B. Iden, 36, 63, 70, 81; PRODUCTIONS: *The Knight of the Burning Pestle,* 81; *Much Ado About Nothing,* 36, 71, 104
Peer Gynt (Ibsen), 106
Perch limes, 21, 100
Perception, competition of senses, 65-68, 108, 132-33
Periaktoi, 117, 119
Peter Pan (Barrie), 96, 228, n.26
Philips, Stephen: *Herod,* 23-24, 40, 45, 47, Illus. 4; *Nero,* 33; *Paolo and Francesca,* 23
Pictorialism: composition, 29; Representationalism, 2, 5, 7, 12, 42, 55, 60, 61, 65, 68, 79, 85, 86, 90, 90-91, 94, 96, 100, 105, 108-9, 111, 114, 116, 130, 149, 154; reforms, 88, 115
Picture-frame stage, 53, 55, 56, 58
Pilgrim Players, 74
Pinero, Arthur Wing, 59; *Iris,* 41

Pinkie and the Fairies (Robertson), 111, 228, n.25
Placards, 61, 65, 71
Planché, J. R., 71, 73, 77
Platform stage, 13, 56, 58, 69-70, 112, 134, 135, 136, 137
Plausibility, 96
Playfair, Nigel, 227, n.4
Playwright's intentions. *See* Intentions
Poel, William, 2, 13, 43, 51, 63, 114, 135, 150, 153; on appropriateness of Elizabethan stage for Shakespeare, 53; on artifice, 42; assists Harvey, 77; on Barker's scene designations, 131; on competition of sensory perception, 66; complimented by Shaw, 56; on continuity, 59; on costume, 57, 83; use of costumed audiences, 81; on Craig, 98-99; on draped stages, 75; eccentric use of space, 70; introduced to Reinhardt, 138; on logic of *Henry V,* 57; on logic of *Two Gentlemen of Verona,* 57; on masques, 52; use of modern dress, 83; on narrative interpolation, 59; on Pinero, 59; on progress, 54-55; "realism of the actual event," 56-57; on Reinhardt, 112-13; rejects placards, 61; on relation of actor to scenery, 43-44; on relation of drama to the stage for which it was written, 152; on Rickett's *King Lear,* 57; on *Romeo and Juliet,* 57; use of tapestry, 61; on textual integrity, 59; on touring, 32; use of traverses, 60-61; on vocal contact of platform stage, 70; PRODUCTIONS: *All's Well that Ends Well,* 83; *The Comedy of Errors,* 70; *Coriolanus,* 83, 153; at Earls Court, 75; *Edward II,* 113; *Everyman,* 71; *Hamlet,* Illus. 13; *Henry V,* 71, 153; at Holborn Empire, 70; at Manchester Repertory Theatre, 70; *Measure for Measure* (E.S.S.), 69-70, 81, Illus. 19; *Measure for Measure* (Manchester), 114; *Much Ado About Nothing,* 70; *The Tempest,* 66, 70, 138, 153; *Troilus and Cressida,* 83, 153, 214, n.11; *Twelfth Night,* 71, 53, Illus. 20; *Two Gentlemen of Verona,* 113, 119, 134, 149, 153, 214, n.11, 218, n. n.69, Illus. 28
Post-Impressionism, 75, 227, n.4
Post-Impressionist Exhibitions, 86, 111
Presentationalism, 138
Probability, 96
Profile groupings, 144
Properties, 130

Proscenium arch, 11, 69-70, 91; abolition of, 9; false, 11, 103, 113, 114, 115, 136, Illus. 13; masked, 78, 112; moveable, 91, 110; as picture frame, 9
Proscenium stage, 62-63, 69, 135, 137
Prunella (Barker and Housman), 98, 228, n.25
Purcell, Henry, *Dido and Aeneas,* 92, 97; *Masque of Love,* 97
Purcell Society, 97, 102
Purdom, C. B., 136

Rackham, Arthur, 120-21
Radicalism, Edwardian, 54-55
Realism of the Actual Event, 56
Realism, 8, 86, 88, 100, 108
Realistic repertoire, 30, 96
Reality of the stage world. *See* Fictive reality
Reinhardt, Max, 43, 86, 111-13, 120, 138, 154, 156; accepts two-dimensional decor, 94; influences Harvey, 77-78, 116; on relation of actor to scenery, 43; use of turntable, 90; PRODUCTIONS: *The Comedy of Errors,* 156; *Hamlet,* 118; *Julius Caesar,* 114; *Oedipus,* 9, 56, 86, 111-13, 118, 119, Illus. 26, 27; *The Merchant of Venice,* 90; *The Miracle,* 86, 111, 112; *Sumurun,* 86, 90, 111, 112; *Venetian Nights,* 111
Repertoire companies, 32
Repertory, 32, 50
Representationalism. *See* Pictorialism
Restoration stage, 60, 114
Reusable scenery, 32-33
Revolve. *See* Turntable
Reynolds, George F., 62, 224, n.55
Richard II, 4, 154; PRODUCTIONS: Benson, 214, n.11; 217, n.61; Tree, 15, 27, 28-29, 148, 214, n.11, 217, n.60
Richard III, PRODUCTIONS: Benson, 14, 35, 217, n.61; Harvey, 20, 79, 80, 154
Ricketts, Charles, 87, 88; on appropriate staging for each play, 155; on Craig, 109; employs Harker, 94; *Pages on Art,* 109; on relation of actor to scenery, 21; PRODUCTIONS: *Attila,* 109, 110; *The Death of Tintagiles,* 109; *King Lear,* 57, 107-10, 117, 154, Illus. 25; *Lanval,* 109; *A Midsummer Night's Dream* (projected), 109; *Saint Joan,* 115; *Salome,* 109
Rignold, George, 47
Ring des Nibelungen, Der (Wagner), 120-21

Index

Robertson, Johnston Forbes. *See* Forbes Robertson, Johnston
Robertson, T. W., 127; *School,* 53; *Ours,* 53
Robertson, W. Graham, 146, 216, n.45; *Pinkie and the Fairies,* 111, 228, n.25; PRODUCTIONS: *As You Like It,* 218, n.69
Robins, Elizabeth, 71
Romantic period, 18
Romantic repertoire, 8-9, 28, 30, 32, 33, 36, 48, 101, 107-8
Romeo and Juliet, 57, 130, 153; PRODUCTIONS: Calhoun (projected), 89-90; Davis/Lawrence, 74; Flanagan, 218, n.68; Hunter/Williams, 74; Irving, 11, 45, 46; Lang, 25, 31; Fred Terry, 74
Rosmersholm (Ibsen), 106
Rostand, Edmond, *L'Aiglon,* 19
Rôze, Raymond, 37
Rostrum, 77, 113, 114, 115, 136
Rothenstein, Albert. *See* Rutherston, Albert
Rothenstein, Will, 98, 99
Ruskin, John, 152
Russian Ballet, 86, 87, 111, 138, 226, n.3
Russian Imperial Ballet, 86
Rutherston, Albert, 74, 140, 142; on artifice, 43; on Bakst, 226, n.3; on decor, 139; on realism, 139; on the Savoy stage, 134-35; on "style," 140; on unity of design, 158; PRODUCTIONS: *The Winter's Tale,* 158, Illus. 33

Saint Joan (Shaw), 115
St. John, Christopher, 100
Salome (Wilde), 109
Samson Agonistes (Milton), 70
Savits, Jocza, 114
Savoy Shakespeare, 74, 75, 113-14, 115, 123, 129, 131, 134, 135, 136, 137, 139-50, 155, 157, Illus. 29, 30, 31, 32, 33
"Scene" (Craig), 89, 95, 103
Scene, changes of, 31, 34, 36
Scene changing, 30, 34, 36-38, 45, 48, 62-63, 88, 89, 111, 114, 115, 117
Scene-waits, 31, 36, 38, 89
Scenic space, 115
Screens, 89, 105
Schiller, Friedrich, *Wallenstein,* 113
Scholarship, relation to stage practice, 49, 59-65, 123
School (Robertson), 53
Separation of stage from auditorium, 8-9
Serial discontinuity, 39
Serlio, Sebastiano, 89, 103

Seven-headed director, 138-39, 157
Shakespeare, William: appropriate staging for each play, 153-55; use of clowns, 148; demands, 30-41, 88; demands of interpretation, 151; dissatisfaction with his stage, 50-52; as managerial status, 4; as pageant-master, 218, n.69; as Romantic, 53-54; transcendence of his age, 152; "word pictures," 58; WORKS: *All's Well that Ends Well,* 4, 83; *Antony and Cleopatra,* 4, 11, 14, 25, 31, 32, 33, 41, 51, 64, 130, 133, 153, 217, n.60, Illus. 1, 2; *As You Like It,* 10, 34, 72, 74, 89, 97, 153, 218, n.68, 227, n.4, 228, n.26; *The Comedy of Errors,* 4, 70, 75-76, 156, 214, n.11; *Coriolanus,* 4, 11, 35-36, 40, 41, 45, 45-46, 64, 83, 153, 214, n.11, Illus. 3, 5, 6, 7; *Cymbeline,* 16, 96-97, 130-31; *Hamlet,* 12, 13, 15, 16-17, 25, 29, 31, 32, 33, 39, 61, 66-67, 71, 73, 73-74, 74, 81, 83, 88, 89, 105-6, 116-21, 127, 130, 131, 133, 134, 144, 148, 151, 153, 154, 217, n.60, 217, n.62, Illus. 13, 14; *Henry VIII,* 18-19, 19, 26, 29, 38, 45, 107, 113, 119, 134, 148-49, 153, 154, 218, n.69; *Henry V,* 38, 40, 47, 50-52, 57, 71-72, 74, 77, 79-80, 153, 154, Illus. 10; *Henry IV, part one,* 47; *Henry IV, part two,* 4; *Henry VI,* 4, 34; *Julius Caesar,* 12, 19, 31, 32, 46, 114, 153, 154, 216, n.59, 217, n.60, 217, n.62; *King John,* 23, 25-26, 33, 47-48, 148, 219, n.79, Illus. 12; *King Lear,* 57, 107-10, 114, 117, 131, 148, 154, 155, Illus. 25; *Love's Labour's Lost,* 4, 214, n.11; *Macbeth,* 12, 29, 31, 32, 35, 37, 93, 95-96, 105, 106, 128, 130, 131, 132, 142, 154, 155, 216, n.59; 217, n.62, 219, n.79; *Measure for Measure,* 14, 15, 69-70, 71, 81, 83, 114, Illus. 19; *The Merchant of Venice,* 14, 15-16, 16, 17-18, 18, 25, 26, 32, 33, 36, 39, 41, 39, 71, 74, 76, 89, 90, 105, 217, n.61; *The Merry Wives of Windsor,* 19, 32, 34; *A Midsummer Night's Dream,* 27, 33, 37, 39, 61-62, 68, 72, 76, 82, 90, 96, 97, 106, 109, 109, n.82, 123, 132, 133, 136, 140, 141, 146-49, 153, 218, n.68, 228, n.26, Illus. 32; *Much Ado About Nothing,* 11, 13-14, 14, 15, 33, 36, 40-41, 70, 99, 101-5, 114, 144, 218, n.68, Illus. 23, 24; *Othello,* 32, 34, 35, 130, 134, 153, 217, n.61; *Richard II,* 4, 15, 27, 28-29, 148, 154, 214, n.11, 217, n.60, 217, n.61; *Richard III,* 14, 20,

35, 79, 80, 154, 217, n.61; *Romeo and Juliet,* 11, 25, 31, 45, 46, 57, 74, 89-90, 130, 153, 218, n.68; *The Taming of the Shrew,* 34, 38, 71, 73, 77-79, 81, 92, 113, 118, 119, 131, 154; *The Tempest,* 4, 27-28, 47, 64, 66, 70, 72, 72-73, 106, 138, 153, 155, 214, n.11, 218, n.68, 219, n.79, 228, n.26; *Timon of Athens,* 4, 214, n.11; *Titus Andronicus,* 213, n.8; *Troilus and Cressida,* 4, 73, 83, 153, 213, n.8, 214, n.11; *Two Gentlemen of Verona,* 4, 33, 57, 113, 119, 134, 149, 153, 214, n.11, 218, n.69, Illus. 28; *Twelfth Night,* 12, 18, 24, 33, 33-34, 34, 36, 46-47, 53, 71, 74, 93-94, 123, 125, 131, 136, 140, 141, 142, 144-46, 147, 148, 155, 218, n.68, 219, n.79, Frontispiece, Illus. 8, 9, 20, 29, 30, 31; *The Winter's Tale,* 10, 17, 19, 24, 33, 36, 39, 74, 123, 131, 136, 140, 141, 142, 143-44, 145, 147, 148, 158, 218, n.68, Illus. 29, 33. For specific productions, consult entries under individual plays
Shakespeare Memorial Committee, 70
Shakespeare Memorial National Theatre (S. M. N. T.), 4, 70, 75. *See also* National Theatre
Shakespeare's England, 75
Sharp, Cecil, 82
Shaw, Byam, 103, Illus. 23
Shaw, G. Bernard, 85; on appropriateness of Elizabethan stage for Shakespeare, 52; on appropriate staging for each play, 153; on artifice, 42; on Bancroft, 56; on borders, 92; on Craig and draped stages, 75; on *Cymbeline,* 16, 130-31; on Daly, 33-34; on the environment as a reflection of dramatic action, 16-17, 100-101; on Forbes Robertson's *Hamlet,* 16-17; on history, 50; on imagination, 66; on Morris, 43; on placards, 61, 65; on Poel, 13, 42, 56, 57; on progress, 54-55; on relation of the actor to scenery, 44; on relation of the artist to his age, 152; on Tree and Irving's revisions of Shakespeare, 151; on *The Vikings,* 100-101; WORKS: *The Admirable Bashville,* 65-65; *Androcles and the Lion,* 96, n.25; *Cashel Byron's Profession,* 64; *Don Juan in Hell,* 109; *Heartbreak House,* 50; *Saint Joan,* 115
Shaw, Martin Fallas, 97
Sherringham, George, 120
Shock, 141-42

Sidney, Sir Philip, *Apology for Poetry,* 61
Sight-lines, 81, 129, 136, 137
Sky-cloths, to denote changes in time, 40. *See also* Cycloramas
Skydome, 112, 118, 119
Smith, H. R., 25, 31
Sophocles, *Oedipus,* 9, 56, 86, 111-13, 118, 119, Illus. 26, 27
Space, differentiation of interior and exterior, 14, 61, 65, 88, 119
Spatial reforms, 88, 111-15, 124, 134-37
Split scenes, 63, 114, 115, 147-48
Spontaneity of response, 124, 126
Stanfield, Clarkson, 110
Stanislavsky, Constantin, 106
Star actor system, 32
Steen, Marguerite, 99-100
Stern, Ernest, 94, 112
Stevenson, Robert Louis, *Markheim,* 12
Stock company system, 32
Stoker, Bram, 20, 36-37
Stoll, Oswald, 86, 111
Strauss, Richard, 87
Strindberg, August, *Lucky Per's Pilgrimage,* 228, n.25
Stuart, Otho, PRODUCTIONS: *Hamlet,* 116; *Measure for Measure,* 14, 15; *A Midsummer Night's Dream,* 228, n.26; *The Taming of the Shrew,* 34, 38
Styan, J. L., 49, 56, 59-60, 135, 148
Style, of a period, 140, 145-46
Subjective vision, 26-29, 105-6
Suggestion of a period, 117, 119, 120, 135, 140
Sumurun, 86, 90, 111, 112
Surfaces, 91, 102, 104-5, 139
Symbolic content of the drama, 13, 25-26, 29
Symbolic scenery, 108, 119, 138, 153, 154
Symposium on the best method of presenting Shakespeare's plays, 53, 90
Symonds, John Addington, 56
Symons, Arthur, 98
Synaesthesia, 104-5
Swan drawing, 54, 60, 63, 64

Tableau, curtains, 41, *see also* Decorative curtains; scene-endings, 22, 55, 58, 117-18, 120, 146; static, 22, 47, 72-73, Illus. 10, 12, see also Narrative Interpolations
Taming of the Shrew, The, PRODUCTIONS: Asche/Stuart, 34, 38; Harvey, 77-79, 81, 92, 113, 118, 119, 131, 154; Webster/Planché, 71, 73, 77
Tadema, Alma. *See* Alma Tadema, Lawrence

Taylor, Tom, 71
Tapestries, 61, 73-75, 78, 103, 131, Illus. 13
Teatro Olimpico, 114
Technical reforms, 85, 88, 89, 90, 93, 100, 110
Telbin, William, 9, 92, 94, 110
Tempest, The, 4, 64, 106, 153, 155; PRODUCTIONS: Benson, 72, 213, n.11; Leigh, 72-73, 213, n.11; Poel, 66-70, 138, 153; Tree, 24, 27-28, 47, 213, n.11, 218, n.68, 219, n.79, 228, n.26
Temporality of drama, 152
Tennyson, Alfred Lord, *The Cup,* 103-4
Terry, Ellen, 152; advocates two-dimensional decor, 44; on appropriate staging for each play, 153; on artifice, 42; as Beatrice, 76; on costume, 18; on fanciful scenery, 98; on Godwin's designs for *The Cup,* 103-4; as Hermione, 19; as Hiordis, 100; as Imogen, 16; on Irving's use of alternation, 35; on Irving's front scenes, 45; Jubilee, 103, Illus. 23; management of the Imperial Theatre, 96-97; as Mrs. Page, 19; on unity of design, 157; PRODUCTIONS: *The Merchant of Venice* (projected), 89, 105; *Much Ado About Nothing,* 99, 101-5, 144, Illus. 23, 24; *The Vikings,* 99-101, 102, 103
Terry, Fred, 74
Textual alteration, 2, 17, 30, 31, 59, 102, 125
Théâtre des Arts, 86
Theatre in the round, 137
Theatricalism, 86
Theatrical means and dramatic ends, 30, 38, 48, 59, 88, 91, 91-92, 93, 127
Thorndike, Sybil, 72
Three-dimensional scenery. *See* Built-up scenes
360 degree reality, 11-12, 22, 104-5
Time, 34, 38-41, 62, 128
Timon of Athens, 4, 214, n.11
Titus Andronicus, 213, n.8
Touring, 32
Traditionalism, 7-48, 49, 50, 55-59, 88, 91, 93, 100-101, 104-5, 105-6, 107-8, 111, 119, 121, 127, 135, 150, 154
Training an audience to be receptive to convention, 127
Translation, 5, 124, 152
Transformation scenes, 22, 80
Transparencies, 28-29

Traverse curtains, 60, 61, 62, 63, 70, 79, 113, 115, 223, n.49, 224, n.55, Illus. 20
Treatment, 156
Tree, Herbert Beerbohm, 2, 7, 85, 114, 148-50, 151; Academy of Dramatic Art, 75; and Alma Tadema, 19; on appropriate staging for each play, 153-54; use of apron, 149; as Caliban, 27; use of clowns, 148-49; on competition of sensory perception, 66-67; on continuity, 31, 219, n.79; on Craig's *Hamlet,* 29; as Fagin, 26; on Hamlet and Richard II, 27; on *Henry V* chorus, 50-51; on illusion, 12; integration of actor and scenery, 21; on individual v. institution, 159; on interpretive mandate, 156; as Macari, 26; use of narrative interpolations, 216, n.59, 217, n.60, 217, n.61, 217, n.62, 39; pageantry, 218, n.68, 218, n.69; patronage of Kirwan, 72; on post-impressionism, 227, n.4; quarrel with Trench, 107, 111; on relation of artist to his age, 152; reuses scenery, 33; scene-changing in darkness, 37; scene-waits, 38; on Shakespeare as pageant master, 218, n.69; as Shylock, 26; use of stage business, 21; use of static tableaux, 47-48; as Svengali, 26; use of tableau curtains to denote passage of time, 41; use of tapestry, 131; time changes, 401 touring practices, 32; on unity of design, 237, n.27; PRODUCTIONS: *Antony and Cleopatra,* 11, 25, 31, 33, Illus. 1, 2; *Hamlet* (traditional), 15, 32, 33, 148, 217, n.62; *Hamlet* (Elizabethan), 61, 66-67, 73-74, 131, 144, Illus. 14; *Henry VIII,* 18-19, 26, 29, 38, 45, 107, 113, 119, 134, 148-49, 153, 218, n.69; *Henry IV, part one,* 47; *Herod,* 23-24, 40, 45, 47, Illus. 4; *Julius Caesar,* 19, 31, 46, 216, n.59, 217, n.60, 217, n.62; *Katherine and Petruchio,* 213, n.9; *King John,* 23, 25-26, 33, 47-48, 148, 219, n.79, Illus. 12; *Macbeth,* 12, 29, 93, 95-96, 105, 106, 154, 219, n.79; *The Merchant of Venice,* 17-18, 25, 33, 36, 39, 41, 217, n.61; *The Merry Wives of Windsor,* 19, 32; *A Midsummer Night's Dream,* 27, 33, 37, 61-62, 218, n.68, 228, n.26; *Much Ado About Nothing,* 11, 14, 15, 33, 40-41; *The Mystery of Edwin Drood,* 33; *Nero,* 33; *Oliver Twist,* 26, 215, n.16; *Pinkie and the Fairies,* 111; *Richard II,* 15, 27, 28-29, 148, 214, n.11, 217, n.60; *The Tempest,*

24, 27-28, 47, 213, n.11, 218, n.68, 219, n.79, 228, n.26; *Twelfth Night,* 12, 18, 24, 33, 34, 36, 46-47, 93-94, 219, n.79, frontispiece, Illus. 8, 9; *The Winter's Tale,* 10, 17, 19, 33, 36, 39, 140
Tree, Maud, 73, 217, n.62
Tree, Viola, 29
Trench, Herbert, 87; on competition of sensory perception, 108; quarrel with Tree, 107, 111; PRODUCTIONS: *The Blue Bird,* 111; *King Lear,* 57, 107-10, 154, Illus. 25; *A Midsummer Night's Dream* (projected), 109
Trilby (after Du Maurier), 26
Tristan und Isolde (Wagner), 89
Troilus and Cressida, 4, 4, n.8; PRODUCTIONS: Fry, 214, n.11, 73; Poel, 83, 153, 214, n.11
Trompe l'oeil, 11, 35, 39-40, 44, 48, 69, 88-89, 91, 93, 93-94, 112, 140
Turandot (Gozzi), 112
Turntable, 90, 94, 137, 125
Twelfth Night, PRODUCTIONS: Barker, 74, 123, 131, 136, 140, 141, 142, 144-46, 147, 148, 155, Illus. 29, 30, 31; Daly, 33-34; Flanagan, 218, n.68; Poel, 53, 71, Illus. 20; Robins/Lea, 71; Tree, 12, 18, 24, 33, 34, 36, 46-47, 93-94, 219, n.79, frontispiece, Illus. 8, 9
Two- v. three-dimensional scenery, 44-45, 46-47, 48, 88-89, 93-94
Two Gentlemen of Verona, 4, 57; PRODUCTIONS: Daly, 33, 213, n.11; Leigh, 213, n.11; Poel, 113, 119, 134, 149, 153, 214, n.11, 218, n.69, Illus. 28

Übermarionette, 157
Unity, 8, 13-22, 26, 34, 55, 56-58, 59; of design, 109, 110, 157-58; of effect, 8, 151

Vanbrugh, Violet, 12, 74, 218, n.69
Vedrenne, J. E., 87
Venetian Nights, 111
Veronese, Paolo, 145

The Vikings, 99-101, 102, 103, 106
Visualization of the scene, 66-68, 132

Wagner, Richard, 87; mystic gulf, 8-9; WORKS: *Götterdämmerung,* 90; *Die Meistersinger,* 18; *Parsifal,* 89, 90; *Der Ring des Nibelungen,* 120-21; *Tristan und Isolde,* 89
Wagon stages, 37, 114
Walkley, A. B., 41
Wallenstein (Schiller), 113
Waller, Lewis, use of narrative interpolation, 217, n.61; scene-waits, 38; use of static tableaux, 47; time changes, 40; PRODUCTIONS: *Henry V,* 38, 40, 47, Illus. 10; *Othello,* 34, 217, n.61
Webster, Ben, 71, 73, 77
Well-made play, 58
Werther (Goethe), 27
White, J. Fisher, 75
Wilde, Oscar, 10, 18; *Salome,* 109
Wilhelm Meister (Goethe), 27
Wilkinson, Norman, 74, 135; on built-up scenes, 139; on decor, 139; on style, 145-46; on unity of design, 158; PRODUCTIONS: *A Midsummer Night's Dream,* 109 n.80; *The Winter's Tale,* 158
Williams, Harcourt, 72, 74
Wing and groove system, 117
Winter's Tale, The, 39; PRODUCTIONS: Barker, 123, 131, 136, 140, 141, 142, 143-44, 145, 147, 148, 158, Illus. 29, 33; Calvert, 74; Flanagan, 218, n.68; Kean, 10, 140; Tree, 10, 17, 19, 33, 36, 39, 140
Word pictures, 66
Woolf, Virginia, 86
Wyndham's Theatre, 9
Wyspianski, Stanislaw, 86

Yeats, William Butler, 98, 120

Zone theory, 58, 62-63, 79, 88, 114, 129, 134

OHIO UNIVERSITY LIBRARY

Please return this book as soon as you have finished with it. In order to avoid a fine it must be returned by the latest date stamped below.

LOAN